THIRD DISPLACEMENT

BOOKS BY JOHN HART

Editor, *The Wiley Blackwell Companion to Religion and Ecology* (2017)

Cosmos Contact: Close Encounters of the Otherkind (trilogy):
Cosmic Commons: Spirit, Science, and Space (2013)
Encountering ETI: Aliens in Avatar and the Americas (2014)
Third Displacement: Cosmobiology, Cosmolocality, Cosmosocioecology (2020)

The Spirit of the Earth: A Theology of the Land (1984)
Ethics and Technology: Innovation and Transformation in Community Contexts (1997)
What Are They Saying About Environmental Theology? (2004)
Sacramental Commons: Christian Ecological Ethics (2006)

THIRD DISPLACEMENT

COSMOBIOLOGY, COSMOLOCALITY,
COSMOSOCIOECOLOGY

John Hart

FOREWORD BY *Jacques F. Vallée*
AFTERWORD BY *John F. Haught*

Cosmos Contact:
Close Encounters of the Otherkind

CASCADE *Books* • Eugene, Oregon

THIRD DISPLACEMENT
Cosmobiology, Cosmolocality, Cosmosocioecology

Copyright © 2020 John Hart. All rights reserved. Except for brief quotations in critical publications or reviews, no part of this book may be reproduced in any manner without prior written permission from the publisher. Write: Permissions, Wipf and Stock Publishers, 199 W. 8th Ave., Suite 3, Eugene, OR 97401.

Cascade Books
An Imprint of Wipf and Stock Publishers
199 W. 8th Ave., Suite 3
Eugene, OR 97401

www.wipfandstock.com

PAPERBACK ISBN: 978-1-5326-3310-2
HARDCOVER ISBN: 978-1-5326-3312-6
EBOOK ISBN: 978-1-5326-3311-9

Cataloguing-in-Publication data:

Names: Hart, John, 1943–, author. | Vallee, Jacques, foreword. | Haught, John F., afterword.

Title: Third displacement : cosmobiology, cosmolocality, cosmosocioecology / John Hart ; foreword by Jacques F. Vallée; afterword by John F. Haught

Description: Eugene, OR : Cascade Books, 2020 | Includes bibliographical references and index.

Identifiers: ISBN 978-1-5326-3310-2 (paperback) | ISBN 978-1-5326-3312-6 (hardcover) | ISBN 978-1-5326-3311-9 (ebook)

Subjects: Unidentified flying objects—Religious aspects. | Space theology. | Life on other planets—Religious aspects.

Classification: BL65.U54 H36 2020 (print) | BL65.U54 H36 (ebook)

Manufactured in the U.S.A.   JANUARY 31, 2020

The Scripture quotations contained herein are from the New Revised Standard Version Bible, copyright © 1989, Division of Christian Education of the National Council of Churches of Christ in the U.S.A., except as noted. Used by permission. All rights reserved.

DEDICATION

*For Janie, in celebration of sharing life and love for forty-four years,
in so many places,
and
For our beloved daughter, Shanti, and our beloved son, Daniel—
You have enlivened and filled with joy and love our shared family journeys:
We are proud of how you have lived life, and anticipate that your spirit of
concern for others and critical inquiry will stimulate further ongoing creative
adventures and notable achievements in years to come*

Contents

Foreword by Jacques F. Vallée ix
Preface xi
Acknowledgments xiii

1. Introduction: Emerging Cosmos Consciousness 1

2. Plurality of World, Plurality of Being, Displacement, *Axis Mundi—Logos-Logoi* in Space *Loci* 28
   GENESIS, JOHN, MAXIMUS CONFESSOR, FRANCIS OF ASSISI, HEUP YOUNG KIM

3. Unidentified Aerial Phenomena: Extraterrestrial and Interdimensional 64
   ALLEN HYNEK AND JACQUES VALLEE

4. Science Discovers ETL and ETI 96
   PIERRE TEILHARD DE CHARDIN, STEPHEN HAWKING, EDWARD O. WILSON, ABRAHAM LOEB

5. Abductions and Indigenous Peoples' Encounters 139
   JOHN MACK, PHILLIP DEERE, DAVID SOHAPPY, ARDY SIXKILLER CLARKE

6. Socioecology, Integral Ecology, Hague Principles, Intergovernmental Panel on Climate Change (IPCC): On Earth and In the Heavens 192

7. Conclusion: Community in the Cosmos Commons 226

Afterword by John F. Haught 243
Appendix 1: Analysis of Alleged ETI/IDI UAP Events in the US and UK 245
Appendix 2: Cosmos Charter 263
Appendix 3: Continuing Considerations and Conversations 273
Bibliography 277
Index 287

Foreword

There is no more interesting subject than the possible existence of other forms of consciousness in the universe. It is the defining question of our generation, and our children's generation. It may represent an extraordinary opportunity—or an awesome threat—to our grandchildren.

Given that premise, there is no greater mystery than the failure of the vast majority of our scientists, over the last sixty years, to detect *any* sign of such consciousness anywhere in the accessible universe, or to publicly state that they have evidence of other-than-human intelligent life in the universe.

Not only that, but we are still unable to prove that *any* form of life, let alone conscious life, exists beyond the Earth. Even with the formidable means that modern science can deploy: the sophisticated radio telescopes, the exquisitely clear optical systems orbiting our planet or spread across high deserts in South America, the powerful computers equipped with artificial intelligence processing millions of images of planetary surfaces and energy emissions from stars, planets, and galaxies, no pattern has emerged to demonstrate that life exists beyond our own little world. The few rocks NASA has been able to bring back from the Moon and the data from Mars probes obtained in several extraordinary missions show tantalizing signs of chemical complexity, and the necessary molecules do exist in space (contrary to what science was teaching just fifty years ago) to build assemblies conducive to life, but these structures belong to physics, not to living things. Even the analysis of Martian meteorites expelled from the planet by ancient impacts, and collected on Earth, has failed to convince the experts.

Such is the grand enigma John Hart poses before us in this book, with an invitation to redefine the problem, to open our minds to a broader understanding of life, consciousness, and spirit, and to consider bold ideas that can take us beyond the boundaries of current technology.

As a young astronomer with the University of Texas, when I first came to the United States in the early days of space exploration, I was tasked with the computations that produced a map of Mars accurate enough to locate and reduce the data from the images of the Mariner probes in the mid-1960s. My mentors were passionate about the possibility that primitive vegetal life, or fossilized signs of an earlier insect or animal life, might exist on Mars. Indeed, the best observations we reviewed from the previous hundred years in preparation for the project showed tantalizing changes in color occurring periodically between certain areas of the planet. Was it life? Was our own terrestrial life seeded from the Cosmos? The challenge remains, and the discovery of water on both Mars and the Moon continues to encourage speculation, but the proof still eludes us.

Yet life must be universal. Chemistry suggests it, physics consents, and the human Spirit calls for such a breakthrough, sometimes in poetry and dream, occasionally in solitary contemplation, often in prayer, and sometimes in despair.

Not only life, but Consciousness in all its glory, equal to ours; or far, far beyond our limited grasp of cosmic realities, in the transcendent realm of the Divine. And if not the Divine, scientists say, at least the Sacred.

Third Displacement is a bold invitation to step away from the necessarily narrow technical experiments of the past and to consider such a wider range of potentialities. As a self-defined "enquiring scholar-activist," John Hart reminds us that the Kepler space probes have now discovered thousands of planets beyond our own solar system, opening a new debate about what cosmic life means. His interests range from the works of Saint Francis Assisi, whose encounter with a flying seraph in a circular sky form caused deep wounds that led to his painful death, to the modern speculations of Stephen Hawking and Teilhard de Chardin. But it is John Mack, the Harvard psychiatrist who dedicated the last part of his life to the study of abductees, who best summarized the passion and the drama of our society's current fascination with alien "contact."

As the Sacred goes, most statements about UFOs on TV specials are primitive at best, and the arguments of the believers fall short of testable scientific criteria. But it is the long-term impact of the images, the sincerity of thousands of witnesses, and the challenge they represent for future science on this planet that matter: Those "Close Encounters of the Otherkind" described by Dr. Hart contain the seed of a new philosophy, more attuned to the expectations of the public, and more respectful of a humanity it can restore to its rightful place among the stars.

Jacques F. Vallée, BSc, MSc, PhD
Astrophysicist and Computer Scientist
San Francisco, CA
1 August 2019

Preface

I began the Cosmos Contact trilogy and its final book, *Third Displacement*, with the intention of exploring with readers the Earth consciousness-disruptive idea that We Are *Not* Alone in the cosmos. In the introductions to *Cosmic Commons* and *Encountering ETI*, I describe my first encounter (a CE-1, in astronomer Allen Hynek's categories) with an intelligently controlled Unidentified Aerial Phenomenon (UAP), in 1963. I did not think at length or in-depth about this until forty years later, after reading a comment by Stephen Hawking that UFOs do not exist. I knew he was wrong: I did not only *think* that UAP exist; I *knew* that they exist. To establish this "beyond a reasonable doubt" does not require a reductionist perspective that only accepts hard evidence—that leaves physical traces—as the way to recognize the present or prior presence of a UAP on a site. Rather, credible witnesses who have been carefully and respectfully questioned—without bias, pro or con, regarding their testimony—especially if several of them have observed the same phenomenon or being(s) simultaneously, from different sites or through diverse optical devices; these factors would provide a firm foundation from which to confirm or dismiss the proposal that a UAP or intelligent other-than-human being(s) had been in the area.

I observed in *Encountering ETI* that I do not *believe* that UAP and ETI exist. Belief has to do with a metaphysical or metamaterial realm of reality, in which what is described is in a transcendent or spiritual dimension, and not in a material reality. Spacecraft are material, physical, or corporeal objects. Their physical existence or nonexistence can be established over time; one does not "believe" that a space shuttle exists, for example.

Over the past decade, I have discovered that my intellectual, social-scientific-spiritual exploration has had far more impacts than I could have anticipated. I have come to new understandings about UAP, spirituality, the Bible, and the world of science, particularly as understood and practiced in astrobiology and astrophysics. My "objective" research has, as a consequence, become deeply personal as I have tried to understand, give new meaning to, or replace prior beliefs and knowledge, now with new eyes, a new vision, and a new consciousness.

In this final volume of the trilogy, then, the reader might well be challenged by the data I present and its possible meanings for the twenty-first century . . . and beyond. I have explored reflectively mysteries of the night sky, and pondered what other dimensions of the cosmos might exist that are not visible to Earth eyes. I had to have an open mind in my explorations, and be willing to accept that what I had once taken for granted as real or true is not entirely so. Through the process, I was at times dismayed, disturbed, distraught, and depressed: it is difficult to part with long-held beliefs and supposed "knowledge." I held on to the spiritual core in my innermost being. In doing so, I was able to see the world and the cosmos with new eyes, free from the old blindness and barriers, and to transition to more creative, responsible thinking. When I wrote *Cosmic Commons*, I did not imagine a trilogy. However, as I discovered and understood more data, I wrote *Encountering ETI* and, finally, *Third Displacement*.

I invite the reader to journey with me on a spiritual, scientific, and spatial voyage of discovery. We will know not where we are going, at times. The way might be difficult, or even perilous—but exciting. The destination we reach might be only a temporary stopover and, even then, not what we anticipated. But our lives will be enriched by where we go and what we see, and by how we try to pull it all together. Over time, we will become new people with a new consciousness in a new world . . . or new worlds.

Acknowledgments

Third Displacement follows *Cosmic Commons* and *Encountering ETI* in the trilogy Cosmos Contact: Close Encounters of the Otherkind. This book and its predecessors came to fruition because of the encouragement and support of numerous people. I am grateful to all of them, but especially to the friends, faculty colleagues, and family members noted here.

While in the process of retiring from teaching at Boston University in June of 2018, I reflected on faculty colleagues and friends who encouraged my exploratory creative thinking and writing in an intellectually and spiritually challenging field—the consideration of impacts on Earth communities, and particularly on Earth communities' spiritual understandings, that the acknowledged presence of extraterrestrial and interdimensional intelligent beings would have. This would be the case, I think, even if the possibility is considered only as a "thought experiment"—as I had done in the first two volumes. My Boston University colleague-friends (and neighbors, in some cases) have been supportive in sometimes stressful circumstances but also for celebratory moments—through dinners, parties, and conversations in halls and offices at the university, and while strolling Boston streets or along the Charles. On- and off-campus, they have been wonderful: Walter Earl Fluker, Martin Luther King Jr. Professor of Ethical Leadership; Andrew Shenton, Associate Professor of Music, James R. Houghton Scholar of Sacred Music; David Campbell, as provost and then as professor of physics, electrical and computer engineering, and materials science and engineering; Claude Hobson, concert pianist and music instructor; Bryan Stone, associate dean for academic affairs, and H. Eugene 'Gene' Stanley, William Fairfield Warren Distinguished Professor of Physics. I appreciated, too, dinners and the friendly folks at the Island Creek Oyster Bar on Kenmore Square, where Chef Nicki Hobson and several servers and managers became family.

I have enjoyed and gained new insights, too, from dialogic interactions with my masters and doctoral students at Boston University: in my classes, in my office, and walking the hallways, and, on occasion, in my apartment when students came for the final session of the semester, and we enjoyed together an informative and convivial gathering.

I am grateful, too, for the encouragement of and occasional conversations with Edward O. Wilson, University Research Professor Emeritus, Harvard University. We wrote complementary complimentary endorsements for each other's 2006 book: *The Creation: An Appeal to Save Life on Earth*; and *Sacramental Commons: Christian Ecological Ethics*.

I was intellectually stimulated by Oxford University faculty and friends who guided the Oxford Seminars in Science and Christianity, which for one month per summer for three summers provided exceptional stimulation and congenial conversation in Oxford. I am grateful particularly to distinguished professors Alister McGrath, John Roche, John Hedley Brooke, William Shea, and Ernan McMullin.

The Center for Theology and the Natural Sciences was very supportive of my work: through personal encouragement, by providing grants for my courses and research, and for sponsoring the Oxford Seminars, with Templeton Foundation funding. I appreciate especially the support I received from Robert John Russell and Ted Peters.

Astrophysicist Jacques Vallée, a friend of several years, has been very supportive. I have enjoyed our dialogue and his professional and personal insights during our postal mail correspondence.

Scientists Joan Bird and William Puckett, a field research team in Montana for the Mutual UFO Network, were very helpful guides for my analysis of Montana UFO claims about a sighting at Bannock.

For almost forty years, I have been inspired and guided by Indian activists and elders, for whose friendship and support I have been very grateful: William Means, Lakota, executive director, International Indian Treaty Council; David Sohappy and Myra Sohappy, Wanapum (River People), extraordinary spiritual leaders, healers, and human rights advocates, and Wanapum fishing rights activists on the Great River, the Columbia; Phillip Deere, Muskogee elder and healer, and spiritual guide for both the American Indian Movement (AIM) and the International Indian Treaty Council; and Pat Kennedy, Chippewa-Cree elder, healer, and activist in Montana and beyond.

I appreciated the editors and employees of Wipf and Stock who have been interested in my work focused on the other-than-human intelligent presence on and around Earth, and in the cosmos more generally. They guided to publication my first book on the topic, a new area for them: James Stock, Charlie Collier, Daniel Lanning, Ian Creeger, and Jacob Martin.

Through the development and writing of the Cosmos Contact trilogy, Charlie Collier has been my editor at Wipf and Stock. He has been patient and encouraging, as *Third Displacement* was slowed or halted temporarily by life's unexpected events, just as he had been when I was writing—with several interruptions—the previous two volumes of the trilogy. I thank Charlie for enduring ever-new deadline requests as life intervened in the flow of my research and writing. For this and for his ongoing encouragement for seven years: Thank you very much, Charlie.

I am especially grateful for my family's support and insights as I wrote the volumes of the trilogy: my beloved wife, Jane Morell-Hart, our daughter, Shanti Morell-Hart, PhD, and our son, Daniel Morell-Hart, EdS. I have been embraced by their love and stimulated by our conversations as I explored unfamiliar territory and pursued an answer to the ages-old question, "Are we alone in the universe as an intelligent species?"

After much research and considered reflection, particularly on scientists' analyses and ideas and traditional Indian elders' words, I formulated my answer to the question, "Are we alone?" The information I gathered as I searched for an answer sometimes has been disconcerting and anxiety-producing, and at other times exciting and hopeful. We are *not* alone in the cosmos.

The exploration and elaboration of my considered response to the question about other-than-human intelligent life in the cosmos is presented in the pages that follow.

John Hart, PhD, Helena, Montana
Emeritus Professor of Christian Ethics, Boston University School of Theology
October 5, 2019

1

Introduction: Emerging Cosmos Consciousness

Humankind around the world has achieved extraordinary progress in space exploration and solar system voyages during the past fifty years. Initially, the US and USSR were the only nations that had the technology and the capability to design, develop, and construct rockets that could carry artificial satellites to orbit Earth, and more powerful rockets that enabled humans' space vehicles to leave Earth's gravity's hold and travel to the moon and, later, into the universe beyond. Within decades of Sputnik's launch and Apollo 11 astronauts' walk on the moon, other countries joined the effort. Today, humankind has international representation in space. Individual nations have particular projects, and international coalitions have others. These have been preceded by intense scientific research and exceptional technological innovation, the result of human imagination and creativity set free to explore multiple possibilities for humans to venture into space. In the process, humanity became more aware and curious—and sometimes fearful—about cosmos immensity and about what other-than-human intelligent beings they might encounter in their exploration.

Humankind Explores Space: Decades of International Accomplishments

Accomplishments by the US space program have included astronaut Neil Armstrong's lunar landing and moonwalk in 1969; the ongoing explorations of Voyagers 1 and 2 within and beyond the solar system; the completed construction and continuing missions of the International Space Station (ISS;

first occupied in 2000); the NASA Mars rovers (and discovery of water on Mars); the Cassini explorer's analysis of Saturn's rings and moons (Enceladus: vapor plumes; Titan: underground bodies of water); exploration of Jupiter's moon via 1997 Galileo flyby (Europa: frozen surface, vapor plumes, subsurface water[1]), and other discoveries through telescopes and electronic equipment on satellites launched by the US National Aeronautics and Space Administration (NASA), France's CNES-GEIPAN (Centre National d'Études Spatiales-Groupe d'Études et d'Information sur les Phénomènes Aérospatiaux Non Identifiés), the European Space Agency (ESA), and space technology on the ISS. Rovers have been placed not only on Mars by NASA, but on the far side of the moon by the China National Space Agency (CNSA). A NASA and ESA joint project to use radar for subsurface exploration of Mars resulted in the discovery of liquid water underneath the planet's south pole—NASA's MARSIS (Mars Advanced Radar for Subsurface and Ionosphere Sounding) was transported to the red planet by the ESA's Mars Express spacecraft.[2] The water detected by the MARSIS instrument on board the European Space Agency's spacecraft is located 1.5 kilometers (~one mile) beneath the ice, in the form of a lake twenty kilometers (12.4 miles) across under the freezing plains of Planum Australe.

Cosmos exploration by the ESA Gaia satellite has discovered more stellar phenomena than any other Earth-launched explorer. In winter of 2018, it discovered an immense nearby "ghost galaxy," named Antlia 2 ("Ant 2"), the size of the Large Magellanic Cloud (LMC). Ant 2 was not previously seen because it is a very low density "dwarf galaxy" that emerged in the early universe; such a galaxy contains very old stars and little metals. Compared to the LMC, "Ant 2 is 10,000 times fainter. In other words, it is either far too large for its luminosity or far too dim for its size . . . Gaia has produced the richest star catalogue to date, including high-precision measurements of nearly 1.7 billion stars and revealing previously unseen details of our home Galaxy."[3]

Extraordinary accomplishments have resulted recently, too, from NASA's search for exoplanets (planets outside Earth's solar system) in the Milky Way Galaxy, using the Kepler and Hubble telescopes, among others. The work of the Kepler exoplanet hunter telescope, which was retired by NASA in November 2018, should be recognized and celebrated. Kepler's mission lasted 9.6 years. During that period, Kepler personnel discovered 2,662 planets ("many of which could be promising places for life"); surveyed more than 530,000 stars; found that the number of planets in our galaxy is

---

1. NASA, "Old Data." A follow-up is forthcoming in the 2020s: forty-five orbits by Europa Clipper to ascertain if life-supporting elements are present in the water.

2. Cooper, "Astrobio Top 10."

3. Collins, "Gaia Spots a 'Ghost,'" paras. 3–4, 6.

larger than the number of stars (prior to Kepler's mission, scientists did not know if even one star, other than Earth's sun, had planets; there was not a single named planet; the first exoplanet to be named was discovered only in 1995, by NASA: 51 Pegasi b). Now, according to NASA, "analysis of Kepler's discoveries concludes that 20 to 50 percent of the stars visible in the night sky are likely to have small, possibly rocky, planets similar in size to Earth, and located within the habitable zone of their parent stars. That means they are located at distances from their parent stars where liquid water—a vital ingredient to life as we know it—might pool on the planet surface."[4] The most recent major NASA achievement, as of this writing, took place on January 1, 2019. The New Horizons voyager, which had previously photographed Pluto in 2015, passed just 2,200 miles away from the surface of 2014 MU69, known as "Ultima Thule" ("beyond the known world"). It is located four billion miles from the sun, in the Kuiper Belt at the outer edge of the solar system.[5] In the icy Kuiper Belt, whose origins date back to the beginning of the solar system and whose occupant entities have remained virtually unchanged since then, scientists hope to learn more about the origins of the sun, as well as Earth and other planets in the solar system.[6]

China's space technology achieved a first for humankind—on the day following the New Horizons flyby of Ultima Thule. The CNSA announced on January 2, 2019, that the Chang'e 4 lunar rover had landed on the far side of the moon, in the Von Karman Crater. This is the moon's deepest crater—caused by a massive meteor strike—whose sides have an abundance of minerals in their layers. Chang'e 4's cameras have been sending pictures back to Earth.[7] Chang'e 4 is named after a goddess in Chinese mythology who lives on the moon. It was China's second lunar landing; the first was in 2015. China is becoming a major player in space exploration: it has hopes to mine the moon, and to set up a base there to launch exploratory missions farther out into the solar system. (US administrations and Congress have forbidden

---

4. NASA, "NASA Retires Kepler." The reader is encouraged to explore the NASA website.

5. Chang, "Journey." See also NASA, "Astronomy Picture," for the New Horizons photo of asteroid Ultima Thule. Other data about New Horizons, related to the picture, is found on the NASA website.

6. Brian May, PhD, an astrophysicist involved with New Horizons, is the lead guitarist for the rock group Queen. He wrote a song and developed a music video, "New Horizons," commemorating the event. It was released at the Advanced Physics Laboratory in Johns Hopkins University from which NASA's New Horizons was controlled, a few minutes after midnight on the occasion of the New Horizons flyby of Ultima Thule: see Fingas, "Queen Guitarist Brian May."

7. See extensive coverage in the *Washington Post* by Kaplan et al., "China Lands Spacecraft," and by Meyers and Mou, "New Chapter," in *The New York Times*.

collaboration between NASA and the CNSA, including by excluding China from participation in the ISS.)

On the horizon is NASA's anticipated 2021 launch of the James Webb Space Telescope, which will be capable of seeing far into space and deep into time: less than 500 million years from the beginning of the 13.8 billion-year universe story. Increased knowledge of distant space and deep time will not only add to humans' wonderment about the vast and complex cosmos, but also intensify the curiosity expressed in the question "Are we alone?" posed by the NASA Astrobiology Institute[8] and, for millennia, by scientists, philosophers, religious thinkers, and other Earth inhabitants.

Those are just a few examples of how research scientists, aided by innovative technologies, have helped humanity to understand, to a greater extent than was possible previously, both the vastness and complexity of the cosmos, and the diversity of, and potential for the presence of life on, numerous worlds recently discovered or projected to be discovered in the near future.

Intelligent Life in Space

During the past four decades, stories multiplied globally that people had sighted UFOs (Unidentified Flying Objects), an acronym often narrowly and erroneously used in common parlance, unfortunately, solely to indicate intelligently controlled spacecraft rather than all unknown (sometimes only temporarily) objects. While artificial satellites, meteors, lunar phases, or Venus were viewed as UFOs in these instances, as was determined by investigating astronomers and meteorologists, at other times scientists could find no scientific explanation for the events described.[9]

A changing cosmos consciousness consequent to these events has been developing among the general public. The impact of related scientific narratives and a complementary flurry of documentaries, television programs, and science fiction (sci-fi) movies have stimulated this progressive consciousness. To a far greater extent than just a few decades ago, people are expressing that they "believe" or, more accurately, that they "think" or "know"

---

8. I served on the NAI Focus Group on Astrobiology and Society as a humanities scholar.

9. Astronomer Allen Hynek, Chair of the Astronomy Department at Northwestern University, and the US government's official "debunker" of all reports of apparently intelligently controlled UFOs, came to realize that there were some events for which he could not find or contrive a scientific explanation; he pressed the US government to establish and fund independent science research. When this did not happen, he resigned from his position and continued his work independently. Hynek developed the "close encounters" categories, the basis for Steven Spielberg's film *Close Encounters of the Third Kind*; Hynek has a cameo role near the film's end.

that intelligently controlled spacecraft have been seen,[10] and that interactive Contact has probably occurred: ETI-TI-IDI (ExtraTerrestrial Intelligence-Terrestrial Intelligence-InterDimensional Intelligence).[11] To a lesser extent, scientists have gone on record suggesting that objective independent scientific research, not government-controlled research, should be undertaken to investigate thoroughly and transparently claims about ETI and IDI sightings. Privately, several scientists have confided to this author their own experiences; they dare not describe them publicly or even to colleagues because of their fear that they would lose their university teaching or research position, government and private foundation research support, or their prestige among colleagues.

Based on scientific evidence and scientists' affirmations, it is possible to assert now that Contact between human beings and intelligent beings from other cosmos places has occurred. This fact, based on solid scientific observations and data, and scientists' extrapolations from the data, stimulates humankind to reflect seriously and deeply, at this moment of human history, about next steps in humanity's journey to understand human place(s) in a suddenly more comprehensible and more meaningful complex cosmos in which extraterrestrial intelligent life and interdimensional intelligent life have made their presence known. What are *they* thinking about us, and what intentions might they have in initiating Contact with us?

In order to explore thoroughly the evidence about ExoEarth beings, a "thought experiment" will be used as a means to facilitate communication and discussion among all who are interested in the subjects of Extraterrestrial Life (ETL), Extraterrestrial Intelligent Life (ETI), and Interdimensional Intelligent Life (IDI). It will begin with an answer to the millennia-old question, "Are we alone?" The answer is, "We are *not* alone. What might we do now? How might we respond to Contact with intelligent Others?" This rubric enables people from diverse backgrounds—unreservedly and without anxiety—to examine the data and evidence, express their opinions, hypotheses, and theories (constantly updated, based on ever-increasing factual data), discuss what they think, describe their experiences, and pose their questions. They will discuss compatible and incompatible ideas and seek some form of common ground, rather than separate into opposing confrontational camps. They will express their understanding of data received, not stating facts absolutely, but facts as they understand them, even when they know that what they are describing did indeed occur. They will discuss implications of ETI and IDI encounters on the grounds of "what if" this or that has taken place.

---

10. See Costa and Costa's *UFO Sightings Desk Reference* catalogue.
11. See Hynek, *Hynek UFO Report*.

The process described allows for freedom of expression, since even if what is stated was in the morning's newspaper, participants in the process would be considering diverse implications for humankind should distinct new data be evaluated and incorporated in their thinking. A news story might be based on "objective" or agreed upon facts, or on an experience of an event that is theorized to be a narrative of an apparent ETI or IDI visitation. The "what if" could be a reaction to a story about a UFO, to a scientist's statement, to the narrative of a "credible witness" to a single incident or multi-incident event, or to an unusual artifact found by the rovers InSight or Curiosity on Mars, or by Voyager 1 or New Horizons in deep space. No personal or professional risk would be taken; in such a setting; it would not be needed or even desirable for people to "credentialize" themselves. Discussion could be about the danger of pathogenic transfer from Enceladus to Earth, or from Earth to Mars (such as when Curiosity's drill was taken out of its secure, sterile storage while on its rocket, and readied for a possible crash landing on Mars: it likely carried microbes from the non-secure area to the Mars surface). Ethical issues could arise from the latter types of events. All thought-experiment-developed discussion would assume that ETL, ETI, and IDI exist, and flow from that foundation to focus on particular occurrences and their potential impacts on human thought in general, Earth's religions, and Earth communities.

The "Third Displacement" concept and its elaboration coincide well with NASA Astrobiology Institute (NAI) explorations and NAI Focus Group expectations, as stated on the NAI website: "How did life begin and evolve?"; "Is there life beyond Earth?"; and, "What is the future of life on Earth and beyond?" It embodies the objective of the NAI Focus Group, "to bring together interested researchers across a broad range of expertise including ethics, sociology, theology, and philosophy, as well as the science of astrobiology, to address the social implications of astrobiological discoveries now and in the future."

New Understandings about Life on Earth, in the Universe, and in the Cosmos

As NASA and SETI scientists analyzed results of research that they were doing on life in space, it occurred to them that a change of terminology was needed to represent new understandings about life on other worlds, in different space contexts. "Biology" traditionally referred to the "science of life" on Earth. This term was inadequate to refer simultaneously to life on humans' home planet and life on other worlds in the universe. *Biology* (life on Earth) became *astrobiology* (life on ExoEarth worlds in the universe more broadly, in space among the near and distant stars). Then many scientists proposed that there is a "multiverse" or there are multiple cosmos dimensions in which yet other worlds are likely found and on some of them, too, intelligent living beings who have the technology to travel interdimensionally through the cosmos. In order to acknowledge the possibility of this hypothesized cosmos reality, and of beings who are thought to have come to Earth and Earth's dimension, a new, more comprehensive understanding of the totality of cosmos living beings is needed. These beings are present on Earth in its dimension, and in space among planets orbiting stars. Other living intelligent beings are likely present, too, not only on other worlds, but in other dimensions of cosmos being in more complex contexts. The study of other-than-human intelligent life is best described as cosmobiology: life among the stars in space, and in other dimensions of existence. This awareness of life's cosmos possibilities stimulated a progression in terminology about life, developed to include all known and proposed variations; humans acknowledge that the forms life takes among the stars, and interdimensionally, likely differ considerably from life on Earth.

Reflecting on this, I decided to include these new understandings in *Third Displacement*. Initially, I was going to retain the customary phrasing of, for example, "astrobiology," and make other areas consonant with it, such as discussing "astrolocality," thereby paralleling existing terminology. However, changing "astrolocality" to "cosmolocality," and "astrosocioecology" to "cosmosocioecology" seemed to acknowledge and clarify cosmos realities more appropriately. I decided to break with traditional nomenclature, since the book does consider the idea of cosmos interdimensionality, and the existence of InterDimensional Intelligent beings (IDI) as well as ExtraTerrestrial Intelligent beings (ETI). Thus, cosmolocality and cosmosocioecology were born, as terminology that would coexist well with cosmobiology.

Natural Rights in and for Nature

Analyses of TI-ETI and TI-IDI Contact[12] include exploration about the extent to which a specific component of integral being[13] (e.g., a planet, star, star system, or species) has integral natural rights (from which *all* natural rights are derived), and requires ethical consideration from both theist and atheist or humanist perspectives. "Natural rights" in this endeavor would include the rights of all biota and their abiotic contexts, not just human rights. In light of recent scientific findings and understanding regarding Earth biota

---

12. "Contact," when capitalized, is the term used to indicate TI-ETI and TI-IDI encounters.

13. Hart, *Cosmic Commons*, 180. See the description and elaboration of "integral being" below. Integral *being* actually is integral *being-becoming*.

(such as intelligence, emotions, moral consciousness and choice, and intra- and interspecies relationality), "natural" should be extended beyond solely human rights and "nature" on Earth, to include "nature" integrally, in its diverse manifestations in the cosmos commons.

Transcendent and Transcosmos Considerations

Two interrelated dimensions of human experience on Earth and in the universe are explored: the *transcendent* and the *transcosmic*. The transcendent refers to engagement with ultimate reality, including in its manifestations as experienced through divine (however understood) immanence in the revelatory Earth commons; the transcosmic refers to speculative extensions—based on scientific data and theories, including those derived from the work of NASA (the US National Aeronautics and Space Administration), CNES—GEIPAN (the older-than-NASA space agency, in France: Centre National d'Etudes Spatiales[14]—Groupe d'études et d'informations sur les phénomènes aérospatiaux non identifies), ESA (European Space Agency), and other space programs—of the transcendent across space and time as explored in dynamic spiritual and ethical understandings, and of materiality across space and in time, as assessed by present, projected, and unanticipated scientific means. The ETL, ETI, and IDI speculation and exploration will be assisted in its analysis and assessment by terrestrial, extraterrestrial, and interdimensional bioethical and ecological ethics (which include engagement with human community cosmosocioecological ethics).

An Integrative Relationship: Interdimensional-Terrestrial-Extraterrestrial Ethics

Earth- and humankind-related *socioecological praxis ethics*[15] expands into a cosmos-centered *cosmosocioecological praxis ethics* in order to extend considerations of humankind's ethical consciousness and conduct outward, into space. This cosmos-aware, cosmos-developed, and cosmos-engaged theory and practice are much needed as humanity constructs space stations, sends mechanical explorers voyaging into space and roving on new worlds, establishes bases and colonies in near and distant places, and searches for human-needed and human-desired natural goods ("natural resources").[16]

14. See the CNES homepage at https://cnes.fr/en.

15. Socioecological praxis ethics, in brief, is the integration of social justice within and among human communities, with the wellbeing of Earth and all living beings (Hart, *Cosmic Commons*, 188–90). In a universe or multiverse context, it becomes *cosmosociological praxis ethics* (Hart, *Encountering*, 281–7). See also below, chapter 6.

16. A "natural good" is something in place that might be used in its context to provide

Richard Randolph, Margaret Race, and Chris McKay state in a 1997 article[17] that theological and ethical discussions of extraterrestrial modification "may help us see our own environmental issues more clearly from this distant perspective." This might be amended and updated to suggest engaging time—the present and the future—as well as terrestrial and ExoEarth experiences, reflections, and projections. Terrestrial ecological and social ethics should be in conversation with ExoEarth ecological and social ethics. Optimally, they should exist in a dynamic, dialogic–dialectic process wherein each informs the other. What humans do on other worlds[18] will probably reflect what they do on Earth, at least initially. Therefore, reflections about the impacts of space exploration may challenge us to modify our human consciousness and conduct, both on Earth and elsewhere. In the longer term, what humans learn as they adapt to other worlds' contexts can, in turn, guide their attitudes, values, and practices on Earth or in similar cosmos contexts encountered in later voyages.

Human researchers and explorers must be conscious of actual or potential dangers from Earth to other worlds, and from other worlds to Earth. They should take into consideration possible impacts on both Earth and ExoEarth evolution, which are likely to be in process wherever life exists, at whatever stage of development. If humans believe they are, as ever-fewer people believe, the only reflective consciousness of the cosmos, then if they act irresponsibly toward themselves and toward integral cosmos being, they might well destroy not only life on Earth, but cosmic consciousness itself. If humans currently are the only form of reflective cosmic consciousness, and destroy life on other planets, they will eliminate a "fallback" evolutionary possibility on another world (whether that life exists as a current mode of divine creativity, or has emerged from a non-transcendent origin and is part of dynamic cosmic diversification and complexification). The consciousness perspective, and ethics that humans take with them for stellar and planetary explorations will influence the manner in which they engage biota and abiotic being. For example, if cosmos-conscious and cosmos-oriented praxis ethics is overridden by economic or military considerations, humans' consciousness of their responsibility within and in relation to integral being would be significantly diminished or disregarded. It is incumbent on humankind to

---

a geophysical benefit, or serve the needs of a variety of biota, not just humankind. A "natural resource" implies something beneficial to humans, and prioritized in this way in humans' thinking; other biota often are excluded from consideration.

17. Randolph, et al, "Reconsidering," 1–8.

18. "World" is used by NASA as a generic term for a planet, moon, asteroid or other "heavenly body," whether viewed from Earth or from an Earth telescope in space, or visited in space.

develop a terrestrially formulated "ethics of encounter" that can evolve and adapt appropriately in response to the nature and diversity of any extraterrestrial Contact or contacts that may occur.

Distant space and deep time will add not only to human wonderment about the vast and complex cosmos, but also intensify the curiosity expressed in the question "Are we alone?" which has been posed by the NASA Astrobiology Institute and was the focus of Kepler telescope searches. Kepler sought habitable planets in space (as noted earlier, it discovered more than two thousand new planets). The primordial NASA question will be explored primarily in terms of "We are *not* alone as intelligent life in the universe; now what?" It focuses on potential societal impacts of discovery of microbial or intelligent life in our solar system (particularly on planetary or lunar bodies) in the foreseeable future, and deeper into space in the distant future.

This exploration and exposition extends my prior work with NASA. Our focus group was charged with considering societal impacts of the discovery of microbial life in space; each member reflected on possible reactions that their specific constituency in their particular fields would have to ETL. Three of us pondered impacts on religion if microbial life is discovered. Along these lines, here we will explore, and to some extent reflect on in-depth, statements and assertions made in the scientific debate about the possible existence of intelligent life in the solar system and the immense cosmos beyond. The scientific consensus today, in the context of the theorized existence of some ten million Earth-like planets in our Milky Way Galaxy alone, is that there is likely microbial life in space; there is no consensus on the existence of intelligent life. However, while a majority of scientists think that there is none, their numbers are diminishing slowly in light of NASA's and other agencies' discoveries and consequent theories. Several renowned scientists who once rejected the possibility of other-than-human intelligent life in the cosmos have changed their view. Several of these scientists' previous and current positions are presented.

Third Displacement is the third volume of the trilogy Cosmos Contact: Close Encounters of the Otherkind.[19] The volumes explore possible ecological, ethical, economic, and ecclesial[20] implications of Earth-ExoEarth intelligent life Contact that would occur when scientists discover either simple or complex forms of life in the universe. Among the latter is the likelihood that a third contextual-conceptual and psychological-spiritual-philosophical shift in human consciousness and humans' sense of cosmic place will occur,

---

19. All the books in the trilogy are published by Cascade Books, an imprint of Wipf and Stock Publishers.

20. Used uncharacteristically generically here to represent all religious and spiritual traditions.

complementary to the aftermath of the First Displacement (Copernican Revolution) and the Second Displacement (Darwinian Evolution). The current volume follows *Encountering ETI: Aliens in* Avatar *and the Americas*, and *Cosmic Commons: Spirit, Science, and Space*. The latter books focused on Contact using a "thought experiment" to consider that intelligent life Contact has occurred already; credible witnesses' reports contribute to the respective books' analyses. This book explores concrete data from scientists, social scientists, and other credible witnesses. The data has been acquired in part through personal interviews, and from journals, books, and newspaper articles. It examines more in-depth the impacts of Contact when it is accepted as a fact, and explores confirming that Contact is a fact. Humans' current understanding of their present and future cosmos locus (humankind as the sole intelligent life—and therefore central in cosmos importance) in thought and in physical place (cosmolocality) will be ever-more disoriented at Contact when new types of living beings (cosmobiology) are engaged among near and distant stars. The disorientation would be significant for some people, and minimal for others (depending on whether they are hostile toward or fearful of, or engage with and adapt to, Contact).

The trilogy title—Cosmos Contact: Close Encounter of the Otherkind—suggests that when Contact occurs between terrestrial intelligent beings and extraterrestrial intelligent beings or interdimensional intelligent beings, this encounter will prompt an enhanced cosmos consciousness on the part of humankind. The reality that "we are *not* alone" will stimulate human thinking to go "outside the box" of its previous Earth-bound and human-centered way of viewing the cosmos and all that might be "out there." (Humans are, of course, "out there" in the perspective of inhabitants of other worlds, to whose environs they journey.) Humankind and Otherkind—the Others or Visitors with whom humankind makes Contact—have the potential, as time passes and they come to know and understand each other better, to recognize that all living beings are members of a relational cosmos community. As expressed in Indian traditions of the Americas, "we are all related"; "all my relations" includes all biota and abiota; and, in the words of Francis of Assisi, all beings are "sisters" and "brothers."

New understandings of *socioecological praxis ethics* (originating in Earth settings) would have to be developed that might adapt to and adopt from distinct and diverse cosmos contexts, and transition, over time, into *cosmosocioecological praxis ethics*. This would guide human consciousness and conduct while humankind explores space, establishes bases on Earth's moon and other places, and colonizes (and possibly, terraforms) habitable planets that have or do not have microbial life. Humans should, through sustained Contact, develop an understanding of cosmic relatedness (cosmosociality, to parallel cosmobiology), and awareness that other evolutionarily advanced beings, too, have an intraspecies consciousness of caring for their progeny (eusociality). A shared consciousness of eusociality might be extended, as a consequence of Contact, to a shared interspecies intergenerational concern (cosmoeusociality). In all of the preceding considerations of other worlds, humanity should bear in mind the interrelationship of social justice and ecological wellbeing (cosmosocioecology).

The exploration of human place(s) in the cosmos helps to recall and elaborate impacts of past major displacements, and to imagine how Contact would be similar to and distinct from them in its consequences. This new displacement might be closer in time than currently conceived, because of NASA's ongoing discoveries in and projections about the existence of Milky Way Galaxy planets in the "Goldilocks Zone": they orbit neither too close to (too hot) nor too far from (too cold) their star to support life as we know it. The discovery of microbial life or intelligent life is not assumed or asserted to be a catalytic event that will cause a major consciousness shift, as did past displacements. Previous displacements were, for most people, abrupt and astounding. At the time of the new Displacement, almost one-half of humans have already been considering that possibility of being displaced, having been stimulated to these considerations by news reports, credible witness narratives, space telescope discoveries, and scientists' speculations about all of the preceding occurrences. Much of humanity has long been considering Contact (especially in native cultures, as described in the traditions and experiences of indigenous populations, for whom it is already considered a past, present, and future reality). When a shift occurs in the extent to which people understand the reality of ETI/IDI impacts, since they have already explored them proactively *a priori* and projected their possible adverse consequences, they would not have to address them urgently and reactively at Contact.

Social Justice Integrated with Ecological Wellbeing

Social issues and social ethics relate to and are integrated with ecological wellbeing. When people reach for the stars, human consciousness should be aware of and creative about ethical principles, elaborated in context, for justice within and among human communities, and among humankind, Earth, Earth's biota, other worlds, and other–than–Earthlike life. Complementary principles should be creatively developed for human conduct on ExoEarth worlds, especially if people anticipate interaction with biota already inhabiting them. In preparation for a diversity of encounters with otherworld beings, explorers should consider the ideas and principles discussed in the

Earth Charter[21] and in the Hague Principles for a Universal Declaration on Responsibilities for Human Rights and Earth Trusteeship[22] including as currently being expanded and expressed more universally in a complementary Cosmos Charter,[23] now in a seminal stage of development.

The Cosmos Charter aspires to effect efficaciously an integration of cosmolocality, cosmobiology, cosmocommunity, and cosmosocioecology for cosmos commons and cosmos relational community wellbeing. The envisioned cosmocommunity, currently an ideal, would be a cosmos relational community, characterized by beneficial relationships between humankind on Earth and humankind dispersed among settlements on distant worlds; among humankind in all places, with other living beings (including ETI and IDI) encountered in them; and with living beings' shared abiotic contexts. The intelligent beings would be engaged, in diverse near and distant places, in dialogic discourse. The resolution of a Third Displacement, then, might well come about through a shift from an Earth-bound locus and thinking to a cosmos relational consciousness in a common cosmos relational community, as humankind comes to inhabit worlds other than its Earth home.

Scientists Encounter Visitors

Throughout the twentieth and twenty-first centuries, most scientists, and people who claimed a scientific perspective (for some, only if scientific findings were in accord with their beliefs and opinions), raised the questions of "Where's the proof?" or "Where's the science?" when discussing the possible existence of Visitors—intelligent other-than-human beings—to Earth, and the reality of intelligently controlled craft—UAP, Unidentified Aerial Phenomenon/a—that were reported in the news. "Proof" and "evidence" generally meant something tangible; credible eyewitnesses' statements—even when made by scientists—did not count. (This attitude continues to be evident today, too.) Astronomer Allen Hynek represented this view initially,

---

21. The Earth Charter is discussed throughout *Cosmic Commons*, but in some depth on 112–13, and 348–50. See the Earth Charter Initiative website for a downloadable copy and continuing updates about the implementation of the Earth Charter around the world: www.earthcharter.org.

22. The Hague Principles were conceived and formalized by a core group of international scholars, primarily from the Netherlands, and released to the public from the Hague on December 10, 2018, the seventieth anniversary of the UN Universal Declaration of Human Rights. See http://www.earthtrusteeship.world/the-hague-principles-for-a-universal-declaration-on-human-responsibilities-and-earth-trusteeship. I endorsed the document on December 9, 2018. See chapter 6 of this book.

23. A proposed first draft of a Cosmic Charter is presented in Hart, *Cosmic Commons*, 358–68.

when he was the US scientific consultant whose official role was, as he proudly proclaimed, to "debunk" stories about UFOs. While in this capacity for more than two decades, he developed the criteria for categories into which encounter claims could be filed: Close Encounters of the First, Second, and Third Kinds (remember Steven Spielberg's movie?). Eventually he realized, as he did his work, that some cases could not be scientifically debunked—he reversed his prior opinion and, when the US government continued to refuse to support an independent scientific evaluation, resigned his government position. He continued his pursuit of evidence—hard data *and* credible witness reports—that Visitors had flown over or come down to Earth.

In recent years, many scientists who did not accept the reality of Visitors because of lack of "hard" (physical) evidence, and often also because they believed that humans were the only intelligent living beings in the cosmos, themselves encountered Visitors, the Others. In some cases, they stated this directly (while rarely acknowledging this publicly). In other cases, they referred to it indirectly, as they began to accept the multitude of credible witness reports, accompanied eventually by visual evidence such as photos (which had not been doctored or photoshopped) and videos (not creatively fabricated). In these cases, scientists did, indeed, encounter Visitors. They had a "conversion," so to speak, from "unbelievers" (who had no credible scientific evidence for why they "believed" now or had not "believed" previously, as is true for every faith) to thinkers, and affirmed the presence of Visitors and their craft. Complementarily, the Kepler, Hubble, and Gaia telescopes in space found thousands of planets, many in the Goldilocks Zone; in fact, there are more visible planets than stars. So, the "lack of planets" and "lack of habitable planets" foundation for previous positions crumbled.

In response to the unbelievers' assertions, in part, and because of my own long-term interest in the sciences, the book has a strong science theme. It includes scientists' assessments of UFO/UAP events which prompted them to change their position: from skeptics or deniers to scientists. Several of these scientists—and a psychiatrist—were distinguished in their profession. They include National Medal of Science recipients; Pulitzer Prize recipients; and those who earned recognition by virtue of distinguished academic chairs, awards, and other honors. Their respective changes of perspective provided much-needed support for people who knew about, or were curious about, stories of Visitors coming to Earth or its solar system environs.

Science-Religion Complementarity

Third Displacement originates and elaborates: social, psychological, and spiritual meanings of "displacement"; the concept of a "third displacement"

INTRODUCTION: EMERGING COSMOS CONSCIOUSNESS 15

in human history; integration of social justice and ecology on Earth and in cosmos contexts; consideration of spiritual and ecological insights from native peoples' elders, and teachings from centuries-old indigenous traditions, and from Christianity; recognition of science-religion complementarity, mutuality, and relationality; cosmosocioecology and cosmosocioecological praxis ethics developed in particular contexts and adaptive to other places; an evolving *Cosmos Charter*; interviews with credible UFO witnesses; presentation of the findings of the official US government UFO "debunker," astrophysicist Allen Hynek, his categories of Close Encounters, and their relevance; use of a "thought experiment" to describe and discuss credible witnesses' reports of ETI and IDI encounters positively, rather than questioningly or disparagingly; acceptance of the reality of ETI and IDI; integrated discussion of ExoEarth intelligent life; ETI, IDI, and TDI (extraterrestrial, interdimensional, and transdimensional intelligent life), as theorized by astrophysicist and computer scientist Jacques Vallée et al.); and discussion of the most recent scientific data on space explorations and planetary investigations that NASA, ESA, and CNES-GEIPAN have gathered (and the latest scientific theories related to them) and continue to accumulate and release to the scientific community and the general public.

Concepts of "cosmos commons," "Cosmos Charter," and "praxis ethics" are interwoven to elaborate innovative considerations of *time* (the relationship of present and future); *space* (human exploration of the cosmos); human-other intelligent being relations (TI-ETI and TI-IDI biota interaction); and *place* (Earth-ExoEarth, TI-ETI and TI-IDI); ecological and economic impacts of human colonization of other worlds (extraction, or extraction and exploitation, of natural goods; alteration of abiotic places; and intrusion in biotic evolution). Projected socioecological impacts of terrestrial-extraterrestrial and terrestrial-interdimensional engagement are related to suggestions for a present-future-present dynamic that would promote ecological responsibility in extraterrestrial and terrestrial contexts; a dynamic *praxis ethics*, originating on Earth but eventually adapting to and adopting from ExoEarth contexts; collaboration of humanist scientists, members of faith traditions, sociologists, environmentalists, and ethicists to process impacts of space exploration and Contact; and proposed dynamic ethical principles and practices to minimize or mitigate harm.

In order to consider in a holistic manner these diverse issues, ecology and social ethics in both Earth—including from native peoples' traditions—and other world settings, and TI-ETI / TI-IDI Contact and relationships, are integrated in these pages.[24]

24. In recent years, other scholars have considered the possible existence of ETI; some dismiss the possibility of TI-ETI Contact. Such books include theologian David

In *Third Displacement*, I continue to explore the existence of intelligently controlled UAP that originate on Earth, in ExoEarth locales, or in other dimensions. I have added considerations of intelligent beings' interdimensional travel in UAP that originate in or at least voyage through a dimension other than that in which Earth is located; the origins and attributes of robots who might be piloting them; and living beings who might be controlling them—from within or from afar. Both ETI and IDI are being studied. When humans encounter either type of intelligent being, and their origin is not yet known, ETI/IDI will be used collectively to indicate either one separately, or both conjointly.

In order to stimulate people's openness to the idea and reality of Contact, the book provides (and has a focus on) the personal narratives and professional insights of scientists who once rejected the ideas of exploratory spacecraft in Earth environs and of intelligent other-than-human beings operating such vehicles in their voyages. Then, scientists came to reason, as new evidence became available or as they examined existing evidence with a new scientific openness, that Earth visits by space voyagers or interdimensional voyagers have in fact been taking place for millennia.

The pages that follow provide new understandings about inter-intelligent species engagements, and expand socioecological praxis ethics (developed in Earth settings) into an innovative *cosmo*socioecological praxis ethics adapted to, adopted from, or integrated with ethical consciousness and conduct originating from diverse cosmos contexts. A draft Cosmos Charter (modeled on the Earth Charter and United Nations space documents, in particular) is included as Appendix 2 to promote integration of cosmolocality, cosmobiology, cosmoeusociality,[25] and cosmosocioecology for cosmos community wellbeing.

Wilkinson's *Science, Religion, and the Search for Extraterrestrial Intelligence* (2013); historian George Basalla's *Civilized Life in the Universe: Scientists on Intelligent Extraterrestrials* (2006); and astronomer David Koerner and neurobiologist Simon LeVay's *Here Be Dragons: The Scientific Quest for Extraterrestrial Life* (2000); the latter two scientists express more confidence than most others in TI-ETI encounters. In the last paragraph of their book, as they reflect on the question of whether or not we are alone, they state that while this question has no answer currently, those who seek one might find that "the trail of discovery hangs heavy with the scent of life," and the seekers might discover "maybe someone wiser" than humans (246).

25. "Cosmosociality" describes a cosmos community characterized by relational consciousness and relational conduct. "Cosmoeusociality" describes an integrated cosmos community in which the interrelated species share the latter characteristics and a common concern for intergenerational responsibility for descendants' wellbeing. The concept and practice of eusociality on Earth has been elaborated by Harvard Emeritus Biologist E. O. Wilson in several works, and in his discussion of characteristics of ExoEarth intelligent beings in *The Meaning of Human Existence*, in the chapter "A Portrait of ET." See below, chapter 5.

Socioecological Ethics in Cosmos Contexts

In this elaboration, considerations of social justice and social ethics will be integrated with ecological wellbeing, and ethical principles will be formulated in context to promote justice within and among human communities and among humankind, Earth, and other-than-human life. Complementary principles will be suggested for human conduct on ExoEarth worlds when people interact with the worlds' existing biota. In all contexts, the guiding objective is to stimulate development of a new relational consciousness for a cosmos relational community. The resolution of a third displacement might well be through a shift from humans' Earth-bound locus and thinking to a cosmos coextensive relational consciousness in the cosmos commons, and cosmos relational conduct in this common space community.

The deeper development of cosmoethics (which goes beyond—literally—astroethics) might be essential in the near future. ETI-TI-IDI Contact has been made already, according to credible witnesses—including scientists—from around the world, and will be made with greater engagement and frequency in the near term, given increasingly common reports and news coverage documenting CE-I (Close Encounters of the First Kind), CE-II (Close Encounters of the Second Kind), and CE-III (Close Encounters of the Third Kind).

Abductions and Encounters

In the first two volumes of the trilogy, I did not consider in-depth abduction claims. At the time, I thought that abduction stories emerged from apparent abductees only when they were hypnotized. Since I knew that under hypnosis, subjects are more exposed to, amenable to, and accepting of suggestions about what occurred during a specific moment or moments, I assumed that the narratives were of questionable accuracy. Enter John Mack. A friend gave me a copy of *Abduction*; I read it, and followed that with *Passport to the Cosmos*. I changed my assessment of the phenomenon. Pulitzer Prize recipient and Harvard psychiatrist Mack provided sufficient evidence and analysis of the experiencers' descriptions of what had transpired that I came to accept abduction narratives as accurate accounts of what people experienced, as did Mack. He said that sometimes the experiencers seem to have been bodily transported to an alien craft, but on other occasions the people seemed to have experienced events and procedures only mentally. Nonetheless, they were still "real" events because the abductees experienced them as such, and experienced trauma whether they were physically or only mentally taken by Visitors, and later when they described to Mack what had transpired.

Mack's work is complemented by the narratives of (American) Indians in the books by Ardy Sixkiller Clarke, Emeritus Professor of Montana State University. Some of the people Clarke interviewed had endured what Mack's clients experienced. Others had other kinds of experiences, including being healed by Others and assisted by them in other ways.

Mack and Clarke had different interview styles and methods. Mack used, usually in an office setting, what his education and prior counseling of patients had trained him to do, including by using regression techniques. Clarke does straightforward interviews of Indian people, including traditional elders and healers. It is a conversational style that both puts the interviewee at ease, and enables thereby a relaxed, but detailed, narrative. Her interviews rarely take place in an office setting: usually, she meets interviewees in a coffee shop for lunch or coffee, at a park campsite next to a campfire, at their home, or even on a horseback ride to the place where their encounter with a Visitor occurred. Mack and Clarke assured the people with whom they spoke that their name and occupation, and the place of the event, would not be mentioned.

Mack and Clarke, then, have complementary accounts of the experiences of people with Others; sometimes the experiencers were willing participants in the events they describe, but at other times they were taken against their will, unable to resist. What is apparent from these events is that there are numerous species of ETI/IDI, some benevolent, some apparently malevolent, but often hiding that beneath a veneer of concern for the people abducted, for the survival of Earth, or for the survival of the human species. A "hybrid project" is described by both Mack and Clarke: some species of Visitors are trying to crossbreed human subjects with members of their own species or other species, to be the future intelligent beings inhabiting Earth. People are lured, it seems, into believing that the procedures and pain to which they are subject are for a "greater good" or "higher purpose."

Robert Wright and Peter Singer, in their *New York Times* op-ed piece, disagreed with Stephen Hawking's proposal that humans should avoid ETI because they are dangerous. They stated in their own assessment of Otherkind that to travel in space a species must first have evolved beyond aggression on its own planet in order to be sufficiently unified to engage in space voyages.[26] Some abductees' experiences, however, contradict both that evolutionary supposition and Hawking's assertion: there seem to be both malevolent beings and benevolent beings voyaging the cosmos.

---

26. Wright, "Ethics for Extraterrestrials."

Interdimensional Voyages

The idea of IDI, InterDimensional Intelligent beings, and awareness of Jacques Vallée's work, came to my attention (as a then-recent researcher into Visitor narratives), while *Encountering ETI* was nearing completion. I inserted into the book a short section on this topic that noted its possibility. However, I stated, too, that I leaned toward ETI, ExtraTerrestrial Intelligent beings, but accepted the possibility of Others using both types of transport. Over the years, it seemed ever more likely to me that IDI indicated a significant Other and that interdimensional voyages, given the vast distances in the cosmos—which have been increasing as the universe continues to inflate, at an increasing rate—are possibly the means of transport for most voyagers. Portals to other worlds—or other dimensions—might also include moments of interdimensional travel. In this book, then, this has a greater focus than space travel. Of course, the extent to which either means of travel is used by Others coming to Earth is, at this point, entirely unknown; it will remain so until there is more extensive communication between TI and Visitors, through Contact, telepathy, or electronic messaging, or by another way of sharing information that is not yet known—not by humans, that is.

Earth in Crisis, Cosmos Considerations: In the Heavens as on Earth

The topic of extraterrestrial/interdimensional intelligent beings' exploration of Earth and the solar system and Contact with humankind might seem somewhat exotic in the present historical moment. On Earth, people are preoccupied with the depth and breadth of problems such as the ecological devastation that threatens Earth and Earth's biota; rampant racism; gross economic disparities between the 1 percent and the 99 percent of the US population; sexual discrimination and domination; and ultraorthodox Christian, Jewish, and Muslim religious fervor. All of these pressing issues have been increasingly exacerbated as a consequence of the election of Donald Trump to be US President, and his post-election speeches and twitter comments. However, as nations begin to explore space more extensively, the potential for greater social and ecological destruction on Earth, and consequently in the heavens, should provoke proactive preventive thinking to avoid Earth's increased devastation and to promote mitigation and conservation now, rather than solely reactive responses to problems that become suddenly present later. Consideration of elements of a socially and ecologically better future should stimulate conceptualization and concretization of a better social and ecological present. International conflict could be avoided if nations were to collaborate on space projects generally, as they have in ISS construction and operation. *Cosmic Commons* and *Encountering ETI* proposed initiating now a dialogic relationship between ideals and practice, between suggestions that humans currently destroying Earth will "do better in space" in future colonization and, correspondingly, how that projected aspiration should stimulate humankind to strive to do better on Earth in the present to address socioecological devastation. The proposals put forward in those books are still relevant today. They have become more urgent as the impacts of human-caused and human-exacerbated global climate change are wreaking havoc on Earth through more violent and frequent storms, dramatic loss of fresh water, droughts that adversely impact agriculture around the globe, diminished air quality, disappearing forests (the "lungs of Earth," since trees and other plant life recycle human-generated carbon into tree-generated oxygen), and regional and international conflicts that have erupted because of the preceding. Humanity must begin to put its ecological house in order now, or humanity and Earth will not have a future. Denial of scientific facts about a devastated climate in order to favor corporate energy companies' owners', executives', and shareholders' greed will lead, ultimately, to ever-increasing harm to Earth and all living beings. Considerations about Contact, therefore, can stimulate care for Earth today, whether or not Contact occurs.

Contemporary Consciousness Catalyst: Foo Fighters Redux?

As World War II was coming to an end in 1944, pilots from different nations among the warring parties began to report that strange objects and lights suddenly appeared near them. The unidentified craft would accompany them for a short time, then race ahead or do maneuvers around them at extremely high speeds. This occurred over Europe and in the Pacific. Needless to say, the pilots were disconcerted and, at times, frightened. The US pilots of the 415th Night Fighter Squadron seem to have experienced more such events than other US aviators or foreign pilots. At first, having seen the objects' proximity and maneuverability, they feared that they were a secret German weapon. This theory was discarded because they were not hostile, and because military base investigators discovered that German and Japanese pilots had observed and reported the same phenomenon. The unidentified aerial phenomena (UAP) were called "Foo Fighters" by fighter plane radar operator Donald J. Meiers.[27] Originally from Chicago, he was familiar with a cartoon series about a firefighter that was published by the Chicago Tribune: "Smokey Stover" by Bill Holman. Some of these cartoons were published in a small book format.[28]

27. Krasney, "What Were the Mysterious."
28. Holman, *Smokey Stover*.

In 2004 (but classified, and not disclosed until December, 2017), US Navy pilots, while flying F/A-18F Super Hornets off the California coast, received orders to investigate an unidentified aerial object that was being tracked by ground radar. US Navy pilot Commodore David Fravor photographed his pursuit of the UAP through his gunsight, which was focused on the UAP. The event captured international attention when Luis Elizondo, the resigned director of the Advanced Aviation Threat Identification Program, a secret US Defense Department agency studying UFO phenomena, reported it to news media and released video from Fravor's plane.[29]

Cosmos Relational Consciousness in a Cosmos Relational Community

Third Displacement strives to provide a realistic assessment of humans' cosmic aspirations, and to propose a reasoned and responsible human reaction to Contact with extraterrestrial/interdimensional intelligent life. Its intention, in this regard, is to avoid or mitigate the kinds of intellectual and psychological cosmic displacements that were engendered by the First and Second Displacements. It will provide an ethical process for space exploration and colonization that could work whether or not other-than-human life is engaged—an original *cosmosocioecological praxis ethics*—to guide (negotiated with ETI and IDI, if available and as necessary) available space exploration, acquisition of extraterrestrial natural goods ("resources"), and equitable sharing of potential common ground. *Cosmosocioecological praxis ethics* will be discussed in greater depth than previously. It has the potential to be a seed that will begin to propagate and to promote a human- and cosmos-community common good in relationships within cosmos integral being.

The ethical component of the current book has a foundation in *Sacramental Commons*,[30] which includes first formulations of "relational consciousness" and "relational community," and "principles of Christian ecological ethics." Complementary principles are expressed in humanist ecological ethics.

---

29. Rosenberg, "Former Navy pilot." In light of the fabrication of Rendlesham Forest events by US spy agencies, a serious (and suspicious) researcher might wonder why the US chose to acknowledge this event more than a decade later, and if Elizondo is still linked secretly to the US Defense Department.

30. Hart, *Sacramental Commons*.

Origins of Third Displacement:
Continuing Cosmos Curiosity—A Personal Journey

I have had a lifelong interest and participation in work for social justice and ecological wellbeing, which I came to call socioecological praxis ethics. My work flows from being a scholar of Christian Ethics, and a socioecological ethicist and scholar-activist. I have been immersed in comparative religious and humanist ethics and (American) Indian[31] spirituality as a college and university professor engaged in on-the-ground justice movements. I have been, too, a "ghost writer" for theology- and religion-environment-ethics statements and documents issued by community and church leaders.

I started pondering the possibility of humans' *third displacement* while participating in the Oxford Seminars in Science and Christianity (summers, 1999–2001), and reflecting on Oxford professors' presentations of the first two displacements.[32] It occurred to me then that Contact (terrestrial intelligent life/extraterrestrial intelligent life engagement) would have as profound an impact on humanity as did the intellect- and psyche-jolts of the first two displacements.

While writing *Cosmic Commons* I conceived, and developed in seminal form, the concept of integral being. In *Third Displacement*, this concept is explored further. *Cosmic Commons* states:

> *Integral being* is the totality of all being. In it all being and beings have originated—it is the "stuff" from which all being has been and is being comprised, formed over eons and intertwined into an intricate web of interrelated being. The cosmos in which humankind lives is the sole cosmos with which humans are familiar, but it might be one of many cosmoses (scientists theorize the possible existence of a *multiverse*, a "universe of universes" of which only one is known to human science). This cosmos is posited to have begun at some "point" just before the singularity, the initial explosion in space (Georges Lemaître's theory

---

31. I have worked for almost four decades with the International Indian Treaty Council (IITC) and the American Indian Movement (AIM); both are traditional Indian human rights organizations. They use the word *Indian* intentionally: as an elder declared at a Treaty Council meeting prior to the UN International Human Rights Commission, "'Indian' is the name by which we were oppressed, and Indian is the name by which we will be liberated." (This story was related to me separately by Lakota and Haudenosaunee Indian activists who were participants in this discussion.) Some Indians reject the term "Native American"; they consider it a further effort at cultural genocide: "Indians" disappear from it and history, as does discussion of injustices they experienced.

32. Two Oxford Seminar professors wrote book endorsements for *Cosmic Commons*: William R. Shea, Galileo Professor of History of Science (ret.), University of Padua, Italy; and John Hedley Brooke, Emeritus Professor of Science and Religion, Oxford University.

of a "primeval atom" exploding on a "day without yesterday") which catalyzed the existence and inflationary expansion of the universe that has continued through eons. Integral being births all being, which emanates from and in it. For the theist, integral being is the dynamic cosmos as a whole, existing in, engaged with, and sacred because of, divine presence; it originates in a creating transcendent-immanent Spirit who permeates all that is. For the secular humanist, integral being is solely the complex cosmos in itself, with all its diversity.[33]

Awareness of the integral being of the cosmos could prompt Earth-bound (materially and metamaterially) people experiencing a sense of displacement because of ETI-TI-IDI Contact to reflect on and embrace a *relational consciousness* and consequently experience the *relational community* in which all members of integral being participate, and might more consciously and conscientiously do so.

I began to think about the book in-depth when I was working on a research grant with scientists from the SETI (Search for Extra-Terrestrial Intelligence) Institute at the Carl Sagan Center (Mountain View, California), who affirmed my ethical insights. Complementarily, little more than a decade ago, José Funes, SJ, the priest-physicist director of the Vatican Observatory, stated in a 2008 *L'Osservatore Romano* interview that there might be intelligent life elsewhere in the universe, and that it is likely more intelligent than humans are;[34] the British and French governments released their respective previously classified files about military and civilian encounters with UFOs; and ice was discovered on Mars by the NASA Rover, possibly indicating the presence or prior presence of life there.

Personal ETI/IDI Encounters

On two occasions, separated by some twenty years, I had Close Encounters of the First Kind with intelligent being-controlled craft passing by in the sky. The first time was in 1963, while I was a Marist College sophomore. The college is situated in Poughkeepsie, New York, on the Hudson River. One clear night with little ambient moonlight, two friends and I decided to go on the riverbank to observe and enjoy the extraordinary beauty of the bright stars, which contrasted sharply with the dark dome of the night sky. (Since we were college students, I want to make it perfectly clear that neither drugs nor alcohol were involved when we saw the event described.) Sometimes, we

---

33. Hart, *Cosmic Commons*, 222n11.
34. Funes, "L'extraterrestre."

saw meteors in the distance. Then, unexpectedly, I saw the brightest, fastest, largest, and lowest meteor I had ever seen, shooting from south to north above the Hudson. I watched its trajectory, awed by its unexpected appearance, and waited for it to fade and fizzle. Abruptly, without banking, slowing, or stopping, it shot straight up, perpendicular to its prior course. Amazed, I said to myself, "That's impossible: I've studied physics, and it would have violated the laws of physics and shattered if it changed direction so suddenly." I blinked several times, dismissed what I had seen as an illusion, and said nothing. After a moment one of my friends queried, "Did you see that speeding bright light suddenly shoot up at a right angle?" Relieved that I had not seen an illusion, I answered affirmatively. One of us said then, "I guess that we saw a flying saucer," and we laughed. I did not think much about the event for the next quarter-century, until I was teaching in Helena, Montana. My ten-year-old son and I were in a mall bookstore. He was in the children's section selecting a book, and I waited for him in the front of the store, by the cash register. I glanced down on the counter there and saw neat stacks of new books. Their subtitle caught my attention: "UFO Sightings in the Hudson River Valley, 1962–65." I paged through the book, whose title I do not recall, and discovered that there had been more than eight hundred sightings in the Hudson Valley in that time span. I thought, "Oh, I was there," but did not buy a book (which I regret to this day). My son rejoined me, I purchased the book he had selected, and we left the bookstore.

The second time I saw a UAP (but did not recognize it as such) was in 2002, when I was traveling by air from Helena to Newark to give a lecture at Drew University. After changing flights in Minneapolis, I had a window seat and was reading a book. About halfway through the flight, out of the corner of my eye, I saw an orange-brownish large vapor trail swiftly pass the airplane, just off the wing. I was surprised that I had felt no turbulence from its speed or proximity. I called the flight attendant over, showed her the vapor trail outside, and asked her if she knew what it was. She looked at it, and said that she did not know but would ask the pilot. She went forward, returned in about five minutes, and said, "The captain says he doesn't see anything." That surprised me and even angered me somewhat: How could he not see an object that close through his window? I returned to my reading and forgot about the incident—until about a decade had passed.

At the time, I was with my family as we roamed our independent ways through the aisles of Powell's Books in Portland, Oregon. I discovered that they had a section on UFO books. I looked them over and found Leslie Kean's book, *UFOs: Generals, Pilots, and Government Officials Go on the Record*.[35] Kean provides three bits of data pertinent to my experience. First,

---

35. Kean, *UFOs*.

even though they do not use fuels that leave a vapor trail, on some occasions ETI/IDI Visitors (or their robotic pilots) release such a trail to let observers note their presence; this is especially dramatic when they do zigzags in the sky with the vapor trail; second, pilots are required by federal law to report any UFOs they see; and third, pilots do *not* report such incidents because they fear losing their job, since airline companies do not want to get involved in stories about UFOs. This meant that the pilot on my flight chose to state falsely, "I did not see anything," because if he had seen the vehicle speeding by off his wing, he would have had to report it to airline officials of an airline that did not want to hear about it, and his position would have been in jeopardy. The captain opted in such a situation, of course, to declare that he did not see anything—so nothing would have to be reported. (It occurred to me later that the flight attendant, who had seen the vapor trail, hinted at this with her words to me: "The captain *says* that he did not see anything."

One representative case along these lines is in Kean's *UFOs*. She describes the 1977 experience of a highly experienced United Air Lines pilot, Captain Neil Daniels. While flying his DC-10 on autopilot during a commercial flight, his plane was pulled off course while a "brilliant, brilliant light off the wing tip" seen by him, his copilot, and his flight engineer flew near his plane. He decided, on landing, not to report the incident, even though it was corroborated by the air traffic controller. He feared the consequences. Months later, while hunting with his United Airlines boss, he decided to reveal what had happened. His boss told him, "I'm sorry to hear that. Bad things can happen to pilots who say they have these sightings."[36]

Stephen Hawking's Deus ex Machina

A particular stimulus for my cosmos-oriented books came in 2007 just prior to my work with SETI scientists. Stephen Hawking, in press interviews in Hong Kong and Cape Canaveral, advocated constructing a moon base and Mars colony because, he said, human survival requires interplanetary settlement commitments: Earth might be destroyed soon by "sudden global warming, nuclear war, a genetically engineered virus." He urged extra-Earth resettlement: "I think that getting a portion of the human race permanently off the planet is imperative for our future as a species." My immediate thought was "It's the same people! Those selected from Earth to go into space are chosen from among those currently destroying Earth. Why or how would they act differently on other worlds?" Hawking apparently assumed that people who leave Earth to explore and colonize other worlds will arrive with an altered consciousness and not overpopulate those worlds, adversely affect their

36. Kean, *UFOs*, 45–46.

climate, or use human technology and new worlds' natural goods ("natural resources") to develop new weapons for a "nuclear war" on a distant planet, or to release a "genetically engineered virus."[37] As I reflected at length on this, I decided to write in depth about it. I include it here in my exploration about the possibility of ETI-TI-IDI Contact because Hawking stated more recently on BBC that there is ETI, but humans should avoid extraterrestrials because they are a threat to humankind.[38]

Indigenous Peoples' Spiritual Leaders: Being at the "Center of the Universe"

The "center of the universe" concept and experience, which I will explore in greater detail later, I learned about from several traditional (American) Indian spiritual leaders with whom I became friends as a result of my human rights work with the International Indian Treaty Council (the first native peoples' organization recognized—more than forty years ago—by the United Nations as a Non-Governmental Organization [NGO]). At a Treaty Council meeting, traditional elders / spiritual leaders / healers from different Indian cultures shared in a small group their experience of "being at the center of the universe"; all agreed that it was not a fixed point in a special place, but a spiritual space that was, often unexpectedly at times, engaged and experienced during prayer. It occurred to me recently that each elder was an *axis mundi* in those moments, a link between two worlds or two dimensions of reality. A rabbi friend told me later as we conversed that a similar understanding of a universe center is present in the Kaballah. A complementary spiritual insight is indicated, too, in the Hindu greeting (first expressed in Sanskrit) *Namasté*.[39]

Homes in the Cosmos

Humans who discover and dwell in diverse cosmos places will adapt to a wide range of newly found otherworld milieus. This adaptation mirrors, to some extent, what other people did who migrated throughout the world, and found viable niches in diverse Earth contexts over the course of human biological and cultural evolution. Humans' social and ecological wellbeing

---

37. Hawking news articles, see chapter 4.
38. Hawking BBC, see chapter 4.
39. In Nepal, I was taught that *Namasté* has multiple layers of meaning: "the Spirit in me greets the Spirit in you; the Spirit in you greets the Spirit in me; the Spirit in me greets the spirit in you; the Spirit in you greets the spirit in me; the spirit in me greets the spirit in you; the spirit in you greets the spirit in me." Material and metamaterial realities are intertwined and in relation.

on Earth and in the heavens would be conceptualized and contextualized through awareness of cosmos integral being, and efforts to live conscious of its almost tangible presence. This will be continually stimulated by cosmosocioecological consciousness, which is itself continually developed, expanded, and enhanced through cosmosocioecological praxis ethics. In the process, initial anxiety generated by the Third Displacement that will occur when humankind comes into Contact with Otherkind is transformed. People learn an adaptive openness to unanticipated experiences and events in newly discovered spiritual, social, and spatial places, complemented by confidence in humans' ability to assess and address them. When this occurs, the sense of Earth *displacement* is itself displaced—by the experience of material and metamaterial cosmos *placement*.

2

Plurality of World, Plurality of Being, Displacement, *Axis Mundi—Logos-Logoi* in Space *Loci*

Genesis, John, Maximus Confessor, Francis of Assisi, Heup Young Kim

In the current historical moment, Earth is the only place in the cosmos where *homo sapiens* lives. Earth is, and always will be, humans' original home and habitat, no matter where they roam in space and time. People live temporarily in space shuttles and the International Space Station, but when they complete their professional work in these human-constructed places they return to *terra firma*, where they live, work, and walk on solid ground, and breathe native air deeply. As human space explorations continue and advance, however, some people will self-displace to a moon base, a Mars colony and eventually, perhaps, to a Saturn or Jupiter moon. The human species will become a living presence in diverse cosmos contexts, on Earth and on other worlds. People on Earth today are, in diverse ways, preparing for what are projected possibilities for humans' roles in different, distinct ExoEarth settings (in their current or a different dimension) in years to come.

As humankind ventures into space, humans' quest for security of place, home, hearth, and security of seemingly stable traditions—intellectual, psychological, and spiritual—might be satisfied, but only tenuously, initially, until people adapt to and become comfortable in new places.

As the cosmos continues to unfold, humans in their original Earth home and in their future, then-current planet home might be displaced in diverse manners by an arriving or invading species that has greater intelligence and superior technology. Conversely, humankind expanding into space might arrive at or invade another world and displace an indigenous intelligent species that has less advanced technology.

Human Displacement

On discovery of extraterrestrial life (ETL), and more especially on Contact with extraterrestrial intelligent life (ETI) or interdimensional intelligent life (IDI) arriving on Earth or encountered in ExoEarth places, humans and possibly the other intelligent species will experience to some extent a sense of displacement from their current understanding of, and beliefs about, their place in the cosmos.

The possibility of humans' displacement after their "discovery" of intelligent extraterrestrial and interdimensional life—or, better expressed, of intelligent beings' mutual discovery of each other—is highly likely. Its forms might include physical displacement, psychological displacement, social displacement, and religious primacy displacement. People in Western cultures long have considered themselves to be the superior species in the universe, even as their self-identified preeminent position gradually has diminished, subsequent to and as a consequence of the Copernican Revolution (the First Displacement), Darwinian Evolution (the Second Displacement), and Cosmic Status Change (the Third Displacement). The shift of perception might well include, in the future, a new Cosmos Spiritual Awareness (the Fourth Displacement).

Peoples' current concepts of "place," "placed," and "displaced" will be challenged. What people presently think is their place on Earth (perhaps through a lens of anthropocentrism, biocentrism, or terracentrism), or in the heavens (with a perspective of anthropocentrism, terracentrism, or cosmocentrism), based on known or theorized contexts, could be called into question significantly as a result of unanticipated hospitable or inhospitable alternate socioecological settings.

Many people—religious or secular humanist—consider *homo sapiens* unique among biota in the cosmos. However, discovery solely of microbes, for people familiar with evolutionary biology, would catalyze a suspicion that such primitive forms of life—whether encountered, or theorized to exist elsewhere—might eventually become intelligent life, and that this might have happened already on other worlds and in other dimensions, given that the age of the universe as a whole is thought to be three times the age of Earth within it.

In such a milieu, human experiences from an earlier historical period might well be analyzed to provide clues about "displaced persons" or "DPs." These could include the experiences of post-World War II Europeans, pre-Israel Jews, post Israel-founding Palestinians, post-European arrival (American) Indians, and twenty-first-century migrants across the world seeking sanctuary from political dictatorship and economic hardship. Unfortunately, in some cases, upon arrival in their hoped-for new home, they are being interned in prison-like camps: they become "strangers in a strange land."

Contact with Visitors: Projected Modes of Displacement

The term "extraterrestrials" has been used for decades to refer to Visitors to Earth who make Contact with humanity from unknown places. In recent years, in light of numerous narratives and speculation about the variety of vehicles used by Visitors, and the diverse ways that they have appeared (and rapidly disappeared), scientists have theorized that they might be extraterrestrial, interdimensional, or transdimensional—or a combination of two or more of these during their journey to Earth. Since little in-depth research has been done yet, to my knowledge, on transdimensional travel, this chapter will focus on *extra*terrestrial and *inter*dimensional beings. The term "extraterrestrial," then, has become outdated. I will use *Visitors* or *Others* as standard words to refer generically to other-than-human intelligent beings whom people have seen, whose distinct modes of travel have been observed, or whose characteristics or technological prowess have been viewed or conjectured. Whoever they are, and however they have come, these Otherkind are Visitors or Others. Therefore, these words are used in these pages to indicate, in the aggregate, distinct and diverse intelligent beings, the Others who have made some form of Contact with humankind.

Potential Visitor Impacts and Influences

Even prior to a confirmed and sustained engagement with ETI/IDI Visitors, many people have feared (as they project that Visitors' conduct could mirror what has been human conduct over millennia) that the relative newcomers to Earth might compel humankind to relocate away from their homeland—in this case, their home planet—or to a different place on their homeland. Humans might have to move to one or more types of different places: a geographic area on Earth or beneath Earth's earth, another planet in the solar system, or another world in a different star system. Human beings are rightly concerned that some type of *physical displacement* might be imposed if the intelligent life encountered has lost its home world because of some catastrophic event(s)—originating in nature or caused by the intelligent beings—and is searching for a new planetary habitat or had lost its niche on its original world—in terms of having space on it in which to dwell, or of availability of sufficient natural goods to provide for its needs—and seeks to expand or relocate its habitable territory. The Visitors' expansion in space and extension to other worlds (or dimensions) might be in person or (because of the Visitors' fear of the danger posed by Earth microbes that had evolved in a far distant and different place from their own), through highly developed robots. The latter likely would resemble, to some extent and with the abilities of, the Visitors who developed them, who had evolved elsewhere in the cosmos via the interaction of their DNA with their own native, microbially hospitable environment.

A human *psychological displacement* could result from an awareness or perception that the intelligent life encountered is far superior intellectually and far advanced technologically. A great sense of inferiority and loss of self-esteem and species-esteem, and of a human worldview that believed humankind to be the most intelligent species extant not only on Earth but in the vast and uncharted universe (without having any data to support such human claims to superiority on such a cosmic scale, only the lack of a previous encounter with highly intelligent other life). A particular jolt might be experienced by those who had asked regarding ETI/IDI, perhaps with an air of superiority tinged with suppressed anxiety, "Where's the evidence?" The question vocalizes a reductionist intellectual position that refuses to accept evidence that is not physically present and immediate (expressed, for example, as "I'll believe they exist if a spacecraft lands on the White House lawn").

If that evidence should suddenly materialize in the form of an intelligently controlled spacecraft, the visual or other physical experience of overwhelming evidence of Visitors would be a shock not only to strongly and even smugly held scientific or spiritual understandings, but to humans' previous sense of their self-worth and their belief in their supposed superior place in the cosmos. It would be accompanied by bewilderment and an overwhelming sense of loss—perhaps even of what they understood before to give meaning to life, or to be the meaning of life. The encounter might prompt fear: extraordinary fear about the unknown, in a new reality not previously conceived or conjectured, complemented by fear about not being able to control planetary (as humans have done to various extents for millennia) and personal environments, despite human technology and intelligence. Fear could emerge, too, about loss of control over human life and culture, and because of a sense of diminution, of suddenly feeling "small" not only on Earth but in the universe. The appearance of overwhelming Visitor technology might initially (and possibly, continually) catalyze fear of conflict with and conquest by the Visitors, based on projecting onto them an anthropocentric–like hostility toward and desire to dominate other living beings. Initially, some people might suffer loss of their religious or spiritual beliefs when faced with the apparently incredible and incomprehensible, when they wonder whether or not faith in a divine Being any longer has meaning and, if so, about what that might be in the "new" universe—which might come to be perceived as transparently multidimensional and interdimensional—suddenly observed and experienced.

A *social displacement* likely would result from humans' loss of their preeminent self-ranking on Earth. Many human beings today see themselves as the alpha species, placed or evolved to be over and to control lesser species. Humans have thought they were the center of the universe (pre-Copernicus); and an original individual creation in God's image (pre-Darwin); when those were discredited, at least they remained the top Earth species because of their intelligence—and thereby being, by extension, the top cosmos species (pre-Contact).

A newly formulated *spiritual-religious unifying consciousness* (the Fourth Displacement), for a new reality and an enhanced cosmos sense of neighbor beings, would likely develop after Contact, linked to and flowing from humans' loss of their belief that they are the top cosmos species. In Christian dogma, humans are the premier spiritual species because the divine Spirit became embodied in creation as part of an intelligent species only on Earth, in all the cosmos; God became incarnate in Jesus of Nazareth, the God-Human. Effectively, this belief implies that the Spirit particularly or exclusively loves only one intelligent species, humankind. It also spurs suggestions, in some Christian circles, that Visitors must be converted to and baptized in the Christian religion. This position claims that the spiritual salvation taught by Jesus is possible only for believers who are members of an institution or community, comprised initially of his human followers. This belief is a misunderstanding and limitation of the activity of the divine creating Word, the *Logos* in the language of the Gospel according to John. The belief implies that the Word physically entered creation only as part of the human "world" and not of the "world" or "worlds" of other intelligent beings. It also gives primacy to one religion, Christianity, over all other religions and spiritual communities—on Earth and in the heavens. However, a particular Christian Exceptionalism cannot logically be accepted as the exclusive form of the Spirit's interaction and interrelationship with the world(s), and be asserted as a Cosmic Christian Exceptionalism.

When their social, spatial, and spiritual self-placements are disproven or at least strongly called into question because of their exclusivity vis-à-vis all other beings, humans initially might be groping for cosmos meaning when encountering Visitors "live and in person." This indisputable evidence of Visitor existence will prompt immediate theorizing about a new way to understand humans' cosmos placement. Humankind then might view itself as "second rate" or, contrastingly, as a complementary component of integral cosmic being, in relational community with other beings, having its own place(s) and responsibilities.

Dangerous Visitors?

In any or all of these scenarios, ETI/IDI Visitors might be thought to be scouting Earth to attack and overwhelm people in the actual geographical place(s) of human habitation, in order to acquire needed or desired goods. This appears to be what humans—as individuals, communities, or a species—dread most, when they are fearful of encounters with Visitors. Such fears might be prompted or exacerbated by events in which human beings on Earth or in Earth skies have interacted with Visitors (as evidenced by recently released [2018] videos and photos that were claimed to be taken by military aircraft or ships around the globe, such as US Navy pilots off the coast of California, and Chilean navy sailors off the coast of Chile), and photos taken by passengers on commercial flights (such as those flying over the Irish coastline in 2018), or by sci-fi films that portray technologically more advanced alien beings, sometimes presented as monsters, invading Earth.

On a simpler biotic level, displacement might be caused by an unexpected ETL microbe-led event, in which initially undetected physically harmful biota, traveling through space on a comet or arriving on a returning Earth-launched satellite, space shuttle, or planetary or lunar explorer to which it had attached itself—wittingly or unwittingly—and been transported to Earth when the originally Earth-launched vehicle returned home, and descended under human control or fell from the sky. (In July 1969, the first samples of "moon rocks" were transported to Earth by Apollo 11 astronauts [two of whom—Neil A. Armstrong and Edward E. "Buzz" Aldrin—had walked on the lunar surface] with great caution, and subsequently displayed in hermetically sealed transparent cases because of concerns that there might be microbes on them that would endanger the health and lives of humans and other Earth biota.)

Discovery of microbial life originating elsewhere in the universe will be received by the general public in diverse ways: curiosity, intense interest, fascination, or fear not only that they might be a biological hazard, but also that in yet undiscovered places on still unknown worlds life might evolve, or have evolved already, as did humankind on Earth, into highly intelligent species—potential future competitors on Earth or on other worlds where they are encountered. Such fear might be accompanied by hope among some people—that the evolved life would prove to be collaborators with humanity in advancing medical knowledge and technology, or engaging in cosmic adventures or ventures. Some people might continue to defend, from religious bases and biases, the theory that humans are the lone living beings in the cosmos, and reject data indicating that cosmolife exists. Others might reject receiving Visitors hospitably because they dread a new kind of *other*, some form of microbial life that is part of their being: microbial life that should be feared because of its ExoEarth origin. It might be biologically incompatible with, and thereby toxically dangerous for, human biological integrity. Possibly, too, adult Visitors might be, in terms of their species, an *evolved Other* with conquest motives and vastly superior weaponry to accomplish Earth's domination.

Close Encounters with Visitors

Intelligent ExoEarth[1] life, this author suggests, will be encountered and then engaged for an extended time on Earth or elsewhere in space in the near future, whether this life be extraterrestrial (ETI), interdimensional (IDI[2]), or transdimensional (TDI)—since *intra*dimensional or *inter*dimensional intelligence could both be expressed as IDI,[3] TDI is proposed as a substitute

---

1. *ExoEarth*: apparently not originating on, nor having evolved within the corporeal/material reality of, planet Earth.

2. While *extradimensional* (EDI) is nicely symmetrical, so to speak, with *extraterrestrial* (ETI), such intelligent beings would more accurately be described, in this author's assessment, as *interdimensional*: they are not beyond or above, that is, *extra* distinct dimensions of reality or even of one reality; rather, they cross over between dimensions, possibly being simultaneously in both at some point, not limited by *time*, *space*, or *place*, and not above nor crossing between or among dimensions of existence, but able to be present in different dimensions transitioning from one to another in a way that humanity is not yet able to understand or undertake; or *intradimensional*, journeying in different time periods within a dimension, but designated *transdimensional* (TDI) to avoid confusion about the meaning of the acronym IDI. Humans, at this time in their physical, social, intellectual, and evolutionary history, lack knowledge of how any of these are possible. Perhaps, too, Visitors are *visible* in more than one dimension, but are at that time physical existents primarily in one. New understandings of physics are needed to consider this. Newton, Einstein, and others broke barriers that limited what is knowable in physics; new discoveries by people who have a further evolved human consciousness await the openminded members of our species who are scientifically capable, intellectually curious, and psychologically courageous in present and future times and places.

3. Acronym proposed by this writer.

designation for "*intra*dimensional" and, moreover, in that case might originate from some place on Earth in present time or future time. Some astrobiologists and astrophysicists anticipate that such Contact might be in a place as close as on Mars; a moon of Saturn, such as Enceladus; or of Jupiter, such as Europa. Consequently, humans might experience in varying degrees a third "displacement": *negatively*, as if being wrenched from a customary social, geographical, psychological, and spiritual locale; or *positively*, as if gaining an enhanced sense of being "at home"—or at least "closer to home"—at long last, in life-to-life cosmic egalitarian relationships, not needing—psychologically or socially—a self-designated "higher status" among living beings. In the latter case, a potentially fascinating and fruitful exploration of encounter interaction could be undertaken because of discovery of a mutual awareness of some kind of spiritual consciousness in the other intelligent being, whether expressed in an organized or institutional form, or in communal or individual practice. A shared consciousness of being related in the integral being of the cosmos might include awareness of complementary perceptions of a spiritual dimension of that being. Then, believers with a particular understanding in a cosmos Spirit and a specific spiritual consciousness would not feel compelled to forcibly convert others to their way of thinking.[4]

Humans Contact Visitors: Religious Trauma?

Currently, some atheist scientists predict and project that encountering intelligent life elsewhere will catalyze a loss of religious faith. They believe that intellectually advanced beings elsewhere in space or in a different dimension will have "evolved beyond" the supposed "need" for such belief. Often those who hypothesize this are people whose own belief is that no spiritual beings

---

4. Throughout human history, most conquerors have forced their religion on the conquered. A notable exception was the Persian conqueror Cyrus the Great (c. 600–529 BCE), by religion a Zoroastrian. The peoples he absorbed into the Persian Empire were permitted to keep their religion, and even their governance, to some extent, as long as they did not try to rebel. He was regarded as a wise and just ruler who did not oppress those conquered—sometimes people in a city governed by a tyrant overthrew their own leader, opened the city gates, and invited Cyrus in. He freed the Jews from their Babylonian exile, and assisted them to go home and rebuild Jerusalem. In the book of Isaiah in the Hebrew Scriptures, God calls Cyrus "my anointed (messiah)": The LORD "says of Cyrus, 'He is my shepherd, and he shall carry out all my purpose'" (Is 44:28); "Thus says the LORD to his *anointed*, to Cyrus, whose right hand I have grasped to subdue nations before him . . . I, the God of Israel, who call you by your name for the sake of my servant Jacob, and Israel my chosen, I call you by your name . . . I have aroused Cyrus to righteousness, and I will make his path straight; he shall build my city, and set my exiles free . . . " (45:1–4, 13, NRSV; italics added). Today, because of wars, racism, religious violence, ethnocentrism, totalitarian governments, etc., some people hope that ExoEarth intelligent beings will intervene on Earth to promote justice and harmony.

or spiritual dimension exists. They do not consider an alternative possibility: ETI and IDI (and TI) might all have come to be evolved beyond institutional religions. In that case, they might find that they have a shared common spirituality that acknowledges a relationship with a Being both immanent in and transcendent to the cosmos.[5] Spiritual evolution might be, in fact, the next stage of human evolution. It could draw *homo sapiens* beyond the limitations of their current mental capacity and cosmic awareness. Teilhard de Chardin's idea of a *noosphere* (community of intelligent beings) would be especially meaningful in both a cosmos and an interdimensional spiritual reality.

Empirical evidence concerning possible Visitor impacts on religious belief has been gathered from data assembled by Pacific Lutheran University theologian Ted Peters. He surveyed 1,325 students in "The Peters ETI Religious Crisis Survey." The results support the possibility that most would not be adversely affected by Contact. He states that "We tested the following hypothesis: *upon confirmation of contact between earth and an extraterrestrial civilization of intelligent beings, the long-established religious traditions of earth would confront a crisis of belief and perhaps even collapse.* The evidence gathered by the Peters ETI Religious Crisis Survey tends to disconfirm this hypothesis."[6]

The Peters Survey focused on the extent to which students' faith would be impacted by *extraterrestrial* intelligent beings. As will be seen below, Jacques Vallée hypothesizes that humans have encountered, too, *interdimensional* intelligent beings (IDI). Vallée wonders, recognizing interdimensional mobility as a possible means of transport and connection between worlds, whether over human history IDI might have influenced human imagination and consciousness to effect or at least stimulate changes for the better in human conduct. This might have occurred, he speculates, in events described and elaborated in stories from folklore and in narratives of religious experience. The latter idea would stimulate, it would seem, even greater discomfort among people who are committed to and secure in particular religious faith traditions.

Recent empirical scientific studies have shown that, in the US at least, people respond more positively than negatively to news about discovery of ETL microbes, or Contact with ETI.[7] They were curious, too, rather than fearful, about the Oumuamua object that traveled swiftly across the solar system in 2017 and exited at a very high speed—196,000 miles per hour,

---

5. For a more extended discussion, see Hart, *Cosmic Commons*, 292–93.

6. Peters and Froehlig, "Peters ETI Religious Crisis Survey," 3.

7. See, for example, recent articles in scientific journals: Saplakoglu, "Is Humanity Ready"; and Kwon et al., "How Will We React."

according to NASA. Some people hoped that it would be an alien probe, and thereby evidence of extraterrestrial intelligent life.

Thought Experiment

In this chapter, the use of a "thought experiment" of a different kind than used previously in this trilogy would be helpful. It would be to consider Contact in a different way than was described in *Cosmic Commons* and *Encountering ETI*. In those books, I suggested that people should consider, as a thought experiment, potential impacts of Contact as if it had already occurred or would soon occur. This would enable them to think about Contact with less anxiety and less allegiance to a prior *pro* or *con* commitment that would influence their considerations.

In the present moment, the thought experiment will be to contemplate impacts of Contact—already experienced, or yet to come—given that now we know that it has been made already. We have changed our fundamental question from "Are we alone?" to "What should we do now that we know that we are *not* alone?" We still need to step back and strive to consider objectively, to the extent possible, Contact events as they have been described by those who experienced them (whether materially or solely metamaterially or mentally)—that is, that they have occurred, perhaps for centuries; they are occurring; and they will continue to occur. By thinking in this manner, we will be challenged in unanticipated ways as we strive to keep an "objective distance." We might choose to do so by regarding them as not "real" but fascinating narratives that are imaginative or symbolic. Or, we might choose to see them as actual events and, in the spirit of a "thought experiment," think about what the implications might be—and potential impacts in our own lives—of relating these events to possible future closer encounters with Visitors. Humans' thinking has reached and gone beyond the caution point suggested by Teilhard de Chardin in his 1953 essay (cited in the next chapter), where he states that even if it seems likely that intelligent life exists elsewhere in the cosmos, "No matter how great a probability may be, we must be careful not to treat it as a certainty—that is obvious . . . There is no question, then, of having to begin work on a theology for these unknown worlds. We must at least, however, endeavour to make our classical theology open to (I was on the point of saying 'blossom into') the possibility (a positive possibility) of their existence and their presence."[8] It is timely now, I would suggest, for those in the field of theology "to begin work on a theology for these unknown worlds," bearing in mind that it must not be an imperialistic theological endeavor such that *Christian theology* as currently understood

---

8. Teilhard, "Sequel to the Problem," 233–34.

by open-minded scholars should be believed to be a universal spiritual consciousness. Rather, it should enter into dialogic discourse with those whose civilizations and spiritual consciousness have developed and matured within their own culture, in relation to how they understand—and are open to insights from—an immanent-transcendent Being, who might be thought to have already become part of their own world.

It might be useful to include, in a thought experiment, elements suggested by John Mack in the preface to *Abduction*. He proposes an approach to considering the narratives of people who describe their experiences with ETI/IDI: "Terms like 'abduction,' 'alien,' 'happening,' and even 'reality' itself, need redefinition lest subtle distinctions be lost. In this context, thinking of memory too literally as 'true' or 'false' may restrict what we can learn about human consciousness from the abduction experiences I recount."[9]

Contact with Intelligent Beings on Other Worlds

Human displacement after encountering ETI or IDI on other worlds or during space voyages might have, initially, several possible outcomes; all depend on the levels of social, intellectual, and technological evolution of the respective species. First, human explorers might have much the same experience in the heavens arriving on an inhabited world as when Visitors arrive on Earth. That is, if the intelligent species seems to be socially, intellectually, and technologically superior to humankind, judging from evidence in their communities, then, even though members of the human species had had the knowledge and technical skills to construct a vehicle, and journey through space (or another dimension) to reach this previously unknown world, they would feel inferior to those they now met. Second, human explorers might think or know themselves to be intellectually, socially, and technologically superior to the newly encountered intelligent species. In this scenario, the resident inhabitants might come to have the same concerns or even fears that humanity has on its own planet, perhaps for many of the same reasons. Third, both intelligent species might be at equivalent stages of social and intellectual, if not technological, evolution. This scenario has the greatest potential to stimulate interspecies accommodation and adaptation.

In any of the preceding cases, the successful outcome of an encounter might depend on the extent of altruism characteristic of either or both species, or the degree to which they had arrived respectively at a complementary understanding of and interaction with the Transcendent-Immanent Being-Becoming Spirit, Energy, or Entity present in the integral being of the cosmos.

9. Mack, *Abduction*, xi.

Singularity and Plurality of World

In oral traditions and in recorded history dating back millennia, people "knew" that a "firmament" served as a kind of roof over the planet, to hold at bay the waters of chaos and provide a base to which all the lights in the sky were in some way attached, and followed their appointed tracks across the heavens. Earth was a unified whole, an integrated body in which everything visible had its place.

In this context, when people spoke of the "world" they meant all that existed. All the stellar, planetary, and other existents were components of this one Earth world; there were no other worlds beyond and independent of Earth. Today, when people look back with twenty-first century eyes and out through telescopes, they understand how their ancestors viewed Earth from their context. Contemporary people realize, unlike earlier humans, the immense distances in the cosmos, and a plurality of worlds. In a nutshell, it might be said that the ancients saw a singular world in which all was contained—effectively, then, a "plurality of world"—while people today see a plurality of worlds.

In ages past, humans, believing in the plurality of entities comprising one world, thought that they had a special, central place in the universe. Observing the night sky, they believed that all of the entities in Earth's visible world, which included everything in the universe as seen in the heavens (that are understood today as visible entities—stars and planets—in space), revolved around them. They believed that they were at the pinnacle of living beings since they were the only being with intelligence. Their role was to rule over other creatures: either because a divine Being had created them to do so, or because they had gradually developed the technology (including for hunting, plowing, building construction, and warfare) that enabled them to control the terrain, and subject other biota to their purposes.

In the present age, humankind realizes that it inhabits one Earth, which is one of eight or nine planets (Pluto's current non-planet status is still being debated by some scientists) in the solar system in which they all orbit their local star. Earth has a certain discrete planetary body, enveloped by an atmosphere in which, barring excessive human-caused pollution or a catastrophic natural event, its air, land, and water exist in balance. In Earth's evening, its moon reflects the sun's light and is part of a diversity of lights in the heavens: other stars, planets, and moons, meteors, comets, and asteroids (and, since the twentieth century, artificial satellites and diverse types of space junk that reflect the sun's rays). People know that all of these are distinct entities.

Plurality of "World" to Plurality of Worlds

The transition from believing in a plurality of world to knowing about a plurality of worlds developed over millennia. The Western world (and possibly, for the first time in human history and for humankind as a whole) first pondered the possibility of a "plurality of worlds" when Epicurus wrote to Herodotus that, since atoms exist in space in infinite numbers, "there are infinite worlds both like and unlike this world of ours." He added that "in all worlds there are living creatures and plants and other things we see in this world."[10] Subsequently, Aristotle weighed in on the issue, disagreeing that there was a plurality of worlds. Complementarily, in diverse early cultural traditions throughout Earth, songs, stories, and art describe or depict otherworldly beings. The discussion—and debate—continued for millennia and briefly entered Christian theology when Thomas Aquinas agreed with Aristotle.[11]

As noted previously, not only in Western thought but in numerous ancient religious traditions, the "world" was not solely planet Earth. What was seen in daylight on Earth and at night in the heavens was understood in its totality as one integral self-contained entity, a "plurality" of world: a complex, integral, self-contained interacting entity that included the sun, moon, stars, constellations, and other space lights that appeared to circle Earth, and meteors and an occasional comet that passed overhead.

Genesis 1 Creation Story

A well-known example of this understanding of the sky as a dome occurs in the Bible in Genesis 1:6–8:

> And God said, "Let there be a dome in the midst of the waters, and let it separate the waters from the waters . . ." So God made the dome and separated the waters . . . God called the dome Sky . . . [second day]
> And God said, "Let there be lights in the dome of the sky to separate the day from the night . . . and let them be lights in the dome of the sky to give light upon the earth." And it was so. God

---

10. Crowe, *Extraterrestrial Life Debate*, 4–5. Discussed in greater depth in Hart, *Cosmic Commons*, 254. Epicurus is the earliest Greek thinker known to have written about a plurality of worlds.

11. Aquinas temporarily was excommunicated, posthumously, by the archbishop of Paris because of this assertion. Theologians soon found a way to accept both views: Christians could believe that it was *possible* that there could be a plurality of worlds, since nothing was outside of God's power; but God chose not to create them. See Hart, *Cosmic Commons*, 254–55.

made the two great lights—the greater light to rule the day and
the lesser light to rule the night—and the stars. God set them in
the dome of the sky to give light upon the earth . . . [fourth day]

As noted, on the second "day"[12] of creation, Yahweh creates a dome amid chaotic waters to separate the waters into those above the dome, and those below it. God calls the "dome" the sky (imagine a bowl inverted atop a plate: a hemisphere is formed. Then, imagine submerging the hemisphere in a tub full of water. This is what is understood by the biblical authors: the hard surface of the dome keeps waters above it in place; the Earth keeps the waters below at bay: springs reveal the waters below emerging in a few places). On the third "day" the land appears when the waters under the dome are gathered together, and the land is called Earth, on which living beings are created; on the fourth "day" Yahweh creates lights—sun, moon, and stars—and places them on the sky dome. The "firmament" in this story is indeed firm, separating "waters above from waters below" and providing a foundation for the lights in the sky.

The distinct stars and worlds that astronomy has discovered since then had been, for ancient peoples, entities that participated in the totality and plurality-in-unity of the heavens and Earth that comprise the "world."

Genesis 1 to John's Logos: *Creator Is Incarnated in Creation*

The Genesis 1 story is foundational for understanding the Christian Scriptures' discussion of the "world" and of God's incarnation in the world to benefit those made in God's image (understood at the time to mean solely humankind).

Genesis 1 begins:

> In the beginning when God created the heavens and the earth,
> the earth was a formless void and darkness covered the face of
> the deep, while a wind from God swept over the waters. Then
> God said, "Let there be light, and there was light [first day]."

The imagery of God creating by speaking is carried forward through the rest of the days of creation.

The Gospel of John builds on Genesis 1, linking creation and incarnation. John 1 begins with an old Christian hymn, which predates the rest of

---

12. "Day" is a metaphor for a (long) period of time: since in the story Earth and sun do not yet exist, the spinning of Earth on its axis as it orbits the sun has not happened yet; so day (ruled by the greater light, the sun) and night (ruled by the lesser light, the moon) could not exist either, in today's astronomical understanding. The imaginative biblical writer uses a familiar understanding of units of time that describe daytime and nighttime.

John's Gospel. The hymn opens with direct references to Genesis 1, in which Yahweh creates, metaphorically, by *speaking* (since the Creator is a Spirit, the Creator would not have a physical body, and therefore not a "mouth" to speak). The imagery of God "saying" creating words is carried over into John 1:1.

In his opening hymn, John narrates his creation story. He integrates the Christian understanding of God the "Father" with that of God the "Son": both are eternal aspects or persons of a triune God. In John 1, the "words" God speaks are viewed as descriptions of the transcendent power of God, which in turn are transformed into the immanent power and presence of God: the Word (*Logos*) who becomes visible by taking on a human form (John 1:1–14).[13]

> In the beginning was the Word [*Logos*], and the Word was with God, and the Word was God. He was in the beginning with God. All things came into being through him, and without him not one thing came into being. What has come into being in him was life, and the life was the light of all people. The light shines in the darkness, and the darkness did not overcome it . . .
>
> He was in the world, and the world came into being through him; yet the world did not know him. He came to what was his own, and his own people did not accept him. But to all who received him, who believed in his name, he gave power to become children of God, who were born, not of blood or of the will of the flesh or of the will of man, but of God.
>
> And the Word became flesh and lived among us, and we have seen his glory, the glory as of a father's only son, full of grace and truth.

The first verse might be expressed as:

> In the beginning was the *Logos*, and the *Logos* was with God, and the *Logos* was God.

The *Logos* is the creative aspect of divine Being, who creates the physical world and then, in Christian belief, becomes part of it. What flows from this is that when the *Logos* comes into the world, this happens on Earth, which in the time of John is the plurality of world, as then understood.

Bearing in mind, then, the concept of a "plurality of world": since all the creation that was visible to John was understood to be part of the Earth world, then John 1 could be understood to mean that the *Logos* became incarnate in multiple worlds, according to each one's need. Given the

---

13. Verses 6–9, about John the Baptist, were added to the original hymn; these are omitted here. NRSV translation.

interlocking dimensions of time, and that in God past, present, and future are one, such incarnations might be either *simultaneous* (all occurring at the same "moment" in cosmic time) or *sequential* (each occurring at a particular, appropriate moment in the sociocultural history of a particular world at a particular time).

The *Logos* incarnate on planet Earth, then, would be complemented by *Logos* incarnate on other entities of the "world" visible in the night sky. It is the same *Logos* manifesting at a moment in which it would be most beneficial for a world's intelligent beings to receive—and follow—the words (teachings) of the Word. God, who loves creation and is solicitous of all creatures on every world that people view as part of the plurality of "worlds," would enter other worlds to guide other intelligent beings to be God's people(s). What ancients saw as one world with some of the world's entities passing overhead on fixed tracks in the firmament, humankind today views and understands to be multiple worlds visible in the night sky: not attached to a firmament or vault in the heavens, but existing as stars with their own (often invisible to human eyes) planets at great distances from Earth, a reality inconceivable for the ancients.

The word *world*, then, can indicate simultaneously "one" and "many": one material world (e.g., Earth in the solar system in which humankind dwells) and many a material world (e.g., planets throughout the cosmos). It could indicate, too, different dimensions of existence (e.g., metamaterial world[s]), and different times during which what exists, exists here and now in a specific moment (which could last for a nanosecond or a millennia), and exists there and then for a specific moment (also of varying durations). God, who entered the Earth world in the person of Jesus of Nazareth, also enters other worlds, as needed, to help particular creatures and creation as a whole.

The mental impression is mind-boggling: all worlds are *loci* of divine Presence manifest throughout the cosmos. A question that flows from this understanding is: Whether one assumes that there is a "plurality of worlds" or a "plurality of world," to what extent is our metamaterial world plural— e.g., in terms of multiple dimensions, and diverse species of intelligent living beings—and simultaneously singular—with complementary or overlapping aspirations, a shared sense of the sacred expressed through spiritual understandings not institutionalized in structured religions?

Paul's letter to the Philippians stimulates similar reflection along these lines, in Philippians 2:5–8. In his letter to the people of Philippi, a city he had visited and in which he founded a community of believers (a "church"), Paul urges the people:

> Let the same mind be in you that was in Christ Jesus,
> who, though he was in the form of God,
> did not regard equality with God
> as something to be exploited,
> but emptied himself,
> taking the form of a slave,
> being born in human likeness.
> And being found in human form,
> he humbled himself,
> and became obedient to the point of death—
> even death on a cross.

A key phrase in the passage is "emptied himself" expressed in the Greek word *kenosis* in John's Gospel. God's self-emptying is God's relinquishment of divine power in order that God-in-Jesus might, in human form (incarnation) become human and share in the human condition. A similar *kenosis* might have occurred in all the worlds that are included in the biblical understanding of "world."

This is not multiple incarnations. The eternal, Transcendent-Immanent divine *Logos* becomes visibly embodied in intelligent species throughout the cosmos, in multiple worlds according to their respective needs. Indeed, in creation itself, the *Logos* relinquishes having a coercive control over living creatures by which they would be forced to follow divine commands in their natural world. God, whose primary attribute is love, who is creative and free to express creativity, enables in creation a derivative creativity: the universe unfolds from its explosive origin (Belgian priest-scientist Georges Lemaître described this origin as an event that occurred on a "Day Without Yesterday" when a "Primeval Atom" exploded[14]) as it expands ("inflates") and provides habitable contexts that enable life to emerge and evolve over time on the cosmos worlds. The cosmos freedom to be creative results in spectacular heavenly bodies and amazing evolving biota. On worlds other than Earth, similar evolution of life is theorized to result from their DNA-environment interaction and interrelationships.

The Divine Being-Becoming Spirit of the Cosmos

Spirit is divine Being-Becoming, transcendent to yet immanent in the universe, and then is simultaneously present-past-future in time, when time comes into being as one of the creatures at the origin of creation.

---

14. Hart, *Cosmic Commons*, 165–69.

The Spirit is not a static impersonal Being, nor solely the Creator Spirit described in sacred texts, from whom came the primeval atom from which the universe emerged in an unprecedented explosion on the "day without yesterday." Rather, Spirit is solicitous and caring while continuing to create, now indirectly, through the elements and energies that continue to unfold from the primeval moment and interact, and also by evolutionary processes that produce new beings who will find a niche and adaptive existence in ever-emerging and ever-emergent cosmos settings. The Creating Spirit's immanent but distinct presence in creation is called *panentheism*. This understanding is distinct from *pantheism*, in which Spirit and the Spirit's creation are one entity.

Divine Cosmos Being

The eternal Spirit of the cosmos is, in John's words, Love. Divine Love becomes manifest when the Spirit creates, through a gradual cosmos process, other living beings, likely in multiple dimensions or, if in one dimension, with the ability, at some time in their ongoing evolution, to come to understand a way to pass into other dimensions.

Divine Cosmos Becoming

At the instant of creation, the eternal Spirit is a *transcendent* Spirit relative to other beings who come into being, emanating from Spirit as distinct forms of being; and an *immanent* Spirit, whose Presence permeates all that comes to be. The Creator is then, relative to all other being, the Transcendent-Immanent Spirit. As creation unfolds into abiotic and then biotic forms, the Spirit, who is Love and in a relational bond of community with all life, experiences what living beings experience. The Creator, then, is Being-Becoming Spirit, whose empathy (Rabbi Abraham Joshua Heschel) for creatures stimulates an always-becoming divine Nature. Spirit is not a rigid, cold, insensitive observer from a heaven above, but a loving, engaged participant in whatever living beings experience. (In Christian theology, God-become-embodied in Jesus of Nazareth experiences pain, love, friendship, and hatred, and endures a torturous death.)

Locus

The word *locus* can indicate simultaneously one "place" with multiple facets (e.g., material location in a material world with a diversity of material beings), or a plurality of "places" (e.g., a place materially present simultaneously—or at different times—in different dimensions of existence), or "place" or "places" that are metamaterially present simultaneously or in variant times (e.g., intellectually in creative thought; spiritually in creative relation with others or an Other; or psychologically, in terms of one's "state of mind" at distinct moments). The late Oxford Anglican priest-theologian-biochemist Arthur Peacocke described the divine Spirit as immanent-transcendent being-becoming. The Being-Becoming Spirit, in a Third Displacement consciousness, would be theorized to be at the center of the cosmos, a center understood not as a specific location or place but as a transcendent place of metamaterial experience of and engagement with divine Being-Becoming. Indian spiritual elders and healers throughout the Americas have described themselves being at the "center of the universe," often unexpectedly, and receiving the "power of the universe" from the Creator Spirit. God/divine Being is believed to be, in this tradition, an immanent Presence in all that is. A divinity's transcendent center and immanent presence are everywhere, and have no limiting boundary anywhere. This immanent Presence might be viewed as effecting *cosmosacrality*.

In the Third Displacement, people would realize—regarding cosmos ethics and understandings of relationality, relationships, and reciprocity, and in considering "sociality," biotic evolution, and the interrelated, interdependent, integrated unfolding of the universe—that they need a more "universal" understanding of "integral being" and "integral universe,"[15] and cosmos "common good."

Logos *and* logoi *in Dialogic Relationship*

In Christian tradition, the divine *Logos* is the power and thread present throughout the cosmos. The *Logos* is the creative power of God that brings forth the cosmos. In Genesis 1, the first creation story in the Bible, the creating God "speaks," as noted earlier, and creatures emerge, both inanimate (such as the sun, moon, stars, planets, and sky) and animate (living beings of different species and characteristics). In the first chapter of the Gospel of John, the metamaterial-creating *Logos* assumes a material form while simultaneously remaining, in its essence, a transcendent Being and immanent Being: *Logos* became flesh, incarnate in the person of Jesus of Nazareth, and lived as a human being among humankind.

In both the Hebrew Scriptures and specifically Christian Scriptures, as described earlier, the *world* was understood to be a composite of all that exists, not just Earth and all biota in Earth's air, land, and water. The sun by

---

15. Hart, *Sacramental Commons*, 138, 221; Hart, *Cosmic Commons*, 392; Hart, *Encountering ETI*, 240–241.

day and all stars by night were viewed as components of *world*. When the *Logos* took on human physicality, the *Logos* became at that moment a part of all worlds seen as part of the Earth world. Thus, scripturally and in the thinking of people in biblical times, the *Logos* can be understood to be present throughout the universe in ways appropriate to the needs of creatures on every planet. The *Logos*, too, would be present in various dimensions of reality: concurrent with this moment in Earth history, or existing in different places simultaneously, across space and time. In that and succeeding eras, a human couple viewing the beauty of the evening sky would see all objects there as part of Earth, attached to the "firmament" that is Earth's sky, and following appointed tracks on and around its surface.

When this is borne in mind, confusion about how Jesus could "save the world" is overcome: the *Logos* in the form of an intelligent species becomes a distinct being on each world simultaneously or in a different, appropriate time, a unifying being who links worlds and times, and is immanent in all of them, on a material or metamaterial, physical or spiritual, visible or invisible plane of loving, relational, cosmos existence.

Maximus Confessor (580–662)

Centuries after the biblical stories were written, their imagery would be a foundation for the teaching of Maximus Confessor, revered as a saint in both Eastern Christianity and Western Christianity. Maximus was born in 580 into a comfortable life, "in a family of high reputation in the imperial capital," Constantinople.[16] Due to the quality of his writing and the scholars with which he is obviously familiar, his biographers have speculated that he "received the sort of broad humanistic education for which the Christian 'university' at Constantinople was renowned."[17] He became the "'protosecretary' in the court of the emperor Heraclius."[18] He left his position just three years later to enter the monastery at Chrysopolis, where he became abbot. He moved into another monastery and then, in 630, when Constantinople was threatened by the Persian army he went to Carthage, arriving in 632 by way of Crete (where he resided for a time) and Cyprus.[19] He entered the monastery of Euchratas. The abbot was Sophronius, who was a leader in the principal doctrinal dispute of the time: did Christ, as God-Man, have one will or two? Sophronius supported the latter, as did Maximus.

---

16. Thunberg, *Man and the Cosmos*, 17.
17. Maximus Confessor, *Selected Writings*, 3.
18. Maximus Confessor, *Selected Writings*, 3.
19. Thunberg, *Man and the Cosmos*, 18.

Maximus had an extensive body of theological and philosophical work. As the fight over the issue of the number of Christ's wills flared up, the opposing sides had support from powerful patriarchs in local cities. Eventually, Maximus was in a region controlled by those who fought for the one-will position, and he was arrested and brought to trial in Constantinople in 653. He was consequently convicted in 655 and banished to Bizya in Thrace. When he continued to maintain his theological position (which had been affirmed by the Council of Chalcedon two centuries earlier, in 451), he was summoned to Constantinople for another trial in 662. He convicted, and his right hand was cut off (to stop his writing and to punish him for not signing a compromise doctrinal statement) and his tongue was cut out (to prevent him from teaching). Then he was exiled to the distant city of Lazica, where he died in the same year. (Thunberg observes that Maximus's ecclesiastical and political enemies "accused him of political crimes rather than heresies, since his spiritual theology, his monastic status and his integrity as a thinker" would have made such an accusation "ridiculous."[20] Maximus's theological position was affirmed almost twenty years later, by the Council of Constantinople, 680–81.[21] Today, and for millennia past, Maximus has been recognized by both Eastern and Western Christianity as a saint, martyr, mystic, and *Confessor*—one who confesses (proclaims loyally and steadfastly declares or affirms) their Christian faith unreservedly, even when threatened, harmed physically, or facing death.

In his work, Maximus describes a dialogic relationship between the creating divine *Logos* and all beings in creation, the *logoi*, which include abiotic and biotic entities. This *dialogos* goes on through time: it is an unending interaction between *Logos* and *logoi*—the creation is incomplete until its culmination in the *Logos*; it is a work still becoming while it is being. The visible creation reveals the materially invisible *Logos*: "The author of existence gives himself to be beheld though visible things."[22] Maximus wonders how anyone seeing the greatness and beauty of creation could not recognize that God's power brought it into existence. People should integrate visible and invisible realities. The human being "unites the created nature with the uncreated through love ... showing them to be one and the same through the possession of grace, the whole [creation] wholly interpenetrated by God."[23]

Orthodox Christian scholar Elizabeth Theokritoff, author of *Living in God's Creation: Orthodox Perspectives on Ecology*, discusses the *Logos-logoi* interaction permeating Maximus's thought in "The Vision of Maximus the

20. Thunberg, *Man and the Cosmos*, 17.
21. Thunberg, *Man and the Cosmos*, 20.
22. Louth, *Maximus*, 110.
23. Louth, *Maximus*, 158.

Confessor: That Creation May All Be One."[24] In the beginning of her chapter, she observes that "Maximus is increasingly regarded as the greatest and most profound of Byzantine theologians."[25]

In the section "The Texture of All Things: The *Logoi* of Beings," Theokritoff declares about Maximus:

> When he maintains that all things participate in God . . . the key to participation lies in the notion of *Logos* . . . Creation "in word (*Logos*) and wisdom" . . . means that each thing is created according to its own principle (*logos*) of existence, which pre-exists in God in the divine Will . . . Maximus expresses this panentheism in strong terms: according to [God's] creative and sustaining "procession" into the creature, the one [divine] *Logos* is many *logoi* . . . the many are one . . . The very texture of the universe is thus God the Word in action . . . [humans will not comprehend] how God who is in truth no one of the things that exist, and properly speaking *is everything and is beyond everything*, is in every *logos* of each thing separately, and in all the *logoi* of things taken together . . . [God] conceals [Godself] in the *logoi* of beings . . . [26]

Theokritoff states, as do biologists and ecologists today who think in a way that complements and affirms Maximus, that in Maximus's understanding "any entity . . . is defined not only by its own *logos* of being, but also by the *logoi* of the things that make up its environment . . . Relationality is at the core of his cosmic vision . . . "[27] She concludes the chapter in a similar vein by observing that "the unifying web of the *logoi* of things pervades the physical universe no less than the spiritual, intellectual, and moral aspects of human life."[28]

Lars Thunberg elaborates similar ideas about Maximus. He states that for Maximus,

> The cosmic Christ [the creating Word, the *Logos* who became part of creation] is at the same time the Christ of the Cross and of the Resurrection . . . [and only through these events] can the world be saved, although it is at all times kept together through its different *logoi* by the *Logos* Creator . . . Through the contemplation of the *logoi* of creation, the soul enters into mystical

---

24. Theokritoff, "Vision," 220.
25. Theokritoff, "Vision," 220.
26. Theokritoff, "Vision," 226.
27. Theokritoff, "Vision," 228.
28. Theokritoff, "Vision," 233.

communion with the *Logos*, who gives Himself to it there in virtue of His primary inhabitation in the *logoi* of all things.[29]

Maximus's understanding of the *Logos*-become-incarnate on Earth, of course, would be phrased differently by intelligent beings on other worlds, who might have complementary ideas about the Spirit's mode of becoming visibly, materially present (if appropriate) on their world.

Thunberg relates Maximus's understanding of creation's ultimate fulfillment in its final Mystical Union with the Spirit, to the "speculations of a Fr. Pierre Teilhard de Chardin on the evolution of the world toward the *Omega* point [which] also seem to have a certain affinity to those of Maximus."[30]

Thunberg uses the words of Maximus to describe the distinction between, and at the same time the interrelationship of, the *Logos* and the *logoi*:

> God is in the *logos* of every special thing and likewise in all the *logoi* according to which all things exist, God who is truly none of the beings and yet truly all the beings and above all the beings. Thus, in a proper sense, all divine energy signifies God properly, *indivisibly and totally via that energy in everything*, whatever the *logos* may be which is capable of conceiving exactly and telling *how* God is it without being divided and without being diversely spread out in the infinite differences of being in which [God] is as Being.[31]

(In chapter 5 below, Bernardo Peixoto, an indigenous leader from Brazil, relates that intelligent beings told him that they came from "nowhere" and therefore, he thought, from "everywhere." He reflects, then, that only God can be from nowhere in particular, and therefore everywhere.)

TI/ETI/IDI *Logoi*

Maximus's thought, by affirming the relationality of all beings and the Spirit's Presence in all, complements the teaching of John that the *Logos* assumed human form in Jesus, becoming visible thereby, and the teaching of Francis that all beings, biotic and abiotic, are "brother" and "sister." All *logoi*, on Earth and in the heavens, are related each to the other, and are in *dialogos* with the Spirit—consciously or unconsciously. The divine *Logos* is in all *logoi*, not solely in *homo sapiens*, nor solely in living beings, but in every abiotic and biotic being. *Logoi* are all the creatures in creation. *Logoi* are distinct from, and immanented by, the *Logos*. The *Logos* is in ongoing dialogic

---

29. Thunberg, *Man and the Cosmos*, 135, 136.
30. Thunberg, *Man and the Cosmos*, 137. Teilhard is discussed in chapter 4.
31. Thunberg, *Man and the Cosmos*, 140.

relationship with the *logoi*, all of whom have emerged from divine creativity. The *Logos* is a visible or invisible presence as *logoi* in diverse cosmos settings. The *Logos* dialogues with *logoi* both in the material world, in which the *Logos* is part of all *logoi*, the Spirit's creatures, and in the metamaterial world (in all its spiritual and other transcendent dimensions). Humans and ETL are kin to each other, therefore, and should relate as such. While not all species of ETI/IDI might be amenable to such interrelationality, or to a community of living and not living beings in the integral being of the cosmos, it is at least an ideal that might come to be realized in the future. Lunberg states that "On account of the presence of the *Logos* in all things, holding their *logoi* together, the world is pregnant with divine reality."[32] Berthold cites related insights from Maximus: "Maintaining about himself as cause, beginning, and end all beings which are by nature distant from one another, [God] makes them converge in each other by the singular force of their relationship to [God] as origin."[33] Maximus declares that "all beings" are held close by God and, although they are "distant from one another" by nature, God stimulates their convergence in each other because of their common relationship with God. Further, "there is but *one world and it is not divided by its parts*. On the contrary, it encloses the differences of the parts arising from their natural properties by their relationship to what is one and indivisible in itself."[34] (This might be rephrased or at least understood, in light of ideas presented previously, that this is a "plurality of world.")

This reality might, after Contact, stimulate intelligent beings who have evolved beyond institutional religious traditions in diverse worlds' settings and share a profound spiritual sense of the cosmos, to draw on that understanding to relate each to the other. Contact could then be congenial rather that confrontational.

As described later (chapter 5), indigenous peoples' spiritual traditions are similar to Maximus's teachings: native peoples teach that all biota and abiota, including diverse cosmic beings, relate to both the Creator and each other.

Nicholaus of Cusa (1401–64)

Nicholaus of Cusa, writing some seven centuries after Maximus, reflected directly on the possibility of life (ETL and ETI) on other worlds:

---

32. Thunberg, *Man and the Cosmos*, 127.
33. Maximus Confessor, *Selected Writings*, 186.
34. Maximus Confessor, *Selected Writings*, 188. Italics added.

> Life, as it exists here on earth in the form of men, animals and plants, is to be found, let us suppose, in a higher form in the solar and stellar regions . . . [W]e will suppose that in every region there are inhabitants, differing in nature by rank and all owing their origin to God, who is the centre and circumference of all stellar regions . . . Of the inhabitants then of worlds other than our own we can know still less [than we know about Earth's biota], having no standards by which to appraise them.[35]

Note how Nicholaus suggests that a "higher form" of life, that is, a more intelligent and advanced type of life, is to be found in distant regions in space: effectively, in today's parlance, "extraterrestrial" or "interdimensional" intelligent life. Further, knowing nothing of DNA or evolution, he says that this higher form of life differs from us; the life about which we are aware is "life as we know it," as NASA's and other scientists declare today. Other insights for people today are that "we are all related" (in integral being, it might be added), having a common origin in God and in the unfolding cosmos; and that when we ponder the vastness of the cosmos, rather than feeling small and insignificant we might consider that we are part of a vast community of living beings, and embrace the immensity before us, whose "centre and circumference" is God.

Francis of Assisi (1181–1226)

People often seem to regard Saint Francis as someone who is oriented solely toward nature and other-than-human living creatures, as depicted in much of the art portraying him. However, he was also greatly concerned about the poor, who were often despised by society.

Regarding his nature theology, theists who accept insights about divine immanence are likely to be able to accept and relate more readily to ExoEarth life, in the spirit of Francis, who perceived all creatures to be "brother" or "sister." This is readily seen in Francis's most well-known work, the *Canticle of All Creatures*:

> *Canticle of All Creatures*
> Most High, all-powerful, and all-good Lord,
> Praise, glory, honor,
> and all blessing
> are yours.
> To you alone, Most High, they belong,

---

35. Nicholaus in Crowe, *Extraterrestrial*, 31.

although no one is worthy
to say your name.
Praised be my Lord, with all your creatures,
especially my lord Brother Sun,
through whom you give us day and light.
Beautifully he shines with great splendor:
Most High, he bears your likeness.
Praised be my Lord, by Sister Moon and Stars:
in the heavens you made them bright
and precious and beautiful.
Praised be my Lord, by Brother Wind,
and air and cloud
and calm and all weather
through which you sustain
your creatures.
Praised be my Lord, by Sister Water,
who is so helpful and humble
and precious and pure.
Praised be my Lord, by Brother Fire,
through whom you brighten the night:
who is beautiful and playful
and sinuous and strong.
Praised be my Lord, by our Sister Mother Earth,
who sustains us and guides us,
and provides varied fruits
with colorful flowers and herbs.
Praised and blessed be you, my Lord,
and gratitude and service be given to you
with great humility.[36]

36. Translated by this writer while I participated in a seminar on the life and historical context of St. Francis; it took place in Siena, Assisi, and Rome. I used the Italian text of Ms. 338 in the Assisi library (Fortini, *Francis of Assisi*, 566–67). I concur with scholars who have translated "per" as "by"; others have translated "per" as "through" or "for." Bearing in mind the stories about Francis's "conversations" with animals, birds, and fish, and his familial relationship with all of them, I think that, as is expressed in Psalm 148, all creatures praise their Creator. Moreover, contemporary scientists have found that animals and birds are social, intelligent, and communicate verbally (which indicates that they first thought about what they wanted to say). "Per," then, expresses the spirit of Psalm 148 and current scientific research.

In paintings and statues, Francis is ordinarily portrayed in the company of birds or a wolf . . . or both. Yet, in the *Canticle*, no biota are mentioned, which is surprising—unless the meaning of the complete song (including words and melody), which Francis sang as he approached villages, is known. Francis's words, as just noted, urge abiotic beings to praise God. Francis begins with beings in the skies, and gradually lowers his vision to see those in the air and then on Earth's surface. Francis addresses, in turn, my lord Brother Sun, Sister Moon and Stars, Brother Wind, Sister Water, Brother Fire, and our Sister Mother Earth. In the last three words, he describes humans' home planet as a living being, just as do indigenous peoples. The melody is taken from a romantic Italian ballad of his time, whose words celebrate animals, birds, and plants. Therefore, when Francis was heard singing as he came near, villagers would recall the original words. When these words and melody were considered together with Francis's new verses, the verbal-visual image would be that *all* entities of the world, biotic and abiotic, are integrated, and are called on to praise God as a familial chorus of creatures.

When Francis teaches that all beings are humans' relatives, their brothers and sisters, he mirrors indigenous peoples' spiritual and cultural understanding, and their millennia-old tradition: "We are all relations." By extension, beings from stars, planets, and other worlds that are not human habitations, including those in other cosmos dimensions, should be welcomed as family, unless and until they are not faithful to their calling to be part of a relational cosmos community, and reject efforts to include them in, or restore them to sociality within, that community.

Displacement

People's self-assessment or self-designation of their place on their home planet was altered by the realization (which was resisted until evidence for it became overwhelming) that they are not preeminent in the cosmos as they understand it. They experienced, then, on an intellectual and spiritual level, dethronement from their perceived imperial status over their Earth realm, and displacement from their preeminent role in the cosmos. In the pages to follow, the First and Second Displacements will be elaborated in terms of the spiritual, psychological, and societal impacts of scientific discoveries by Copernicus, Galileo, and Kepler in astronomy, and Charles Darwin in biology. These considerations will include exploration of the possibility that humankind would be "re-placed" in the human intellect or religious consciousness when future places—philosophical or planetary—are pondered, whether or not they exist in concrete reality or, if existing, are actually occupied by some form of living being. Elaborated, too, are ways in which humans, as a species and as communities, social groups, families, or individuals, could adapt to materially, socially, or spiritually disorienting new places, through analyzing factors that cause religious/spiritual displacement. Alternatively, the new human locus (physical, psychological, spiritual, and philosophical) could generate a sense, consciousness, and experience of being part of an extensive cosmos relational community. In this scenario, cosmobiological discoveries initially would affect society adversely, perhaps particularly in diverse faith traditions, but then generate excitement, and engagement to overcome anxiety and stimulate acceptance. Current perceptions of cosmolocality will be materially and metamaterially altered, but then might be replaced by a *cosmos relational consciousness* in a *cosmos relational community*.

Displacement: Cosmically Decentering Humankind

In pre-sixteenth century consciousness, diverse human civilizations understood humanity to be at the pinnacle of the natural world. Initially, humans believed that they were at the center of the cosmos. The sun, moon, stars, and all worlds visible in the night sky apparently revolved around their planet—and therefore, around themselves as the dominant (and dominating) species on Earth.

In the sixteenth and seventeenth centuries, however, scientists Copernicus, Galileo, and Kepler (for whom is named the recently decommissioned planet-hunter telescope) discovered that Earth was not the center of the cosmos around which all other worlds and stellar bodies revolved. This was humankind's First Displacement. This information catalyzed a psychological and cultural shock: Earth and humans were not at the center of the vast universe after all. Rather, people lived on a planet that orbited a local star, along with other planets, in an integrated heliocentric system—one of many such that are present throughout the universe. Humankind felt displaced from its premier cosmic place.

People continued to believe, nevertheless, that at least they were unique among living beings: they were created separately from other biota and further, in Christianity, God had become enfleshed—incarnate—in human form. In addition to being social and spiritual "images of God" as expressed in Genesis 1, their status had been further enhanced by God's incarnation in Jesus, a physical "image of humanity," metaphorically speaking, who revealed in his divine-human life and his teachings how all people should live. Effectively, in Christian teaching, Genesis 1 (Yahweh "speaks," and people are created in Yahweh's "image"), John 3:16 ("God so loved the world" that God entered into it), and John 1 (the creating "Word became flesh and lived among us") are foundational to understand some Christians' current efforts to "save the souls" of other intelligent species encountered in space.

Then, in the nineteenth century, Darwin's theory of evolution by natural selection posited that humankind, along with all other living beings, had evolved from earlier biota; they were part of a natural selection process. Darwin's proposal that humans had evolved from prior primates stimulated humankind's Second Displacement. People who accepted Darwin's theory had to transition from believing that they were a unique, distinct divine creation to knowing that they were one form of life's gradual development, from simplicity to complexity, over eons, part of an evolving Creation, not a special divine creation.

After accommodating in varying degrees to the first two displacements, humans retained the belief that at least they had a special cosmic status and place because they were the only intelligent species in the vast universe. However, some people around the globe described seeing spacecraft whose maneuvers were beyond both the laws of physics as then understood, and the capabilities of human technology. A disturbing possibility occurred to them, and to some scientists: there were beings not of this world who were significantly more advanced (and likely more intelligent) than humans. Twentieth-century scientists who were open and willing to consider this realized that the cosmos, about fourteen billion years old, was three times the age of Earth, a mere 4.5 billion years old. The possibility of a Third Displacement, which resulted from a progression from a belief that humans had the highest cosmic intelligence to a growing awareness that probably they have only the highest Earth intelligence, became alarmingly (for some humans) possible. Humans would be cosmically decentered and downgraded in status, and could not rationally retain belief in their intellectual superiority and their assumed, self-described preeminence over all life—not only on Earth, but in the entire universe.

Humans might experience, inalterably, a Third Displacement—psychologically, physically, socially, and culturally—upon discovering biota elsewhere in space. This type of displacement likely will be even greater than prior displacements. In fact, a major "displacement" might result even from discovery solely of microbial life in space, let alone intelligent life, as described earlier.

The First and Second Displacements resulted in spiritual, psychological, and societal impacts. This was a consequence of scientific discoveries by Copernicus, Galileo, and Kepler in astronomy, and Charles Darwin in biology. The consequences included, over time, exploration of the possibility that humankind would be "re-placed," in the human intellect or religious consciousness, when future places—philosophical or planetary—are considered.

This would occur whether or not such places exist in concrete reality or, if existing, are actually occupied by some form of living being.

Humankind has begun to explore, at least intellectually, psychologically, and spiritually, the ways in which, as a species and as communities, social groups, families, or individuals, people could adapt to materially, socially, or spiritually disorienting new places, through analyzing factors that cause religious/spiritual displacement. How adaptive might humans be if their customary and comforting worldviews were threatened or being altered, in whole or in part, by discovery of microbial life on other worlds (including planets, moons, asteroids, etc.) in the heavens?

In a Third Displacement, Maximus's *dialogos* between *Logos* and *logoi* would be seen in a new light: the *Logos-logoi* relationship is simultaneously *Logos-loci*, in all dimensions of existence. The *locus* and *loci* of *Homo sapiens*, in whatever context, are immanented with the presence of the *Logos*. Similarly, the *locus* and *loci* of ETI/IDI are immanented by the *Logos*. The *Logos* immanents different levels and dimensions of *loci*: in the plurality of "world" and in all the distinct cosmos contexts of material existence and material-metamaterial existence.

Theologos *and* Theodao

Contemporary Asian Christian thought offers a complementary but more comprehensive understanding of divine Being in itself and in relation to all beings. Korean Christian thinker Heup Young Kim suggests a fusion of ideas from Buddhism, Daoism, and Christianity that has been emerging from Asian Christian cultural contexts. He views the concept of *Logos* and the study of theology as bases for a singularly Western culture-developed tradition. These should be superseded by a more universally approachable and apprehensible—and universal, in his view—understanding of what he terms *Theodao* (theology of Dao).[37] The Spirit as *Logos*—the eternal creating Word—is described in the opening hymn of John's Gospel ("In the beginning was the Word, and the Word was with God, and the Word was God"); the hymn, in Greek, rephrases and complements the Genesis 1 creation story, in Hebrew, in which Yahweh creates by speaking ("God *said* . . . and it was so"). The Spirit as *Dao* is expressed in Asian languages in sacred texts and other writings. Kim suggests that the integration of the words and theological understandings presented as *Dao* and *Logos* would present, as *Theodao*, a globally acceptable reference to divine Being.

---

37. Kim, "*Theodao*." Kim is Professor of Theology at Kangnam University, Yongin, South Korea, and was the president of the Korean Society for Systematic Theology.

Theodao and Daologos

Another possibility for unifying East-West Christian thought, this writer suggests in response to Kim, would be to represent the Spirit of the universe as *Daologos*. This would represent a further step toward all humans having a more global understanding of the transcendent-immanent divine Being: the different concepts and constructs of the Dao and the *Logos* would be melded into one: *Daologos*. The name of the creating Being, now represented by diverse words—God, *Dao*, Allah, Yahweh, *Logos*, Wakantanka, and so on—could be integrated in a single word—*Daologos*—which would facilitate conveying, to ETI/IDI, an integrated human spirituality and religions' foundational teachings, from East and West (but still not inclusive of all religions' faith traditions, or of a global spiritual understanding).

Daologos, who permeates the cosmos, is immanent thereby in ETI/IDI and TI, and all other biotic and abiotic being. It would be more fitting, perhaps, for ETI/IDI and TI, from their first encounter and thereafter, to learn, and to greet each other with *Namasté* or its cosmic equivalent expressed in whatever word, in the Others' respective customary types of communication, that would convey the same meaning and message. In *Namasté*, no specific verbal reference is made to any Being, in any culture: "Spirit" presents a concept of Being that is likely universally understood.

Theanthropocosmic and Pneumabiocosmic

Kim suggests, too, that a new *theanthropocosmic* vision of God, humanity, and the cosmos in communion would be an appropriate cosmology for Christianity, more especially in the current era when ecology and science are prominent.[38] While the "the" of *theanthropocosmic* represents the Spirit, the "anthropo" is problematic, in this writer's view. It appears visually to be a variation of "anthropocentric" ("man-centered"); "anthropo," because of its male-oriented or male-centered meaning, is a prefix much in disfavor among feminists, women in the general global population, and men who seek to express a more inclusive understanding of divine Being.

A more global and, potentially, universal evolution of this concept, more consonant with consideration of dialogic intercultural conversation about a Spirit immanent in the cosmos and all biota, might be expressed as a pneumabiocosmic or pneumadaocosmic vision of the interrelated Spirit, all life, and the cosmos in dynamic interrelation. "Pneuma" is the Greek word for Spirit or spirit or soul; "pneumatology" is a term referring specifically to study of the (Holy) Spirit. Such a dialogic communion is expressed in

---

38. Kim, "*Theodao*," 105.

Maximus's understanding of the *Logos-logoi* relationship. A complementary description of this relationship is expressed in the Hindu greeting *Namasté*, as noted previously. Its multiple levels of meaning, dialogue, and relation (as explained to me in Nepal two decades ago) are that "the Spirit in me greets the Spirit in you; the spirit in me greets the spirit in you; the Spirit in me greets the spirit in you; the Spirit in you greets the spirit in me; the spirit in you greets the spirit in me." *Namasté* conveys a relationship in which I, you, and the Spirit commune in a continuous dialogic relationship, which is acknowledged respectfully on occasions when we meet directly.[39] ("Pneuma" could replace "Spirit," and "pneuma" could replace "spirit," except that this Greek word would not be globally known or understood.) Each time you and I greet each other in this way, we are declaring our shared identity and shared spiritual consciousness, and strengthening our spiritual bond.

Along these lines, a consequent intellectual assessment of Spirit experience and cosmos relationality would be focused on how, when disorienting space encounters occur, a perceived experience of interactive dialogue with a *Logos* Spirit would be different from and less tenuous than what occurs in reflecting on religious doctrine or participating in religious ritual in Earth communities. In such circumstances, humans have regard only for their and their species' place in a dynamic universe where other life exists. *Namasté* and other expressions of a bond among intelligent species' individual members and communities would acknowledge that a human-Spirit relation and another intelligent being-Spirit relation would not emerge from any intelligent biotas' self-valuation of their material existence and their psychological "place" vis-à-vis other biota and other worlds. An anticipatory projection could be developed, too, that would describe how contact with ExoEarth microbial life would stimulate integration of traditional beliefs and texts with new data and experiences. This could facilitate creation of a transitional spirituality as Earth consciousness gradually (or suddenly) becomes subsumed into cosmos consciousness.

Axis Mundi and Being-Becoming at the Center of the Cosmos

Humans' discovery of living beings in space would free humans to have a spiritual consciousness as an *axis mundi*, in a different way than conceived previously through the ages: they would consciously link Earth with other

---

39. This understanding complements well Jewish thinker Martin Buber's concept of an I-Thou relationship—in people's mutual engagement, in people's engagement with other living beings, and in people's engagement with divine Being. If the "Thou" of Buber's I-Thou were to be extended to include all beings in the cosmos, this phrasing would promote a sense of cosmos interrelationality and ecological consciousness and conduct.

worlds, through scientific discoveries, Contact on Earth or in the heavens, or an intuitive sense of connectedness to ExoEarth life, microbial or intelligent. Unlike ways in which *axis mundi* has been understood in traditional religions of the world, people who experience this connection would not be solely making a connection between Earth and heaven, but between Earth and the heavens. The *axis mundi* would not be *material* and visible (such as represented in religious thought by sacred mountains, trees, church steeples, temple spires, and mosque minarets) but *metamaterial* and invisible: intellectual, psychological, or spiritual, an immanent-transcendent, *material-metamaterial* relationship and even, conceivably, an *interdimensional* relationship.

An excellent elaboration of understandings of *Axis Mundi* over milennia is presented in the *New World Encyclopedia*; the entry is edited and summarized:

> The axis mundi (also cosmic axis, world axis, world pillar and center of the world) is a symbol representing the center of the world where the heaven (sky) connects with the earth . . . The term *axis mundi* derives from the Latin words "*axis*" and "*mundi*" or world, together meaning "pivot point, or line, connecting the earth and the sky/heavens." . . . Because the axis mundi is an idea that unites a number of concrete images, no contradiction exists in regarding multiple spots as "the center of the world." The symbol can operate in a number of locales at once . . .
>
> The human form can function as a world axis . . . Disciplines such as Yoga and Tai Chi begin from the premise of the human body as axis mundi . . . World religions regard the body itself as a temple and prayer as a column uniting earth to heaven . . . A common shamanic concept, and a universally told story, is that of the healer traversing the axis mundi to bring back knowledge from the other world . . . It is the essence of the journey described in *The Divine Comedy* by Dante Alighieri . . . Anyone or anything suspended on the axis between heaven and earth becomes a repository of potential knowledge.[40]

While I was sitting in a circle of elders from diverse Indian nations at Chippewa-Cree elder Pat Kennedy's peace gathering decades ago, several elders said that they had been at the "center of the universe." It is not one central place in the cosmos. Rather, as Bernardo says in John Mack's *Passport to the Cosmos*, it is "anywhere and nowhere," so elders in different places on Earth equally have access to being at a cosmic "center." I recalled this incident when I read the *New World Encyclopedia* entry, where it states that

---

40. New World Encyclopedia, "Axis Mundi," paras. 1, 3, 5, 8, 10, 11.

"multiple spots" can simultaneously be the "center of the universe," and "the human form can function as a world axis." Each and every elder, even had they been praying to the Creator simultaneously at different places around Earth, would be an *axis mundi*, a link between the spiritual and physical dimensions of reality, at the center of the universe. A few years later, after I had hiked to the top of Mount Helena and was praying with my arms upraised, I saw the world before me as an integrated circle of sky, clouds, trees, and mountain top (it reminded me of looking through a fish eye lens on a camera). As I watched, in my mind I had an image of a line going diagonally through a circle, and I was located where the line emerged, pointing upward. I realized the image represented the *axis mundi*. With this image in mind, as I felt power surging through me from my feet through my upraised arms, I thought, "I'm at the center of the universe."

Cosmolocality

"Cosmolocality" indicates a locale in the cosmos, a place or point in the time-space of the cosmos as a whole. Over millennia, Westerners initially considered their locality to be the center of the universe: all heavenly bodies, the sun, the moon, the stars, planets, and all else that was visible to them appeared to circle Earth, their home and habitat. This belief in their *cosmolocality* at the center of the cosmos—at least in terms of the physical universe available to their gaze—gave them a sense and a belief that they were the preeminent existents in the material universe. The First Displacement altered that belief. Because of the discoveries and teachings of Copernicus and then Galileo, humankind gradually had to accept that their planet orbited a local star along with other planets.

The Second Displacement provided a second corrective to their previously conceived ideas, beliefs, and conjectured cosmic status: they were not unique in creation, a special creation of God. Rather, they had emerged well into Earth's history, as did all other life. Charles Darwin provided a scientific, psychological, and ideological jolt to humankind's self-understanding, an awareness still not accepted in the twenty-first century by some members of religious traditions. Most humans have become aware that their conjectured planetary locality was not as lords over creation, but as a species integrated, interdependent, and interrelated with all other species in a circle (or perhaps in a spiral) of life, in a succession of presents. As more data was acquired, humans realized that they had the same origin as all life—in the primeval ocean from which all had emerged—and that humankind gradually had evolved from primates. However, humans thought, at least human beings are the only intelligent beings not only on Earth but in the entire universe.

This new cosmolocality (and cosmocentrality) served humankind until narratives about sightings of intelligently controlled spacecraft increased in public awareness. Despite governments' denials and attempt to cover up such events, people around the world accepted them as true to reality. Humans' theorized cosmolocality and cosmocentrality, as the preeminent intelligent species, came to be an endangered species' self-evaluation.

The developing Third Displacement became the strongest challenge yet to humans' sense of their cosmolocality being cosmocentrality. It is denied out of fear of the "other," because some religious traditions glorify humans, and because of some scientists' and other people's concerns about not being "number one" in the cosmos. It became evident that extraterrestrial beings that travel in spacecraft far superior in technology, maneuverability, and flight capabilities to what humans have invented to date—or even postulated—are highly likely to be more intelligent than are human beings.

It is evident, then, that although a being's physical locality might remain the same for a time, their psychological, social, or intellectually understood locality can be altered because of factors not known or even theorized previously. While cosmolocality might be slightly different, in terms of the vast cosmos, between people on Earth and people in a Mars colony, these humans remain linked as a species and a human community. If humans landing on or colonizing Mars encounter other intelligent beings, both might share in this place the same cosmolocality in terms of physical place in the cosmos, but each would have a different place of origin, and might have a far different cosmolocality in terms of their scientific knowledge, technical expertise, and ability to easily relocate themselves to faraway places. The other intelligent beings would have a different cultural identity and evolutionary development. A shared physical cosmolocality obviously does not mean, then, a congruence of other aspects of what comprises coherently their integral cosmolocality[41] in time and space. A being's actual *material* locality here in this local place is distinct from their imagined *status* locality in the cosmos of which this place is a part.

As reports and narratives about intelligently controlled Unidentified Aerial Phenomena (called initially—and continually—UFOs) increased in number and detail, the US government decided to have a special "scientific consultant" analyze and evaluate them . . . and dismiss them. Distinguished astronomer Dr. Allen Hynek was invited to hold this position. He accepted and did this work while simultaneously acting as chair of the Astronomy

---

41. Might there be, also, a "cosmotemporality," a common "time" that permeates the universe and is not limited or altered by local time, solar system time, galactic time, etc., of existents within the vast universe? Perhaps "uni" might refer to the shared time aspect of being, or the shared "beingness" of life, however and wherever constituted and situated.

Department at Northwestern University. He would subsequently have astrophysicist Jacques Vallée as a colleague in the department. They became the first scientists to study the "UFO phenomenon" extensively. Their stories follow.

3

Unidentified Aerial Phenomena: Extraterrestrial and Interdimensional

Allen Hynek and Jacques Vallée

Distinguished scientists began to consider carefully and in depth, during the 1960s, the nature and origins of Visitors to Earth. The scientists (often in secret for fear of adverse professional consequences) wondered what intentions the Visitors might have in coming to Earth and making Contact with humankind, and what might be the impacts and influences of that Contact. Allen Hynek and Jacques Vallée, for more than a decade colleagues in the astronomy department at Northwestern University, are prominent members of this group of scholars.

Allen Hynek

Dr. Josef Allen Hynek (1910–86), better known as J. Allen Hynek or simply Allen Hynek,[1] was an astronomer who believed initially that all people who claimed to have witnessed a UFO in the skies were either delusional or had misidentified celestial objects as UFOs—artificial satellites launched by the US or USSR; lunar phases; the planet Venus; or meteors and other natural phenomena observed in near and distant space.

---

1. Hynek's published works include *The Hynek UFO Report*; *The UFO Experience: A Scientific Inquiry*; and *Night Siege: The Hudson Valley UFO Sightings* (with Philip J. Imbrogno and Bob Pratt).

Mark O'Connell elaborates well the life of Allen Hynek in *Close Encounters Man*.[2] The author does more than just narrate Hynek's biography; he links that life story to its historical context on several levels: developments and discoveries in science and technology, some of which originated with Hynek; sociohistorical events in terms of politics and national conflicts; and literary developments in science fiction—science at times seemed to influence, and at other times to be influenced by, the imagination and creativity of sci-fi authors. Hynek's fascinating biography is interwoven with a historical narrative and a description of the changing public awareness and acceptance of the reality of intelligently controlled UFOs. This is interspersed with UFO narratives that entered the public consciousness—and attracted Hynek's interest and, at times, in-depth investigation. Consequently, a deeper public consideration emerged of potential consequences of real-life encounters with extraterrestrial or interdimensional intelligent beings. Some researchers speculated, on the basis of testimony presented by credible witnesses, that the diverse intelligent other-than-human beings whom witnesses had seen represented distinct species from different worlds.

In the bio, O'Connell notes a fascinating historical coincidence: Hynek was born in Chicago in 1910, while Halley's Comet was visible overhead. His parents took their newborn son to the roof of their apartment building while they observed the comet. Hynek passed on in Scottsdale, Arizona, in 1986—the year when the comet was next visible (Hynek himself stated periodically throughout his life that he hoped to be alive to see the next passing of the comet). In between the comet's visits, Hynek's formal education included an MS in astronomy from the University of Chicago in 1932, and a PhD in astronomy in 1935 from the Yerkes Observatory on Lake Geneva in nearby Wisconsin. He did his doctoral research at Yerkes, having received the much-coveted prestigious fellowship in observational astronomy and astrophysics. There, he used the forty-inch refractor telescope—the largest of its kind in the world—for his research. O'Connell observes that "science and mysticism came together every night in the eyepiece of his telescope . . . time vanished, dimensions contracted." Hynek himself noted later in life that "the whole thing had a sort of mystical quality."[3] An article he wrote based on his dissertation was accepted and published by the prestigious *Astrophysical Journal* of the University of Chicago. His associated work in spectroscopy at the Perkins Observatory led to his appointment to a teaching position at The Ohio State University. In 1942 he took a position at the Applied Physics Laboratory of Johns Hopkins University to work on defense projects being

---

2. O'Connell, *Close Encounters Man*. O'Connell also wrote the summary bio of Hynek on the CUFOS website: O'Connell, "J. Allen Hynek."

3. O'Connell, *Close Encounters Man*, 18.

developed during World War II. He helped to develop the proximity fuze for the first atomic bomb. Subsequently, he returned to The Ohio State University to teach astronomy.

In 1948, while he was an astronomy professor at Ohio State, Hynek was enlisted by the United States Air Force (USAF) to be the official scientific (astronomy) consultant on UFOs for the US government and the USAF. For much of the twenty-two-year period that followed, he held this position through Project Sign, Project Grudge, and Project Blue Book, the successive iterations of the government program established to address citizen reports of Unidentified Flying Objects. He relished this work, calling himself the "official debunker" of UFOs. During this time he transitioned from Ohio State to Northwestern University, where he had accepted an offer to chair the department of astronomy; he held his academic and government positions concurrently for more than twenty years.

While serving in his government advisory capacity, in which he sought to judge objectively the credibility of thousands of UFO-ETI reports he had received and reviewed over the years, Hynek realized that numerous cases could not be explained by scientific means. He pressed the US government/ Air Force unsuccessfully for a more extensive, intensive, and independent scientific study about the real and purported evidence of an ETI presence in the heavens or on Earth. In his research reports, he provided insights such as that US military and US government officials investigating and evaluating UFO reports held the opinion that "It can't be, therefore it isn't."[4] As a consequence, a kind of "fake science" emerged, propagated by Hynek himself when he described reported objects with terms such as "atmospheric eddy" or "swamp gas." Consequently, Project Blue Book was disparaged and dismissed in scientific circles as "the Society for the Explanation of the Uninvestigated."[5]

A complementary phrase is used by some scientists who have asked, "Where's the proof?" or "Where's the evidence?" to imply that controlled UFOs, and ETI/IDI explorers, do not exist. There are several underlying flaws in their disparagement of the possible existence of ETI/IDI, and of intelligently controlled UFOs. The countering phrase succinctly provides a starting point for the questions posed: "Absence of evidence is not evidence of absence." Among the questions' flaws: an assumption that no one has seen UFOs that are intelligently controlled—despite numerous reports by

---

4. Hynek, *Hynek UFO Report*, 23; this phrase is the title of chapter 3 in Hynek's book. This was the supposedly "scientific," "guiding principle" for his work, in which he was claimed to be a serious investigator of UFO and ETI reports. The official Pentagon policy came to be to "debunk UFO sightings" (24).

5. Hynek, *Hynek UFO Report*, 31.

credible witnesses about objects near and far that did maneuvers impossible to achieve by existing Earth aircraft or then-current pilots' abilities. Over time, the evidence came to include photos or films showing spacecraft hovering, or exercising the maneuvers cited (including zigzags or sudden perpendicular changes in direction, all at extreme speeds unattainable by previously present or currently available Earth technologies). Other unfounded assertions by scientists (and government personnel) were that there have been no measurable physical or radiation traces where craft have landed, or that radar from military and civilian sources, on the ground and in aircraft, had not found evidence of Visitor-controlled UFOs. It should be noted, in this regard, that some scientific evaluations and radar reports are known to have been suppressed or censored by government agents as described by, among others, Jacques Vallée.[6] Decades of UFO files from the British, French, and other governments' files provide abundant narratives describing—and photos depicting—an ETI presence and activity.[7] Suppression of such evidence by governments has been amply documented. In the past several decades, too, several scientists' and citizens' organizations have been established that collect information about UFO/ETI/IDI events—in all of Hynek's Close Encounters categories—and publish them online.[8] In light of the evidence just cited regarding Visitors' encounters with human observers, it is evident that there is no "absence of evidence." Similarly, in past decades, numerous scientists self-assuredly declared that no planets besides Earth existed in the universe or, if they did, they had no resident biota. Today, however, NASA and the ESA find new planets almost daily, many in the "Goldilocks Zone" in which life, with characteristics that life has on Earth, could exist.

"Close Encounters" Categories

Dr. Hynek received thousands of UFO reports from around the world. Some were similar enough and sufficiently credible that he decided to put them in distinct groupings. When the observed objects were five hundred feet away or closer, the incident was classified as a "Close Encounter of the First Kind" (CE-I). If craft landed and left some physical traces of their presence, which evidence scientists could examine with relevant technology, they were

6. Vallée, *Revelations*, discussed below.

7. Leslie Kean's *UFOs* is a good source for photos, and for statements and testimonies by government officials, commercial pilots, and senior military commanders from several countries.

8. These include the science-based Center for UFO Studies (CUFOS) founded by Hynek, which has the most rigorous scientific examination of reports; and the Mutual UFO Network (MUFON), which discloses, describes, and sometimes investigates UFO reports from around the globe.

"Close Encounters of the Second Kind" (CE-II). If the incident included direct contact between ETI/IDI and TI, they were "Close Encounters of the Third Kind" (CE-III). The category of CE-III so intrigued film producer and director Steven Spielberg that he produced a film whose title used that category: *Close Encounters of the Third Kind* (1977). Its principal protagonists are portrayed by actors Richard Dreyfuss, Terri Garr, Melinda Dillon, Bob Balaban, and François Truffaut (ordinarily a film director, but in the film he portrays the perspective and scientific rigor of astrophysicist Jacques Vallée, Hynek's colleague in the astronomy department at Northwestern University in real life). Dreyfus's character's story is an amalgam of multiple stories told by actual UFO witnesses. In the credits, Hynek is listed as a consultant for the film; he has a cameo role toward the film's end, as a scientist proceeding with other scientists down an airfield runway to meet the landed UFO and greet the members of its crew, who descend a ramp from the spacecraft. Hynek stands out because, although he says not a word, he is wearing a dark suit and tie amid a sea of white lab coat-attired scientists. (ETI beings are presented here as benevolent, curious spacefarers who are studying human societies and scientific accomplishments, and seek to take with them, on their departure from Earth, ordinary citizens interested in exploring the cosmos.)

In order to clarify the meaning of the acronym "UFO," which in the public mind had come to mean an ETI-controlled spacecraft, Hynek stated:

> *We can define the UFO simply as the reported perception of an object or light seen in the sky or upon the land the appearance, trajectory, and general dynamic and luminescent behavior of which do not suggest a logical, conventional explanation and which is not only mystifying to the original percipients but remains unidentified after close scrutiny of all available evidence by persons who are technically capable of making a common sense identification, if one is possible.*[9]

CE-I, Close Encounters of the First Kind, are described by Hynek as follows:

> Here we have a close encounter with a UFO but there is no interaction of the UFO with either the witness or the environment, or at least none that is discernible. The encounter must be close enough, however, so that the UFO is in the observer's own frame of reference and he is able to see details. The chance, therefore, of this sighting being a misidentification of Venus or a conventional aircraft, etc., is quite small, particularly if the sighting is made by several persons.[10]

9. Hynek, *UFO Experience*, 10. Italics in original.
10. Hynek, *Hynek UFO Report*, 19–20.

In a CE-II Encounter,

> the UFO is observed interacting with the environment and frequently with the witness as well. The interaction can be with inanimate matter, as when holes or rings are made on the ground, or with animate matter, as when animals are affected (sometimes becoming aware of the presence of the UFO even before human witnesses). People, too, can be affected, as in the many reported cases of burns, temporary paralysis, nausea, conjunctivitis, etc. But in order for a CE-II to have taken place, the presence of the UFO must be established at the same spot in which the physical effects are noted. That is, if a burnt ring on the ground is noted, it must be at the exact place where the UFO was sighted hovering, or if an automobile ignition system is interfered with, such interference must have occurred at the time and place of the UFO sighting.
>
> The observed physical effects in these cases (often called "physical trace cases") must not be explainable in some other obvious way. That is, if holes in the ground ("landing marks") are found, these marks must be unique, and not like marks found elsewhere in the vicinity.
>
> Close Encounters of the Second Kind are of particular interest to scientists who can, in a sense, bring the UFO "into the laboratory." Burnt grasses, samples of disturbed soil, etc., can be tested with a view toward determining what caused the burn, what pressures were necessary to produce the imprints on the ground, and to finding what chemical changes occurred in the soil samples by comparing the affected soil with control samples from the vicinity... A catalogue of over eight hundred cases in which the UFO was both seen and left physical traces has been compiled.[11]

In a CE-III event,

> Here there is not only a close encounter with the UFO, but with its apparent "occupants" or "UFOnauts." Close Encounters of the Third Kind bring us to grips with the most puzzling aspect of the UFO phenomenon: the apparent presence of intelligence other than our own, intelligence we can recognize but not understand. Hundreds of close Encounters of the Third Kind have been reported all over the world in the past decades. A catalogue of over one thousand cases has been compiled...

---

11. Hynek, *Hynek UFO Report*, 20–21.

In Close Encounters of the Third Kind, where the occupants make their presence known, we find reported creatures who resemble humans but are predominantly shorter and slimmer, capable of communication in their own way and on their own terms. Their interaction with humans has been reported to be largely impersonal, neither overtly friendly nor hostile.

Clearly, Close Encounters of the Third Kind hold the most fascination for us because they bring into focus most sharply our fear of the unknown, the concept of other intelligences in space, and the possibility of intelligent contact with such beings, with all that such contact might imply for the human race.[12]

Scientists, ufologists, writers, and members of the general public still use "close encounter" categories when describing or categorizing people's claims of UAP engagement; they facilitate categorization and cross-event and cross-category assessment, documentation, and investigation.

As stated in *Cosmic Commons*,

Hynek's writings provided a previously lacking depth and probing analysis based on the scientific method he used as he reflected on and elaborated several topics. In *The UFO Experience*, he describes a "credibility index" by which he judges event reporters' degree of believability in what they say has occurred.[13] He notes that there are variations in how multiple reporters describe an event, just as there are discrepancies in descriptions of witnesses to an accident, fire, or robbery; but similarly, he observes, that just as there is no doubt in the latter events that it was indeed a fire and not a bank robbery being described, so, too, are credible witnesses all describing a UFO event.[14]

Hynek comments, too, on the "strangeness" of events or parts thereof:

Still, there exist UFO reports that are coherent, sequential narrative accounts of these strange human experiences. Largely because there has been no mechanism for bringing these reports to general attention, they seem to be far too strange to be believed. They don't fit the established *conceptual framework* of modern physical science. It is about as difficult to put oneself into a "belief framework" and accept a host of UFO reports as having described actual events as, for example, it would have

---

12. Hynek, *Hynek UFO Report*, 21–22. For more complete descriptions and analyses of UFO event categories, including Close Encounters, see Hart, *Cosmic Commons*, 308–15.

13. Hynek, *UFO Experience*, 18–20.

14. Hynek, *UFO Experience*, 20.

been for Newton to have accepted the basic concepts of quantum mechanics ... the strangeness spectrum of UFO reports is so narrow that ... a *definite pattern* of strange "craft" has [been reported] ... If UFOs indeed are figments of the imagination, it is strange that the imaginations of those who report UFOs from over the world should be so restricted.[15]

In the first chapter of *UFO Experience*, "The Laughter of Science," Hynek describes US government pressure that has been effective to silence faculty in colleges and universities. Ridicule by colleagues of a faculty member who mentions their interest in the possible existence of intelligently controlled UFOs is sometimes parroted by the media and in deprecatory comments expressed by members of the general public. This is seen far less today, among the general public: most people do think that intelligently controlled UFOs and ETI beings have visited and are visiting Earth. However, it is still the case in academic circles. Hynek observes:

> The scientific world has surely not been "eager to find out" about the UFO phenomenon ... The almost universal attitude of scientists has been militantly negative. Indeed, it would seem that the reaction has been grossly out of proportion to the stimulus. The emotionally loaded, highly exaggerated reaction that has generally been exhibited by scientists to any mention of UFOs might be of considerable interest to psychologists ... giggles and squirming suggest a defense against something the scientists cannot yet understand ... such exhibitions by mature scientists are [perhaps] expressions of deep-seated uncertainty or fear.[16]

In discussions with scientists, I discovered that the reactions described by Hynek are at times their way to hide facts and realities of UFO phenomena which they have established privately for themselves. They fear that they might be the next objects of ridicule, and might lose their academic position, their research funds, their scholarly status, or their possibilities of future grants from their academic institution, private foundations, government agencies, or corporate supporters of scientific inquiry.[17]

Acknowledging difficulties in the reception he receives in scientific circles, Hynek comments that

> The facts are not strictly scientific. Yet the data nonetheless form a fascinating and provocative field of study for those whose temperaments are not outraged by the character of the information.

15. Hynek, *UFO Experience*, 23.
16. Hynek, *UFO Experience*, 6–7.
17. Hart, *Cosmic Commons*, 310–11.

And it should be remembered that there are those whose fields of study abound with equally "unsatisfactory" data. Anthropologists, psychologists, and even meteorologists deal daily with evidential and circumstantial data that must be fitted together like pieces of a jigsaw puzzle.[18]

Reflecting further on negative reactions of scientists to his work, Hynek declares that the "history of science has shown that it is the things that *don't* fit, the apparent exceptions to the rule, that signal potential breakthroughs in our concept of the world about us. And it was these cases that should have been studied from many angles."[19] In a 1953 article Hynek wrote along these lines: "Ridicule is not a part of the scientific method, and the public should not be taught that it is . . . The steady flow of reports, often made in concert by *reliable* observers, raises questions of scientific obligation and responsibility."[20] He adds that "It should be emphasized that in science one never knows where inquiry will lead—('if we know the answers in advance it isn't research')—that a primary aim of science is to satisfy human curiosity, to probe the unknown, and to open new paths for intellectual adventure."[21]

Sometimes, dealing with the unknown can be disturbing intellectually and psychologically, and Hynek speculates, "Is it the confrontation on the animate level that disturbs and repulses us? . . . Encounters with animate beings, possibly with an intelligence of different order from ours, gives a new dimension to our atavistic fear of the unknown. It brings with it the specter of competition for territory, loss of planetary hegemony—fears that have deep roots."[22] Further,

> When the mind is suddenly confronted with "facts" that are decidedly uncomfortable, that refuse to fit into the standard recognized world picture, a frantic effort is made to bridge that gap emotionally rather than intellectually (which would require an honest admission of the inadequacy of our knowledge) . . . When we are faced with a situation that is well above our "threshold of acceptability," there seems to be a built in mental censor that tends to block or to sidestep a phenomenon that is "too strange" and to take refuge in the familiar . . . The history

---

18. Hynek, *UFO Experience*, 33–34.
19. Hynek, *UFO Experience*, 194.
20. Hynek, *UFO Experience*, 207.
21. Hynek, *UFO Experience*, 207.
22. Hynek, *UFO Experience*, 138–39. Hart, *Cosmic Commons*, 312.

of science is replete with "explainings away" in order to preserve the *status quo*.²³

Hynek recalls, too, that despite astronomers' public statements—or lack thereof—regarding visits by other-than-human intelligent beings, privately they acknowledge, usually anonymously, that they have seen, through their telescope, anomalous objects in space. In a confidential poll he took of astronomers, 11 percent of his respondents acknowledged that they had seen anomalous objects. His poll complemented the results of the Stanford University 1977 Sturrock Survey.²⁴

As a consequence of these explorations, Hynek came to alter his position on UFOs:

> The transformation from skeptic to—no, not believer because that has certain "theological" connotations—a scientist who felt he was on the track of an interesting phenomenon was gradual, but by the late '60s it was complete. Today I would not spend one additional moment on the subject of UFOs if I didn't seriously feel that the UFO phenomenon is real and that efforts to investigate and understand it, and eventually to solve it, could have a profound effect—perhaps even be a springboard to a revolution in man's view of himself and his place in the universe.²⁵

By contrast, members of the staff for the official activities of the USAF projects were expected to dismiss what people claimed to have seen. Their superiors and supervisors had decided *a priori* that UFOs did not exist, and so reports about them "*had to be nonsense.*" He asserts that their guiding principle was "It can't be, therefore it isn't"; everyone "learned to follow suit or else."²⁶ Hynek considers, too, peoples' fears about acknowledging the existence of ETI, with or without direct Contact with them, and wonders:

> Why should it be more difficult for us to accept encounters with "creatures" than with "craft"? Probably because once we dare to admit that beings alien to ourselves exist, we are forced to face our deepest fear of the unknown, along with our more basic and specific fears of competition and hostility. But, as in the other types of UFO experiences, we cannot ignore the reports which *do* exist, for they are made by seemingly credible persons and are widespread.²⁷

23. Hart, *Cosmic Commons*, 170.
24. Hynek, *Hynek UFO Report*, 14.
25. Hynek, *Hynek UFO Report*, 17.
26. Hynek, *Hynek UFO Report*, 23.
27. Hynek, *Hynek UFO Report*, 189.

Hynek came to realize as a scientist that, given the credibility of witnesses who described what they had seen, their testimony should be respected. In a 1978 address to the UN General Assembly, Hynek declared that "the UFO phenomenon, whatever its origin may turn out to be, is eminently worthy of study." He notes that the French government determined that what people had seen "involved a material phenomenon that could not be explained as a natural phenomenon or a human device." Hynek concluded: "I began my work as Scientific Consultant to the U.S. Air Force as an open skeptic, in the firm belief that we were dealing with a mental aberration and a public nuisance. Only in the face of stubborn facts and data similar to those studied by the French commission . . . have I been forced to change my opinion."[28]

Allen Hynek's extensive experience, professional credentials, and openminded research led to his transformation from a "debunker" of UFO stories to an advocate of independent scientific research into the phenomenon. Accompanied by his professional credentials, this helped him to have great credibility in his consequent statements and assertions about UFOs. For the remainder of his life he pushed for serious scientific study of UFO phenomena based on the scientific method of research; went on investigative journeys to UFO event sites; and founded the Center for UFO Studies (CUFOS), which continues his work to document scientifically well-evidenced UFO phenomena.

Astrophysicist Jacques Vallée, recognized today as the top UFO investigator and researcher in the world, was Allen Hynek's colleague at Northwestern University; they remained close friends until Hynek's death.

Jacques Vallée

Jacques Vallée (1939–present) was born in France. He received a BSc in mathematics from the Sorbonne in 1959, and an MSc in astrophysics from Lille University in 1961. He accepted then a position at the Paris Observatory, and served, too, on the staff of the French Space Committee. While there he watched, with other astrophysicists, films of anomalous objects that were taken through the Observatory telescope. The director, seeing this, seized and destroyed the films. This adversely impacted Vallée, but it stimulated, too, a lifelong interest in intelligent other-than-human beings. He moved to the United States in 1962 to teach astronomy at the University of Texas, Austin. While at the university, he codeveloped for NASA the first computer-based map of Mars. He went thereafter to Northwestern University, where he taught in the astronomy department (chaired by Allen Hynek)

---

28. Hynek, "Address."

and simultaneously studied for a computer science and artificial intelligence PhD, which he received in 1967.[29]

Vallée currently is a private investor and executive manager of Documatica Financial, based in San Francisco, which focuses on healthcare and high technology startups. From 1987 to 2010 he served as a general partner of several venture funds in Silicon Valley. Since 1987, he has spearheaded early-stage investments in over sixty high technology start-ups, serving on the board of many of them; a third of these companies reached the public markets. He is a member of the science board for the French Genopole, based in Evry, France, which specializes in genomes and biotechnologies; and he is a trustee of the Institute for the Future.

Vallée has had a long-term interest in astronomy and in the frontiers of astronomy research. He has written twelve nonfiction books on Unidentified Aerial Phenomena, including his trilogy *Dimensions, Confrontations,* and *Revelations*.[30] He is a member of the expert committee of CNES-GEIPAN (Centre National d'Etudes Spatiales[31] [the French equivalent of NASA]- Groupe d'études et d'informations sur les phénomènes aérospatiaux non identifies[32]), the oldest governmental group in the world that has continuously monitored reports of unexplained aerial phenomena. He serves on the scientific advisory board of Bigelow Aerospace in Las Vegas, Nevada. He has written seven science-fiction novels, including *Le Sub-espace* (under the pen name Jerome Seriel), which was awarded the Jules Verne Prize (1961) in Paris, and *Stratagem* (2007), published in French and English.

InterDimensional Intelligence

Vallée analyzed ETI phenomena and found insufficient information in ETI theories to explain some of the data assembled. He proposes that, in addition to extraterrestrial travel, intelligent biota likely journey in another cosmos dimension and, perhaps, in a distinct dimension of human consciousness.

Jacques Vallée posits, then, that what humankind has perceived, encountered, and described was likely not, in most cases, Extra*Terrestrial* Intelligence (ETI) but rather Extra*Dimensional* Intelligence (EDI) or

29. "Jacques Fabrice Vallée."

30. In addition to his listed space trilogy, Vallée authored *Messengers of Deception: UFO Contacts and Cults*; *Invisible College: What a Group of Scientists Has Discovered about UFO Influence on the Human Race*; and *Wonders in the Sky: Unexplained Aerial Objects from Antiquity to 1879 and Their Impact on Human Culture, History, and Beliefs*.

31. CNES: Centre National d'Etudes Spatiales.

32. GEIPAN is a unit of CENES, and stands for "Groupe d'Études et d'Informations sur les Phénomènes Aérospatiaux Non-identifies." See their website at http://www.cnes-geipan.fr/.

Inter*Dimensional* Intelligence (IDI)[33] which existed in a parallel universe or universes; intelligent beings travel interdimensionally rather than or more often than extraterrestrially. He suggests that perhaps, at times, Contact was made solely or primarily in the (human) mind of the one who experienced it. In *Third Displacement*, IDI will be the term used to indicate intelligent beings who travel the cosmos primarily interdimensionally.

In a 1989 presentation at the Eighth Annual Conference of the Society for Scientific Exploration, held in Boulder, Colorado, Vallée presented a paper that catalyzed a virtually instant negative response by both scientists who accepted the extraterrestrial hypothesis, and scientists who rejected it in favor of natural phenomena explanations of what people saw—despite what people stated that they had seen. In his paper, "Five Arguments against the Extraterrestrial Theory,"[34] Vallée stated, on the basis of his analysis of the events, that although it was highly possible that intelligent beings did live in the universe elsewhere than on Earth, the ETI hypothesis was faulty on several accounts. This is summarized in his paper's abstract, and discussed in depth in the text that follows:

> (1) unexplained close encounters are far more numerous than required for any physical survey of the earth;
>
> (2) the humanoid body structure of the alleged "aliens" is not likely to have originated on another planet and is not biologically adapted to space travel;
>
> (3) the reported behavior in thousands of abduction reports contradicts the hypothesis of genetic or scientific experimentation on humans by an advanced race;
>
> (4) the extension of the phenomenon throughout recorded human history demonstrates that UFOs are not a contemporary phenomenon; and
>
> (5) the apparent ability of UFOs to manipulate space and time suggests radically different and richer alternatives, three of which are proposed in outline form as a conclusion to this paper.

Vallée then elaborates difficulties inherent to each category. In "Close Encounters Frequency" he calculates, based on the thousands of reports globally that are primarily about night sightings from rural areas in Europe,

33. Author's acronyms, and analysis and summary of Vallée's speculation on intelligent not-human beings. Other possible terms: IntraDimensional Intelligence (IDI) or TransDimensional Intelligence (TDI), encounters which might occur solely in engagements of consciousness, in a cerebral realm.

34. Vallée, "Five Arguments." Published later as an Appendix to *Revelations*, 239–57.

the Americas, and Australia, that there should be as many as fourteen million incidents of close encounters on Earth in forty years of event tabulation. While some of his assumptions might not be correct, even if that estimate were to be drastically reduced, the remaining number of projected landings would still merit his query (based on his projections): "What objectives could extraterrestrial visitors to the earth be pursuing, that would require them to land 14 million times on our planet?"[35] He notes that Earth's surface is clearly visible from space; that humans have been broadcasting information on radio and television for decades; and that samples of Earth's physical properties could be obtained unobtrusively with just a few visits to Earth's surface by robotic rovers such as those used by human explorers of Mars who do not leave Earth. In the section on "Physiology," Vallée evaluates the reported humanoid form of extraterrestrials. He states that they would likely *not* look "like us" because of the interaction of their DNA with their home planet's environment, the comparative mass of both planets, and their planet's proximity to their home star. He adds that their display of human-like emotions "suggests not only biological similarity but extensive social acculturation."[36]

Vallée Responds to Vallée

To a certain extent, Jacques Vallée provides possible responses in his own work to some of his preceding points. For example, he speculates about how, at times, ExoEarth intelligent beings seem to have the capability to project holograms of themselves and their craft, in which the actual physical appearance of beings and vehicles is transformed in human perception: beings become humanoid in the case of the former, journeying in craft appropriate to a specific historical era in the latter—although, in that case, with far greater capabilities than the visible craft would have had in their actual historical era. For example, craft that appeared to be "airship(s)" in appearance, which were seen in different, widely separated locales, flew against the wind and dropped anchors from above to catch boulders on Earth below. The "captain," "crew," and "passengers" seemed to be humans, and spoke the local language. Perhaps, then, Vallée's comments about "humanoids" should refer primarily to their external appearance, not to their actual form which would, presumably, be adapted to extraterrestrial space travel or interdimensional travel. ExoEarth intelligent beings, while not being identical in anatomy and physiology with humans (because evolution proceeds from the interaction of DNA and ecologically present microbes, which would differ in distinct planets), might still have some basic similarities.

35. Vallée, "Five Arguments," 109.
36. Vallée, "Five Arguments," 112.

Biologist E. O. Wilson asserts this possibility, based on his knowledge of the characteristics of numerous biota on Earth.[37] If Wilson is correct, then alien intelligent beings, while not looking like humans, might have some similar traits that are necessary to survive and to retain or expand their niche vis-à-vis other biota on their home planet. So, "holograms" and comparative biological evolutionary transitions, even in distinct planetary contexts, offer possible responses-in-progress to Vallée's second point.

In regard to "Abduction Reports," Vallée states that such reports now number in the thousands. Often, they include narratives in which Visitors do medical examinations on the experiencers, take blood samples from them, cause them to miss or to think they had missed long periods of time, and, at times, have sexual interactions of various types with them. Some of the Visitors have stated that they are creating a "hybrid race." In his evaluation of this, Vallée states that an advanced civilization should have medical techniques much beyond humans' technology: since doctors on Earth can take samples without leaving permanent scars and causing trauma, and through molecular biology could develop a genetic fingerprint and produce test tube offspring that could be cloned "*ad infinitum*," so too should other intelligent species have available advanced biotechnology to fulfill those purposes. Visitors also should have techniques to take what they need without cruel experiments on abductees' bodies.[38]

It occurs to this writer that perhaps some intelligent beings might travel interdimensionally or transdimensionally solely mentally, not needing physicality to visit dimensions and places other than their own. Their entire communication and interaction with humanity, including the fabrication of era-appropriate craft and the use of mental manipulation, would be mind-to-mind, without humans recognizing this. Then, in the course of their intrusions into human consciousness, the use of what is, effectively, torture of human subjects might be a control tactic to force humans' submission to their will rather than an actual occurrence. And, it might be done by just one or a few species among Otherkind, not all species or their individuals.

When exploring "History," Vallée states that ETI-related events did not begin after World War II, as was assumed by many ufologists. He discusses how the reports emerged long ago, as early as in the ninth century. He notes that some European researchers have, as a consequence, suggested a "Psycho-Sociological Hypothesis" that "the entire UFO phenomenon" was a "projection of the consciousness of the witnesses."[39] These researchers proposed a *symbolic* interpretation of what witnesses claimed to have seen. They noted

37. See chapter 5.
38. Vallée, "Five Arguments," 113.
39. Vallée, "Five Arguments," 114.

that cultures around the world at different times have described "an ancient tradition of little people that fly through the sky and abduct humans."[40]

In "Physical Considerations," Vallée observes that the phenomena "include not only strange flying devices that are described as physical craft by the witnesses but also objects and beings that exhibit the ability to appear and disappear very suddenly, change their apparent shapes in continuous fashion and to merge with other physical objects." While such descriptions violate known laws of physics, if they can be confirmed "either by direct observation, by photographic evidence or by the weight of statistics they may represent an opportunity to test new concepts of physical reality."[41]

Vallée concludes the article by suggesting new hypotheses about claimed human-alien encounters. He speculates that they might describe a "control system" used by humans or aliens, or be a natural occurrence. It could originate from alien intelligence or from a "human collective unconsciousness," as per C. G. Jung. Finally, extraterrestrials might travel by space-time manipulation, "notably the use of four-dimensional wormholes." In this instance, they could appear simultaneously in different periods of human history, and be from "anywhere and anytime," even from Earth.[42]

In his books and interviews,[43] Vallée elaborates his views more extensively, and in greater depth.

Dimensions: A Casebook of Alien Contact

In the first volume of his "Alien Contact Trilogy," Vallée states compellingly and early on what will be an undercurrent throughout *Dimensions* and the rest of the trilogy: "If there was ever a situation in science that called for the careful sifting and screening of data and for the questioning and testing of every hypothesis, it is the situation presented by the UFO phenomenon."[44] In chapter 1, "Ancient Encounters," Vallée describes events witnessed by noted people over the centuries, including Paracelsus and Goethe, and into the twentieth century, about which he notes that since 1946 these stories have

40. Vallée, "Five Arguments," 114.
41. Vallée, "Five Arguments," 114–15.
42. Vallée, "Five Arguments," 116. Bernardo Peixoto, a Brazilian-born indigenous leader, described to John Mack a conversation with his abductors. He asked one of them where they came from; he replied, "We come from nowhere," which made Bernardo feel very uncomfortable. He thought that the only way that beings could come from nowhere would be "because they are everywhere." Interestingly, Bernardo's people in the Amazon region were called Uru-ê Wau-Wau, which is translated as "people from the stars." Their ancient legends describe a visit by Sky People. See chapter 5.
43. Batchelder, "Legendary Interview."
44. Vallée, *Dimensions*, 4.

been "rather common in all parts of the world."[45] These include the well-known story of New Mexico highway patrolman Lonnie Zamora. In 1964, he saw a spacecraft land and four humanoids emerge. Then they reentered their vehicle, and disappeared at great speed. (Zamora was so sure that he had seen non-human beings that he went to his parish priest for counsel before giving the information to authorities.) Vallée observes that to "a physicist, of course, they appear unbelievable," but that "there are several cases on record in which similar accounts are associated with traces that can hardly be questioned."[46] Among the cases, he discusses an intentionally isolated survivalist-like family in Kentucky whose members shot to no avail at short creatures approaching their home; the family fled inside their house, barricaded the door, and continued shooting at the beings from inside their house (as evidenced by bullet holes in window screens), with no noticeable effect; and several cases in France, including events when humanoid-like beings were observed.[47] Vallée concludes the chapter by offering a further possible purpose of ETI events: "And if a superior race does in fact generate what we are now observing as the UFO phenomenon, perhaps it is precisely with the purpose of changing the course of human destiny by presenting us with evidence of our limitations in the technical, as well as the mental, realm?"[48]

In succeeding chapters, Vallée narrates more stories that have emerged from around the world over centuries. Many describe "little people." He discusses Phoenician amulets and cylinders which depict winged craft and winged people; some are on view in the British Museum in London. Regarding the amulets, he states that he tends toward "a literal, rather than purely symbolic, interpretation of the scenes depicted," and is "tempted to accept as a working hypothesis that *in times remote contact occurred between human consciousness and another consciousness, variously described as demonic, angelic, or simply alien*."[49] He relays descriptions of airships seen in the United States in the late 1890s (reported in numerous newspapers), including "a staggering number of observations"[50] in the Midwest. He presents the story of Erasmus Darwin, grandfather of Charles Darwin, who reports a large cylinder that "strike[s] the earth with a stream of electricity perhaps two to ten yards in diameter."[51]

---

45. Vallée, *Dimensions*, 23.
46. Vallée, *Dimensions*, 23.
47. Vallée, *Dimensions*, 23–28.
48. Vallée, *Dimensions*, 28.
49. Vallée, *Dimensions*, 37; italics in original.
50. Vallée, *Dimensions*, 42.
51. Vallée, *Dimensions*, 65.

In his explorations of UFO phenomena, Vallée continues to speculate about their implications and meanings beyond what might be extrapolated from witnesses' descriptions of intriguing objects and the living beings flying them. He states in regard to UFO occupants' origins, that to say that they are from a planet other than Earth is "not a good answer."[52] Rather, he suggests, "UFO occupants . . . are not extraterrestrials. They are denizens of another reality."[53] He notes further that "the chameleon-like character of the secondary attributes of the sightings: the shapes of the objects, the appearances of their occupants, and their reported statements *vary as a function of the cultural environment into which they are projected.*"[54] He wonders if it is "possible to make three-dimensional holograms with mass, and to project them through time."[55] He continues:

> To put it bluntly, the UFO phenomenon does not give evidence of being extraterrestrial at all. Instead it appears to be inter-dimensional and to manipulate physical realities outside of our own space-time continuum.[56]

Confrontations: A Scientific Search for Alien Contact

The prologue to this second volume of the trilogy describes Vallée's and his wife Janine's 1980 ascent of Morro do Vintem hill in Brazil, across the bay from Rio de Janeiro. They were on their way to investigate a site where in 1996 two men, whom locals said had been expecting some sort of communication from an alien craft, had been found dead. They were wearing suits, lying atop a bed of leaves; handmade lead masks were nearby. There were no signs of violence. Witnesses had seen a large oval object descend to the hilltop, then rise and leave. In the years after the bodies were found, no vegetation has grown on the site. Vallée comments that circumstances surrounding the event might not only provide proof of UFO existence, but prompt a drastic revision of hitherto held beliefs that alien beings were "gentle visitors," "scientific explorers," "mischievous aliens," or "shining presences," such that the alien hypothesis might have to include "a more complex and dangerous picture."[57] Later, he concludes the introduction with an observation that

---

52. Vallée, *Dimensions*, 80.
53. Vallée, *Dimensions*, 109.
54. Vallée, *Dimensions*, 159. Italics in original.
55. Vallée, *Dimensions*, 161.
56. Vallée, *Dimensions*, 136. Italics in original.
57. Vallée, *Confrontations*, 3.

"whatever else they may be, UFOs represent a technology capable of harmful actions."[58]

In the introduction Vallée describes, too, his growing interest in UFO phenomena after he became an astrophysicist, and his changing perception of the meaning of people's experiences. He notes that he was inspired by "Teilhard de Chardin's gentle view of a great spiritual potential permeating the cosmos. I believe that life and consciousness are manifested in distant worlds."[59] Vallée describes how his method of investigation differs from the ways much of the work in ufology is done: "[E]ssential information was obtained (1) by the author himself, (2) from firsthand sources, and (3) at the site; furthermore, all potential lines of conventional explanation have been followed to the best of my ability."[60] Vallée assures the reader that he investigates as a well-qualified research scientist, not as a believer in UFOs who might not rigorously examine UFO reports, sites, and purported witnesses.

In subsequent chapters, Vallée describes numerous narratives from around the world in which credible witnesses describe the motions of intelligently controlled objects or lights in the sky. He does so with a scientist's professional competence, curiosity, skepticism, attention to details, and openness to going beyond solely physical evidence in order to analyze the narratives of witnesses to extraordinary occurrences. He follows this process so that he might determine not only if the events indeed might have occurred as described, but also to consider the credibility of witnesses whose narratives elaborate events of a kind not previously described or even considered speculatively. Vallée's openness in this process sets him apart from most scientists who think that credibility rests solely upon physical traces of a spacecraft's presence or actions, or space visitors' conduct.

In his discussion of reports about UFO events, and his critical analysis of what they describe and the credibility of witnesses attesting to them, Vallée notes:

> perhaps the major obstacle we find in this research is the preconceived notion that UFOs, if they are not imaginary, *must* necessarily represent advanced spacecraft from another planet. This notion represents the worst example of a jump to a conclusion in the face of insufficient data. *Although I am certain that UFOs are not imaginary, I will be disappointed if they turn out to be nothing more than advanced spacecraft* . . . they promise to be much more: a challenge to many of our concepts in physics,

---

58. Vallée, *Confrontations*, 23.
59. Vallée, *Confrontations*, 17.
60. Vallée, *Confrontations*, 22.

perhaps a clue to the existence of unknown dimensions beyond space-time.[61]

Vallée states that evaluation of a UFO event includes more data than just that received from credible witnesses:

> The sighting of a UFO is a complex event that cannot be analyzed purely on the basis of the story told by the witnesses. Their testimony, with its own terminology and structure, contradictions, and internal validation, is an important aspect of the case; but other dimensions, such as the physical layout of the site and the social framework around the witnesses, are equally important.[62]

In *Confrontations*, Vallée highlights in several passages his criticism of ufologists who rush uncritically to "prove" both that a UFO-related event occurred, and that the event's description fits into their preconceived understanding of what the components of the event should have been. At times, the ufologist team includes people with apparently little or no prior experience in interviewing or even interacting with "abductees" or other credible observers of UFOs or their occupants. Sometimes, an inexperienced "hypnotist" attempts to use hypnosis to acquire data affirming the ufologists' preexisting beliefs. He cites UFO skeptic Philip Klass who "has raised the important question of 'pseudo-memories' that can so easily be planted in a subject's mind under hypnosis."[63] Vallée notes a division in the UFO community itself between a majority of investigators who generally accept data gathered from witnesses via hypnosis, and a minority that "questions the validity of the hypnosis technique and the preconceptions that seem to propel the whole research into the extraterrestrial framework."[64] People who think they have been abducted, for example, are likely familiar with books and televised stories and "a majority of them do 'recall' highly structured situations and similar beings."[65] Vallée states that although he has not sought out abductees, several have contacted him; he referred them to hypnosis experts, and studied the results with the abductees.

Vallée describes several situations and interviews in which ufologists' enthusiasm moved them to affirm not only their own understandings, but also to "verify" that witnesses had certain common components of their

---

61. Vallée, *Confrontations*, 53.
62. Vallée, *Confrontations*, 83.
63. Vallée, *Confrontations*, 172.
64. Vallée, *Confrontations*, 172.
65. Vallée, *Confrontations*, 172.

experiences if they had seen a UFO or its occupants (whether or not they had been abducted). An example of such behavior occurred near Gilroy, California. Vallée drove to the place to investigate, but "the case was so badly mishandled by some of the local UFO investigators that I waited three years to conduct an independent assessment of the data."[66] When he finally visited the affected family and listened to their narrative, he heard, too, what they experienced afterward "at the hands of UFO enthusiasts, reporters, and crackpots . . . the Urantia cult held a prayer meeting on their lawn, and several card-carrying ufologists from the major civilian groups pestered them."[67] Worse yet, "representatives of a nationwide UFO organization . . . brought with them an amateur hypnotist." He put one of the witnesses in a trance, and "the hypnotic session quickly turned into a disaster." The subject "became very agitated; her body temperature dropped drastically, much to the alarm of the investigators who did not know how to bring her out of the trance." When awakened at last, she was at risk for "cardiac problems." The hypnotist and other "investigators" took their tape recorders and "flew out the door, leaving her in a fit of anguish." The incident, Vallée declared, "reinforced my belief that when a sighting is highly publicized, the witnesses are best left alone for some time. Not only is it more ethical to proceed this way, but the quality of an investigation can improve once interest has died down."[68]

In the aftermath of this experience, Vallée was angry and frustrated. He states that "in their eagerness to obtain definite answers, or simply to validate their own preconceptions about the extraterrestrial nature of the phenomenon, many investigators rush in demanding answers." Rather, he says, they should delay the inquiry for days or weeks, as basic ethics would require. However, he laments, "in the last few years, the number of untrained, unqualified hypnotists roaming the countryside in the name of UFO research has greatly multiplied."[69]

In his assessment of his interaction with professionals, Vallée states that he gained "a healthy respect for the complexity of the human mind and a great deal of skepticism regarding the methods used by some ufologists . . . The experts I consulted, when I showed them the current UFO literature, were amazed and upset at the superficial conditions under which UFO investigators used hypnosis. Unanimously, they considered it unethical for anyone who had already reached a strong personal conclusion about UFOs to interrogate a witness under hypnosis."[70] Vallée, it should be remembered,

66. Vallée, *Confrontations*, 88.
67. Vallée, *Confrontations*, 90–91.
68. Vallée, *Confrontations*, 91.
69. Vallée, *Confrontations*, 93.
70. Vallée, *Confrontations*, 173.

does not disagree with *all* use of hypnosis, only its use by improperly prepared practitioners working with ufologists who have already made up their mind—not only about the presence of UFOs, but also about what sorts of "experiences" witnesses might have had—or *must* have had.

In his comments on consideration and discussion of the existence of UFOs and intelligent other-than-human beings, Vallée provides important insights: since the human mind is complex, a person might be influenced, when questioned about their experience under hypnosis or when otherwise pressed about what they recall about an event, to assume that they must have seen or felt what their questioner presents to them; they are sure that they have had an experience and want, albeit subconsciously, to fit the profile assumed to characterize someone who seems to have already been confirmed to have seen UFOs or made Contact with UFO occupants.

Numerous abductees report that they have "missing time," for which they cannot account, during their experiences. Vallée states that

> I have a problem with the very concept of "missing time" for the simple reason that the time in question has never been shown to be missing in the first place *in the time line of the abductee* ... it is not necessarily true that time is passing at the same rate within the region of space occupied by the phenomenon. Some theories of UFOs, whose authors I respect, would, in fact, demand relativistic effects under which the abductee might spend only a few minutes or a few seconds inside the phenomenon during the full hour of "reference."

Vallée goes on to say that the abductee might add additional events and therefore time to his experience, drawn from "collective unconscious material or personal fantasies."[71]

As he reflects on the experiences he investigated in *Confrontations*, Vallée observes that

> My own private conjecture, which deviates considerably from the accepted dogma among UFO believers, is that *we are*

---

71. Vallée, *Confrontations*, 174–75. This writer recalls a complementary view, expressed in books about dreams that I read decades ago. Unfortunately, I do not remember the texts or their authors, but a general consensus of their respective writings was that seemingly lengthy experiences in dreams occurred, in conscious time, during a much shorter period. A dream-remembered hours-long experience, as related in the dreamer's narrative, might have lasted only for minutes of the time of which the dreamer was a part during waking hours. Comparatively, if an abductee recalls events that lasted for an extensive period of time that was required to interact with their abductors (including, for some, to undergo sexually related, intrusive, and traumatic medical examinations), this might only be an hour or so of their ordinary awake time in the place from where they were abducted.

dealing with a yet unrecognized level of consciousness, independent of man but closely linked to the earth . . . I do not believe any more that UFOs are simply the spacecraft of some race of extraterrestrial visitors. This notion is too simplistic . . . Instead, I have argued that an understanding of the UFO phenomenon would come only when we expanded our view of the physical universe beyond the classic four-dimensional world model of spacetime. Like other paranormal phenomena, UFOs seem to be able to operate outside of known spacetime constraints. In this sense, they provide science with an extraordinary opportunity to enrich its physical models and perhaps to give us a new picture of our relationship to the universe, a new avenue of communication with forms of consciousness we have not yet recognized, perhaps including undiscovered levels of our own human consciousness.[72]

Revelations: Alien Contact and Human Deception

Vallée's trilogy concludes with *Revelations*. In it, he integrates ideas from the previous two books with an assessment of the behind-the-scenes realities of several UFO narratives. Utilizing once again his incisive and insightful scientific mind and expertise, he uncovers multiple cases in which the perceptions and consciousness of ufologists and the general public were manipulated by US government entities and agents. The latter used intricate and elaborate schemes to stimulate belief in UFO events, including by disseminating false data about spacecraft landings that had not occurred. While secretly fostering these false UFO narratives, government representatives simultaneously continue to state that there were no such things as UFOs or intelligent other-than-human beings, thereby evading notice when people have doubts about events and speculating about government complicity in orchestrating them, as a tactic to hide and cover up actual events.

Vallée declares at the outset of *Revelations* that

> [Some cases] were found to have been engineered by government agencies engaged in psychological warfare exercises on which they declined comment, conveniently burying them behind the curtain of classified intelligence. This bears emphasizing: *some UFO sightings are covert experiments in the manipulation of the belief systems of the public.* And some cases simply *did not happen*. The stories about them, numerous rumors of crashed saucers and burned aliens, were not so much the result

---

72. Vallée, *Confrontations*, 99–100.

of delusions as the product of *deception*: rumors deliberately planted in the eager minds of gullible believers to hide more real facts about which it was felt the public and the scientific community had no "need to know."[73]

He states further that humanity needs to "solve the problem of detecting and communicating with the other forms of consciousness that probably fill the universe."[74]

Vallée explores, in-depth, occurrences that, ufologists affirm, confirm their hypotheses and beliefs. As he probes background events behind these stories using available data and his own experiences with government agents and their tactics, he uncovers an extensive plot—or integrated plots—to divert the public and scientists from investigating genuine events and instead be guided toward examining details of spurious UFO events. When the latter were dismissed as hoaxes or misunderstandings of what had occurred, already-skeptical scientists and members of the general public, unsure about the reality of UFOs, became more oriented toward questioning and dismissing any such events; they lumped them all in the same category of disproven deceptive stories. In some cases, the targets and victims of this tactic have been serious scientists who would otherwise be scientifically intrigued and fascinated by, and interested in researching, data assembled from around the world regarding extraterrestrial/multidimensional/interdimensional visits—in the skies, on the ground, or in the water, from the heavens or via Contact on Earth—by other-than-human intelligent beings.

Longtime UFO analysts and investigators reject his proposals, Vallée declares, because their *beliefs* in elements of UFO phenomena cloud their view and understanding of *actual events*: they want these to be true in order to reinforce their beliefs. His theories are rejected, too, by the now-diminishing number of scientists who do not accept the possibility in any case that intelligent life exists elsewhere in the universe—even as ever-more numerous planets are found by NASA and ESA in the Goldilocks Zone.

Representative cases among those Vallée investigates in *Revelations* include the UMMO narratives and documents from around the world, and the Rendlesham Forest events in England.

---

73. Vallée, *Revelations*, 8.
74. Vallée, *Revelations*, 10–11.

UMMO Stories

In his analysis of the UMMO narrative with its purported events from around Earth,[75] Vallée dissects details and finds, as he has in numerous other cases, the hand or fingerprints of government agents and of a secret government agency that appears to be involved in the events. The interest in the immediacy and excitement of such sudden stories distracts the general public and scientists, and diverts them from considering events that are more likely to have occurred—and ultimately discourages scientists from investigating actual events, as they do not want to be fooled again.

Nevertheless, as Vallée reports, many ufologists and interested members of the general public believe that UMMO events and UMMO communiques are truthfully conveyed, and indicate other-than-human intelligent beings' interest in saving humankind and Earth from the inevitable destruction that will occur if humanity continues on its rampant self-destructive and Earth-devastating course of action.

Rendlesham Forest Activities

In his assessment of the Rendlesham Forest incidents,[76] Vallée notes numerous discrepancies in details provided by US military personnel who claimed that they observed UAP, including some who said they had approached a landed saucer-like object. One of them, Sergeant James Penniston, claimed that he had touched it (and had made drawings, at the time, in a notebook that he still has: this is not a likely occurrence in the military, especially if it truly wanted to dissuade people from taking UFO reports seriously). In subsequent years, several of those involved were interviewed; some published their own book on their experiences.[77] In summary, what was claimed,

---

75. Vallee, *Revelations*. His extensive, detailed, largely negative analysis comprises the entirety of chapter 4, 91–121.

76. Vallée, *Revelations*, 154–65; this chapter is tellingly titled "Special Effects."

77. In my own earlier writing, particularly in *Encountering ETI* (127–30) and in my graduate-level university course on UAP events and encounters, I expressed the idea that the preponderance of evidence indicated an actual event in Rendlesham Forest, although I was troubled by discrepancies in the reports and by incomplete data. I had noted, in the latter regard, that in 2008 when the British government, in response to a Freedom of Information Act request, released decades of its investigation of UAP reports, the Rendlesham Forest events were missing. It seemed to me when I read this that the US government had pressured its NATO ally, whose base it had been using, not to release information about the events. After I read *Revelations*, it seemed to me that perhaps the British government released nothing about Rendlesham because there was nothing to release: the events publicized appeared to be a US fabrication. *Revelations* prompted me to probe the entire UAP narrative more in-depth, and to revisit some of my previous misgivings about the accuracy of the sequence of and details about the events, as they had been described. See Appendix 1.

published, and publicized about Rendlesham[78] was that over three days in December 1980, USAF members stationed at Bentwaters and Woodbridge, two air bases separated about a mile from each other by Rendlesham Forest in Suffolk county, observed mysterious lights in the sky and in the forest.

In his critical assessment of the situation, Vallée notes that observers were assembled at a particular point, from which they saw ground fog or mist. But,

> There was no UFO in view anywhere, yet an elaborate scene was being staged. Guards, officers, and other personnel had been assembled, unarmed in an area where some sort of fog—as in the Pontoise case—had mysteriously developed. It is difficult not to imagine that they had been brought deliberately, not to guard anything, but to witness a very special phenomenon, and that it was their reactions to the forthcoming event that were being covertly tested . . .[79]

> Far from being surprised by the sudden appearance of an unidentified object over their base, the U.S. Air Force had clearly anticipated and prepared this encounter. A large number of military personnel from various backgrounds had been assembled . . . They were carefully placed at prearranged locations . . . Once the men had seen whatever they were supposed to see, they were pulled out and debriefed.
>
> This is not what would happen if a real UFO did land. But it is exactly the sequence of actions one would expect if the reactions of the men to a prearranged stimulus were being tested.[80]

In terms of promoting a false event, the Rendlesham Forest incidents were a significant success for the US military; the story has been told time and again as a factual event. In *Revelations,* Vallée describes US military and spy agency efforts to confuse the public about actual UFO/ETI/IDI events by covertly creating and disseminating false UFO stories. As described earlier, Vallée notes that often these US operatives stimulate interest in these false UFO narratives to divert people from thinking about or investigating actual UFO events; he thinks that the Rendlesham Forest event was one of these fabrications, and UMMO was another.[81] Military officers and scientists are

---

78. See, for example, Bruni, *You Can't Tell the People*; Kean, *UFOs*; and Pope et al., *Encounter in Rendlesham Forest*. Burroughs and Penniston were present when the events occurred.

79. Vallée, *Revelations*, 158–59.

80. Vallée, *Revelations*, 160.

81. Many ufologists would disagree with Vallée's critique. This writer thinks it plausible.

among the unwitting accomplices to these efforts. In discussing Rendlesham events, Vallée states that "To me, the most plausible theory is that the US military has developed a device or collection of devices that look like flying saucers, that they are primarily intended for psychological warfare, and that they are being actively tested on military personnel."[82]

It should be noted that Vallée's *Revelations* originally was published prior to two well-documented books on Rendlesham Forest: Georgina Bruni, *You Can't Tell the People*, and Pope et al., *Encounter in Rendlesham Forest*.[83] In *UFOs*, Leslie Kean dedicates a chapter to the story of "The Extraordinary Incident in Rendlesham Forest," written by retired officers Colonel Charles I. Halt and Sergeant James Penniston.[84]

A specific occurrence that stood out for me in Pope et al.'s book was Penniston's narrative about touching a landed craft and feeling data transferring from it to his mind as he stood frozen in place. The message he received, in binary code[85] (with which, he said, he had not previously been familiar), provided a new twist on Visitors' mode of going from their time and place to Earth in 1980: the UAP occupants indicated that they were time travelers who came from the future. Another distinctive memory by a member of the USAF, as described in Bruni's book, was Adrian Bustinza's recollection that he saw Colonel Halt, while facing the landed and apparently damaged craft, telling its occupants (verbally or telepathically) that Halt would "contact the electronics division and get a part."[86]

In terms of Visitors encountered in Rendlesham Forest events described in different sources, there appear to be at least four possibilities of their origins: extraterrestrial; interdimensional (from concurrent spatial dimensions); transdimensional cosmic time (from Earth's future time to Earth's present time); and spy agencies' labs, including beneath the airfield, where there is a massive underground with multiple levels, to which access is still restricted. It might well be, of course, that all four are accurate descriptions of the diverse sources and travel modes of distinct intelligent species who have come from different times and places in the cosmos—or are products of the

---

82. Vallée, *Revelations*, 157.

83. Books about Rendlesham Forest are discussed, analyzed, and assessed in Appendix 1.

84. Keane, *UFOs*, 179–88.

85. Photos of the handwritten code in Penniston's notebook are in Pope et al., *Encounter in Rendlesham Forest*, 263–70.

86. Bruni, *You Can't Tell the People*, 202. A curious statement: how would the USAF have in stock a "part" needed by an alien craft? Or, is it really a US craft parading as a UFO, for which a part would be available?

complex creative and deceptive work of the human mind, in the service of a government entity.

It is initially difficult, for those who have come to understand that there are intelligent beings who traverse the cosmos, and do so in interstellar, interdimensional, or transdimensional spacecraft, to accept that a story of a UFO event, previously understood to be a historically accurate narrative, is a fabrication by covert intelligence/spy operatives.

Although I had had some questions previously about Rendlesham, my UFO blinders, bias, and enthusiasm for the idea of extraterrestrial beings, and my desire to have evidence of actual events that confirmed that hypothesis, initially clouded my vision and my assessment of events; I had accepted that there had been ETI/IDI Visitors, but had not considered other possibilities. I recognize now that my uneasy feeling as I considered some Rendlesham data and events—particularly Colonel Halt's comment about a replacement part, and Penniston's ongoing possession of his notebook—should have been pursued to see if, in fact, they could endure rigorous analysis.

Rendlesham Forest Deception

The supposed close encounters that occurred in 1980 in England, on or around Rendlesham Forest in Suffolk County, East Anglia, then, appear to have been government-orchestrated by the United States and, possibly, the United Kingdom. Residents in the area where the Royal Air Force (RAF) bases of Woodbridge and Bentwaters are located, separated by the forest, saw unexpected moving lights in the sky and on the ground, at times seemingly coming from intelligently controlled craft. RAF Woodbridge and RAF Bentwaters were occupied at the time by the United States Air Force, as part of joint NATO operations. As described previously, Jacques Vallée provided a strong critique of the supposed events. He determined that it was an operation of US spy agencies, not a visit by UAP and ETI/IDI. In past decades, and possibly during the time of the events, the bases had had secret military and scientific operations, dating back to the 1930s. The latter included successful efforts to alter the weather by seeding clouds with silver to cause rain, among other activities; to affect the ocean; and to influence magnetic and gravitational energy—possibly even into other dimensions of the universe. Personnel at the bases during these times constructed and operated UFO-like contraptions.

In the first two volumes of the Cosmos Contact: Close Encounters of the Otherkind trilogy, I discussed the 1947 events near the Roswell Army Air Base in New Mexico. Since the Rendlesham Forest events were described as "England's Roswell," I determined to analyze them more closely, which I have done here and in Appendix 1. Analysis of the reasons for US spy agencies' expertly designed and executed deception has not brought to light the US government's reasons for their operation. It needs further examination, by independent researchers.

All that having been expressed, I continue to think and affirm that there are other-than-human intelligent beings who are capable of traveling the vastness of the cosmos. The manner by which they do so—extraterrestrial, interdimensional space, and/or transdimensional/intradimensional time— are seemingly not available to twenty-first-century humans on Earth in our current biological, intellectual, and technological evolutionary state.

Secret Association of Scientists: Investigations

In *The Invisible College*, Vallée describes a loose-knit behind-the-scenes group of scientists who collaborate in discussions about events related to intelligent life from space. Their identities are kept confidential in order that their reputation might not be attacked by those who claim to rationally evaluate and then reject the possibility of ETI/IDI existence; or work for the government to discredit objective scientific research into ETI/IDI; or fear the implications of scientific verification and validation of the existence of other-than-human intelligent beings. Scientists in any of these scenarios do not want an objective scientific analysis of UAP/ETI/IDI experiences people narrate, or of events they have seen. Invisible College members are concerned, too, that their academic positions or reputation might be jeopardized by self-described "objective" scientists, including faculty colleagues, associated researchers, and administrators at their academic institution or research institute. The invisible college scientists and their potential colleague adversaries all fear—justifiably, given government attacks on UFO/ETI work—loss of prestige, professional reputation, or needed financial support from public funding agencies and private grantmaking foundations.

Vallée's Arguments Assessed

Jacques Vallée's argument for extradimensional, transdimensional, or interdimensional intelligent beings is compelling, but perhaps not complete. Some species might be extraterrestrial in terms of their own origin world, but not in Earth's dimension until they have departed from their home dimension and reemerged near Earth; others might be entirely extradimensional relative to Earth until they become interdimensional for traversing space, and transdimensional when they have entered into humans' dimension as they come into Earth environs. The most encompassing designation might be intra- or interdimensional intelligent beings (signified by IDI, which can indicate either or both) who are or become at ease in exploring dimensions other than their own. The interdimensionality might be in terms of *place*—moving between concurrently coexisting dimensions—or in terms of *time*—moving between or among places that are in different past, present, or future times, which are, effectively, in one time-space/place continuum.

The sci-fi film *Interstellar*, about wormhole/"event horizon" possible impacts and uses, suggests a means by which human spacecraft might enter into and eventually emerge from a wormhole. Toward the film's end, the principal protagonist is locked in a dimension from which he cannot yet emerge and, from within the walls of his Earth home while he is in that dimension, communicates on a basic level with his daughter, who lives in his origin dimension. From within the walls, he is able to see different stages—past, present, and future—of moments in time, and chooses a particular moment to push, from within the wall of the house, books in her room off the shelves and onto the floor. This was done in order that a visible symbolic representation of mathematical formulae would be evident on the shelves. The film offers a fascinating story of interdimensionality but remains today, for humankind's technology and hopes, science fiction.

Hynek and Vallée: Complementarity and Congruence

Allen Hynek affirmed the existence of extraterrestrial life throughout most of his professional career. In his experience with official government projects in which his work was to analyze UFO events reported by members of the general public, he saw NASA and the USAF eventually publicly accept that there was ETL. They also publicly and, at times, forcefully and even forcibly rejected possible extraterrestrial or interdimensional existence of other-than-human intelligent beings, and of intelligently controlled UAP, whether extraterrestrial or interdimensional.

Jacques Vallée's early experience as an astrophysicist working at the Paris Observatory while on the French Space Committee, when the director seized and destroyed film of anomalous objects in space that scientists were viewing, piqued his ongoing interest in ExoEarth beings; this was reinforced by his subsequent participation in reviewing and evaluating stories of UFOs as described by credible witnesses whose testimony was often corroborated by physical evidence that could be scientifically analyzed. Vallée suggests that, based on available evidence, intelligent beings likely travel interdimensionally much more often than extraterrestrially. Vallée argues several times in *Revelations*, too, that ufologists, once they become "true believers" who have become experts in UAP events, lose their objectivity as they try constantly to assess new events through their UFO eyes—thereby being blinded by their beliefs, and unable to accept that events which they "know" are about Contact with UAP and ETI are, to an objective external observer, not only not definitively so but, on numerous occasions, erroneous narratives by members of the public. This happens because of some people's scientific ignorance, lack of knowledge about meteor or artificial satellite activity, or experience of government deception because they have seen seeming UFO events that were contrived by members of the US military and spy agencies to appear to be genuine manifestations of space voyagers.

In some eras, conditions on Earth seem to indicate that humanity needs to be "rescued" by ExoEarth Visitors to prevent Earth's destruction by members of the human species. This situation can lead to more openness to the Other, accompanied by hope in a better future that, it is assumed, would be catalyzed by intelligent beings concerned about the future not only of humans, but of all biota and their Earth home. On the other hand, people's openness might make them vulnerable to manipulation by intelligent Others, who play on their altruism to guide them to follow a course of action desired by the Others.

Allen Hynek and Jacques Vallée agree that highly intelligent, older (perhaps by millions or billions of years), other-than-human intelligent species have, over millennia, visited Earth, perhaps from places in which they lived on or beneath the surface of Earth. Vallée is particularly concerned to know why members of these species have sought for millennia to influence and even guide human social and spiritual consciousness, to an end still unknown.

Hynek and Vallée collaborated on *The Edge of Reality: A Progress Report on Unidentified Flying Objects* (1975), which presents a facilitated dialogue they had had. At the time of this writing forty-four years later, the book is outdated in terms of data such as what is known about ETI/IDI, and about the number of inhabitable worlds—including planets and lunar satellites, among others—that seem possibly or likely to exist in the Milky Way Galaxy and beyond. Their volume is helpful for understanding how Hynek and Vallée, respectively, approached analytically and theorized scientifically then-current reports about interstellar and interplanetary events.

As research into and debate about the origins of Visitors continues, ETI, IDI, and TDI proponents—as well as those who think that Visitors arrive in all three ways—share in common a core understanding. All assert that other-than-human intelligent beings have come into Contact with human beings, no matter the means by which they journeyed or the place(s) from which they have come.

Complementary research into, hypotheses about, and intellectual pondering concerning other-than-human intelligent beings and their interaction with humankind have come from other noted researchers from diverse fields (as will be seen in chapter 4). In the aggregate, stimulated by intriguing discoveries by NASA, ESA, and other space agencies, ever-increasing numbers of scientists now are taking UAP and UAP-occupant events more seriously, deeming them to be worthy of open, openminded, and serious scientific investigation.

4

Science Discovers ETL and ETI

Pierre Teilhard de Chardin, Stephen Hawking,
E. O. Wilson, Abraham Loeb

The presence or absence of life beyond Earth in the vast cosmos has been debated for millennia. Ancient Greek philosophers, medieval Christian theologians, and scientists during the last one hundred years have weighed in on the discussion. In the twenty-first century, several scientists, religious leaders and scholars, secular humanists, historians, and serious thinkers among the general public have expressed firm or flexible positions on the topic.

In order to probe deeply the issue of life in space, people on this quest have posed thought-provoking questions to sharpen their thinking. Over the past decade, this was often prompted or stimulated by the ever-increasing number of planets found by NASA's Kepler Planet Hunter Telescope (retired in 2018) and Hubble Space Telescope, and additional space-based telescopes used by the European Space Agency and the International Space Station, among others. Consequently, several distinguished scientists have changed their thinking regarding the possible presence of intelligent life elsewhere in the universe. The most fundamental and most thought-provoking change has been the transition from questioning "Are we alone in the universe?" to stating "We are *not* alone in the universe. How might we respond to this new knowledge and challenge?"

New queries have emerged, built on the foundation of past thinking: What might intelligent life be like on other worlds in space or in spacecraft traversing the cosmos in our dimension (ExtraTerrestrial Intelligence, ETI) or traveling in the cosmos interdimensionally (InterDimensional Intelligence, IDI)? What diverse forms has life taken and might life take as it evolves beyond Earth (ETL)—to what extent will they be similar to or dissimilar from Earth's biota and, if intelligent, how like humankind will they be? Will new types of biota be visible or invisible to human eyes with or without telescopes, microscopes, and other instruments and, if not visible, in what other ways might they be discerned? Does life—including intelligent life—exist not only in distant galaxies, but in a (perhaps local) different dimension than that in which Earth and Earth's biota exist? (If in a different dimension, how has it been discovered, and how might it be discovered and analyzed via apparent or conjectured visible or otherwise noticeable influences on Earth and on alien worlds visited, or observed from afar?) What should human responses be to accepted physical evidence, and to other credible evidence and credible witnesses' statements, that ETI/IDI has been visiting Earth, traveling here from nearby Mars or one of the moons of planets in this solar system, or from distant galaxies such as Orion or Proxima Centauri? Would humankind be displaced from its customary physical places by more advanced species' superior military force armed with weaponry previously not seen? To what extent would people be traumatized psychologically and spiritually, and overwhelmed intellectually, by the revelation that another species has surpassed them in accomplishments in the "human"ities ("intelligities"?), arts, sciences, and technology?

Humankind: Sole Intelligent Life?

A fundamental question that most human beings have posed for millennia is, are we alone? Is there other intelligent life in the universe? Indigenous peoples around the globe answered that question hundreds and even thousands of years ago, as evidenced by their oral traditions passed on for generation upon generation: We are not alone. Star People have been visiting us; sometimes, they intermarried with our ancestors. Visitors from the skies still visit us (in chapter 5, indigenous elders and ordinary people describe their encounters—and those of their ancestors—with Star People).

We are not alone as an intelligent species in the cosmos. Scientists have confirmed that this is true, supporting thereby teachings of traditional native peoples around the world whose oral traditions about Star People are centuries or even millennia old. What now?

To date, there are no globally accepted answers to the questions posed, nor is there even consensus on possible responses to them. Contact has not been sustained sufficiently, nor verified extensively, nor accepted as a reality, long enough for people to interact at length (even speculatively) with Visitors who are intelligent Others, and grapple with the questions through a dialogic exchange of ideas through species-specific engagement and interaction. However, the questions and tentative responses to them offered by serious researchers (those who enter thoughtfully into considerations and conjecture, and evaluate evidence with their mind open to new insights, rather than with an inflexible position from which they study data intent on "proving" what they "know" is fact) at least indicate directions in which research into the issues might proceed.

A Century of Scientific Speculation

Several scientists during the twentieth and twenty-first centuries began to consider seriously, and explore thoughtfully (at first, tentatively and cautiously), the possibility that intelligent life exists in ExoEarth contexts. Distinguished representatives of those who have been engaged in this scientific speculation and progress include geologist-paleontologist Pierre Teilhard de Chardin; mathematician and cosmologist University of Cambridge professor Stephen Hawking; emeritus Harvard professor, National Medal of Science awardee, and Pulitzer Prizes recipient Biologist E. O. Wilson; and astrophysicist and chair of the astronomy department at Harvard University Abraham (Avi) Loeb. Some began as strong skeptics about ETI, and gradually changed their position as more scientific data, and credible witnesses' event narratives, became available to them.

Pierre Teilhard de Chardin, SJ (1881–1955)

Pierre Teilhard de Chardin, a Jesuit priest, geologist, and paleontologist, pioneered efforts to integrate coherently Christian theology and Darwinian evolution. Teilhard advocated strongly for their interrelation in his intellectual and intercontinental scientific journeys. The result of his explorations was an extensive body and variety of writings, international lectures, and participation, as a geologist, in significant scientific expeditions.[1] The vast majority of his writings were published posthumously, since his public life, verbal expressions of his thinking, and his writings were subject to Vatican and Jesuit control and censorship. Consequently, he gave his manuscripts to friends, who began to publish them soon after his death.

Teilhard was born in 1881 in Auvergne, France, a beautiful bucolic setting in which his lifelong love of nature began, and his sense of a divine

---

1. A more extensive and in-depth discussion of Teilhard is in Hart, *Cosmic Commons*, 156–75.

presence in nature was awakened. He entered the Jesuit novitiate in 1900, and was ordained in 1911. He did in-depth scientific research in Paris at the Institut Catholique and the Sorbonne. He was drafted into the military in 1914, and became a stretcher-bearer—at the front lines, as per his request. He participated in major battles, including the second battle of the Marne in 1918. Even while in the military during World War I, he continued to write scientific articles and collected specimens of pre-human remains that were churned up to the surface of battlefields by artillery shells, or unearthed when trenches were dug. Pondering the meaning of the universe, he wrote in 1916 *La vie cosmique* (*Cosmic Life*). His heroism under fire as he went from the trenches into the field of battle to rescue wounded soldiers earned him the prestigious honors of a Croix de Guerre and the title of Chevalier of the Legion of Honor. After the war he resumed his scientific studies; he received his doctorate in geology in 1922. He went to Tianjin in 1923–24, his first expedition in China.

Teilhard's geology expertise provided a foundation for his work in biology and paleontology; for a time, he held the chair in geology at the Institut Catholique. Intellectually, he had been led by his studies and his involvement in scientific field research to accept the Darwinian theory of evolution; this was an unusual position for a Christian to take, let alone a Catholic priest, in the 1920s. His advocacy for an integration of Catholic theology and biological evolution led to his forced resignation from the Institut Catholique, and his return to China, now as an exile from France. While there, he was invited by Pei Wen-Chung to be the geologist on an expedition that would come to find the then-earliest human remains known: *Sinanthropus pekinensis*, Peking Man. This was particularly ironic in that he had been exiled to China because of his ideas on evolution, and while there he was part of the team that unearthed compelling scientific evidence for human evolution.

Teilhard: Science and Spirituality

Teilhard de Chardin is well-known as a Jesuit priest-scientist who sought to guide the Catholic Church to accepting the reality of life's evolution on Earth—and endured censorship and exile as a consequence of public statements to that effect. His lifelong spiritual quest has not received as much attention. It is difficult for people to consider that, in addition to being an accomplished scientist, Teilhard was a Christian mystic. There was no "conflict between science and religion" in his thinking and his professional life. While several authors have noted this complementarity and even congruence of fields, only recently has the topic been explored in depth by a scientist, Kathleen Duffy, SSJ, a physicist and simultaneously a member of a Catholic congregation of religious sisters. Her life parallels Teilhard's, except for the types of suffering he endured from Vatican officials and the Jesuit order because of his pioneering efforts to link the Christian theological tradition with the science of evolution.[2]

Teilhard had an extraordinary perception and experience of the depth and dimensions of cosmos being and energies. He penetrated intellectually and spiritually to the heart of matter, where the essence of what he saw was revealed as distinct streams of energy, threads of the material of the cosmic fabric. In one meditative experience, Teilhard left

> the zone of everyday occupations and relationships where everything seems clear, I went down into my inmost self. To the deep abyss whence I feel dimly that my power of action emanates ... I became aware that I was losing contact with myself. At each step of the descent a new person was disclosed within me of whose name I was no longer sure ... I had to stop my exploration because the path faded from beneath my steps, I found a bottomless abyss at my feet, and out of it came—arising I know not from where—the current which I dare to call *my* life.[3]

As he looked into the abyss, he experienced "the distress characteristic to a particle adrift in the universe."[4] Then, as he neared the beginning of time,

> all cosmic structure dissolved into a sea of elementary particles.[5] [The lack of unity distressed him and he reversed direction. As he journeyed toward the future following the origin of time-space,] he watched the elementary particles fuse into fragile streams [and coalesce] ... [he] "focused on those that would eventually form his own current."[6] They extended "from the initial starting-point of the cosmic processes."[7] As time progressed, they came alive—they began cascading in torrents, swirling in eddies, pulsating with life and with spiritual power. Teilhard could feel the energy of life gushing from his core. The more Teilhard explored the cosmic landscape, the more an intangible spiritual layer became apparent. The power and beauty of this spiritual energy opened his eyes to the inner face of evolution:

---

2. Theologian Ursula King's *Spirit of Fire: The Life and Vision of Teilhard de Chardin* is an excellent description and analysis of Teilhard's life and of his integration of scientific knowledge and Christian mysticism. Her book complements well Kathleen Duffy's work.

3. Teilhard, *Divine Milieu*, 76–77; cited in Duffy, *Teilhard's Mysticism*, 84.

4. Teilhard, *Divine Milieu*, 78; Duffy, *Teilhard's Mysticism*, 84.

5. Duffy's description in Duffy, *Teilhard's Mysticism*, 84.

6. Duffy, *Teilhard's Mysticism*, 84.

7. Teilhard, *Writings in Time of War*, 228.

"Everywhere in the stuff of the universe there necessarily exists an internal conscious face lining the external 'material' face habitually the only one considered by science."[8] As he allowed the beauty of the cosmos to flood his spirit, he became more and more capable of accessing matter's inner dimension, of exploring evolution's inner face.[9]

As Teilhard reflected on the origin of life in Earth's waters and its beginning evolution, he realized that matter and spirit co-evolve. Teilhard "learned to look at the evolutionary phenomenon as a whole, to place the human phenomenon within the context of the total story of the Universe. In fact, he found that once the evolutionary cosmos is looked at as whole, 'as a single organic object,'[10] the world becomes 'an interdependent mass of infinitesimal centers structurally interconnected by their condition of origin and their development.'[11] . . . For Teilhard, 'Matter and Spirit are not only complementary aspects of a single reality; they also evolve in complementary ways.'"[12]

Teilhard, although not a musical composer, described aspects, and his own experiences, of cosmic being and presence in musical terms. As he listened attentively to the sounds of nature, he observed that

> all the sounds of created being are fused, without being confused, in a single note which dominates and sustains them . . . so all the powers of the soul begin to resound in response to its call; and these multiple tones, in their turn, compose themselves into a single, ineffably simple vibration in which all the spiritual nuances—of love and of ecstasy, of passion and of indifference, of assimilation and of surrender, of rest and of motion—are born and pass and shine forth.[13]

Duffy states, in paragraphs worthy of being quoted in their entirety, that

> Not only did Teilhard experience the Divine Presence radiating from within all things, but he also heard this Presence pulsating at the heart of matter (HE, 123).[14] "There is a . . . note," he

---

8. Teilhard, *Human Energy*, 26.
9. Teilhard, *Human Energy*, 36; Duffy, *Teilhard's Mysticism*, 84–85.
10. Teilhard, *Science and Christ*, 89.
11. Teilhard, *Human Energy*, 38.
12. Teilhard, *Writings in Time of War*, 155; Duffy, *Teilhard's Mysticism*, 87.
13. Teilhard, *Divine Milieu*, 120. Cited in Duffy, *Teilhard's Mysticism*, 32.
14. Teilhard, *Human Energy*, 123.

says, "which makes the whole World vibrate" (LTF, 31)[15] with "a vibration that passes all description, inexhaustible in the richness of its tones and its notes, interminable in the perfection of its unity" (S, 39).[16] The resonance that lies muted in the depth of every human" (W, 101)[17] caused the very core of his being to vibrate in response (HU, 46).[18] Like a musical instrument, his spirit resonated with the unique tone emitted by the Divine Presence, and within his whole being, he felt reverberate 'an echo as vast as the universe' (W, 101).[19]

For Teilhard, the duty of the mystic is to be aware of the inner rhythm of the world and to listen with care for the heartbeat of a higher reality (W, 119).[20] As a result of this kind of listening, he was drawn out of himself "into a wider harmony . . . into an ever richer and more spiritual rhythm" (W, 117),[21] so that he eventually became "caught up in the essential music of the world" (W, 101)[22] and responded to "the fundamental harmony of the Universe" (LTF, 59).[23] At this privileged place, he tells us, "the least of our desires and efforts . . . can . . . cause the marrow of the universe to vibrate" (D, 115).[24] "Indeed," he wrote, "we are called by the music of the universe to reply, each with his own pure and incommunicable harmonic" (HE, 150).[25]

Teilhard's thoughts on Universe harmony, Divine Presence, and vibrations are fascinating in how they resonate with the perceptions of experiencers Sara and Peter, as described in psychiatrist John Mack's *Abduction* in his interviews with them, and in his analysis of "vibration" descriptions. While he had no experience of being abducted by other-than-human intelligent beings, Teilhard did state that he thought that they were present in the cosmos.[26]

15. Teilhard, *Letters to Two Friends*, 31.
16. Teilhard, *Science and Christ*, 39.
17. Teilhard, *Writings in Time of War*, 101.
18. Teilhard, *Hymn of the Universe*, 46.
19. Teilhard, *Writings in Time of War*, 101.
20. Teilhard, *Writings in Time of War*, 119.
21. Teilhard, *Writings in Time of War*, 117.
22. Teilhard, *Writings in Time of War*, 101.
23. Teilhard, *Letters to Two Friends*, 59.
24. Teilhard, *Divine Milieu*, 115.
25. Teilhard, *Human Energy*, 150. Duffy, *Teilhard's Mysticism*, 32–33.
26. It occurs to this writer that the different resonances experienced by Sara might become harmonious throughout the cosmos as per Teilhard's description of an ultimate harmony emerging from a cacophony of competing tones. The latter seems to be present today, as described by Sara.

Teilhard and ETI

Teilhard began early in his career to speculate about the possibility of extraterrestrial intelligent life. In 1920 he wrote (in an unpublished essay) that it seemed likely that elsewhere in space intelligent life exists: "[I]t is almost impossible to conceive that, among the millions of Milky Ways which whirl in space, there is not one which has known, or is going to know, conscious life."[27] More than thirty years later, his speculation on the possibility of the evolution of intelligent life elsewhere in the cosmos was expressed more fully. In mid-1953, while in New York, he wrote "A Sequel to the Problem of Human Origins: The Plurality of Inhabited Worlds."[28] As with his other works, it was not published during his lifetime. His scientific knowledge regarding biotic evolution on Earth (reinforced by paleontological data from his field expeditions), the age of Earth and the universe (informed by geological data from his expeditions), and his understanding of the cosmic time required for Earth to form and, much later, for life eventually to come into existence, stimulated him to consider similar possibilities elsewhere in the cosmos. His ideas here were, as was the case with his thinking about the relationship of evolution and theology, well ahead of his time and place. They were written just six years after news of a crash of an alien craft near Roswell, New Mexico, in 1947; this had been followed by other UFO reports and scientific and theological speculation about extraterrestrial life possibilities—including in a *Time* magazine article (September 15, 1952) which he cites. He died just two years after he wrote the essay.

Teilhard observes that "There are millions of galaxies in the universe, in each of which matter has the same general composition and is going through essentially the same evolution as that inside our own Milky Way."[29] This leads him to speculate that "*If* [emphasis in original] proteins appear as early and wherever possible, and *if* life, once existing, evolves as high as possible," including "up to 'hominization' if it can," and *if* there exist billions of solar systems where life can emerge and become "hominized," then "our minds cannot resist the inevitable conclusion" that if some form of technology could somehow detect the "radiation of the 'noospheres'" [places in space where thinking occurs], "it would be *practically certain* that what we saw registered ... would be a cloud of thinking stars."[30] He states further that what once could only be imagined "is seen by us in the twentieth century to be *by*

---

27. Teilhard, "Fall, Redemption, and Geocentricism," 38.
28. Teilhard, "Sequel to the Problem," 229–36.
29. Teilhard, "Sequel to the Problem," 230.
30. Teilhard, "Sequel to the Problem," 230–31.

a long way the most probable alternative,"[31] and adds: "In other words, considering what we now know about the number of 'worlds' and their internal evolution, the idea of *a single* hominized *planet* in the universe has already become in fact (without our generally realizing it) almost as *inconceivable* as that of a man who appeared with no genetic relationship to the rest of the earth's animal population."[32] In these words, Teilhard affirms both human evolution on Earth and the existence of evolved intelligent life elsewhere in the cosmos.

Teilhard speculates along these lines that "At an average of (at least) one human race per galaxy, that makes a total of millions of human races dotted all over the heavens."[33] However, he cautions, "No matter how great a probability may be, we must be careful not to treat it as a certainty—that is obvious ... There is no question, then, of having to begin work on a theology for these unknown worlds. We must at least, however, endeavour to make our classical theology open to (I was on the point of saying 'blossom into') the possibility (a positive possibility) of their existence and their presence."[34]

In his developing cosmos-focused evolutionary understanding, then, Teilhard almost unreservedly affirmed the existence of intelligent—"hominised"—extraterrestrial life. He did not speculate about what its characteristics might be, except that it would have evolved human-like intelligence. Decades would pass before other scientists, whether secular humanists or religious humanists, would dare to openly suggest—usually very cautiously, at first—what Teilhard considered a reasonable, likely possibility. In fact, for decades since it was formulated in 1961, the "Drake Equation," which provides a mathematical calculation that supposedly negates the possibility of intelligent life elsewhere in the cosmos, has been oft-cited in efforts to reject that possibility.[35]

---

31. Teilhard, "Sequel to the Problem," 231.

32. Teilhard, "Sequel to the Problem," 231.

33. Teilhard, "Sequel to the Problem," 232. Here, it is possible that Teilhard means by "human life" what he states earlier to be "hominised" or "intelligent" life, probably not literally "human life." However, the interaction between DNA and environment, which effects evolution, was likely not known to him. DNA's role in genetic inheritance was first demonstrated a decade before his essay, in 1943. The genetic implications had been elaborated in the same year that Teilhard's essay was written when, in 1953, James Watson's and Francis Crick's research, assisted by Rosalind Franklin's and Maurice Wilkins's work, enabled scientists to determine more extensively the role of DNA in biotic evolution. See "DNA."

34. Teilhard, "Sequel to the Problem," 233–34.

35. An excellent elaboration of the Drake Equation, and recent space telescope discoveries that provide a response to it, are found in Howell, "Drake."

TI/ETI/IDI—Common Quest: Universal Spirituality

Christian thinking is now at the stage, given the remarkable ETI/IDI events of the last century, "to begin work on a theology for these unknown worlds"— preferably, more constructively and ecumenically, and supplemented, after future Contact, by conversations with those worlds' as yet unknown intelligent biota. There should be recognition, in this process, that beings encountered and engaged might have their origins in civilizations that are tens of millions or even billions of years old, and that some others will be known only through architectural archaeological artifacts: they might have perished over millennia. They might still contribute to the conversation through information about their culture and reasons for its disappearance, which could inform theological understandings and interpretation of "traditional" doctrines. Many world religions understand that the transcendent-immanent Spirit of the universe (called by different names, with diverse meanings attached to those names) loves and is solicitous of all living beings, not just humans and other intelligent beings; their scholars and laity should recognize that intelligent life elsewhere in the cosmos also communicates with the Spirit, and has developed its own form(s) of spirituality. These might or might not have been organized into religious institutions; the Others might have a diversity of ways in which they acknowledge and celebrate divine Being. Intelligent biota from elsewhere in the cosmos do not need or desire to be "converted" to Christianity or any other Earth-originated and Earth-based religion or humanist faith tradition. Earth believers' religious or atheistic imperialism of any type would rightly be rejected by members of religious, spiritual, or secular humanist traditions that come into Contact with humankind from elsewhere in space-time. The Europeans' and Euroamericans' destruction of native peoples' religious beliefs and practices on Earth in the aftermath of fifteenth-century voyages of "Discovery"[36] and continuing today, should not be replicated in the heavens.[37] No "universal" religion or spirituality has been developed on Earth, nor will it be in the foreseeable future, that will be accepted by all, some, or even any members of a newly-encountered intelligent species. (Humankind has not achieved this unanimity of belief on Earth; it cannot expect to propagate a shared spirituality or religion in the heavens without having done so.) First steps on the way toward this cosmos consciousness and relational community might be undertaken at Contact or soon thereafter. This would be possible if all participants in dialogue are open and eager to learn and to reflect on the insights, beliefs, and practices of intelligent Others from distinct and distant cosmos settings.

36. Hart, *Cosmic Commons*, 59–88.
37. Hart, *Cosmic Commons*, 117–42.

Stephen Hawking (1942–2018)

The late Cambridge theoretical mathematician and cosmologist Stephen Hawking was born in Oxford on January 8, 1942, the three hundredth anniversary of the death of Galileo.[38] When he was only eleven years old, he went to University College, Oxford, in hopes of studying mathematics. That field was not then a possibility at University College, so he focused on physics. Three years later, he received a first-class honours degree in natural science. In 1962, he went to the University of Cambridge to focus on cosmology. He earned his PhD there in 1965. He was elected a Fellow of the Royal Society in 1974. He taught at Stanford University from 1974–78, then returned to Cambridge as Lucasian Professor of Mathematics (1979–2009), a position held by Isaac Newton in 1669. He finished his academic career in Cambridge as the Dennis Stanton Avery and Sally Tsui Wong-Avery Director of Research in the Department of Applied Mathematics and Theoretical Physics, and Founder of the Centre for Theoretical Cosmology.

Stephen Hawking gained international recognition for his thinking on black holes and the space-time relationship. His brilliant mind was not limited by his ALS physical infirmity, diagnosed in 1963. His best-known work, which contributed substantially to his field and to his stature among scientists and the general public, is *A Brief History of Time: From the Big Bang to Black Holes* (1988).[39] In 2013, his self-reflective autobiography, *My Brief History*, was published.[40] In 2014, *The Theory of Everything*, a movie about his life, was released.[41]

Hawking's Deus ex Machina

In his first comments on life in space, Hawking focused on humans' need to escape into space in the near future because of the devastation they are causing on Earth. In comments in 2006 at the Hong Kong University of Science and Technology,[42] he declared that life on Earth is at an ever-increasing risk of being wiped out by a disaster such as "sudden global warming, nuclear war, a genetically engineered virus," or another type of catastrophe. Similarly, in 2007 at the NASA base on Cape Canaveral, Florida, just prior to his zero-G

---

38. Biographical data is drawn from Hawking's website at http://www.hawking.org.uk/about-stephen.html.
39. Hawking revised and expanded this classic as Hawking, *Illustrated*.
40. Hawking, *My Brief History*.
41. March, *Theory of Everything*.
42. Hui, "Physicist Hawking."

(zero gravity) airplane flight,[43] Hawking said that because of the danger of humankind's self-extinction, "I think that getting a portion of the human race permanently off the planet is imperative for our future as a species." This was an "imperative" because of humans' continuing and accelerating destruction of their Earth home while ignoring what they were doing.

The comments by Stephen Hawking in Hong Kong and at Cape Canaveral stimulated my decision to write cosmos-oriented books. In 2006–07, just prior to my work with NASA and SETI scientists, newspaper articles about his trips to China and Florida were published. In them, as just described, he advocated constructing a moon base and Mars colony because human survival requires exoplanetary colonization to save some humans. My immediate thought on reading his assessment and proposals was "It's the same people! Those who go into space are currently destroying Earth. How would they act differently on other worlds?" Hawking seemed to assume that people who leave Earth to explore and colonize other worlds will have a different consciousness and conduct than those left behind: they will not overpopulate those worlds, adversely affect their climate, or use human technology to extract, in a planet-devastating way, planetary natural goods from the worlds which they would come to inhabit. Contrary to Hawking's assertions, however, on those worlds, too, they will likely have brought with them, or develop on-site, new weapons for a "nuclear war," or release there a "genetically engineered virus." As I reflected at length on this, I decided to write in depth about it.[44] It occurred to me that Hawking's idealistic assumptions—that human consciousness and conduct would be different when traversing the cosmos and settling on other worlds—were unrealistic: how would humans be converted from the greed and rapaciousness that became endemic in human exploration and colonization of Earth? I wrote that humankind should not flee their destruction of Earth, and escape to the stars to start anew. Rather, people should strive for a change in consciousness, and hence of conduct, on their Earth home, transform their societies, and renew, not abandon, their world. I suggested that his human emigrant proposal was a *deus ex machina*, comprised of the proposal and the space vehicles that would carry it out.

43. Boyle, "Hawking Goes Zero-G."

44. Hart, "Cosmic Commons," 371–72. A more extensive and in-depth elaboration and discussion of Hawking's ETI thinking is found in Hart, *Cosmic Commons*, 7–14, 138–39 and throughout the book; and in *Encountering ETI*, especially 8–18, 135–42, 225–27; this section is adapted, in part, from the works cited.

Hawking: There Is No ETI

On the topic of the possible existence of ETI, Stephen Hawking first dismissed the likelihood of intelligent life in space, then changed his view. In February 2008, he declared that he did not take UFO stories seriously: "we don't seem to have been visited by aliens. I am discounting the reports of UFOs. Why would they appear only to cranks and weirdos? If there is a government conspiracy to suppress the reports and keep for itself the scientific knowledge the aliens bring, it seems to have been a singularly ineffective policy so far. Furthermore, despite an extensive search by the SETI project, we haven't heard any alien television quiz shows. This probably indicates that there are no alien civilizations at our stage of development within a radius of a few hundred light years. Issuing an insurance policy against abduction by aliens seems a pretty safe bet."[45] His deprecatory and even sarcastic comments and his attempts to ridicule the phenomena ("alien television quiz shows") or those who stated that they had witnessed them ("cranks and weirdos") generated more critical responses than they gained affirmation. Obvious critical comments included that not just those he labels "cranks and weirdos" describe anomalous objects that they have seen in the heavens, but military pilots; professional people, including scientists; and ordinary, respected citizens. Moreover, the fact that data is lacking might be precisely because objective evidence is being suppressed—as credible witnesses to Roswell events, among others, have declared is occurring—and this has proved to be, for decades, a "singularly *effective* policy."

Hawking: ETI Does Exist—Avoid Them

Stephen Hawking reversed his position rejecting the possibility of ETI existence just two years after his disparaging 2008 remarks about alien existence and about the people who stated that they had seen evidence of it. In his 2010 BBC program broadcast on the Discovery Channel, "Into the Universe with Stephen Hawking,"[46] he states,

> Are we alone? . . . I think probably not because of one fact: the universe is big, really big . . . So to my mathematical brain, the numbers alone make thinking about aliens perfectly rational. The real challenge is to try and work out what aliens might actually be like, living on some far-off world. The possibilities are infinite, and infinitely intriguing. Alien life could range from simple green slime . . . to more advanced animals, something

---

45. Hawking, "Questioning the Universe," 4:59–6:00.
46. Williams, "Aliens," 1:28–5:00.

with a bit more bite. But of course, that's just the start of what could be out here. It's such a massive universe, it's logical to wonder if there are intelligent beings, perhaps even civilizations like those in science fiction TV shows and movies. "Star Wars" and "Star Trek," two of my personal favorites, may be closer to reality than we think. Similar scenarios are, at least, conceivable. But think about it more . . . there could be life forms so strange we wouldn't even recognize them as life.

What we might do, he suggests, is to reason from here, our Earth home, because it has the only examples of life that we know.[47] The laws of physics appear to be the same everywhere, and so, too, might be the laws of biology;[48] however, the details would be different. "We can use life on Earth as a kind of 'alien hunters' handbook,' a field guide to what alien life is, and how it works, no matter where it occurs." He raises the idea of *panspermia*, that "life originated elsewhere and could have been spread from planet to planet by asteroids."[49] Once life arrives, it organizes for survival, including finding sources of energy in food. Over time, evolution of life occurs. Life seems to need water, which is "very common in space," notably frozen water. He raises the question, "Has alien life evolved as we have, and developed intelligence?" Hawking continued to dismiss stories of human encounters with ETI, wondering where the evidence is for such Contact. He thinks that there would be newspaper articles reporting such events, and he claims that governments could not hide it. After speculating that aliens might have discovered the power of the atom, he wonders if they might have destroyed their civilization; if they are cruising the cosmos, it might be because their own world is gone. Hawking subsequently advises against humanity seeking to make Contact with ETI. He warns that because intelligent explorers likely destroyed their own world, they would be aggressively seeking places in which to live, or at least from which to extract natural goods, and would attack humans to obtain what they need. (E. O. Wilson would disagree, because of the threat of Earth's microbes adversely affecting such Visitors; see below.) Hawking projected anthropomorphically that ETI's conduct would be similar to that of Europeans who went to the "New World" in the fifteenth and sixteenth centuries: the result of encounters between native peoples and European explorers/colonists was the devastation of the lives and cultures of the original

47. E. O. Wilson concurs. See below.
48. See Teilhard's speculation above.
49. In the fifth century BCE, the Greek philosopher Anaxagoras proposed that life on Earth began via *panspermia* (seeds of life traveling through the universe seeded different worlds). For a very brief description of the concept, see Fizbit, "What Is the Theory of Panspermia?" Panspermia is described in depth in "Probability of Pasnpermia."

inhabitants of Turtle Island, now called the United States (he does not mention that Spanish colonists sought to designate indigenous peoples "beasts who talked" in order to enslave them: Spain had already abolished slavery of indigenous peoples in its colonies). In the end, the impact of contact in 1492 and thereafter "didn't turn out very well for the Native Americans."[50] On the other hand, he speculated, if aliens had not destroyed themselves, they might now be colonizing the cosmos. They might have found a way to overcome vast cosmic distances by traveling through wormholes that provide shortcuts. After his warnings about the dangers of ETI, however, Hawking concludes "Into the Universe" on a positive note: "Let's just hope that if aliens do find us, they'll come in peace."[51] A BBC story in 2010 reviewed "Into the Universe" and reinforced Hawking's warning about ETI dangers to humankind.[52]

Hawking Contradicted: ETI Evolved Beyond Violence

Distinguished biologists Robert Wright and Peter Singer responded to and rejected Hawking's basic premise, that intelligent beings voyaging space had destroyed their own home planet. Their views (written by Wright) were presented in a *New York Times* op-ed piece, "Ethics for Extraterrestrials." In it, they took exception to Hawking's statement about cosmos-cruising, humankind-threatening ETI. Wright suggests that ETI might be benevolent rather than malevolent. He discusses Peter Singer's view that as humans progressed significantly in the social systems they developed and their concomitant social conduct, their views and practices were altered. Dramatic changes were made from the time of the Greek city-states where citizens viewed as subhuman their social equivalent in opposing states, to the twentieth century in which humanity regarded as people those other than themselves who were members of diverse races, colors, and creeds. Singer states that this indicates a natural process in the evolution of intelligent beings, who eventually use their reason and interaction to discern that moral concern is socially beneficial; they will even extend such concern to all sentient being. Following his summary of Singer, Wright expresses his own view: "pragmatic self-interest," not reason, promotes moral progress. He integrates Singer's perspective with

---

50. Hawking expressed these sentiments in Williams, "Aliens," 54:58–55:02. The contrasting views of Hawking, and Wright and Singer, are described in several online sources, including Wright, "Ethics for Extraterrestrials"; Leake, "Don't Talk to Aliens"; and "Stay Home ET." An in-depth discussion of the Hawking statement and Wright's and Singer's responses is in Hart, *Encountering ETI*, 141–43.

51. Williams, "Aliens," 55:45–50.

52. Hrala, "Stephen Hawking Warns."

his own, and concludes that humankind will need such moral enlightenment, however evolved, to progress sufficiently—technologically and socially—to journey from its solar system out into space. He reasons that his and Singer's theories, necessary for human social development and technological advance, could be extrapolated to ETI. Without evolving as described in these steps, ETI would not have the technological capability to venture vast distances. In a hopeful contrast to Hawking, Wright anticipates that ETI would not be the menacing, conquering species whom people on Earth should fear.

Wright and Singer think that intelligent species' evolution is the reason why benevolence would characterize them. Singer suggests that intelligent species rationally conclude that ethical sociality will benefit them as a species (and therefore they would act similarly when meeting other intelligent species), and Wright states that moral evolution enables this to be the case. It might be derived from both scientists' thinking that humankind should be optimistic that ETI would not be aggressive and bellicose toward intelligent beings they meet on other worlds or on their home planet. Rather, ETI would accommodate to and even be benevolent toward humans, and promote universal interspecies harmony. Confronting this hope, however, as will be seen in the next chapter, is unnerving evidence about Contact in some areas that seems to indicate that not all ETI species would be benign: the positive evolutionary trajectory theorized by Wright and Singer might not have been operative on some worlds. In such cases, the most aggressive species, concerned about its survival if not its dominance over other species, would likely eliminate competitive species that need a similar habitat and food sources.

Hawking Seemingly Reverses His Position . . . Again

In 2015, Hawking appeared to reverse his position again, according to *Time Magazine* in its story about his support for an ETI search.[53] He joined Russian billionaire technology entrepreneur Yuri Milner at a press conference in London to announce a massive outreach to promising Goldilocks Zone planets to contact ETI. The $100 million effort, "Breakthrough Listen," is one of several "Breakthrough Initiatives" that Milner is funding. It will not send signals from Earth into distant space, but launch thousands of fist-sized probes, fueled by laser-beam energized light sails, and highly electronically technologized, toward targeted areas. The places would have been selected because space telescopes had discovered planets there that appeared likely to have life. Upon arrival in the region, the probes would listen for indications of intelligent life. The project will take years to become operational. Probably

53. Greenberg, "Stephen Hawking."

decades down the line, this effort will be followed by "Breakthrough Message," which will actively seek ETI responses to messages sent by people on Earth. But even while endorsing "Listen," Hawking offered a caution, reminiscent of his 2010 fears:

> If you look at history, contacts between humans and less intelligent organisms have often been disastrous from their point of view, and encounters between civilizations with advanced versus primitive technologies have gone badly for the less advanced … [Citizens of an ETI planet who view an Earth message] could be billions of years ahead of us. If so, they will be vastly more powerful, and may not see us as any more valuable than we see bacteria.[54]

Despite these misgivings, Hawking still justified Breakthrough Listen, as part of the enduring human quest for knowledge: "We are alive. We are intelligent. We must know."[55] Given Hawking's decades-long accomplishments and publishing record, and the popular topic of seeking intelligent life in space, numerous media outlets covered the story.

Hawking's Relatively Final Position

In 2016, Hawking emphasized once again his concern about ETI. As described by Josh Hrala on an online Science Alert site,[56] Hawking states in an online film, *Stephen Hawking's Favourite Places*, that "As I grow older I am more convinced than ever that we are not alone. After a lifetime of wondering, I am helping to lead a new global effort to find out." Then he goes on to say that "The Breakthrough Listen project will scan the nearest million stars for signs of life, but I know just the place to start looking. One day we might receive a signal from a planet like Gliese 832c, but we should be wary of answering back." Hrala observes that "despite Hawking's extraordinary effort to find intelligent life in the Universe, he is one of the most outspoken critics of actually trying to communicate with them, an act that he says would potentially endanger humanity, because a distant alien civilisation might view us as inferior, weak, and perfect to conquer."

In 2017, Hawking reiterated this point strongly, almost seeming anxious about his commitment to Milner's Breakthrough Listen initiative, and reverted back to his previous fears about alien Contact. An online article by Kathleen Villaluz, "Stephen Hawking Warns the World Against Contacting

54. Greenberg, "Stephen Hawking," para. 2.
55. Greenberg, "Stephen Hawking," para. 2.
56. Hrala, "Stephen Hawking Warns Us," paras. 4–5, 9.

Aliens,"[57] discusses his ongoing anxiety. She, too, describes the documentary *Stephen Hawking's Favorite Places*, in which Hawking "embarks on a journey in outer space aboard his spacecraft covering various mysteries found in the universe such as black holes and exoplanets. The physicist believes that a distant world, Gliese 832c, may be host to extraterrestrial life and that at some point Earth could potentially be contacted by creatures on the exoplanet." However, Hawking warned that humans must be cautious when engaging with unfamiliar forms of life. "Many have speculated on what it would be like to encounter extraterrestrial life but Hawking has his own prediction on how man and extraterrestrial life could potentially clash." He states that, at some future time, "we might receive a signal from a planet like this, but we should be wary of answering back. Meeting an advanced civilization could be like Native Americans encountering Columbus. That didn't turn out so well." Villaluz notes that Gliese 832c, then only recently discovered (2014), is thought to be among the "three most Earth-like planets, and is sixteen light years away from Earth," and that Hawking thinks that it is "the best place to scour for extraterrestrial life" and might be a destination for human migration as human-caused global warming devastates Earth.[58]

Hawking and Visitor 'Oumuamua

In December 2017, Hawking and Breakthrough Listen joined with scientists around the world who had been startled to discover and sought to investigate a previously unknown type of object speeding across the solar system at 196,000 miles per hour. Since it did not meet customary criteria for the characteristics and conduct of an asteroid, speculation arose that 'Oumuamua ("scout"), first viewed by astronomers at the University of Hawaii, might be a probe from an alien world's civilization. *The Sun* newspaper described the coalition in a feature article, with photos, by Guy Birchall: "The British genius is leading a team of scientists who are scanning the baffling space rock for any signs of extraterrestrial life."[59] The article states that Hawking "is among the leading space experts today using top-of-the-range technology to scan a vast cigar-shaped object for signs of alien life. Thought to be an interstellar asteroid the object is about a quarter of a mile long, 260ft wide and hurtling through our solar system."[60] The scientists used technologically advanced scanners and radio telescopes to analyze the interstellar voyager, including the world's largest maneuverable radio telescope, at Green Bank,

57. Villaluz, "Stephen Hawking."
58. Villaluz, "Stephen Hawking," paras. 3–5.
59. Burchall, "Out of This World."
60. Birchall, "Out of This World," para. 1.

West Virginia. Birchall quotes Breakthrough Listen's Yuri Milner, who said that "Researchers working on long-distance space transportation have previously suggested that a cigar or needle shape is the most likely architecture for an interstellar spacecraft, since this would minimise friction and damage from interstellar gas and dust."[61] While there is still some minimal scientific speculation about a possible connection between 'Oumuamua and intelligent beings outside the solar system, the general scientific consensus in November of 2018 was that this is not the case. 'Oumuamua traveled so rapidly across the solar system that little (publicly disclosed) scientific data was acquired from it. Theories had included that it was an asteroid or a comet; the latter seems to be what was provisionally theorized to be the case.

It is intriguing that a distinguished group of curious scientists from around the globe took 'Oumuamua seriously, and investigated it as a possible alien-constructed artifact. Apparently, there is an increasing number of scientists who accept the possibility that ETI is present in the cosmos and were willing to have their names associated with an effort to explore this possibility through a thorough analysis of 'Oumuamua. Highly respected cosmologist Stephen Hawking was a major participant in this group. Having once declared that only "cranks and weirdos" saw UFOs, he came to fully accept their reality. Moreover, he continued to advocate, until his death—with some anxiety and reservations—making Contact with ETI. He became fully immersed in seeking data about UFOs and their occupants, whom he assumed to be highly intelligent. Likely, he thought, they surpass humans' intelligence because of their far-longer existence as civilizations in the cosmos. He was convinced that these other intelligent beings inhabit worlds in the cosmos. His scientific curiosity and quest for knowledge remained in a tug of war with his concern for the wellbeing of the human species should Contact be made.

Stephen Hawking: New Socioecological Concern

As previously described, Stephen Hawking had advocated establishing a base on the moon and a colony on Mars to save selected humans from human self- and planetary-destruction. He proposed that the humans chosen should escape from Earth to another world; he did not suggest a potentially planet-preserving alternative, that all humanity should attempt to eliminate or mitigate Earth's devastation and save their own planet.

However, on December 1, 2016, Hawking published an essay, "This Is the Most Dangerous Time for Our Planet," on the front page of the online version of *The Guardian* (US edition) which strongly pressed for humankind's

---

61. Birchall, "Out of This World," para. 6.

attempt to address social ills and ecological crises.⁶² The article advocated a startling and welcome reversal of his earlier position; its subheading highlighted this immediately: "We can't go on ignoring inequality, because we have the means to destroy our world but not to escape it." The *deus ex machina* thinking and proposal of his previous statements were rejected, and were replaced by some down-to-Earth comments; these indicated a conscientious consciousness not evident in his previous statements. Reflecting on the Brexit vote and the Trump victory, he observed that people's "absolutely understandable" underlying concerns were "the economic consequences of globalisation and accelerating technological change."⁶³ He noted the continuing loss of jobs: in manufacturing, for example, people are being displaced by machines and by developments in artificial intelligence. He described, too, "awesome environmental challenges."⁶⁴ After reiterating that humans have the technology to destroy Earth, but not yet to escape it, he rejected his previous *deus ex machina* proposal: "Perhaps in a few hundred years, we will have established human colonies amid the stars, but right now we only have one planet, and we need to work together to protect it."⁶⁵ In this welcome change of view, Stephen Hawking called for trying to resolve Earth's pressing socioeconomic and socioecological issues, rather than to escape them.

In 2017, while being interviewed on the occasion of his seventy-fifth birthday, Hawking addressed once again the danger of global warming. The birthday celebration is covered in a story and video on BBC News by Pallab Ghosh, BBC Science correspondent: "Hawking Says Trump's Climate Stance Could Damage Earth." In the video, Hawking declares that "We are close to the tipping point where global warming becomes irreversible. Trump's action could push the Earth over the brink, to become like Venus, with a temperature of 250 degrees and raining sulfuric acid. Climate change is one of the great dangers we face, and it's one we can prevent if we act now. By denying the evidence for climate change, and pulling out of the Paris Climate Agreement, Donald Trump will cause avoidable environmental damage to our beautiful planet, endangering the natural world for us and our children."⁶⁶

---

62. I am grateful to Nobel Physics Laureate Shelly (Sheldon) Glashow for telling me about the article. Fortuitously, we were sitting next to each other at a dinner party in a home near Boston. We had been conversing about our respective interests and I mentioned ETI–IDI and Hawking's "save some of us" suggestion. Shelly had read the *Guardian* essay shortly before the dinner; he retrieved it for me on his cell phone, and on the spot sent to me an email link to it.

63. Hawking, "This Is the Most Dangerous Time," para. 7.

64. Hawking, "This Is the Most Dangerous Time," para. 13.

65. Hawking, "This Is the Most Dangerous Time," para. 14.

66. Ghosh, "Hawking Says," paras. 8–9.

Stephen Hawking, prestigious scientist, progressed from ETI denial to ETI acknowledgment, and brought to bear in UAP and ETI/IDI investigations his intellect, renown, "mathematical mind," and support for the cosmic quest to respond to the question, "Are we alone?" In the context of his comments about humans' planetary conduct, Hawking had a similar change of mind: at first, he promoted humans' departure into space in the near future, to escape human-caused Earth destruction; then, he advocated that humanity care for its home planet, but kept in reserve the possibility that it might be necessary for people to migrate to other worlds in the future. Hawking's progression in his thinking, but ambiguous sentiments about Contact's impacts, reflects to some extent how other reflective people ponder Contact. His reputation and influence should prompt the interest of a wider audience in the possibility and potential of a third displacement if Contact occurs. Concurrently, it might stimulate consideration of positive outcomes if humankind puts its own house in order and seeks its place in the cosmos commons—as an integrated, interrelated, intelligent species within the integral universe.

E. O. Wilson

E. O. Wilson, Emeritus Professor of Biology, Harvard University, coined the term *sociobiology*. He was awarded the National Medal of Science in 1976. The author of more than thirty books,[67] he received the 1979 Pulitzer Prize for General Nonfiction for *On Human Nature* (1978), and shared the 1991 Pulitzer Prize for General Nonfiction with Bert Hölldobler, his coauthor for *The Ants* (1990).

Edward Osborne Wilson was born in Birmingham, Alabama, on June 10, 1929. He grew up with an intense interest in science, especially biology. This prompted him to go on solo hikes into Alabama wetlands where, on one occasion, he had a near-fatal encounter with a water moccasin: when he lifted it out of the water to throw it away from him, a dangerous game he enjoyed playing, it was larger and heavier than it had appeared. When it was above the surface and began to turn to strike, he hurled it away. He did not play this game thereafter. Wilson received his BS (1949) and MS (1950) from the University of Alabama. His earned his PhD (1955) at Harvard University, and the following year was appointed as an assistant professor of Biology there. He became Associate Professor of Zoology in 1958, and Professor of Zoology in 1964. He was named Curator on Entomology in Harvard's

---

67. Biographical information for E. O. Wilson is selected from his bio on the website of the E.O. Wilson Biodiversity Foundation link to his CV—see the bio here: https://eowilsonfoundation.org/e-o-wilson/. This very brief summary is just the tip of the iceberg of his work he did and the honors he received during his extraordinary career.

Museum of Comparative Zoology in 1973. A succession of distinguished appointments followed: Frank B. Baird Jr. Professor of Science (1976); Mellon Professor of the Sciences (1990); Pellegrino University Professor (1994), University Professor Emeritus (1997), University Research Professor (1997), and Research Professor Emeritus (2002). He worked with the World Wildlife Fund in several capacities (1974–95). He received numerous prestigious science and environmental organization awards and prizes from around the world.

E. O. and ETI

E. O. Wilson's initial assessment of extraterrestrial intelligent life was that its existence was doubtful because it had not been empirically established by scientific evidence. Then, in *The Social Conquest of Earth*, he suggests periodically that ETI might exist. But he describes humankind as "far and away life's greatest achievement," adding "We are the mind of the biosphere, the solar system, and—who can say?—perhaps the galaxy."[68] He thought that this view would continue to prevail because there was yet no globally accepted scientific evidence of ETI.

Wilson stated in *Social Conquest*, too, regarding the possible existence of ETI, that people should "ask seriously why, during the 3.5 billion-year history of the biosphere, our planet has never been visited by extraterrestrials. (Except perhaps in fuzzy UFO lights in the sky and bedroom visitors during waking nightmares.)"[69] Here, Wilson seems to make an oblique reference to the work of a Harvard University faculty colleague, psychiatrist John Mack,[70] whose writings describe his sessions with people who said that they had been abductees (a word Mack replaces with his preferred term, "experiencers," which implies a less intrusive taking of people from highways or homes to interrogate them or perform experiments on them). Wilson asks, too, a question that UFO skeptics (including Stephen Hawking in his early speculation, as noted above) raise often: "why has SETI, after searching the galaxy for years, never received a message from outer space?" His response is both to affirm the SETI search, because "the theoretical possibility of such a contact exists and should be continued," and to reject an objection to SETI

---

68. Wilson, *Social Conquest*, 288.

69. Wilson, *Social Conquest*, 296. This and the quotes that follow are from the same page.

70. Wilson and Mack had been faculty colleagues at Harvard University, in different departments. Both were Pulitzer Prize recipients. They would have been familiar, to some extent, with each other's work. See chapter 5 for a more thorough elaboration of John Mack's thought and work.

that it is not needed because "a scenario to explain the absence of extraterrestrials is that we are unique in all the galaxy going back through all those billions of years; and that we alone became capable of space travel, and so the Milky Way now awaits our conquest. That scenario *is highly unlikely*" (emphasis added). He offers an alternative view:

> I favor another possibility. Perhaps the extraterrestrials just grew up. Perhaps they found out that the immense problems of their evolving civilizations could not be solved by competition among religious faiths, or ideologies, or warrior nations. They discovered that great problems demand great solutions, rationally achieved by cooperation among whatever factions divided them. If they accomplished that much, they would have realized that there was no need to colonize other star systems. It would be enough to settle down and explore the limitless possibilities for fulfillment on the home planet.[71]

Wilson offers similar advice to humankind in his next book which, in contrast to *Social Conquest*, affirms strongly an ETI presence in the universe.

E. O.: ETI Exists

In *The Meaning of Human Existence*, Wilson considered ETI existence more extensively. He went beyond the *Social Conquest* paragraph that rejected the possibility that "fuzzy lights in the sky" were the only purported evidence of ETI. Rather, he devoted all of chapter 10, "A Portrait of ET," to analysis of likely characteristics of extraterrestrial intelligent life. His reflection is based on "life as we know it"; people, he said, have no other basis for projecting what life might be like on other worlds (an idea expressed, too, by Teilhard and Stephen Hawking; see above). He thought that life might have evolved somewhere in distant space: there is a slight chance that it emerged within a radius of 100 light years from the sun, but a much greater chance that it evolved within 250 light years. He stated: "Let's grant the dream of many science fiction writers and astronomers alike that civilized E.T.s are out there."[72] He thought that this proposal could be explored and projected by combining

---

71. Wilson, *Social Conquest*, 296–97. After reading Wilson's remarks in *Social Conquest*, since we were acquaintances and wrote complementary complimentary blurbs for each other's 2006 book and corresponded periodically, I sent him an email stating that there were more details than "fuzzy lights" to indicate the presence and activities of Otherkind, and I described some of them. He did not respond directly to me, but in his very next book, *Meaning*, he has an entire chapter that states that intelligent beings exist elsewhere in the cosmos, and posits possible common characteristics they share with life on Earth.

72. Wilson, *Meaning of Human Existence*, 113.

knowledge of the process of human evolution and the evolution of millions of other species in the diversity of Earth life. It is possible thereby "to produce a logical albeit very crude hypothetical portrait of human-grade aliens on Earth-like planets."[73] (He does not ponder the possibility of *panspermia*, as Hawking did.) He goes on to suggest likely characteristics of ETI,[74] drawing on his expertise as an evolutionary biologist. These would include:

- *E.T.s are fundamentally land-dwellers, not aquatic*: they needed to be in order to develop an energy source, such as controlled fire, to assist technological advancement;

- *E.T.s are relatively large animals*: small animals mean smaller brains, less intelligence, and less memory storage;

- *E.T.s are biologically audiovisual*: to enable auditory communication and unaided visual perception;

- *[E.T.'s] head is distinct, big, and located up front*: this enables quick scanning, integration, and action, provides high capacity memory banks, and enables key sensory input;

- *[E.T.s] possess light to moderate jaws and teeth*: evolving ET had an omnivorous, balanced diet, and "relied on cooperation and strategy rather than brute strength and combat";

- *[E.T.s] have a very high social intelligence*: they live in groups and have a complex social network, which advantages groups and individuals;

- *[E.T.s] have a small number of free locomotory appendages, levered for maximum strength with stiff internal or external skeletons composed of hinged segments (as by human elbows and knees), and with at least one pair of which are terminated by digits with pulpy tips used for sensitive touch and grasping*: these traits enable invention of artifacts that have a distinct nature and diverse designs;

- *[E.T.s] are moral*: they have cooperation among their members, some self-sacrifice, and a moral code—these are characteristic of highly social Earth species.

Wilson concludes the chapter declaring (contrary to and a balance for Hawking's fears of roving extraterrestrials) that humans have nothing to fear from ETI in terms of them conquering Earth. He provided "two good reasons why galactic conquests have never happened, nor even begun, and

---

73. Wilson, *Meaning of Human Existence*, 113.

74. Wilson, *Meaning of Human Existence*, 113; 113–17 elaborates these more extensively.

hence why our poor little planet has not been colonized and never will be."[75] The first was that organic beings have a "fatal weakness": their bodies carry microbiomes, symbiotic microorganisms, and so would have to bring with them crop plants, algae-equivalents, or even synthetic organisms so they would have food. Earth (and any other world not their own) has its own biological context, formed in distinct evolutionary processes; these would be incompatible with the living needs of alien life, whether intelligent or plant. Any effort to transplant would lead to a "biological train wreck."[76] (Sci-fi enthusiasts might recall here how Earth's people were saved from destruction in H. G. Wells's novel *War of the Worlds*: microbes killed the invaders.) A "vicious biological incompatibility . . . would doom interplanetary colonists."[77] Second, ETs intelligent enough to develop technology and vehicles to explore space would have realized the "lethal risk inherent in biological colonization."[78] They would have had to stabilize, ecologically and politically, their home planet—as suggested by Wright and Singer, above, in their response to Hawking. Neither Wilson nor Wright and Singer discuss the possibility that the "stability" might have resulted because a dominant, aggressive species competing with other species for needed natural goods or for hegemony on their world succeeded because they conquered (or extincted) competitor species—and might continue this type of conduct elsewhere, on other biota-inhabited worlds, especially if the biota were intelligent. Subsequently, they would use robots to explore other worlds to determine their habitability or even whether any needed or wanted natural goods that were to be found there could be exploited to their benefit. There would be no need to invade other planets unless they had destroyed their own. As Wilson states, if such an aggressive species were to invade other worlds, they would likely be biologically—microbially—endangered on arrival. Similarly, these factors would make it very difficult for humans to colonize other worlds in the future—or even to visit and explore them without advance assessment by robot explorers.

Wilson provided, in words complementary to those of Hawking at the conclusion of his *Guardian* article, a warning to those who think they can destroy Earth and migrate elsewhere: "There live among us today space enthusiasts who believe humanity can emigrate to another planet after using up this one. They should heed what I believe is a universal principle, for us and for all E.T.s: there exists only one habitable planet, and hence only one

---

75. Wilson, *Meaning of Human Existence*, 119.
76. Wilson, *Meaning of Human Existence*, 120.
77. Wilson, *Meaning of Human Existence*, 121.
78. Wilson, *Meaning of Human Existence*, 121.

chance at immortality for the species."[79] The "enthusiasts" have not considered adverse—especially, deadly—microbes that would likely defend their territory, albeit intuitively or instinctually, not because of an intellectual assessment of their altered ecological context.

On October 23, 2014, Big Think interviewed E. O. Wilson about *Meaning*. In his on-camera mini-lectures, which occurred shortly after the book was published, Wilson elaborated on what he had suggested about ET in the book.[80]

Wilson was very direct and affirmative about ETI life right at the outset of his Big Think presentation in his first sentence: "ET is out there." His reasoning is that

> there just has to be, in the hundred million star systems in the galaxy we dwell in, other cases of life originating, because we now know there're so many planets, that almost certainly you're going to have some of the planets that are Goldilocks—that is, the right position nearest their sun, the right size, and so on that can have the potential to create life, and of those it seems—and we don't have any basis for this, except intuition—that given enough millions of years (in our case we've had half a *billion* years since life came on the land) to produce a human grade eusocial species.[81]

Wilson then described the process he used in his book to propose and project ETI existence: he studied the origins and evolution of life on Earth, going back more than 450 million years, beginning with plants and on through multiple lines of animals. In light of his research, he stated, "I think that we can reasonably conclude that *eusociality*, when it did develop . . . is what they all have in common."[82] Wilson goes on to enumerate and discuss the characteristics of intelligent life, as described in *Meaning*. He says that ET have to be land animals: advanced societies need fire, a transportable energy source that could be used to fashion tools and then more intricate technology; the needed fire could not exist in marine settings. ETI has a head, up front, with a central organizing system that extends throughout their whole body; walks upright to free its limbs and fingers; a small number of limbs, perhaps up to eight, with fingers or tentacles that have soft pulpy tips (an Earth primate characteristic) for grasping and manipulating objects, especially food; ETIs

---

79. Wilson, *Meaning of Human Existence*, 121–22.
80. Big Think, "E.O. Wilson." The text of his narrative is transcribed here from the video and edited by the author.
81. Big Think, "E.O. Wilson," 0:01–1:06.
82. Big Think, "E.O. Wilson," 2:15–44.

would have to be omnivorous in order to have enough diverse food sources, and a large population to evolve and grow into a civilization. They must have the right size, appropriate to their planet, for mobility. Moreover, "they will have *moral instincts*, that is, they will be able to be generous, to at least some extent, caring, and altruistic not just to individuals of their own species, but to other species."[83] Probably "all of the eusocial creatures that produced advanced societies did so by group selection, and a capacity for moral instincts."[84] This follows evolutionary patterns: "By Darwinian superiority of cooperation within a group you have the capacity for a moral system within a group" and, to a lesser extent between groups.[85] "Selfish individuals beat altruistic individuals in a group where both exist . . . But in competition between groups, which is absolutely intense . . . groups of altruists defeat groups of selfish individuals."[86] In evolution, the behaviors balance each other, and their instability leads to the creative behaviors and development characteristic of civilization.

E. O. Wilson added his considerable scientific expertise in biology and the weight of his substantial professional credibility to strengthen people's thinking that there are extraterrestrial intelligent beings: ETI is real and, just as is the case for humankind, has a place in the cosmos. While reports of sightings of intelligently controlled UFOs must still be evaluated as to their merits, they cannot rationally be dismissed out of hand because some people, however well-educated and well-intentioned, do not *believe* that they exist.

Science and Religion Complementarity

Thoughtful consideration of the relationship between the ideas expressed by humanist scientists and by scientists who write from a religious tradition uncovers the compatibility of their insights.

As a priest-scientist, Teilhard de Chardin integrated science and faith: "Considered objectively, material facts *have in them something of the Divine*."[87] In a complementary way, E. O. Wilson stated in *The Creation* that representatives of science and religion should

> meet on the near side of metaphysics in order to deal with the real world we share . . . I suggest that we set aside our differences in order to save the Creation. The defense of living Nature is

83. Big Think, "E.O. Wilson," 7:23–40.
84. Big Think, "E.O. Wilson," 7:48–56.
85. Big Think, "E.O. Wilson," 8:09–22.
86. Big Think, "E.O. Wilson," 8:48–9:40.
87. Teilhard, "Modes," 29.

a universal value . . . it serves without distinction the interests of all humanity . . . The Creation—living Nature—is in deep trouble.[88]

You may well ask at this point, why me? Because religion and science are the two most powerful forces in the world today, including especially the United States. If religion and science could be united on the common ground of biological conservation, the problem would soon be solved. If there is any moral precept shared by peoples of all beliefs, it is that we owe ourselves and future generations a beautiful, rich, and healthful environment.[89]

Abraham (Avi) Loeb (1962–present)

Avi Loeb[90] is Frank B. Baird Jr. Professor of Science (a position held previously by E. O. Wilson) and Chair of the Astronomy Department, Harvard University. He is Director, Institute for Theory and Computation (ITC); Founding Director, Black Hole Initiative (BHI); Chair, *Breakthrough Starshot* Advisory Committee; and Vice Chair, Board on Physics and Astronomy, National Academies.

Loeb attracted international attention in 2019 when he suggested, after 'Oumuamua was discovered hurtling through the solar system, that an alien craft might be in our solar system neighborhood.[91] A front-page article in the *Washington Post* that reported this caught my attention: "Harvard's Top Astronomer Says an Alien Ship May Be Among Us—and He Doesn't Care What His Colleagues Think." I read it with great interest and subsequently contacted him at Harvard via email for additional information about his work. He graciously sent me links to various published articles, some of which were coauthored and printed in scientific journals, such as the *Astrophysical Journal*, and others of which were published in periodicals, such as *Scientific American*, more accessible to the general public. Loeb is a distinguished scientist who is located in what is currently a small niche in scientific circles: he is open to human Contact with intelligent beings (whose existence he thinks likely: humans should have a "cosmic modesty"—they should not

---

88. Wilson, *Creation*, 4.

89. Wilson, *Creation*, 5.

90. See Loeb's professor profile page here: https://astronomy.fas.harvard.edu/people/avi-loeb. See also Harvard University, "Profile." Loeb narrates his biography, from his childhood on an Israeli farm to being a Harvard professor.

91. Selk, "Harvard's Top Astronomer."

think that they are the only intelligent beings in the universe); to confirmation that objects (such as 'Oumuamua) are alien probes; and to sightings of and encounters with other craft which are under intelligent beings' control from within or from afar—even as close as in or near the solar system.

Loeb's perspective differs markedly from that of the scientists who publicly reject any possibility of Visitors' existence, let alone their visibility in the heavens, because they require "hard evidence" (Allen Hynek's CE-II category). Until that happens, they say, effectively, "Where's the proof?" Physical proof of some sort must be in hand; credible witness reports, or even other scientists' assessments of available data, are not sufficient.

Loeb's view differs, too, from that of scientists who accept more readily the direct statements of credible witnesses who are convinced that they have seen intelligently controlled UAP, or scientists whose analyses of astronomical data gathered by telescopes around the world lead them to accept that life, including intelligent life, might be abundant in the universe. They base their assessment on scientific evidence, such as that there are billions of planets in the Milky Way Galaxy alone, among which are billions in the Goldilocks zone; they share Stephen Hawking's assertion, based on reasoning by his "mathematical mind," that it is "rational" to say that life, including intelligent life, exists on other worlds. A complementary component of scientists integrates "hard evidence" and credible witness reports that they have been pursuing directly by interviewing the witnesses; these scientists include astronomer Allen Hynek and astrophysicist and computer scientist Jacques Vallée.

Selk's *Washington Post* article mentions that when he visited Loeb and became curious about papers on Loeb's desk, Loeb told him that those equations are a calculation that supports his theory that, in Selk's words, "an extraterrestrial spacecraft, or at least a piece of one, may at this moment be flying past the orbit of Jupiter." When 'Oumuamua became more visible to space telescopes as it flew across the solar system unaffected by the sun's gravity, Selk reports that because of Loeb's reputation, his "extraordinarily confident suggestion that it probably came from another civilization could not be easily dismissed." Selk notes that Loeb had cowritten an article in November, with his colleague Shmuel Bialy, in the *Astrophysical Journal* letters section, in which they suggested that "Considering an artificial origin, one possibility is that "Oumuamua' . . . is a lightsail, floating in interstellar space as a debris from an advanced technological equipment."

In an essay published at Harvard, "Are We Really the Smartest Kid on the Block?"[92] Loeb wonders whether inhabitants of now-disappeared ancient civilizations in the universe were more intelligent than humankind is today.

92. Loeb, "Are We."

He notes that the kinds of headlines and stories on the front pages of our newspapers might prompt us—and beings in space who might review them and the types of television programs that humans have been inadvertently broadcasting into space—to question ourselves about our intelligence level.[93] He goes on to state that when seeking signs of intelligence in the universe, "the key challenge to improving our awareness of other civilizations is whether we are intelligent enough to adequately interpret their signals or a piece of their technological equipment." He suggests what might be the consequences of some scientists' refusal to acknowledge that other intelligent life exists, and have decided beforehand that it does not:

> If we assign a zero prior probability for evidence coming our way, as some scientists did in the case of 'Oumuamua by stating "it's never aliens," we will indeed never find any evidence for aliens . . . In effect, the adoption of self-imposed blinders signals lack of intelligence . . . The problem with adopting the wrong attitude is that it delays scientific progress. By bracketing the range of possibilities in advance, we might never discover the unexpected.

Loeb goes on to state that "an obvious obstacle to identifying our neighbors is the limitation of our imagination to what we find at home." Rather, he suggests, scientists should be "searching with our best telescopes for unusual electromagnetic flashes, industrial pollution of planetary atmospheres, artificial light or heat, artificial space debris, or something completely unexpected." His exasperation with scientific self-limitation parallels Allen Hynek's frustration when he was the US government's scientific consultant on UFOs. His role was to investigate witnesses' stories that they had seen UFOs that were apparently intelligently controlled, and "debunk them" scientifically. Hynek observed that he and other government-related scientists were not supposed to analyze these reports with an open mind. The government, and scientists other than Hynek, had determined a priori that there was no intelligent life in space, and therefore there could not be intelligently controlled UFOs.

In an extensive, insightful, and in-depth transcribed interview with Ben Johnson for the Endless Thread program, "Harvard Astronomer on Why Aliens Aren't Science Fiction,"[94] Loeb argues in the section "On Uncertainty in Scientific Research" that scientists should release information about

---

93. In a related comment, John Hedley Brooke, Emeritus Professor of the History of Science, Oxford University, told me, when I requested from him a book blurb for the cover of *Cosmic Commons*, that he thought that the greatest proof that there is no intelligent life in space is that there is none on Earth. He did write the book endorsement.

94. Swartz, "Harvard Astronomer." WBUR is Boston's NPR station.

current scientific speculation, rather than wait until they have resolved a particular matter. His view is that "I think we would get much more credibility if we were to show the process of uncertainty and the fact that scientists do not agree with each other when the evidence is not clear."[95] In the section of the interview specifically titled "On Why Aliens Are More Than Science Fiction," Loeb states that "I don't see extraterrestrials as more speculative than dark matter or extra dimensions. I think it's the other way around . . . And the reason is that we exist and that we know that about a quarter of all the planets in the Milky Way galaxy have conditions similar to those on Earth."[96] (Loeb's words recall Stephen Hawking's conclusions, based on thinking about this with his "mathematical mind": since humankind exists, and there are so many Goldilocks-zone planets in the Milky Way, it is likely that there are other intelligent beings in space.) In the section "On Whether Life On Earth Came From Somewhere Other Than Earth," Loeb provides a concise assessment of *panspermia*:

> That's quite possible. In fact, we know that all forms of life on Earth have the same chirality, it's all left handed, the molecules [are] arranged in some special way. And one way to do that is by bringing life from outside and planting it here. What could do that? A piece of rock that flew from Mars, for example, landed on Earth. And we know that such rocks exist that could have carried life in [them]. But another possibility is directed seeding of life . . . another civilization sending out life in tubes . . . I wouldn't say it's likely but it's possible.[97]

Loeb considered *panspermia* in greater depth in two recent coauthored articles: "Implications of Captured Interstellar Objects for Panspermia and Extraterrestrial Life"[98]; and "Galactic Panspermia."[99] Their respective conclusions merit reflective consideration.

In "Implications," after extensive scientific investigations coupled with mathematical computations, the authors conclude:

> We have found that it would be easier to detect smaller interstellar objects at closer distances by means of reflected sunlight, while larger objects at greater distances are more detectable

---

95. Swartz, "Harvard Astronomer," para. 5.
96. Swartz, "Harvard Astronomer," para. 6.
97. Swartz, "Harvard Astronomer," para. 19.
98. Loeb and Lingam, "Implications of Captured Interstellar Objects."
99. Ginsburg et al., "Galactic Panspermia." (Other scientist authors referenced in the article have been omitted to conserve space; they are found in the original "Galactic" article.)

through their thermal radiation due to radiogenic heating. The calibrated number density of interstellar objects, based on the detection of 'Oumuamua, allowed us to estimate the capture rate of such bodies by means of three-body interactions for both our Solar system and stellar binaries such as the nearby α-Centauri. We have found that a few thousand captured interstellar objects might be found within the Solar system at any time. The largest of these would be an object with radius tens of km. For the α-Centauri A&B system, we have found that even Earth-sized objects could have been captured through this process and that Moon-sized objects may currently exist in circumstellar orbits . . . Our findings have potentially important implications for the origin and evolution of life on Earth. If a km-sized interstellar object were to strike the Earth, we suggested that it would result in pronounced local changes, although the global effects may be transient. Habitable planets could have been seeded by means of panspermia through two different channels: (i) direct impact of interstellar objects, and (ii) temporary capture of the interstellar object followed by interplanetary panspermia. There are multiple uncertainties involved in all panspermia models, as the probability of alien microbes surviving ejection, transit and reentry remains poorly constrained despite recent advancements. The Solar system acts as a fishing net, enabling us to search for traces of extraterrestrial life locally (due to the presence of captured interstellar objects) as opposed to sending interstellar probes. The same approach is also applicable to the search for extraterrestrial artifacts within our Solar system.

In the complementary conclusion of "Galactic," Loeb and his coauthors state:

There is no doubt that rocky material can easily be exchanged between nearby planets, such as Mars and Earth or the planets of the TRAPPIST-1 system. Thus, nearly all papers on panspermia focus on Galactic Panspermia interactions within a Solar system . . . In this paper we conclusively show that panspermia is viable on galactic scales . . . objects with lower velocities are in general far more likely to be captured. However, for sufficiently long biological survival lifetimes, the probability of capturing a life-bearing object . . . can be significant . . . However, the capture probability for an intergalactic object is extremely low. If bacteria and other possible extremophiles have sufficiently long survival lifetimes, the GC can act as an engine for panspermia and seed the entire galaxy. While the exact survival lifetimes of bacteria [are] unknown, it is clear that bacteria can survive for at least millions of years ... although panspermia appears most likely to transfer bacteria and other microbes, it may also transfer more complex organisms. Consequently, viruses will invariably be a part of panspermia ... Biological studies strongly suggest that viruses have long been an influential driving mechanism for the evolution of life on Earth, including human evolution ... Every place where there is life on Earth, there are also viruses. An integral part of the biosphere, viruses are by far the most prolific entities on Earth ... and can survive in extreme environments such as Arctic conditions [and] around hydrothermal vents ... There are a number of possible ways to detect extrasolar objects that could potentially contain biotic material. Arguably the simplest method is simply detecting an object passing through the solar system. The first such fortuitous encounter was with 1I/2017 U1 ('Oumuamua) ... there may exist ~103 'Oumuamua–like captured objects currently within our Solar system ... If panspermia operates on galactic scales, it may be that there are little or no habitable exoplanets without life. Consequently, if a survey of exoplanetary atmospheres across the Milky Way found that nearly all habitable planets had biosignatures, this would be strong evidence for galactic panspermia ... Intelligent and technologically sophisticated species that are long-lived will at some point either need to settle a new planet, or simply wish to do so (directed panspermia). Distinguishing between natural panspermia and directed panspermia will be challenging. However, detecting biosignatures on a planet that is not within a habitable zone might be indirect evidence for directed panspermia. Such an argument is significantly strengthened if the same signature is detected on a nearby habitable planet.

Panspermia seems ever more likely a source of life on Earth and other worlds, then, but not necessarily the only source.

Philosophy and Science: An Extraordinary Correlation

A remarkable cross-millennia connection has been made between philosophy and science—from the speculations of philosophers in ancient Greece to the scientific data of astrophysicists in the twenty-first century. *Panspermia*, first proposed more than two thousand years ago by Greek philosophers, is being confirmed by scientists today as a viable theory of one possible origin of life on Earth—and elsewhere, too, not only in the Milky Way Galaxy but in the vastness of the cosmos.[100] Along the way, between the time of

---

100. People familiar with the Ridley Scott sci-film "Prometheus" might recall its first

the ruminations of the philosophers and the research of the scientists, the idea of a "plurality of worlds" was debated. It reached a climax in the thirteenth century when medieval theologians considered the question. Thomas Aquinas opposed the idea, drawing on Aristotle, and was posthumously excommunicated for this position—temporarily—by the Catholic Church. His assertion seemed to contradict the doctrine of an omnipotent God. Church theologians resolved the issue by teaching that while God could have created a plurality of worlds, God chose not to do so. In the past century, because of scientific and technological advances, the debate has been definitively resolved in favor of a plurality of worlds.

Space telescopes continue to find increasing numbers of planets, many of which have at least microbial life, some of which might have intelligent life. It is likely that, by the end of the twenty-first century, Contact will have been made between TI and ETI/IDI, and have been sustained for a sufficiently long time that there is no longer any doubt that ETI/IDI exists. Thinking optimistically, it might be that the outcome of the encounter will have been beneficial for all species.

Cosmic Seeding and Creation Stories

In the twenty-first century, scientists' conjecture about the possibility—or even likelihood—of *panspermia* is on the rise, although still confined to the speculations of a small minority of scientists. Stephen Hawking and Avi Loeb, as noted earlier, are among the scientists who speculate about *panspermia*. But, as footnoted earlier, articles about *panspermia* were published in such science-based magazines as *Astronomy* and *Astrobiology*; this might indicate a more extensive interest in the topic than currently known, among scientists and the general public. However, universal acceptance of *panspermia* is not inevitable and, even if it is shown to have occurred and is still occurring, it is not necessarily the sole source of life on cosmos worlds. For one thing, even if it is occurring today and has been occurring for millions or billions of years, it still had an origin point—a cosmos moment when life emerged from the chaotic beginning of the seen and unseen cosmos. For another thing, it might be possible too, then, that however that occurred eons ago, it might still occur today: in other worlds, life might have originated, or continues to

---

scene, when a humanoid descends to a planet on a pod from a spacecraft. He dives into a waterfall and, in the pool below, his body disintegrates into its component molecules. Water-dwelling life begins to come into being. It is likely that few moviegoers realized that *panspermia* was illustrated in the scene. Later in the film, the human astronauts voyage into the cosmos in search of the "engineers" who are said to have originated the beginning of life on the humans' planet.

be originated, from abiotic sources, and eventually evolves into intelligent life. (Currently, substantial biological research focuses on just how biota emerged from abiotic milieus.)

Should *panspermia*, as the only way or as one of the ways life came to be on cosmos worlds, come to be accepted as scientific fact—for all life in the universe, or for some life on some worlds in the universe—a rethinking of some religions' understandings of a Creator's work of creation might have to occur. *Ex nihilo* (or, as this writer thinks, perhaps *ex deus*, since creation is birthed by or emanates from Spirit creativity) would still be a possibility as the primal source of the *spermia* wandering the cosmos, but not the only possibility. In this case, "let there be life" would describe metaphorically a biotic beginning billions of years ago or more: Life, or the seeds of life, might be still understood to have been created by the Spirit, but long before Earth, and worlds similar to Earth in other galaxies, emerged.

Panspermia, then, would not contradict the underlying myth and message of Genesis 1 and other creation stories. Rather, it would mean that the seeds of life came into being during the eons after the "Primeval Atom" explosion (later called derisively the "Big Bang") on a "Day Without Yesterday," first theorized by Belgian priest-scientist Georges Lemaître (1894-1966),[101] that occurred almost 14 billion years ago. It would have come about before the formation of the Milky Way Galaxy and, billions of years later, the solar system in which Earth is located.

The Genesis 1 creation myth's presentation of Yahweh's creating words, "Let there be light" and "let there be a greater light to rule the day and a lesser light to rule the night," might be seen today to refer to the formation of the galaxy and solar system, not the origins of the universe as a whole—or, allegorically, the words could be a reference to the multiple origins of universes, galaxies, and solar systems. This understanding need not, necessarily, contradict a biblical literalist's understanding of the story; it would extend that understanding to multiple origin points, over eons, in the universe's story.

As did Teilhard, I have wondered to what extent biblical and theological narratives might be understood (or reimagined) to be complementary to or compatible with scientific knowledge as it evolves and expands. A certain flexibility of teachings is required, which allows for an adaptation to or incorporation of new understandings. In the Middle Ages, scientists such as Isaac Newton (1642-1727) said that they were "thinking God's thoughts after Him." They were not imposing science on religion as their work expanded, and embraced and enhanced scientific knowledge. Sometimes

---

101. Lemaître, "Homogeneous Universe." Lemaître had earned two PhDs, one in mathematics at the Université Catholique de Louvain, and the other in science at the Massachusetts Institute of Technology. See Hart, *Cosmic Commons: Spirit*, 165-69.

science seemed to be heretical in the view of some church leaders. The words of Augustine in his discussion of the relationship between science and Bible in his commentary on Genesis are instructive here. Augustine taught that when there is a conflict between science and the Bible, the Bible should be understood allegorically. The Bible is neither a science book nor a history book. It contains elements of both science and history, as understood in the several time periods during which it was being written, but is fundamentally a religious book. Its religious teachings and illustrative myths are intended to convey its writers' insights, not to be read as literally "true."[102] The parables of Jesus are understood similarly, not as statements about actual historical events, but as moral narratives drawn from real-life situations.

Science, Religion, and Space: The Vatican Observatory

Science-religion and TI-ETI Contact discussions have begun to include insights about ETI existence from scientists who have been members of or related to a religious tradition. The Vatican, for example, has been studying the universe for several centuries, striving to understand creation better. The Vatican Observatory, founded in the late nineteenth century, is now at the heart of this endeavor. For almost a century, at least, a part of this study has apparently included a search for possible extraterrestrial intelligent life—perhaps, in part, because astronomers viewing the night sky through Observatory telescopes in Rome and at the University of Arizona have unexpectedly seen UAP that are anomalous, following no known laws of physics and therefore apparently intelligently controlled. In 2008 the then–Director of the Vatican Observatory, astronomer José Gabriel Funes, SJ, unexpectedly told a reporter[103] that ETI beings probably exist and are more intelligent than humans.[104] He stated further that ETI should be regarded in the spirit of St. Francis, who taught that people should relate to all creatures as "brother" and "sister." The Vatican Observatory seems today to be infused with the spirit of Teilhard de Chardin as it integrates science—including evolution and astrophysics—and faith in its diverse projects.

---

102. Biblical "inspiration," "myth," and "interpretation" are discussed in Hart, *Cosmic Commons*, 149–53.

103. Funes, "L'extraterrestre è mio fratello." English translation by the author. An earlier discussion, and the original paragraph in Italian, is found in Hart, *Cosmic Commons*, 263–65.

104. See the Vatican site on ETL at: https://www.vofoundation.org/faith-and-science/life-in-the-universe/extraterrestrial-life/. There are several articles on a variety of ETL topics. See generally the Vatican "Faith and Science" website at: https://www.vofoundation.org/faith-and-science/.

Pope Francis I on Extraterrestrials

Pope Francis explored the topic of ETI existence in an address to the Pontifical Academy of Science on October 27, 2014. In his comments, he linked evolution on Earth to evolution on other worlds in the cosmos; he affirmed that both processes had occurred. He stated, in this regard, that "Evolution in nature is not in contrast with the notion of creation." He understands that evolution, not specific individual creations, is the way that God's creativity continues. He rejects creationist literal interpretations of the Genesis creation stories, observing that "When we read in Genesis the account of creation, we risk imagining God as a magician, with a wand able to make everything. But it is not so."

Francis described a complementarity between creation-evolution on Earth and on other worlds in the universe:

> [God] created beings and allowed them to develop . . . and to arrive at their fulness of being. He gave autonomy to the beings of the universe at the same time at which he assured them of his continuous presence, giving being to every reality.[105]

This brief passage contains several significant elements. God created all beings, and "allowed them to develop": evolution, as science has learned and the Catholic Church has affirmed, is the process by which creatures "develop" over time. This development through evolution is not controlled by God: creatures have "autonomy" in the process. This autonomy is given, too, to the "beings of the universe," that is, to intelligent living beings that have evolved on other worlds: they, too, understand that God's continuous presence is immanent in the universe, "giving being to every reality."

Intelligent ETI and IDI, then, have evolved on their worlds just as intelligent TI have evolved on Earth. If humans accept this, then while they are, naturally, realistically cautious at Contact, they should not be overly fearful of encountering ETI on Earth or in the heavens, nor doubt that ETI and IDI have been Visitors to Earth.

Science-Based and -Related Astrobiology-Focused Investigations

After centuries in denial, the scientific community in recent decades has affirmed that ETI/IDI exist in space or in other dimensions than the one in which humankind exists.

---

105. *ExoNews TV*, "Pope Endorses Evolution." The Vatican's news story on the Pontifical Academy event has been removed from the Vatican website.

Breakthrough Initiatives

A series of privately funded activities oriented toward finding intelligent life in space, the Breakthrough Initiatives, was founded in 2015 by Russian computer technology billionaire Yuri Milner and his wife, Julia Milner. The research and ideas of Avi Loeb and the late Stephen Hawking were discussed earlier in this chapter; both were members of its initial (and ongoing) Management and Advisory Board. Loeb continues in this capacity.

Breakthrough Listen describes its rationale (which includes questions posed earlier in this chapter), and its own and other Breakthrough projects on its website:

> *We are here.*
>
> Circling one star among hundreds of billions, in one galaxy among a hundred billion more, in a Universe that is vast and expanding ever faster—perhaps toward infinity. In the granular details of daily life, it's easy to forget that we live in a place of astonishing grandeur and mystery.
>
> The Breakthrough Initiatives are a program of scientific and technological exploration, probing the big questions of life in the Universe: Are we alone? Are there habitable worlds in our galactic neighborhood? Can we make the great leap to the stars? And can we think and act *together*—as one world in the cosmos?
>
> *Where is everybody?*
>
> So wondered the great physicist Enrico Fermi. The Universe is ancient and immense. Life, he reasoned, has had plenty of time to get started – and get smart. But we see no evidence of anything alive or intelligent in space. In the last five years, we have discovered that planets in the habitable zone of stars are common. Based on the numbers discovered so far, there are estimated to be billions more in our galaxy alone. Yet we are still in the dark about life. Are we really alone? Or are there others out there?
>
> It's one of the biggest questions. And only science can answer it.
>
> Breakthrough Listen is a $100 million program of astronomical observations in search of evidence of intelligent life beyond Earth. It is by far the most comprehensive, intensive and sensitive search ever undertaken for artificial radio and optical signals. A complete survey of the 1,000,000 nearest stars, the plane and center of our galaxy, and the 100 nearest galaxies. All data will be open to the public.
>
> Breakthrough Message is a $1 million competition to design a message representing Earth, life, and humanity that could

potentially be understood by another civilization. The aim is to encourage humanity to think together as one world, and to spark public debate about the ethics of sending messages beyond Earth.

Where can life flourish?

In August 2016, a potentially habitable Earth-like planet was discovered orbiting Proxima Centauri—the Sun's nearest neighbor. Based on the most recent astronomical data, it is likely that there are other such planets in our cosmic neighborhood. With technology now or soon available, it will be possible not only to find them, but to analyze whether they have atmospheres—and whether those atmospheres contain oxygen and other potential signatures of primitive life.

Breakthrough Watch is a multi-million dollar astronomical program to develop Earth- and space-based technologies that can find Earth-like planets in our cosmic neighborhood—and try to establish whether they host life.

Can we reach the stars?

Life in the Universe does not only mean extraterrestrials. It also means us. No other beings have yet visited us—but neither have we stepped out to the galactic stage. Are we destined to belong to Earth for as long as we survive? Or can we reach the stars?

If we can, the natural first step is our nearest star system, Alpha Centauri—four light years away.

Breakthrough Starshot is a $100 million research and engineering program aiming to demonstrate proof of concept for a new technology, enabling ultra-light unmanned space flight at 20% of the speed of light; and to lay the foundations for a flyby mission to Alpha Centauri within a generation.

The Breakthrough Initiatives were founded in 2015 by Yuri and Julia Milner to explore the Universe, seek scientific evidence of life beyond Earth, and encourage public debate from a planetary perspective.[106]

Breakthrough Initiatives projects are visionary and, simultaneously, science- and technology-based in their current and projected activities. Its members consider on-the-ground Earth realities experienced by humans, and imagine out-in-space cosmos explorations to find and communicate with ETI/IDI. The Breakthrough projects are inspired and guided by hope for a future in which the human conflicts on Earth, and ecological devastation

---

106. See the "About" page on the Breakthrough Initiatives website: https://breakthroughinitiatives.org/about.

of Earth, will have ceased because humanity will have come together to embrace a species unity and engage in planetwide and exoplanetary projects. This would be an advance over the modest steps taken already through humanity's shared work in constructing, deploying, and utilizing the scientific resources and technologies of the International Space Station.

Center for UFO Studies (CUFOS)

The Center for UFO Studies[107] was founded by Allen Hynek in 1973. On its website, CUFOS describes its work: "The Center for UFO Studies (CUFOS) is an international group of scientists, academics, investigators, and volunteers dedicated to the continuing examination and analysis of the UFO phenomenon. Our purpose is to promote serious scientific interest in UFOs and their study, and to serve as an archive for reports, documents, and publications about the UFO phenomenon." A non-membership organization, CUFOS invites people "to become involved in CUFOS activities, which can include archival work, assistance with our UFOCAT database, historical case research, current research in both the physical and social sciences on various types of UFO reports, or statistical analysis of sighting data. To volunteer your assistance, contact us at Infocenter@cufos.org."

Mutual UFO Network (MUFON)

The Mutual UFO Network[108] was founded originally as the Midwest UFO Network in 1969. Its members realized quickly that membership and discussions needed to be expanded, and it transitioned into the Mutual UFO Network. Its mission is the "Scientific Study of UFOs for the Benefit of Humanity." Its goals are "I. Investigate UFO sightings and collect the data in the MUFON Database for use by researchers worldwide. II. Promote research on UFOs to discover the true nature of the phenomenon, with an eye towards scientific breakthroughs, and improving life on our planet. III. Educate the public on the UFO phenomenon and its potential impact on society." MUFON has a television station and a monthly journal.

MUFON trains field investigators to go to sites where UFOs have been reported to have appeared, evaluate area evidence, and assess the credibility of witnesses who claim to have seen a UFO. One such MUFON field

107. See the CUFOS website at http://www.cufos.org/.
108. See MUFON's website: https://www.mufon.com/. The site provides a history of MUFON and its ongoing work to investigate UFO stories—through conferences, publications, and members' collaborative efforts. It has continually updated reports on UFO sightings from around the world, which are printed in a monthly report to members.

investigation, to the site of a purported UFO sighting in Montana in 1870, is described in Appendix 1.

SoCIA

The work of CUFOS and MUFON is complemented by an interdisciplinary organization of scientist, social scientist, and humanist college and university faculty members organized in 2016: SoCIA (Social and Conceptual Issues in Astrobiology).

The SoCIA website[109] states that the organization's efforts complement NASA objectives:

> NASA's chief scientist recently announced what those in astrobiology have known for some time: "I think we're going to have strong indications of life beyond Earth within a decade, and I think we're going to have definitive evidence within 20 to 30 years." If she is right, we are on the brink of one of the most important discoveries in human history. Should this come to pass, we will immediately confront a series of extremely complex challenges that cannot be resolved without strong input from disciplines other than the sciences. NASA's vision for astrobiology, as well as nascent European efforts, are far ranging and include broad questions about the future of life in the universe. Yet these issues have received much less attention than the hard science. SoCIA . . . is designed to help correct this deficit, starting a wider conversation on these matters, and perhaps even sowing the seeds for a new academic society.

The questions posed by SoCIA overlap or complement those of NASA and other scientists reflecting on life in the cosmos:

> What is life? What are our ethical obligations to extraterrestrial life? To non-living features of the extraterrestrial environment? Should humans seek to exploit and/or colonize space? If so, how should this be done? Are there truly universal principles of biology, psychology, morality, etc. that would apply to extraterrestrial life? What impact will the discovery of extraterrestrial life have on human society? On religion? What is the status of astrobiology: a science, a proto-science, a speculative enterprise, or what? Should we be actively searching for extraterrestrial life? Messaging potential alien homeworlds?

---

109. See SoCIA's website at https://socia.space/.

Distinguished scientists and humanists have come to realize that they should think seriously about the possibility and project the characteristics of ExoEarth life. Considerations of astrobiology, based in part on extrapolations from Earth's biota, provide a way for science to understand (or at least to propose), at least tentatively, what might be characteristics of other life in the cosmos. These are complemented well by the necessary accompaniment of a humanist consciousness and reasoning. Together, the sciences and humanities enable humankind to develop an integrated, coherent approach to engaging with life—as we know it or decidedly different than how we know it—as humans venture into the cosmos . . . or open themselves to close encounters of the third kind with ETI on Earth.

A shortcoming of SoCIA, as with NASA and other government-based agencies, is that it generally avoids any considerations of the existence of InterDimensional Intelligent Life or ExtraTerrestrial Intelligent Life (except for the last question above, which hints that there might be ETI who might hear and—positively or negatively—respond to the messages humans send). NASA's and SoCIA's respective positions on ETI, and their practices that follow from them, enable these organizations to evade publicly the harder questions. In the past, a difficult question for both to consider publicly would have been, "How might humans respond or react when TI/ETI/IDI Contact occurs?"—as if this had not happened already. Today, the question should be, How might humans respond or react to TI/ETI/IDI Contact in light of evidenced CE-I and CE-II encounters and credible witnesses' reports? It might be that, under the guise of a "no scientific proof of Contact" stance, deeper psychological factors, as discussed earlier, are at work, as well as fears of professional consequences for even mentioning curiosity about, let alone scientific investigations into, Contact narratives. As seen, too, the US government tries to cover up the information it has, and uses covert spy agencies to falsify Contact events, in order to hide what has been occurring, and to discredit credible witness reports.

A hopeful element in all of this is that NASA still does extraordinary space exploration with telescopes, space voyagers, and rovers; this provides excellent information for every interested scientist to probe the solar system and beyond in more depth. SoCIA, for its part, gathers an interdisciplinary group that will be compelled to study Contact events when they become globally obvious. This already-existing interdisciplinary organization that focuses on the inevitably-come-true Contact in a few years will be of immense importance to the human psyche and the human quest—to find a new niche, or to have a continuing niche in a cosmos far more complex than imagined previously.

Scientists' analytical search for physical evidence of ETI/IDI, and the associated work by organizations comprised of scientists and humanists from diverse fields, are complemented by narratives related by Indians from the US, as well as by indio/as from the Americas south of the Rio Grande. In the next chapter, the stories and experiences of native peoples who have had direct or indirect encounters with Otherkind are presented.

Indigenous peoples' narratives about Star People interacting with native peoples have been passed down through millennia in oral traditions. Elders and healers Phillip Deere and David Sohappy Sr., and people interviewed by Ardy Sixkiller Clarke, elaborate these historical accounts. Harvard psychiatrist John Mack became interested in diverse people's stories about "abductions" (including stories of indigenous elders from three continents), and interviewed them. Elders' narratives and Mack's other interviewees' stories follow.

5

Abductions and Indigenous Peoples' Encounters

John Mack, Phillip Deere, David Sohappy, Ardy Sixkiller Clarke

Stories about people being abducted by intelligent alien beings began to catch the attention of the news media in the twentieth century. Initially, most of the general public derisively dismissed them or ignored them. Scientists characteristically asked, absent abundant material proof that these events had occurred, "Where's the evidence?" Eventually and inevitably, news stories by credible witnesses were complemented by science fiction novels, short stories, and movies. Gradually, as non-fiction narratives grew in number, some people began to accept them as true. In 1994, Harvard psychiatrist and Pulitzer Prize recipient John Mack published *Abduction*, which became a national best-seller. It stimulated, even among some scientists, acceptance of the possibility that other-than-human intelligent beings have been visiting Earth—or at least Earth's solar system neighborhood. Some of the Visitors, it was reported, had literally taken people for a ride aboard their spacecraft.

Acceptance of the reality that Visitors were visiting Earth was a relatively recent phenomenon. It was augmented by reports that a saucer-like object or two crashed on a cattle ranch near Roswell, New Mexico, in 1947. Outside Euroamerican-dominated cities, towns, and news media, however, such stories were not new. Traditional Indian peoples in the United States, and in the Americas more broadly, had passed down through generations oral narratives that described "star people" or "sky people" who occasionally visited indigenous peoples and, in some oral narratives, had sexual intercourse with them and are understood to be their ancestors. At times, in recent decades, ETI/IDI beings have abducted selected people for short periods of time ... or permanently. These narratives are being studied more closely now by professionals from the sciences and social sciences.

In this chapter, abductee (or "experiencer"—John Mack's term) stories will be described, and compared and contrasted with native peoples' narratives. There is some overlap evident in the stories, but also some difference. An interesting result of abductees' experiences is that many of them became interested in Indians' spirituality and ecological practices, noting how these are intertwined. After Contact, most abductees have become involved with native peoples' elders (spiritual and cultural leaders) and also engage, many for the first time, in projects to care for Earth, all peoples, and all living beings.

John Mack

John Mack (1929–2004) and Allen Hynek, from their widely divergent respective fields of psychiatry and astronomy, shared an initial assumption that people who claimed to have seen UFOs were either delusional or greatly mistaken. As happened with Hynek when he was confronted with evidence indicating otherwise, Mack changed his position. He came to recognize that UFOs were material phenomena, perhaps coming from a different dimension of reality, and were controlled by intelligent beings.

John Mack was born in New York City.[1] He received his bachelor's degree from Oberlin College (1951), his medical degree from the Harvard Medical School (cum laude, 1955), was a graduate of the Boston Psychoanalytic Society and Institute, and was board certified in child and adult psychoanalysis. In 1977, Mack received the Pulitzer Prize in Biography for *A Prince of Our Disorder*, the life of British officer T. E. Lawrence (known as Lawrence of Arabia). A social progressive, he was a member of Physicians for Social Responsibility (recipient of the 1985 Nobel Peace Prize). He was involved, along with astronomer Carl Sagan, in an act of civil disobedience in 1988 when, along with seven hundred other academics, they trespassed on a Nevada nuclear weapons test site and were arrested. As part of his academic work, he founded the Department of Psychiatry at Cambridge Hospital, which is now the Harvard Medical School teaching hospital. In 1994, Daniel C. Tosteson, Dean of Harvard Medical School, surreptitiously

---

1. Much of the biographical material on John Mack is derived from his biography on the John Mack Institute website: http://johnemackinstitute.org/biography-of-john-e-mack-m-d/.

appointed a committee to investigate Mack and find sufficient evidence to fire him because of his writing and lectures about UFO experiencers. After Mack found out about this effort and began to organize his defense, and the public learned about his case, the Dean reversed his position and instead affirmed Mack's right to academic freedom. He declared that Mack "remains a member in good standing of the Harvard Faculty of Medicine." The effort to dismiss him ended. Mack was killed in 2004 when struck by a drunken driver in London, where he had gone for an academic presentation.

Mack's explorations of the UFO phenomenon are elaborated principally in two books: *Abduction: Human Encounters with Aliens* (1994) and *Passport to the Cosmos: Human Transformation and Alien Encounters* (1999). (The latter title is reminiscent of Jacques Vallée's earlier book, *Passport to Magonia: From Folklore to Flying Saucers* [1969], which discusses the historical transformation, over centuries, of human perceptions of extraordinary objects they had observed in the skies and unusual beings they had seen on the ground.)

Abduction

In *Abduction*, Mack presents the narratives of representative people who state that they had been taken from Earth by extraterrestrial beings, and relocated to a spacecraft—once or several times. They are interviewed by Mack, then a distinguished Harvard University psychiatrist who was skeptical at first that "abductions" were real events; he thought that they were delusions. Then, in 1990, artist, writer, and ufologist Budd Hopkins described to Mack what the experiencers had related to him. Remarkably, people from around the United States who had had no contact with each other reported similar events and experiences. Some had sought psychiatric counseling. Subsequent to his meeting with Hopkins and his interviews with abductees, Mack selected for psychiatric assistance and study people who appeared to be the most credible and trustworthy participant-witnesses. He invited them to counseling sessions with him at Harvard. In these psychiatric evaluation meetings, he discovered that the abductees (or experiencers, as he preferred to call them) described consistently, without alteration, the event(s) they had experienced. They provided the same core details about the incidents whether they spoke to him with or without being brought by psychiatric analytic procedures to a regressive state. He used this comparative process several times in an individual's and individuals' separate treatment sessions. He used relaxation techniques, and sometimes hypnosis, to bring them to a deeper level of consciousness. He realized that the experiencers' narratives of events were identical over several sessions, becoming more in-depth over time. Moreover, diverse experiencers, who had had no prior contact with each other, provided overlapping and even identical descriptions of what they had undergone. One particularly telling incident along these lines occurred when an interviewee described the layout of the spacecraft to which they had been taken. Mack showed the experiencer a drawing. They[2] were amazed that he had so quickly drawn the craft's interior as per their description. He told the interviewee that he had not done the drawing just then as per what they had described—rather, another experiencer in an earlier session had provided this to him. Complementarily, experiencers "Dave" and "Julia" independently drew the same type of probing instrument that had been inserted into them; Dave drew it closed, and Julia, open.[3]

Mack describes his interview methods and sessions and, after each one, his reflections on them. At book's end, he discusses the narratives as a whole, and their impacts on him.

Representative experiencers' narratives provide insights into experiencer events and the insights, many complementary, that they had. Mack devotes individual chapters to specific representatives to tell their stories, and elaborates his analysis of them as he researches the abduction phenomenon. Space limitations preclude a more extensive description of chapters' contents:[4]

- "Sheila N." in chapter 4: Mack observes that "Sheila's case illustrates some of the issues that psychiatrists and other mental health professionals confront when working with abductees" and it "demonstrates typical features of the abduction phenomenon. These include frightening dreams that seem more real than ordinary nightmares, memories—some available consciously with others emerging under hypnosis—of intrusions into her bedroom by humanoid beings, and being taken into a strange enclosure and subjected to intrusive surgical-like procedures . . . The abduction phenomenon runs counter to the notions of reality of the Western scientific worldview. We believe it is simply not possible for these events to be taking place . . . But as Freud once said, theory does not prevent facts from showing up."[5]

- "Scott" in chapter 5: Scott had multiple experiences beginning at about age six; later, as an adult, Scott said that the trauma aspect of his experiences

2. Mack does not disclose the identities of the experiencers; "they" and "their" will be used to indicate, generically, male and female interviewees.

3. Mack, *Abduction*, 264.

4. Since multiple statements are included in the "experiencer" summaries, page ranges are provided for each person, rather than individual citations. The reader is encouraged to read Mack's books for an in-depth elaboration of these and other interviews.

5. Mack, *Abduction*, 69–90.

had "opened up the real stuff, the spiritual behind it"; at a different session with Mack, he described a blue light coming into his room one night, and "unexplained needle marks that had appeared on his arms several times"; during one abduction experience, after semen had been taken from him mechanically, the beings communicated with him telepathically that they were using him "as a father ... making babies"; Scott said that later, during a different session when he was older, the beings told him that humans were destroying Earth just like the abductors had destroyed their own planet and had to live underground, and now they intended to "live here" without humankind, unless "humans change".[6]

- "Joe" in chapter 8: Joe, as other abductees, had "many unexplained childhood nosebleeds"; on occasion Joe felt himself transition to an "alien form," in which he felt comfortable; travel through space occurs when "you just think yourself there"; Joe said that the hybridization program was evolutionary, to perpetuate the human seed and "crossbreed" with other species on the ships and elsewhere in the cosmos; "Joe's abduction-related experiences are as real—more real, he said on one occasion—than those that occur purely on the physical plane of reality, and there is no indication that he is psychiatrically disturbed or that these experiences are the product of some sort of psychopathology. As in virtually all abduction cases, this leaves us with the choice of searching—vainly, I think—for ways of explaining the phenomena within our existing world view, or, instead, of collapsing our rigid separation of psyche and reality, of inner and outer, and opening ourselves to expanded ontological possibilities."[7]

- "Dave" in chapter 12: "David has been drawn in particular to Pemsit Mountain, Pennsylvania, a place of Native American tradition and magic near his home, where many of his experiences have occurred. The universe has become for Dave a place filled with mystery and strange intelligence"; as have other experiencers, in regression Dave recounts events from earlier lives; "He grew up feeling a strong kinship with the Native Americans of the region"; Dave saw UFOs several times in his childhood and youth; Dave said that he wanted to go up to "the end of Pemsit Mountain"—its top, where rocks are exposed, is "a big power spot—that's why they go there ... I think they go there for energy." In a later regression, Dave recalled an earlier life, before white people came to the area, where he was a youth whose name, Mack reported, was "Panther-by-the-Creek, of the Susquehannock tribe living near Pemsit Mountain; there, eagles lived along the river in the cliffs"—he was studying to be a medicine man, many of whom went to the mountain on vision quests; he was killed in battle, however, in a war with the Iroquois, and felt himself "floating up

6. Mack, *Abduction*, 91–108.
7. Mack, *Abduction*, 177–200.

in the air" and "dissipating, spreading out all over like a fog of crystal . . . it was peaceful"; "The Indians felt the eagles were important spiritually, that they symbolize something, part of the Great Spirit . . . When you're Indian and you're real close to the earth, you're real spiritual . . . you get away from that you're more material, and that's to your detriment"; Mack notes further that "in our last regression, he found out that the Native American medicine men knew of the alien beings and also looked upon them as 'guardians' or protectors of nature . . . Needless to say, none of this makes much sense in the framework of the Western ontological paradigm . . ."; Dave wrote in a letter to Mack that Pemsit Mountain is "a big power place. That's why the visitors go there . . . Power is a mystery we will never understand. We can only learn to handle it."[8]

- "Peter" in chapter 13: On his spiritual journey, Mack states, Peter has come to perceive "other dimensions of realities beyond the manifest world." He perceives a dual human-alien identity. He has "been afflicted by vivid, disturbing apocalyptic images of the destruction of the earth"—Mack and Peter explored whether these should be considered "literal prophecies or as metaphors or warnings of possible futures"[9]; when he was married, he had seen a UFO outside his window—he found afterward "two small red lesions like healing pimples behind his ear that were distinct from insect bites in the rapidity with which they healed and the symmetry of their arrangement"; and had his first recalled abduction experience, an intrusive and traumatic one, at about nineteen or twenty: he recalled it well while in regression; Peter, as had other abductees, felt the power of strong vibrations,[10] which shook his body; he said that the beings "were not here to hurt anybody" but are aware and fearful of "our anger and our ability to hate and kill," and also "want our love and how it is we love and care and have such compassion"; they are trying "genetically" to take "the highest human qualities and separate them from the lower human qualities and somehow, I want to say, reincorporate them into our race"; in a presentation on "The Alien Abduction Phenomenon" at the Harvard Divinity School, Peter said that he had "discovered his place in the universe," and that "we are not alone in the universe, that God created many creatures in His likeness . . . God created a lot more in the universe than we can ever imagine. Like thousands of others like myself who have had the

8. Mack, *Abduction*, 264–92. Dave's words reminded me of my own experience with Wanapum elder David Sohappy on Mount Helena.

9. Haudenosaunee elder Oren Lyons, the "Faith Keeper" and a friend of mine who was interviewed for Bill Moyers's television program years ago, stated several times that prophecies about Earth's devastation uttered centuries ago by Handsome Lake, a Seneca prophet, would come true: but, "it is up to each generation to ensure that they do not come true during their lifetime."

10. For more on vibrations in the cosmos, see Teilhard's vision and comments in chapter 4, above.

experience, have seen God's creation in other forms ... I am connected to a creation process that is far greater than anything I have ever been asked to imagine in any of my other previous exposures to any spirituality."[11]

- "Carlos" in chapter 14: Carlos prefers to use "encounter" rather than "abduction" when referring to his experiences with aliens, and "encontrant" instead of "abductee"; Mack observes, as a prelude to what he will report from Carlos: "What is unique to the investigation of the abduction phenomenon, and well-illustrated by this case, is the necessity for human consciousness to expand in order to allow us the capacity to conceive beyond our present technological abilities and perceptions of reality"; an Anglican priest invited Carlos to go to Scotland to do a painting for a church; while there, he went to the island of Iona and, as had been suggested to him, he walked, on the day after he arrived, to a specific beach to sing Gregorian chant hymns—then, as he had been told would happen, a seal (seals were said to have the soul of one of the monks killed in a Viking raid) emerged from the water and paralleled Carlos as he walked along the beach and back; that night Carlos went out on the pier where he had arrived, and saw a luminous pink haze in a bubble shape out on the water; it gradually approached and then enveloped him. In the haze, he realized that he was an orphan boy, and saw two monks and another orphan boy: all were in the sixth century, the era of Saint Colomba, who is associated with Iona; suddenly, Vikings came in a small boat, killed one monk and the other boy, and ran past the second monk and Carlos who were lying face down on the beach; Carlos blacked out, and then was on the dock again; the next morning, before departing the island, Carlos went to the beach and, atop the rocks, sang two Gregorian chants: immediately "a huge, white sea lion with large, white tusks rose up out of those black waters and scared the hell out of me. I didn't understand this." Two months later, when he was preparing to teach a class, a freshman came to his office to inquire about taking a class with him: it was the young monk that he had seen in the sixth century, who recognized him, too; Carlos was well-educated, with MA, MFA, and PhD degrees; Carlos's "concern is for wisdom in action about the earth, other species, and the ecological universe within which the earth and its inhabitants are a part"; Carlos says that "I am connected to my environment which includes all creatures"; Mack observes that "Carlos, like so many abductees, has developed an acute ecological consciousness. He is deeply concerned with the earth and its fate ... His experiences seem tied to the fate of the earth and the tearing of the cosmic fabric that the destruction of its life-forms is bringing about"; Carlos thinks that it may be necessary for humans "to gain a sense of where we belong in the universal order."[12]

11. Mack, *Abduction*, 293–334.
12. Mack, *Abduction*, 335–68. Note that the last of Carlos's understandings

- "Arthur" in chapter 15: Mack says that Arthur "grew up with a passionate love of nature and spent a great deal of time in the woods . . . he had a special relationship with animals . . . like a kind of contemporary St. Francis." Arthur extrapolated, from the way he cultivated a trusting relationship with animals, ways to communicate with Visitors: "The way you communicate with these beings is telepathically, but the only way that you can achieve that telepathy is by eliminating fear. That fear will block it. You won't be able to communicate with them until you can get rid of the fear" and other "negative emotions . . . Arthur tended, like many abductees, to get significant throat and sinus infections. On one occasion, an instrument was pressed against his head and he felt a "shock" as information was conveyed to him: it "doesn't hurt. Just your entire brain, every cell lights up, or you see you're in this like infinite plasma of incredible light particles"; Arthur was told: "Do what you can to stop the destruction and promote the life of the earth"; Mack concludes the chapter by stating that "Arthur's case raised questions about forgetting and the triggering of memory" years later.[13]

Abduction: Themes and Psychiatric Insights

Common themes in the abduction stories are that humans are destroying their planet and themselves, and that a hybrid species is being developed by Visitors to replace humankind or join humankind on Earth and, in contrast to what humans are doing by themselves to Earth, to care for Earth's and the Earth community's wellbeing. Mack observes that "Virtually *all* the abductees with whom I have worked closely have demonstrated a commitment to changing their relationship to the earth, of living more gently on it or in greater harmony with the other creatures that live here."[14] Concerning the reality of the experiences themselves, Mack states: "We can continue to try to make the phenomenon fit the world as we have known it . . . or we can acknowledge that the world might be other than we have known it. Then we are free to see where our thinking leads us."[15] With that freedom, "The abduction phenomenon also raises interesting questions about the nature of memory and the control of consciousness. What are the forces that keep the memory [of abduction] out of consciousness during the years—more than twenty-five in these two cases—during which there is seemingly no recall

---

complement the concept of a Third Displacement that stimulates exploring for and finding humans' niche in the cosmos community of being(s).

13. Mack, *Abduction*, 369–86.
14. Mack, *Abduction*, 398.
15. Mack, *Abduction*, 400.

of the events in question?"[16] Regarding the traumatic experiences and pain that abductees recall, Mack states: "It is possible that experiencing terror, or 'pushing through' it, is an intrinsic or necessary aspect of breaking the psychological boundaries that limit our perception of reality."[17]

> Experiencers come to have a new understanding of the relationship between the physical and spiritual realms of reality. The acknowledgment of the existence and presence of alien beings stimulates people, "after the initial ontological shock," to "the opening of consciousness to a universe that is no longer simply material . . . the universe is filled with intelligences and is itself intelligent. [Experiencers] develop a sense of awe before a mysterious cosmos that becomes sacred and ensouled. The sense of separation from all the rest of creation breaks down and the experience of oneness becomes an essential aspect of the evolution of the abductees' consciousness."[18] Abductees "seem to feel increasingly a sense of oneness with all beings and all of creation. This is often expressed through a special love of nature and a deep connection with animals and animal spirits . . . The aliens themselves, as we have seen, may appear at various times to the abductees in animal form."[19] Experiencers "shed their identification with a narrow social role and gain a sense of oneness with all creation, a kind of universal connectedness . . . [They] become open to the presence of a divine source, which fills their being and gives a sense of connection with a universal consciousness from which they have come and to which they will return."[20] Regarding possible reasons for the abductions, Mack states: Abductions seem to be concerned primarily with two related projects: changing human consciousness to prevent the destruction of the earth's life, and a joining of two species for the creation of a new evolutionary form.[21]

In the last section of *Abduction*, titled "The Paradigm Shift," Mack wonders what is needed to "bring about the shift in consciousness, the change of paradigm that is implicit in what the abductees have undergone. It would appear that what is required is a kind of cultural ego death, more profoundly shattering . . . than the Copernican revolution which demonstrated that the

16. Mack, *Abduction*, 401.
17. Mack, *Abduction*, 402.
18. Mack, *Abduction*, 407.
19. Mack, *Abduction*, 408.
20. Mack, *Abduction*, 409.
21. Mack, *Abduction*, 413.

earth, and therefore humankind, did not reside at the center of the cosmos. UFO abductions and related phenomena suggest first that humans are not the preeminent intelligent beings in a universe more or less empty of conscious life ... we are participating in a cosmos that contains intelligent beings that are far more advanced than we are in certain respects and have the power to render us helpless for purposes we are only just beginning to fathom."[22] He concludes the section, and the book, with thought-provoking ideas:

> I have the sense—might I say faith—that the abduction phenomenon is, at its core, about the preservation of life on Earth at a time when the planet's life is profoundly threatened ... The connecting principle, the force that expands our consciousness beyond ourselves, appears to be love ... As our psyches open, we could abandon the dualistic thinking that has divided mind from matter and the physical from the spiritual world ... The abduction phenomenon, it seems clear, is about what is *yet to come*. It presents, quite literally, visions of alternative futures, but it leaves the choice to us.[23]

Passport to the Cosmos

In the five years between publication of *Abduction* and *Passport to the Cosmos*, John Mack worked with over one hundred people whom he had not previously interviewed. In introductory remarks in *Passport*, he states that "the alien abduction phenomenon can be defined as the experience of being taken by humanoid beings, usually but not always against the person's will, into some sort of enclosure where a variety of procedures and communications occur."[24] He observes that,

> When I first heard of the alien abduction phenomenon, I tried to fit it into my knowledge of psychopathology. But no consistent psychiatric disturbance has been found that could account for these reports, nor has a major psychological study of the population demonstrated more psychopathology than a matched comparison group ... I soon realized, therefore, that no plausible fit was emerging. A purely intrapsychic or psychosocial explanation—that is, one that did not include the possibility of another intelligence or force entering the experiencers' lives, as

---

22. Mack, *Abduction*, 420–21.
23. Mack, *Abduction*, 422.
24. Mack, *Passport to the Cosmos*, 3.

if from outside—was not consistent with my diagnostic assessment of what these clients were presenting.[25]

He notes, too, that "In the world in which I was raised and schooled, the idea of life, beings, energy—really anything at all—emanating from an unseen reality and manifesting materially was just not possible. Yet something precisely like this seems to be what is occurring in the case of the alien abduction phenomenon."[26] Mack leaves open the possibility that abduction experiences are not physical events: "I do not consider that abduction reports necessarily reflect a literal, physical taking of the human body . . . nor do I look upon experiencers as victims, although I strive to be empathic in relation to the pain and trauma they may have undergone . . . I have come to regard the phenomenon not merely as a negative and cruel intrusion, which it can be, but also as one that can bring about new understanding of ourselves and our identity in the cosmos."[27]

Mack elaborates and reflects on his work with experiencers. He states that "a modified hypnosis or relaxation exercise may be used to help focus the client's attention upon their inner experiences and memories, but it should be emphasized that about 80 percent of the information is obtained through conscious recollection. In this slightly altered state of mind, it is easier for the individual to recall more fully their experiences, which are usually not deeply repressed . . . We are careful not to lead individuals or to encourage them to 'produce' an abduction story—we use neutral, encouraging comments and questions."[28] At the end of chapter 2, he provides brief bios of some twenty-five experiencers; he uses pseudonyms, unless they chose otherwise, to protect their identity.[29]

Traditional Indigenous Peoples' Elders: Spiritual Leaders, Healers, and "Experiencers"

One aspect of Mack's work particularly interested me (because of my decades of involvement with the International Indian Treaty Council [IITC],[30] a non-

25. Mack, *Passport to the Cosmos*, 4–5.
26. Mack, *Passport to the Cosmos*, 8.
27. Mack, *Passport to the Cosmos*, 29.
28. Mack, *Passport to the Cosmos*, 30.
29. Mack, *Passport to the Cosmos*, 39–49.
30. I have been involved with the Treaty Council since 1980, including as a Member of the Delegation of the IITC to the UN International Human Rights Commission in Geneva, Switzerland (1987, 1990) and a Treaty Council-invited witness at the UN Consultation on the Declaration of the Rights of Indigenous Peoples, at Sinte Gleska University on the Rosebud Reservation in South Dakota (2009). Through participation in IITC annual

governmental organization accredited to the United Nations): his association and friendship with native elders from around the world whom he had come to know. The principal ones, to each of whom he dedicates a chapter in *Passport*, are Bernardo Peixoto, Uru-ê Wau-Wau people, Pará Brazil; Sequoyah Trueblood, Choctaw, Cherokee, and Chickasaw peoples, Oklahoma (both Bernardo and Sequoyah "had mixed indigenous and white parentage" and "had been baptized"[31]); and Vusamazulu Credo Mutwa, Zulu, South Africa. These native elders all had experienced "abductions" by humanoid beings. Mack provides an introduction to his work with these elders in chapter 7, "Shamans, Symbols, and Archetypes."

Bernardo Peixoto

In chapter 8, "Bernardo Peixoto," Mack relates how he met Bernardo in 1996 at a conference in Boston. Bernardo's people's name, Uru-ê Wau-Wau, translates to "people from the stars." Their oral tradition teaches that in the distant past, "a *huskera*, something from the sky that makes no sound and was not a bird, landed in the Amazon basin, and *makuras*, small glowing beings with large eyes who came from the sky, taught the Uru-ê Wau-Wau how to plant seeds and grow corn." Another name for the occupants of the vehicles is *atojars*, "entities that come from the sky" or "people with so much knowledge that they cannot be from Earth."[32]

Bernardo's father was Portuguese; his mother was Uru-ê Wau-Wau. The elders (spiritual leaders, tradition bearers, and, often, healers) of her people told her that Bernardo had the experiences and personal characteristics to be a shaman. They taught him the particular, deeper knowledge he needed, especially about healing herbs and sacred plants. They taught him, too, about healing powers, and about little people, "*curipiras*, who came from another realm," among whom were the *ikuyas*, spirits who take human form in order to be seen."[33] Later, as his mother was dying, she told him and his father that he had to experience the white people's culture so as to eventually protect the Uru-ê Wau-Wau. His father subsequently sent him to a Catholic school to learn to be a priest, so he could be both shaman and priest. After five years, he decided he would rather be an anthropologist. He pursued studies in that field and received his PhD from Belém de Pará University. Because

---

conferences around the United States, I came to know and become thereafter lifelong friends with Muskogee elder Phillip Deere (1926–85), the spiritual guide for the IITC, and Wanapum elders David (1925–91) and Myra (1926–2005) Sohappy.

31. Mack, *Passport to the Cosmos*, 157.
32. Mack, *Passport to the Cosmos*, 158–59.
33. Mack, *Passport to the Cosmos*, 160.

of his knowledge of native peoples' languages, he became an interpreter for the Brazilian government. During this work, he was shocked by how many peoples were forced from their lands by entrepreneurs exploring their extended territories in order to extract oil, timber, and other natural goods. Cultures were destroyed and natural ecologies were devastated. Bernardo decided to dedicate his life to righting those wrongs. He moved to the United States in 1990. His knowledge of indigenous cultures provided him with the credentials to teach at the Smithsonian Institution. He was engaged in this work when Mack met him in Boston.

In 1998, Bernardo told Mack about a profound experience he had years earlier. He prefaced his account by sharing stories from traditional healers about their frequent interactions with unidentified flying objects which were silent or emitted a buzzing or humming sound. He himself had seen at times "great blue balls of light, moving slowly or very rapidly, close to the water or 'swirling over the tops of trees.'"[34] He described his own experience with humanoid beings who had long arms and wore luminous suits. The beings "appeared to have a kind of aura or capsule of pure light around them. They had large, slanted black eyes." Mack continued:

> Bernardo asked the beings where they came from, and they told him, "We come from nowhere," which made him feel very uncomfortable. For the only way that beings could come from nowhere would be "because they are everywhere." [Mack says that Bernardo was] bothered considerably because according to tribal mythology his people are descended from humanoid beings that came from the stars. But beings descended from entities that are nowhere and everywhere is an altogether different matter.[35]

There is a remarkable correspondence between what the beings said to Bernardo and what was stated more than five hundred years earlier by Nicholas of Cusa. In his 1440 book *De docta ignorantia* (*Of Learned Ignorance*), Nicholas writes that wherever someone is in the universe, they would tend to think that they are stationary, "in a sort of immovable centre," while all entities in the heavens move around them. He continues: "In consequence, there will be a *machina mundi* whose centre, so to speak, is everywhere, whose circumference is nowhere, for God is its circumference and centre and He is everywhere and nowhere."[36]

---

34. Mack, *Passport to the Cosmos*, 161.

35. Mack, *Passport to the Cosmos*, 162.

36. From *De docta ignorantia*, chapter 12. See "Conditions of the Earth" in Crowe, *Extraterrestrial Life Debate*, 30.

Bernardo tells Mack that *ikuyas* are messengers of the Spirit, "from whom we are all descended." Bernardo inferred that the statement that his people are descended from beings who came from the stars "might be largely metaphoric." When Bernardo returned to his village, he told the elders what he had experienced. They were not surprised; they said that he had seen *ikuyas*, with whom they are accustomed to converse. They took him to a sacred cave that had engravings that were "hundreds or thousands of years old, that looked like representations of the *ikuyas*."[37] As Bernardo reflected on this event later, he thought that "if these beings came from nowhere and were everywhere, then perhaps *all* of us were descended from them."[38]

Bernardo continued to advocate for indigenous peoples, and to organize people from outside the Amazon to support their struggle to save their native territory and culture and, by extension, to protect the entire rain forest region. Through succeeding years, he had other encounters with the *ikuyas*, through which his healing powers were enhanced. In addition, he experienced diverse cultures and regions by journeying in his mind in a transcendent state, and through these travels he learned that we are all one, not solely humans, but all living beings: that is how we are from "nowhere and everywhere." The chapter has a substantial number of other stories about the Uru-ê Wau-Wau and other indigenous people: individual and community experiences, oral histories, and spiritual traditions.

Sequoyah Trueblood

Chapter 9 presents the story of Sequoyah Trueblood, whom Mack met in 1997. By then, Sequoyah had taken and taught courses at Harvard. He understood his life's role to be to help people to transcend their suffering in order to discover "who we really are in spirit."[39] Suffering, he said, results from people thinking that they could do better at running the universe than the Spirit, and consequently turned "their backs on the original instructions of the Creator." Like the Uru-ê Wau-Wau, the Cherokee (and Lakota/Dakota) "believe that they are descended from star people.[40] When he was a child, Sequoyah was treated brutally and sexually by his maternal grandmother and his alcoholic parents, but "in the summers he would live in a tent with his brother and paternal grandmother, who taught him the use of medicinal

---

37. Mack, *Passport to the Cosmos*, 163.
38. Mack, *Passport to the Cosmos*, 164.
39. Mack, *Passport to the Cosmos*, 169.
40. An elaboration of this ancestor tradition is found in a story told in Clarke, *Encounters with Star People*, 48, in which the elder Black Elk speaks about Star People.

plants."⁴¹ On several occasions, Sequoyah sensed that he was being aided by protective entities. He understood them to be, Mack says, "beings that were involved in an important journey to another reality." Sequoyah told Mack that "So-called extraterrestrials [are] another face of spirit, just as are we sacred two-leggeds . . . I define *spirit* as the mind of God in motion here on Mother Earth." Spirit can manifest "any form it wants to, and the star people are spirit made visible . . . [our] bodies are just the way that the spirit has chosen to do it on Earth."⁴² Sequoyah participated in and had piercings during Sun Dance ceremonies for many years, including when he was an elder.

Sequoyah had had several unusual experiences while he was growing up. At fourteen, as he roamed the forest near his school, he met a man on the trail who told him not to worry, that he was "being taken care of," and then disappeared.

While in his teenage years, Sequoyah went duck hunting with a man and two women. They were sleeping at night on a frozen lake when, unexpectedly, the ice beneath them thawed and their shelter overturned into the water. The man and one woman made it to shore; Sequoyah was trapped under the ice. He panicked, but a voice calmed him by telling him "it would be all right," and that he would have numerous "extraordinary experiences" in life. And, he was told, "other beings" would always be around him. He surfaced from beneath the ice and saw the second woman on a barrel that had been part of their ice shelter. She said he had been underwater for ten minutes, and she had thought that he had drowned. He then pushed the barrel closer to shore, and the man and other woman pulled them to safety with a rope. Sequoyah said he did not feel cold throughout the ordeal.

Sequoyah and his girlfriend eloped when he was seventeen; they had four children in the following decade. The first one was born in 1958, the year that he enlisted in the military. While in the service, he became a drug addict. After his military experience, he was arrested and imprisoned several times for "possession and transfer of illicit drugs."⁴³ For twenty-three years, he was a Green Beret; he was assigned to an "elite unit" in 1967, with the rank of captain, because of his leadership and combat skills. In Vietnam, he took amphetamines to stay awake and alert during missions, and became addicted. On secret, dangerous missions, his life seemed protected by unseen forces, as sometimes those all around him in his unit were killed, while he was unscathed. In combat zones, "he witnessed many atrocities committed by US forces against enemy soldiers and Vietnamese civilians."⁴⁴ One night

41. Mack, *Passport to the Cosmos*, 171.
42. Mack, *Passport to the Cosmos*, 171.
43. Mack, *Passport to the Cosmos*, 170.
44. Mack, *Passport to the Cosmos*, 173.

his unit was awakened by North Vietnamese soldiers attacking them. He saw two of them coming at him and quickly shot them in the head. With an interpreter's help, he went through their wallets and found their letters and photos from home, just as he carried in his wallet. It was a devastating experience. As he was sobbing, a "luminous being" appeared next to him and told him not to worry because "you're being taken care of." Thereafter, he never shot his weapon in combat, and sometimes he took no weapon on his missions, because he "was being watched over."[45] He returned to the United States in 1970, rejoined his family, and continued on secret missions around the United States and in Korea for nine years. Even though he was a drug addict, he was still able to function well, and received commendations for his role in secret operations. Eventually, though, he was arrested, convicted, and put in the federal penitentiary in Fort Leavenworth, Kansas, for twenty-two months for possession and sale of drugs. (He said that he was "set up" because he knew too much about secret operations.) In prison, he overcame his addiction.[46]

Sequoyah recalls only one "full-fledged" abduction experience, which occurred in 1970 in the United States after he returned from Vietnam; it occurred during a period when he was not consuming alcohol or taking drugs. In his narrative, unlike other indigenous elders, he makes no distinction between the spirit world which he experienced, as elaborated in his tradition and in the preceding narrative, and beings that are regarded by others as "extraterrestrial," who took him into a spacecraft. He thinks that there are numerous inhabited worlds in the universe, some of whose living beings are often among humankind, and take a humanoid form to relate to people and guide them back to Source.[47] Mack states that,

> According to Sequoyah, we are all in a sense extraterrestrial, for star beings took part in the creation of the human species and have always been our teachers. Because of the perilous state of the planet, they are showing themselves more and more now to those who will acknowledge their presence and share their teachings.[48]

45. Mack, *Passport to the Cosmos*, 174.
46. Mack, *Passport to the Cosmos*, 175.
47. Mack discusses "Source" at length in chapter 12, "Returning to Source." In the first paragraph, he states that "Virtually all religious and spiritual traditions in societies around the world and through time have in common knowledge of a supreme or ultimate creative principle or intelligence which is variously called the Divine, the Source (or just Source), the One, Home (especially favored by abduction experiencers), the Great Spirit, the ground of being, or God" (Mack, *Passport to the Cosmos*, 220).
48. Mack, *Passport to the Cosmos*, 175–76.

On July 4, 1970, in Laurel, Maryland, Sequoyah had a sudden urge to go to Norman, Oklahoma and did so. In the house of a friend, he lay down on a bed to rest.

> Then he saw a kind of vortex of swirling lights "like a rainbow," into which he was sucked. [He] then found himself standing in a beautiful garden surrounded by hedges. He was now wide awake . . . In front of him was a silvery saucer-shaped craft and a shimmering small silver-looking being standing on steps that were coming down from the bottom of the craft. The being looked grayish and had a large bald head with large eyes. Sequoyah sensed that it was "androgynous" . . . the being communicated telepathically that it was from "another place" and had been sent to take him there because "they" wanted to talk with him . . . He agreed to go, and walked up the steps with the being into the craft.
>
> Once inside the craft Sequoyah heard no sound, but through a small round window he saw the moon, the sun, and "millions of stars" instantly go by. Then they were hovering over a beautiful white city in what he felt was another planet in another realm or universe.[49]

Sequoyah met several of the city's people, who seemed to be male and female, were "fair skinned," and whose hair glowed as if with sunlight. There was no war or disease in the city, he was informed. There seemed to be no time. The inhabitants needed no food; the air they breathed was converted to nutrients they needed. Led by his guide, Sequoyah walked through and outside of the city to a forest, within which was a clearing in which there were several people. He was told that he was taken to the city so that he could see "the potential of the human race on Earth" and "be reintroduced to his native heritage" and learn to teach people on Earth (at first, native peoples and then others) "about the great peace and love that fills all creation."[50]

Sequoyah was invited to stay, but chose to return to Earth and his family, and his home and car. He realized that he was attached to material possessions. He was told then that "you're only here temporarily. These bodies of yours are just tools that you've been given to learn with." He then returned to Earth on the craft, and arrived in the garden. "He went again through the vortex, and was once again on the bed from which he had left."[51]

Sequoyah rehabilitated himself in prison. He was subsequently released and discharged from military service, in 1981, but was rearrested on two

---

49. Mack, *Passport to the Cosmos*, 176.
50. Mack, *Passport to the Cosmos*, 177.
51. Mack, *Passport to the Cosmos*, 178.

occasions. He was extradited to North Carolina. Eventually he was released into the custody of the Cherokee Nation to initiate healing programs for youth. Over the next several years he was taught by traditional elders from different Indian nations. Mack describes Sequoyah's extraordinary record of service both while in, and after release from, prison. He became versed, over the years, in numerous native traditions. Mack declares that Sequoyah's life of service was "one that in my experience has hardly any parallel."[52] Further, "His universe is dominated by spirit, and the forms of the material world are transient . . . Sequoyah lives in a world of myth and symbol filled with visible and invisible beings from many realms, which are among the forms that spirit can take." He says that "One of the things they're teaching us is that 'hey, you guys are pretty arrogant here' thinking you're in this universe, this Creation, all by yourself." He states, too, that "Everything comes from the Creator, from that one Source. "The flame of love—that's the Creator burning within us . . . there's no such thing as death, there's only transformation going on."[53] Sequoyah, Mack states, is a bridge between native peoples and white people, "but also, like Bernardo and Credo, between the unseen world of spirit and the manifest world of matter."[54] Mack concludes his consideration of Sequoyah's life and work with the observation, "Sequoyah's journey is always supported by his relationship to the Creator and the beings, visible and invisible, through which the Creator manifests."[55]

Vusumazulu Credo Mutwa

In chapter 10, "Vusumazulu Credo Mutwa," Mack describes his visits and conversations with an elder who is probably the most renowned *sangoma* (traditional religious leader and healer) in Africa. Born into a Christian family and raised a Christian (his father was a Catholic catechist, who later became a Christian Scientist), he rejected Christianity as a young man "and became a *sanusi*," someone who "uplifts" his people.[56] *Vusumazulu*, a title that he received when being initiated as a *sangoma*, translates as "awakener of the Zulus." He was given the Christian name "Credo" ("I believe") at his baptism. *Mutwa* means "little bushman." Among his followers, he has the honorific title *Baba Mutwa*.[57]

---

52. Mack, *Passport to the Cosmos*, 180.
53. Mack, *Passport to the Cosmos*, 181.
54. Mack, *Passport to the Cosmos*, 182.
55. Mack, *Passport to the Cosmos*, 184.
56. Mack, *Passport to the Cosmos*, 185.
57. Mack, *Passport to the Cosmos*, 185.

Credo Mutwa was born in 1921 in Natal, South Africa. His parents were not married, a fact which shamed him as he grew up. His maternal grandfather, Zeko Shezi, a Zulu elder, healer, and warrior, trained Credo for his role as a healer. As a child, he often had companions who educated him telepathically; some of them had blue skin. He was educated in a Catholic school, to the equivalent of the ninth grade in the United States, in six years.[58] When he conversed with Mack and reflected back on those years, Credo said that that education, linked to his later experiences, made him seem to be "caught between, on the one hand, Western thought, including the Christian religion, and African thought, which accepts these things without question."[59]

At age twenty-two, he became gravely ill, and had nightmares and visions. A Zulu aunt treated him, after Christian Scientist prayers and Western medicine failed. This experience stimulated his initiation as a *sangoma*: he began to understand his power as a healer.[60] Consequently, he was attacked by African Christians numerous times, and was so severely injured on several occasions that he almost died. "Once, he says, a Christian fundamentalist came close to stabbing him, calling him venomous, a Satanist, and an enemy of God."[61]

Credo believes that a great intelligence, "something which covers several galaxies," created Earth. He teaches, too, that in African legends, "star people" have come in "magic star boats" for thousands of years. Credo believes (similarly: Jacques Vallée and other Western thinkers) that, in Mack's words, "extraterrestrial beings have covertly influenced and 'manipulated' all human cultures and civilizations profoundly for hundreds if not thousands of years, operating in the shadows."[62] He said that "people's lives have been 'changed by entities that were not of this world.'"[63] Credo saw UFOs numerous times. He derides US Air Force claims that UFOs are weather balloons: "A weather balloon doesn't have portholes that are visible through a powerful pair of binoculars."[64] His direct encounters with them have alternated between positive and negative: "He holds extraterrestrial beings responsible for ruining his love affairs, spoiling his marriages, and damaging his penis. At the same time . . . they are sources of vital knowledge, have given him

---

58. Mack, *Passport to the Cosmos*, 189–90.

59. Mack, *Passport to the Cosmos*, 190. This is a common experience of indigenous people who have lived in both worlds: Western culture and traditional native culture.

60. Mack, *Passport to the Cosmos*, 190.

61. Mack, *Passport to the Cosmos*, 191.

62. Mack, *Passport to the Cosmos*, 193.

63. Mack, *Passport to the Cosmos*, 194.

64. Mack, *Passport to the Cosmos*, 195.

powerful skills, and provide important warnings to the human species, which he urgently believes we should heed."[65]

Credo relates to Mack several stories of being taken by the *mantindane*, the name Africans give to the beings whom they sometimes see on the trail, in their homes unexpectedly, or on aerial craft to which they are taken. On one occasion Credo was helpless on a table on a craft, and semen was extracted by a female being through a device attached to his penis. He is both angry with and sympathetic toward the *mantindane*. He declares that "these beings scar you for the rest of your life. You're not able to relate properly to ordinary human beings after they have had a session with you"; and that "these creatures are moved by a desperate need." While white people in Africa call them "aliens," he says, "We don't call them that . . . These beings are not cold, it's only that they've got feelings that we don't even imagine." They are "solvers of great problems" and their technology may be "several million years ahead of us."[66]

When Mack asked Credo why people in the West would not acknowledge that intelligent beings exist elsewhere in the cosmos, he replied that "The entire Western civilization is based upon a blatant lie, the lie that we human beings are the highest evolved forms in this world, that we are alone and that beyond us there is nothing."[67]

John Mack Reflections

When he reflected on his interviews with the three indigenous elders, Mack observed:

> The most important lesson for me and for our society, I think, lies in the fact that these men corroborate the reality of the abduction phenomenon. They make clear that it is not simply the product of the Western imagination or our interest in aerospace technology, and that elements of the phenomenon may be universal—that is, not entirely culture-dependent. [The three elders

---

65. Mack, *Passport to the Cosmos*, 195.
66. Mack, *Passport to the Cosmos*, 200.
67. Mack, *Passport to the Cosmos*, 201. When I pondered the statements of Bernardo, Sequoyah, and Baba Mutwa, and related them to my experiences with traditional Indian elders, I considered how their respective stories of Contact mirrored the traditions of their peoples going back millennia. I wondered why European culture had not, over the ages, had similar experiences and recorded them. I realized then that they had: in stories viewed today as "folklore." This interpretation of "fairy tales" or "folk tales" has been presented before, in books by distinguished authors who have researched the subject. They include Vallée, *Passport to Magonia*; Vallée and Aubeck, *Wonders in the Sky*; and Crowe, *Extraterrestrial Life Debate*.

hope] that I may bring this knowledge to my culture, which is so skeptical of anything that cannot be proven in material terms . . . These shamans see the pain and suffering of their crises, initiations, and other life experiences as essential dimensions of learning and growth. Western society, however, tends to see pain and suffering mainly as obstacles to be removed on the way to well-being. I have found the shamanic perspective helpful in working with abductees in our culture.[68]

In the next chapter, Mack discusses the experiencers' trauma, and the transformation that it apparently effects in people. Among other things, "these disturbing elements seem to carry with them the possibility of profound personal transformation and spiritual growth."[69] He states further that Jim Sparks, one of the experiencers, "captured for me most clearly the way in which an experiencer's terror is connected with the shattering of a worldview." Sparks told Mack that the experiences were initially "a traumatic culture shock of what the world or the universe, at least in my perception, is about, which is nothing like I would have imagined . . . [After] getting over the trauma, it was all about getting over the confusion as to who I am in the universe and all the other things that go with it . . . it's man who puts limits on what God did and didn't create, and what He does outside this planet. So who's to say what God has done out there? . . . It just means that God has created more than you have knowledge of until now."[70]

In these words, Sparks describes experiences that collectively illustrate a positive outcome of a Third Displacement. He was shocked traumatically at first, as the world as he understood it disappeared dramatically. Then, he came to have a greater sense of who he is in the universe. In being displaced from his earlier consciousness of and presence in his place, he found a replacement niche in which he had greater awareness of the immensity and complexity of the universe, and of the diversity of intelligent beings who inhabit it and voyage through it—extraterrestrially or interdimensionally.

In chapter 12, "Returning to Source," Mack states that

> What seems to be unique about the abduction phenomenon, as documented throughout this book, is its reality-shocking content, its energetic intensity, and its potentially rapid transformative power. This may enable individuals who, generally speaking, have not undertaken a path of spiritual practice to connect or reconnect with Source dramatically and quickly

68. Mack, *Passport to the Cosmos*, 202–3.
69. Mack, *Passport to the Cosmos*, 207–8.
70. Mack, *Passport to the Cosmos*, 210.

when they confront and work through the mind-shattering terror that often, at least initially, is produced by the encounters.[71]

Mack states, too, that

> [T]he alien abduction phenomenon can potentially be one of the most powerful agents of spiritual growth, personal transformation, and expanded awareness that is now affecting people on this planet ... The alien beings are usually perceived by experiencers, not as spirits or godly creatures, but as emissaries or messengers from the creative principle, which they most often seem to call "Source." For Karin, the beings function as "the go-between. It's the translator" or a "kind of interpreter," bridging the gulf that has developed between humans and "the One" ... Other experiencers note that the beings seem to have a connection with spirit or Source that we do not have or have lost ... Karin adds that "The Creator [has] messengers of all sorts that are calling us to continue our evolution."[72]

Along these lines, Mack states that "abductees consistently report that the beings seem closer to the Godhead than we are, acting as messengers, guardian spirits, or angels, intermediaries between us and the Divine Source."[73]

In the conclusion to *Passport to the Cosmos*, Mack reflects back on the experiencers he has met, and forward to what might be the meanings and implications of what occurred. He observes that what is most important about these events is not the events in themselves:

> Rather, the most important truths for our culture may lie in the extraordinary nature and power of the abductees' experiences, the opening that these experiences provide to other deeper dimensions of reality, and what they may mean for our culture and the human future ... Whatever words we may use to describe this realm or realms, it appears ever more likely that we exist in a multidimensional cosmos or multiverse, within which space and time appear to be constructs of the mind that order or simplify the chaos of energy and vibration in which we are immersed.[74]

Mack goes on to critique, as he did earlier in both *Abduction* and *Passport to the Cosmos*, the unnatural separation of the manifest and the invisible,

---

71. Mack, *Passport to the Cosmos*, 221.
72. Mack, *Passport to the Cosmos*, 222, 223.
73. Mack, *Passport to the Cosmos*, 276.
74. Mack, *Passport to the Cosmos*, 268, 269.

the material and the spiritual, as fostered and enforced by a science-focused materialist view of reality. He declares, along these lines, that

> the "alien abduction phenomenon" [appears] to belong to that class of phenomena that do not respect the epistemological and ontological walls that we have erected between the unseen realms of the cosmos and ourselves. The aliens, whatever or whomever they may be, cross this barrier with ease and apparent insouciance. The abduction phenomenon is not the only one that does this. As I have noted, crop formations, near-death experiences, some forms of healing at a distance, telepathic communication, and the mind-affecting-matter experiments of parapsychology are a few of the other activities of nature that do not seem to respect this barrier.[75]

Mack states that, after his interviews with the experiencers and his evaluation of what they told him,

> the more deeply I have explored this phenomenon over the past decade, the less certain I have become about when the abductees are speaking of something that happened to them literally in this material reality and when they are communicating in metaphoric language events they experienced as utterly real in a physical sense but that happened to their subtle, astral, or energetic bodies, which may be the actual locus of the sense of self . . . Finally, I cannot avoid the fact that not much sense can be made of any of this material without positing an ultimate or overarching creative principle or intelligence in the cosmos that is doing it through this and related phenomena that break into our material reality from unseen realms. Once we can acknowledge at least the existence of such an intelligence—which the upbringing of my childhood and youth largely denied—many of the pieces of the alien abduction phenomenon seem to fall into place.[76]

In the final page of *Passport*, Mack states that "Abductees and those, like myself, who work with them are often drawn to Native American spiritual leaders, for they appear to have a deep and enduring familiarity with the entities we call alien and the role they have played in enabling them to maintain their own connection with the Creator."[77]

75. Mack, *Passport to the Cosmos*, 270.
76. Mack, *Passport to the Cosmos*, 271–72.
77. Mack, *Passport to the Cosmos*, 280. The relationships I have had with Indian elders have been for me, too, moments of friendship, guidance, and inspiration.

John Mack's books have had a strong influence on me in terms of my coming to understand and accept the reality of abduction experiences. Prior to reading *Abduction* and *Passport to the Cosmos*, I had thought that the experiences were only uncovered through hypnosis. His exposition is unnerving, initially, but ultimately, after reflection, substantially informative and insightful.

John, Maximus, and Francis

Earlier in this book, the words and theological speculations of the Gospel writer John were presented. Among the latter were that God, the divine *Logos*, loves the (plurality of) "world" with all creatures living therein and, in fact, entered God's creation as a creature. Ancestors of Christians, Jews, and members of other faith traditions understood, at the times their respective sacred books were written, that the "world" of their teachings was not solely Earth and all living on it, but the seas, the skies, and the stars. Earth was a hemisphere with solid ground underfoot and a firmament overhead. Across the world's half-dome "roof," stellar and lunar beings followed their divinely established tracks across the sky. Other worlds were visible and interspersed among their "lights." The firmament above held back the waters above, except as God allowed them to descend as gentle rain or as a destructive thunderstorm.

The composite, structured world, however, was far more complex and complicated than the ancients realized. As discussed earlier, this was the reason that the internally integrated, single "world" as they understood it was actually a "plurality of world(s)": some "stars" were really planets, many of which had living beings, among whom were intelligent beings. Therefore, when Yahweh declares in Genesis 1 that God looked at *everything* that God had made and called it all "very good," much more is included in that assessment than humanity realized at that time and for millennia afterward until, in the Western world and eventually beyond, the First Displacement occurred.

Maximus the Confessor elaborates on and deepens understanding about the Creator's relationship to creation. The divine *Logos*, immanent in the cosmos while yet existing transcendentally—a transcendent-immanent divine Being—is intimately related to all creatures, the *logoi*, who are, in a sense, extensions of the *Logos*—sparks of the divine flame. All that is "very good," as declared by Genesis, is now understood further, through Maximus, to be in ongoing *dialogos* with the one who called it "very good," as stated in the Bible. Maximus taught, as discussed previously, that all creatures, the *logoi*, through their *dialogos* with the *Logos*, are intimately related to each other. Increasingly, humans are accepting that intelligent beings other than humans populate space—and other dimensions of the cosmos—and so are included in the "very good" creatures noted in Genesis, and in the *Logos-logoi-logoi-Logos* interrelational community.

Saint Francis provides a complementary teaching, embodied in the totality—verses and melody—of his *Canticle*, as described previously. In his *Canticle*, Francis sings that *all beings* are *brother* and *sister* to each other. Abiotic creation is included in the words he sings, and biotic creation in the original words of the song, becoming present in the melody to which they were once sung, now become the musical foundation of Francis's song. In it, he celebrates every individual *logos* who is simultaneously a member of a *logoi* family. The meaning derived from integration of the understandings of John, Maximus, and Francis is that every *logos* and *logoi* is "very good," in *dialogos* with the *Logos* and with all *logoi* in a relational community, and in a familial relationship within that community. This understanding profoundly describes and integrates how terrestrial, dimensional, extraterrestrial, and interdimensional beings are ultimately related in the integral being of the cosmos, permeated by the Spirit Transcendent-Immanent in whom all creatures, as Paul declares in Acts, "live and move and have their being."

When these intersecting understandings are integrated consciously, humankind can understand who humans are and where they "fit" in a cosmos in which all of God's creation is *very good*; where the creating word of God ("God *said* let there be . . . and it was"), the *Logos*, to whom all are related, so loved the world that divinity became a part of humanity; where all beings, animate and inanimate, all loved by God, on Earth and in the heavens, are "brother" and "sister" to each other: humankind, Earth, all other worlds and their inhabitants, and all who roam the multiverse in humans' and others' craft. Human knowledge and understanding, and that of all other intelligent species, continue to evolve in an unfolding cosmos. In it, Contact between and among intelligent beings potentially will enrich and enlighten each and all.

John Mack and Jacques Vallée

John Mack and Jacques Vallée agree that people have come into Contact with ETI/IDI over millennia; Mack adds that they had been taken involuntarily from customary places by Otherkind, physically, psychically, or psychologically. He describes Visitors' treatment of "abductees" ("experiencers"), which is often terrifying, physically and psychologically painful, and sexually abusive. Ordinarily, Mack explains or justifies these events by stating the Others' rationale for the suffering—development of a hybrid human/ETI/IDI species must be engineered with a dual purpose: to provide for the Others' future generations' species wellbeing by restoring ETI/IDI's lost emotional capacity (they have evolved to become too rational, in the sense of losing emotive and altruistic aspects of their being); and to enable some humans to survive humans' ongoing self-destruction as people inflict devastation on their home planet. Humans taken aboard spacecraft (physically or mentally) must endure fear, suffering, and personal violation for these greater goods; this will give them a consciousness of working for a higher purpose. The human-Others hybridization program will benefit both TI and ETI/IDI.

Mack says, too, that the terrifying and painful aspects of humans' treatment on board the Visitors' craft are needed to purge their self-imposed obstacles to becoming a better person, more relational not only to humans but to other biota and Earth herself. I disagree with Mack's rationale. The physical and psychological abuse seem to me to be cruel, even sadistic, and I question whether that had to be the mode or context of "instruction." It also seemed that different species of Otherkind were engaged in abductions: some were compassionate and less intrusive, others were cold and abrupt, treating human subjects roughly, seeming to view them as "inferior."

Jacques Vallée, too, questions Others' practices and ultimate motives: would an advanced society truly not have developed genetic modification technologies that are less violently intrusive and less violating of person, especially in sexual interaction, to accomplish their hybridization program?[78] Mack might respond that the aliens do not "need" to do these procedures, since they are much more advanced than humans, but that humans need to have these physically, emotionally, intellectually, and spiritually trying experiences in order to move beyond a consciousness that puts humans at the center of the cosmos, denies that other intelligent beings exist, separates matter and spirit, lacks spiritual understanding, and does not see how interconnected they are with all being and Being.

While reading Mack's work, I wondered if the human subjects of experimentation and physical violence who were being forced to hybridize themselves were, in actuality, being duped into procreating offspring intended by the invading species to replace humans on planet Earth. The hybrid species was expected to have, through interbreeding, the habitat and the evolutionary context-adapted DNA to occupy Earth. As this occurred, human "parents" of hybrid offspring would no longer be needed. In a worst-case sci-fi novel scenario, the hybrids might then eradicate or extinct the human species. Finally, some of the methods used by Visitors to coerce their human subjects bordered on the sadistic. The Visitors showed them incredibly long

---

78. Vallée, *Revelations*, 56–57.

needles; ignored their anguish; and extracted samples from them, including reproductive fluids.

A Hybrid Project for Whom?

I wondered, as I read the Visitors' rationale for the hybrid program, how it would be used to populate Earth. The Others said that humankind was destroying its planet: through violent conflicts and by ecological devastation. Humans were warned that if they did not change, Earth would be destroyed by their actions; But, concurrent with these warnings, hybrids were being developed. A somewhat obvious question is, if humans continue on the same path, then Earth will be destroyed and there will be no place for the hybrids to live. Therefore, the destruction had to be stopped: for the wellbeing of the human species, or for the benefit of the hybrid species, or both. Therefore, to save Earth and have a place for the hybrids, would some process of genocide, or incarceration, or exile to a secure place on Earth or in space, or some other type of imposed displacement, need to be undertaken? If the choice had to be made to save Earth or to save humankind, it seems that the Visitors would save Earth. For humanity, the obvious step would be one advocated for decades by concerned people, especially environmentalists and human rights advocates: renew planet Earth and develop human societies permeated by justice. Absent a conversion to consciousness of their place in the cosmos and their relationship to all beings, people will perish on a desolate planet. Would the Visitors truly want people to be converted to be responsible caretakers of their planet? What would happen to the hybrids then?

A flaw in the hybrid process seems to be evidenced by the listless, dazed state of some of the hybrids bred to this point, as seen by experiencers to whom they are shown. As biologists, geneticists, and medical personnel have discovered in areas of genetic and biomedical research, some genes helpful or needed for human survival seem to be inextricably bonded to genes harmful to human wellbeing. For example, the same gene or gene combo can prevent malaria and Tay-Sachs disease in Africans and African Americans. Removing this genetic marker to prevent T-S would remove the protection against malaria. Similarly, if alien experimenters are trying to breed hybrids who have human emotions by transferring genes they have identified for this purpose, they might also, in hopes of preventing the social violence that has become ever more endemic in human individuals and societies, promote undesirable traits, such as the listlessness observed in some hybrids by experiencers. This is not unlike, it appears, drugs that are used in mental institutions to keep patients docile by suppressing their violent emotions and consciousness, and thereby rendering them to be seemingly always unconnected to others and, in some ways, almost lifeless.

Mack on the one hand acknowledges that hybrids appeared listless, and some were physically deformed;[79] on the other hand, he rejects the claim that "hybrids" seem listless or dazed: he asserts that hybrids developed later were much improved.[80]

Considered together, the somewhat overlapping and sometimes contradictory ideas and perceptions of John Mack and Jacques Vallée can be unnerving to some extent, and prompt questions such as: To what extent, if any, at this time of limited TI/ETI/IDI interaction, would people view Others' intentions as brutal or beneficial? Are ETI and IDI beings "con artists" able to convince people that what they endure is for some higher, human-saving purpose undertaken by an altruistic, compassionate being, while the ETI/IDI's overriding concern is really only for their own species? Ultimately, in the final chapters of *Passport to the Cosmos*, Mack assesses positively the actions and practices of the "abductors." He and the experiencers themselves, as a group, think that those with whom experiencers are in Contact are messengers of Source, and are closer to Spirit than humans are. The messengers are trying to help us to save ourselves before we destroy ourselves . . . and our Earth home.

Mack notes, too, in *Passport to the Cosmos*, the visiting beings' urgency about the importance of protecting Earth in the present and into the future. In chapter 1, when discussing experiencers' events, he notes their "relationship to the planet's ecological crisis."[81] In chapter 5, "Protecting the Earth," he says, "Indeed, it seems to me quite possible that the protection of the Earth's life is at the heart of the abduction phenomenon . . . My conviction of the centrality of the earth-saving dimension of the UFO abduction phenomenon derives from the vividness and power of the messages that experiencers receive and convey about the jeopardy to the planet's life."[82]

Although he uses the terms "abduction" and "abductees" because of their familiarity to the general public, Mack prefers "experiencers" to "abductees."

A more apt term for those who are taken against their will might be "transporteds"—however the experiences occur, in a material sense or a metamaterial sense. This expresses the shift of place that occurs in the minds of the transporteds, wherever and however that shift takes place; "abduction" has, in general parlance, the meaning of a felony seizure, against their will,

79. Mack, *Passport to the Cosmos*, 121–22.
80. Mack, *Passport to the Cosmos*, 122–24.
81. Mack, *Passport to the Cosmos*, 4.
82. Mack, *Passport to the Cosmos*, 88.

of those who are taken, and "experiencer" focuses more on what transpires in the locale to which they are physically or mentally taken. Other terms for this experience could include "cosmos consciousness-displaced" people: they have been taken away from the Earth place in which they were living to a place or places in a different world, a different dimension, or a different realm of consciousness—or, to all of these simultaneously.

Mack thinks that, in some cases he studied, people had with other beings an interdimensional experience rather than an extraterrestrial experience, or a mental experience rather than a physical experience.

Indian Elders in North America:
Spiritual Leaders, Human Rights Activists, Healers

In *Passport to the Cosmos*, John Mack interviewed indigenous elders from three continents about their respective experiences with Otherkind: Bernardo Peixoto (South America: chapter 8), Sequoyah Trueblood (North America: chapter 9), and Vusumazulu Credo Mutwa (Africa: chapter 10). Mack's assessment and interpretation of these elders complements what is expressed in the lives of traditional elders in the United States who integrated in their lives a deep spirituality, healing power, and social activism: Muskogee spiritual leader Phillip Deere from Oklahoma, and Wanapum spiritual leader David Sohappy Sr. from the Columbia River region. Other centuries-old oral traditions about diverse native peoples' Contact with ExoEarth beings were recorded and published by Ardy Sixkiller Clarke, PhD, Emeritus Professor, Montana State University.

Phillip Deere

Phillip Deere (1926–85) was a globally acknowledged and admired Muskogee elder from Okemah, Oklahoma. He was the spiritual leader for both the community activist organization American Indian Movement (AIM) and its complement, the International Indian Treaty Council (IITC) NGO.[83]

Phillip Deere recorded for me an oral history narration of the ages-past migration of the Muskogee Indians from the Pacific coast to the Atlantic coast.[84] In the oral narrative that Phillip[85] recounted, he describes

83. A more extensive discussion of Phillip Deere is provided in Hart, *Sacramental Commons*, 45–57; Hart, *Cosmic Commons*, 257–58; and Hart, *Encountering ETI*, 264–65.

84. Phillip recorded his people's migration story for me in my home in Great Falls, Montana, in February, 1984, during his visit to speak at a conference that I had organized. I had the tape transcribed at the time.

85. Indian elders are usually addressed as "Grandfather" or "Grandmother," but both

an unusual incident that occurred during his people's migration. The cross-continent trek occurred in the distant past, perhaps thousands of years ago. Phillip, who had the entire two-hour narrative committed to memory as part of the oral history of his Muskogee people, described how during their migration they encountered Other beings. As I listened to him making the cassette recording, he looked over at me and said offhandedly, "Maybe they came from another planet." He then turned back to the microphone and continued the migration story. His casual acceptance of the event indicated that it was just part of the Muskogee people's history, nothing about which people should be particularly excited or alarmed. (It was for me, however, very thought-provoking.) Years later, I wondered if he had memorized, too, oral-history narratives about Star People interaction with the Muskogee.

In the summer of the same year, at an International Indian Treaty Council conference on the Sisseton-Wahpeton Reservation that straddles the states' line between North Dakota and Minnesota, Phillip and I sat by his campfire and exchanged ideas on various topics for more than two hours. During the conversation, we spoke about our respective reflections on the Spirit. Phillip shared with me that the Muskogee understand that the Creator Spirit is "the Great Mystery." No one can see the Great Mystery, or limit what this Being is like by describing this Spirit. People should realize that the Spirit is throughout creation. Phillip told me, too, that "The Creator as 'The Great Mystery' can be anywhere and everywhere."[86] This means, effectively, that The Great Mystery is from no specific place, or 'nowhere'. Phillip's words complemented Bernardo Peixoto's words, when Bernardo, as relayed by Mack, described his experience with beings from elsewhere in the cosmos. They told him that they were from "nowhere." He took this to mean "nowhere and everywhere," a description that profoundly affected him.

Ardy Sixkiller Clarke

Dr. Ardy Sixkiller Clarke is Professor Emeritus, Montana State University, and former Director of the Center for Bilingual/Multicultural Education there. She was awarded the Distinguished Faculty Teaching Award in 1986. Her academic degrees are in the fields of history, English, psychology, and educational leadership. She has been a high school teacher, counselor, and administrator; university professor and administrator; licensed therapist and

---

Phillip Deere and David Sohappy preferred to be addressed by their name; among their people, however, younger members of their respective communities likely addressed them by the familiar "Grandfather" or "Grandmother" as a respected family elder for all the people.

86. Cited earlier in Hart, *Cosmic Commons*, 257–8.

psychologist; and social science researcher. She authored twelve children's books, and the academic text *Sisters in the Blood: The Education of Women in Native America*. She is a consultant to American Indian nations and indigenous communities worldwide.[87]

Dr. Clarke draws upon the oral histories of her own traditional elders, and elders from other Indian cultures who describe their people's interactions with Star People. These interstellar or interdimensional beings have visited native peoples for thousands of years—indeed, some elders taught that there were bonding relationships between some Indians and space visitors. This resulted in mixed-DNA offspring, many of whose descendants are known as such to their people today. Therefore, Star People are also Star Ancestors for some native people. Clarke's interviews are presented in her books, each focused on a specific population.[88]

Clarke, a Montana native, confidentially interviewed numerous Indian elders from throughout Montana, quietly and secretly to preserve witnesses' identities and confidentiality, during her spare time while on high school and college student recruiting trips for Montana State University and after she retired. Using her background, knowledge, and experience in doing social science research interviews, she professionally conversed with Indians who had come to trust her because she had become well-known and respected in Indian communities. Clarke's interview narratives complement well John Mack's interviews more than a decade earlier. Both present stories from "abductees" or "experiencers."

Mack concludes his work about the experiencers' incidents on a very positive note: he views the physical and psychological abuse that they endured as a traditional "test" to make them able or worthy to receive special powers, and to be stimulated to dedicate themselves to work to save the ever-increasingly devastated Earth environment. Their dedication included and required that some would participate in a "Hybrid Project," in which the human–alien species would be integrated to become the new Earth population.

Clarke's interviewee's experiences and their analyses of them provide a balance to Mack's acceptance of the seeming necessity for the trials endured by the abductees. Her Indian and indigenous peoples' experiencers, by contrast, often evaluate less positively—and even entirely negatively—the intruders into their lives. In contradiction to Mack's subjects, some interviewees call the aliens "evil" and say that they deceive people into thinking they are benevolent intruders when they prompt people's involvement in both a

---

87. Biographical details are taken from the back of Clarke's books, my correspondence with her via email, and her website: www.sixkiller.com.

88. Clarke, *Encounters With Star People*; Clarke, *More Encounters with Star People*; and Clarke, *Sky People*.

project that will save members of the (genetically altered) human species, but also the Earth context for hybrids' future habitat.

Encounters with Star People

In the first paragraph in the Preface of *Encounters with Star People*, Clarke writes about the stories of Star People she learned as a child, which stimulated a life-long interest in Indians' encounters with them:

> I first learned about the "Star People" when my grandmother told me the ancient legends of my people. My childhood reality included narratives that traced the origins of the indigenous people of the Americas to Pleiades; stories of little people who intervened in people's lives; and legends about the magical gift of the DNA of the "Star People" that flowed in the veins of the indigenous tribes of the Earth. I embraced the stories of the celestial visitors who lived among the Indian people as part of my heritage.[89]

Clarke describes how, as a professor at Montana State University, she wondered if other Indians had stories about Star People. She traveled around the Americas and beyond, and recorded and simultaneously took notes as she collected more than one thousand stories. These were told to her by people from all walks of life; she kept their identity and location confidential by using pseudonyms when she attributed the sources of the narratives, and different geographic places when stating where the events took place. While some stories are pre-Roswell in origin, most relate events that occurred between 1990 and 2010. She did not use hypnosis in her one-on-one meetings, nor ask leading questions. As an Indian herself, who understood customs whereby she would become accepted as part of different communities, Clarke had ready access to the narrators and their communities. She was also a well-known and respected educator who traveled around Montana in that capacity, which enabled her to be in communities unobtrusively on university or local school business, and do her interviews during her personal time, in homes or in accessible spaces in schools. Clarke presents ordinary peoples' straightforward narratives, which she recorded on tape and transcribed later, supplemented by notes that she took while they spoke.

In the first account in *Encounters with Star People*, a husband and wife—Sarah, a high school teacher, and Tim, an officer of the tribal police— told Clarke about an incident that occurred years earlier when they were on their way to Billings to celebrate their twentieth wedding anniversary. As

---

89. Clarke, *Encounters with Star People*, ix.

they went around a turn in the highway, their pickup headlights illuminated several dead cattle on the road. They stopped, Tim took a portable spotlight and a .357 magnum pistol, and they went outside to look at the cattle, three in number. The cows were mutilated: parts of their bodies had been removed with surgical precision—eyes, legs, and a head were gone. There was no blood at the site, and no footprints of any kind in the grass around the cattle. They returned to their pickup, mystified, and Tim turned the ignition key. Nothing happened. Then they saw a light approaching low in the sky, and became nervous. A large, cylindrical object came into view, which was "the length of a football field, at least." It circled the pickup, then stopped above and shined an extremely bright light upon it. They have no memory of what happened next, until they found themselves parked on the opposite side of the highway. The cattle had disappeared. The ignition worked now, and they continued their drive to Billings, thinking that they had arrived before 11 pm. When they registered and queried about room service, they were told it would start at 6 am. They looked at their watches: the time was 3 am. They did not know until then that they were missing any memory of the last four hours. Tim realized when they were in their room that Tim's gun was missing. They went out to search the pickup, to no avail. They drove back to the site where they had been stopped, and searched for Tim's pistol. Sarah found it in the grass; it appeared that it had been thrown there. Tim examined it: the gun barrel was melted closed. After Tim and Sarah had lunch with Clarke, they went outside and Tim showed her the gun with the melted barrel.[90]

In chapter 2, "An Encounter That Pre-Dates Roswell," Clarke describes a conversation in Montana with an elder, Harrison, in which he spoke about being aboard a crashed starship on his grandfather's ranch. His grandfather saw the ship crash into the side of a mountain. He went to investigate and met men, about seven feet tall, with very white skin. They had been in their craft when it crashed after being dropped off by a mother ship, one of four circling Earth. He went to see them periodically. Months later, they were rescued. When Harrison visited in the summer, his grandfather took him to the ship, still deeply embedded in the mountainside, but camouflaged. Harrison went inside, found seventeen seats, and sat in one—it closed on him, fitting snugly, and he was frightened; but when he tried to rise it immediately released him. He sat down several more times, and discovered that it always held him in place, anticipating a voyage, and released him when he started to rise. Soon after, the Army Corps of Engineers, which had confiscated his grandfather's land for a reservoir, flooded the site.[91]

---

90. Clarke, *Encounters with Star People*, 2–5.
91. Clarke, *Encounters with Star People*, 7–17.

The next chapter presents accounts of entire families disappearing from their villages in Canada and the northern United States. No trace of them was ever found. Some of the disappearances were in news stories around the world. On one occasion in Canada, the Royal Canadian Mounted Police went to a family's home hours after they were reported missing. They found no one and nothing out of the ordinary.[92]

In chapter 4, "The Man Who Shot An Alien," Clarke describes her meetings with an octogenarian, Chauncey, whom she called "the man who proved to be one of the most unforgettable I have ever met in my life." He had a dog named Blue Son. As they had lunch in his home, she asked him about the time he shot an alien. He smiled and said that he had never shot an alien, but had fired his gun to chase the alien away. The human-like being had come near his home at night; he discovered this when Blue Son barked and Chauncey opened the door to let him out. The dog ran around the corner of the house. Chauncey followed holding his rifle, and saw the being bent over Blue Son. Chauncey thought that Blue Son was dead, and shot at the being, who then stood upright and walked slowly from the shadows into the moonlight toward Chauncey. He wore a jumpsuit made of a dark fabric. The being described to Chauncey "somehow" that he was from the stars. He meant no harm and was curious about Blue Son; apparently, he had not seen a dog before, or perhaps even a pet. Chauncey had Blue Son perform a few tricks after they had walked together toward the craft, which seemed too small to travel from the stars. The being told Chauncey that he had descended from the base ship, which was still in the sky. He pointed at his craft and then at Blue Son; Chauncey realized then that "he wanted my dog. I shook my head and rested my gun across my arms. He understood, and left." Chauncey said that he had seen numerous other starships in the following years, but they never came near his home.[93]

In "An Alien, a Spacecraft, and an Alaskan Blizzard," Clarke narrates her Alaska meeting with Ross, a snowplow driver. While driving in a blizzard, trying to keep the highway open, Ross saw a large craft in the middle of the highway ahead. He flashed his lights; the craft did likewise in return, then suddenly took off straight up. Ross, shaken, started to continue his plowing, when someone pounded on his door. He saw outside his window two hands—each of which had four fingers. He did not want the being to freeze to death, so he invited him to sit in the passenger's seat. Ross was about to open the door, but before he could do so, the being was inside sitting next to him. The being was fascinated by the operation of the snowplow, and observed that it was primitive: he wondered why humans did not use

---

92. Clarke, *Encounters with Star People*, 19–24.
93. Clarke, *Encounters with Star People*, 25–29.

magnetic propulsion instead of oil-based machines. He told Ross that he, too, could learn how to appear and disappear if he used his brain. On the return trip, the ship appeared again in the middle of the road. Ross stopped, and the being disappeared from the seat and reappeared next to the ship. He waved to Ross, disappeared inside, and the craft took off.[94] This chapter that described Contact with a friendly Visitor was followed by one about aliens of a different sort.

In "They Are Among Us," Leland, who had fought in World War II and now made drums, told Clarke that alien visitors "are not the Star People the old ones taught us about. The Earth is being invaded." Leland described spacecraft that he saw from a window in his home; they came at night and dropped off a big car with passengers. The car left and returned later with only the driver on board. Leland changed a flat tire for them on one occasion before they departed for town. The driver, and four passengers whose faces were not visible but who appeared to be women, did not speak; the driver gave ten shiny silver dollars to Leland when he finished changing the tire. When Clarke ended her visit, Leland told her, "Indians know about the Star People . . . But these star travelers are different. They're not our ancestors." Clarke visited Leland on other occasions over the following two years. When she went two months before he died, his friend Walter was there. The spacecraft had returned two weeks before; Walter, too, had seen the beings. Walter thought that "humans . . . were cooperating in the alien invasion."[95]

Chapter 7, "A Star Traveler," relates the experiences of Clarke's friend Billy, which complement "experiencer" narratives of John Mack in *Passport to the Cosmos*. Clarke states that "Star Travelers are persons who claim to have experienced contact with extraterrestrials, but unlike those who have earthly experiences of abductions aboard spacecraft, star travelers are individuals who willingly journey throughout the universe with Star People. Typically, they maintain they have been given messages, warnings, or profound bits of wisdom by the extraterrestrials."[96]

Billy told Clarke that the Star People had been taken him on trips to other worlds. He saw "a new world, a world they have made for us." He goes on to say that Earth will be destroyed, but that the Star People will save the Indians from the destruction to come, and take them to their new home. They told Billy to prepare for this event, and to disseminate the information to other Indians. He was a musician, and played his guitar for Clarke while he sang songs from his forthcoming album; they were about the coming of the Star People to rescue Indians. Clarke liked the songs, but Billy's producers

94. Clarke, *Encounters with Star People*, 31–37.
95. Clarke, *Encounters with Star People*, 39–44.
96. Clarke, *Encounters with Star People*, 45.

told him that they would be bad for his career. When the album was released, the songs had been altered. Clarke did not see Billy again. He released one final album, and then died at age forty-seven because of the effects of alcohol abuse that had disrupted his life prior to releasing his three albums.[97]

The chapters thereafter continue to provide Indians' stories about their encounters with Star People. The next one for consideration here is chapter 16, "Abductions of a Different Kind." Clarke interviewed Antonio and Jennifer, both from New Mexico but unknown to each other, who had separate experiences with Visitors. Antonio, now a school teacher, had his first experience when he was seven years old. As he rode his horse back from a grocery shopping mission that he had made to town, his horse spooked when an extremely bright light shone on them from above. The horse threw Antonio and the bag of groceries; in the dark he groped for and gathered the groceries and placed them in the bag. He stood up and started to walk home when he saw two figures approaching. They took him, now frightened, to the center of the light that had scared his horse. He felt himself being lifted up and into their craft. He remembered nothing about what transpired, only his walk home on the trail and his arrival home. His father was angry: Antonio was several hours late from his shopping expedition. Antonio never told his father about his experience with the bright light and the strangers. In succeeding years, Antonio was taken numerous times; although angry, he could not resist. They disrupted his life whenever they wanted, to subject him to procedures "that no one else has ever done to me." He describes the beings' appearance as insect-like, with large eyes and thin arms and legs. Sometimes he saw other abductees of different ethnicities on board; none were Navajo (as he is) or Mexican in appearance—they were never allowed to converse with each other. He views Star People now as evil, not protective.[98]

Jennifer, a bright college student who had dropped out of school, was working at a gas station when Clarke went to see her at the request of her father. When Clarke asked why she decided not to return to college for the fall semester, Jennifer replied that "something happened" that made her think that college no longer mattered. Jennifer suggested that they meet at a restaurant for dinner. Jennifer and her cousin Rosebud were waiting when Clarke arrived. Jennifer had heard that Clarke was researching UFO stories, and said she had one. She and three cousins, who were riding their horses together at night near their grandmother's house, decided to enter a canyon where they had gone before. A mile into the canyon, they saw bright lights emanating from a large circular craft. They dismounted. Three of them stayed hidden in the rocks, but Jeff stood up and walked toward the spacecraft. Jennifer

97. Clarke, *Encounters with Star People*, 45–50.
98. Clarke, *Encounters with Star People*, 111–13.

ran after him, about a dozen feet behind him, when suddenly, he vanished. She retreated and hid among the rocks with her friends. Jeff was not seen again for a few hours. After he emerged from the light and rejoined his three cousins, they rode back to their grandmother's home. Jeff could not recall anything about what had transpired inside the craft. They promised him that they would never tell anyone. Jennifer and Rosebud, both of whom had been present for the incident, had contrasting views of the Visitors. Rosebud thought they were on a peaceful mission; Jennifer regarded them as "a threat to the human race." Jennifer returned to school. At the university, she majored in physics and minored in astronomy.[99]

Clarke begins chapter 24, "The Little People Are the Star People," describing distinct Indian cultures that have variant understandings of the "little people." Most Indians describe them positively, others negatively, and yet others, such as the Cherokees, understand them to include different types, friendly and unfriendly.[100] In her first week in Bozeman, where she had gone to teach at Montana State University, Clarke met Tom, a graduate student. Clarke befriended Tom and his wife. She asked him if his people had stories about the little people. He said the stories were many, but he had had only a single direct experience, when he was ten years old. On a snowy morning, on his way to school, he decided to cut class. He took an alley route to escape town unnoticed. As he walked quietly behind "old man Wolf's place" to avoid detection, the elder called out to him, warning that the little people were up on the mountain. Tom knew that for centuries his people had good interaction with the little people, who were their "helpers, but then something happened" and they left for a long time. The little people who came next were not friendly: they kidnapped children, who never returned. Wolf, who was known to have a long relationship with the little people, was warning Tom. He invited Tom to breakfast, promising that he would accompany Tom up the mountain.

As they climbed together, Wolf would indicate, with his cane, footprints in the snow: little people, rabbits, coyotes. After a two-hour climb, Wolf cautioned that they must carefully and quietly approach a clearing ahead, a meadow where the little people landed their craft when they were on the mountain. They found the meadow empty. They tracked the little people's footprints to the middle of a large circle in the meadow, in which the grass was burned. Wolf said that the little people had returned home. At that point, Tom saw briefly the glint of a metallic object in the blue sky, and then the

99. Clarke, *Encounters with Star People*, 113–17.

100. This perspective seems, to this writer, most likely to be the case. Diverse stories that feature distinct species of Others are told by different peoples, and are narrated, too, by different individuals within a single culture.

craft departed at a very high speed. Wolf and Tom returned to Wolf's place and had lunch together.

Every year thereafter, when the first snowfall covered the mountain, Wolf and Tom climbed up the meadow. Although sometimes they found and followed little people footprints up the mountain to the clearing, they never saw a spacecraft again. Their last trip happened a few months before Tom graduated from high school and had been drafted to go to Vietnam. Wolf passed on while Tom was overseas. After he returned, Tom went up the mountain every year when the first snow came, as he and Wolf had customarily done. Tom never saw the little people, although on several climbs he saw their footprints. He said to Clarke, "I have never caught a glimpse of them, but I know they are there, just as I know that every fall, when I make that trip, that Wolf is beside me, teaching me about the forest and the ways of the Blackfeet people. *Sometimes you don't have to see something to know that it exists.*"[101]

In the final chapter, "American Indians and the Cosmic Connection," Clarke describes understandings of star people that are held by people from diverse Indian nations; some of these stories, she says, are noted by Lakota scholar Vine Deloria Jr. and astrophysicist Jacques Vallée.

More Encounters with Star People

While *Encounters with Star People* focused on rural and reservation Indians, *More Encounters with Star People* presents narratives from Urban American Indians whom Clarke interviewed. She notes in the introduction, regarding urban Indians, "Unlike those who lived on the reservation, there was a greater concern about the intention of the extraterrestrials."[102]

In the first chapter, "Traveling the Universal Highway," Clarke describes a trip she made to Writing-on-the-Stone Park, Alberta, Canada, near the Montana/Canada border. She met an Indian, Tom, when she stopped to take some pictures. He told her that a portal to the universal highway, a "road" used to travel among galaxies, was located nearby. The portal opened from time to time, on no apparent schedule. They conversed for a while, during which time he said he was a veteran of the Iraq War who had been saved by a Star Traveler when a portal opened in a building he entered to escape from an ambush. After they had conversed for a while, Tom and the Star Traveler walked through a tunnel to a large clearing, in which a spacecraft was sitting. The Star Traveler offered to take Tom away from the war and back home.

101. Clarke, *Encounters with Star People*, 167. Italics added: Clarke comments further on this phrase at the story's end.

102. Clarke, *More Encounters with Star People*, xiii.

Tom declined. Later, the Star Traveler returned with Tom to the United States, and they traveled all around Montana, staying with Indian families. Tom invited Ardy to camp for the night, and she accepted. As they continued their conversation, Clarke said, suddenly UFOs appeared at midnight, having come through the portal. A large ball of light emerged, and then five smaller balls emerged from the large ball, did intricate maneuvers, zigzagged, and departed in different directions; the large ball then disappeared. Clarke notes that she saw Tom numerous times in the following years. She wondered if he was a Star Traveler, but did not ask.[103]

Chapter 5, "He Made Me Feel Like He Was An Old Friend," is unique among Clarke's stories in that a Visitor discusses *panspermia*, thereby linking with the ideas of Hawking and Loeb, among others. It describes an incident reported to Clarke by a hospital doctor, Billy. He told her that he had met an alien who said that he traveled the cosmos "seeding" life, practicing *panspermia*. He transported, to uninhabited but habitable planets, animals and human volunteers who wanted to go elsewhere: those who had no family, or wanted a "new start in life." He said, too, that there are "several thousand intelligent life forms and they do not like the attention that human abduction has brought to the existence of space travelers." He said that his own people liked to travel and explore, not to change an existing culture.[104]

In chapter 15, "We Are the Protectors," Walter and his father Sam, ninety-two years old, live on a family ranch next to a reservation. For generations, they have been Protectors of and friends with Star People who come periodically to get water from their holding pond. Sam and Walter have been on the spacecraft. The water the Visitors take is stored in the walls of their spacecraft. It is used to meet a variety of needs, including fuel. The ranch is secluded: away from the highway and out of sight of military helicopters that search for UAP. Sam said that "there are people like us all over the world, generations of families who protect the Star Visitors. They can come and go on Earth and are protected from the authorities."[105]

In chapter 17, "Masters of Deceit," Drew, a high school English teacher in rural Montana, described her abduction experiences over seven years. She said her abductors periodically took her aboard their craft to examine her. She states that while they observed her, she observed them, and was attentive to their telepathic communications among themselves. She determined that "they are not benevolent creatures. But they are able to convince abductees that they are compassionate and benign through mind control. That allows them to carry out their bizarre experiments and leave their victims feeling

103. Clarke, *More Encounters with Star People*, 1–10.
104. Clarke, *More Encounters with Star People*, 37–42.
105. Clarke, *More Encounters with Star People*, 121–31.

they are privileged or chosen. They often implant the idea that they are helpful aliens who bring messages of peace and warnings about the environment. These are all planted ideas to make the abductees appear special." Drew discusses numerous negative analyses of her abductors and the reasons for their conduct. She notes thereafter that "I'm speaking only for those extraterrestrials I have encountered, and I believe there are other entities from space visiting Earth with different agendas."[106]

Clarke interviewed Jimmy, a seventy-year-old elder and healer, in chapter 21, "There Are Many Alien Species." Jimmy was a leader among his people, and "a spiritual advisor to presidents." He had spoken positively about the Star People over the years, but recently expressed reservations about alien visitors: a "new kind of extraterrestrial" was visiting Earth. He said that they "have no regard for us as a species. They consider us no better than someone might regard a bug." Jimmy knew that they abducted humans. Clarke asked him if he was telling her "that Star People are devious and dishonest?" He replied, "No, not the Star People. The Star People are those who came before us. They are the ancestors. I am talking about some of the other species that inhabit this great universe. They make their victims believe they are special or chosen . . . humans accept their lies and say they are peaceful and loving. There is nothing loving about them."

Jimmy described how Alfred and his family, his nearest neighbors, discovered that Samantha, their sixteen-year-old daughter, disappeared one night. Alfred called Jimmy, who helped them look for her the next day, scouring the area on horseback, to no avail. That night, his neighbor called to say that she was back, with no memory of what had happened. She disappeared multiple times during the next few weeks. After a month, when Jimmy went to his neighbor's house one night shortly after speaking with Alfred on the phone, no one was there. He decided to wait on their porch that night, his shotgun on his lap. He saw a bright light shining behind the house, crept around, and saw a "circular spacecraft. I saw a bright light come down from the bottom of the craft and floating on the light was the family. They were confused, but when the craft departed, they walked into the house." Jimmy knocked on the door, and Alfred opened it and invited him inside. Alfred and his family had no recollection that they had been gone. Two days later Alfred called. He said that Samantha was pregnant, and he and his family were moving to New Mexico. Jimmy agreed to watch over their home. He saw the aliens come on two occasions. Later, Alfred called Jimmy and said that Samantha was not pregnant. Clarke told Jimmy, after he had finished, "That's an incredible story." He replied, "Incredible, but true. I have no reason

---

106. Clarke, *More Encounters with Star People*, 143–58.

to make up stories at my age. We humans are in danger. We just don't know it . . . I think they are slowly substituting the humans of earth with aliens."[107]

The final chapter to be discussed here (appropriately so, since I live in Montana and am writing about Others who have been coming to Earth here), is chapter 24: "A Hunter, An Alien, And A Montana Blizzard." Cody was going hunting in the Bear Paw Mountains, Montana. (He told Clarke that his Indian appearance and heritage come from his Chippewa-Cree mother. His father taught him ranching, and Cody's degree was in animal husbandry.) He invited Clarke to go with him to the site. He provided the horses for them, and they rode thirty minutes into the Bear Paws after departing from a trailhead. She followed him to the edge of a cliff. "This is where it happened," he said after they had dismounted, and added that it had been a year earlier.

He and three buddies were scheduled to go on their annual elk hunting trip. They had been friends "since the first day of kindergarten." They travel individually to their mountain base. Cody was the first to arrive at their meeting and parking place; it was getting dark and heavy snow began to fall. His horse, Peanut, was becoming agitated as Cody put his hunting gear on him to go to the campsite. Fifty feet after they began, "the snow was blinding," and Cody lost his bearings and sense of direction. Peanut balked, not wanting to continue. Cody dismounted and walked ahead, leading the horse. Unable to see the trail, Cody lost his footing and fell over the cliff, landing two hundred feet below. He tried to stand up, but discovered his ankle was broken and swelling, and the bone had pushed through his skin. He slept wrapped in a space blanket which he had in a pocket; other than a bottle of water, it was his only remaining gear.

The snow kept falling heavily, and he grew nauseous. During the second night he felt hopeless, "and prayed to God to look after my wife and children." Then, "about midnight of the second night," as he prayed while lying on his back unable to move, he saw a light overhead; he thought that rescuers had found him. The light focused on him, and "I thought I saw movement in the trees. I called again and suddenly this strange being appeared at my side. He told me not to be afraid, but that he would help me . . . I saw a humanoid figure with a strange glow around the edges of his frame. He placed his hands around my ankle, and extreme heat shot through my foot, ankle, and leg . . . The pain was gone. [Clarke asked if the being spoke; Cody replied,] "Not that I recall. I knew he was friendly. He told me not to be afraid, that he heard my call for help, and that he was there to help me, but verbal speaking did not occur . . . I must have passed out, because when I woke, I was back at my rig. My ankle was no longer broken. It was totally mended. I looked for Peanut. He was beside the horse trailer. That's when I saw the craft. I saw it move

---

107. Clarke, *More Encounters with Star People*, 179–85.

above the trees, fly toward me, and hover for a few seconds over my pickup. It turned on its side and then zoomed off toward the west and disappeared before my eyes. I put Peanut in the horse trailer, climbed inside my pickup, and sat there for several minutes trying to wrap my head around the idea that I had been saved by an alien. I knew no one would believe me. I thanked God and the alien, turned the key, the engine started, and I headed for home."[108]

Cody never told anyone about the incident, not even family or friends. He showed Clarke a faint, thin scar on his ankle, "which ran up the side of his foot to an inch above his ankle." Cody told Clarke: "That is the only thing left after the alien used his hands on my ankle. I swear the bone was protruding outside my skin . . . " He had gone to have a medical doctor examine the scar. "He had no explanation. He took an x-ray of my ankle and confirmed there had been a serious break but had no explanation for the healing. He called it an unexplained miracle." Cody said that if Clarke published his story in her book, it would "let people know that not all aliens are bad . . . This being cared about me. He saved my life . . . Maybe it is true what the elders say. The star travelers do look after us."[109]

Jimmy's and Cody's stories present contrasting images of the Others who are Visitors to Earth. They thereby balance understandings that malevolent *and* benevolent alien beings come; there is no "stereotypical" alien to be discussed and analyzed.

The narratives presented here from *More Encounters* indicate the variety of the stories Clarke recorded, and subsequently published in the book. Several of the witnesses noted that there are numerous intelligent species in the universe. In some cases, Visitors are benevolent; in others, they are malevolent. Because of the mind-control abilities that all of them apparently have, the malevolent ones can be "masters of deceit" in what they tell humans.

Sky People

The settings for stories in *Sky People* are indicated in the names of the parts of the book: Part I: Walking With the Ancients: Exploring Belize; Part II: Walking With the Ancients: Exploring Honduras; Part III: Walking With the Ancients: Exploring Guatemala; Part IV: Walking With the Ancients: Exploring Mexico. Clarke provides a rich array of fascinating and detailed narratives from each country. A story from each country follows.

In Belize City, in an unanticipated event observed by Clarke, tourists, and city residents, a UFO hovered above the city for about five minutes.[110]

---

108. Clarke, *More Encounters with Star People*, 203.
109. Clarke, *More Encounters with Star People*, 204, 199–204.
110. Clarke, *Sky People*, 24.

In Part I, chapter 4, "Men Who Walked Through Mountains," Alexandro Jean, manager of the small hotel where Clarke stayed in Belize City, had heard that she was interested in UFOs. He told her about an encounter he and three friends had when they were eighteen years old. They went to "an abandoned Maya city near [their] village"; they periodically went to an ancient Maya temple to get drunk. This time, they never got to drink. They started noticing a strange odor as they approached. When they emerged from the jungle, they saw a spacecraft in the temple plaza. Four men with human forms and human-like features—they were tall and thin, with a broad forehead and thin, light-colored hair—examined their craft. As they walked around it, their grey uniforms (the color of the craft) changed color: green next to trees' foliage, the color of the stones of the temple when they were next to it. The Visitors went together toward the main temple, which had a stone staircase ascending to an entrance. Alexandro and his friends knew the site well; they had discovered a hidden entrance to the temple behind the staircase. The space men did not climb the stairs: they walked through them and disappeared. The four youths, startled and speechless, went toward their secret entrance, fearful that the spacemen would steal artifacts from within. As they went closer to the temple, the spacemen appeared again, on the outside. They walked to a short mountain covered with grass and trees that was behind the main temple; the "mountain" was actually a smaller stone temple. Without slowing their pace, they walked into the mountain. One of the four teenagers, Javier, decided to go into the spacecraft, and ran toward it. Just then, the spacemen "reappeared out of nowhere." They saw the young men and disappeared without interacting with them. Within a minute, the spacecraft began to rise up. It stopped briefly above them as if studying them, zigzagged in the sky, and rapidly disappeared. The boys ended their drinking party—at which they had no drinks—and returned home. They never went drinking together again.[111]

In Part II, chapter 10, "An Encounter With the Old Ones," a hotel housekeeper in Copán, Honduras, asked Clarke if she was *indígena*, an indigenous woman. Clarke responded that she was a "USA *indígena*." The housekeeper told her that "If you go to the ruins at night, you might see the old ones. Our [Maya] priest said you must be *indígena* or they will not show up." She added that only indigenous people have seen the old ones. Clarke asked, "Who are the old ones?" The housekeeper replied,

> They are the old ones. The gods. They appear in many forms ... Sometimes they come from the sky. Sometimes they come from the jungle. Sometimes they come as lights ... Our priest

---

111. Clarke, *Sky People*, 47–54.

told us weeks ago that you would come ... He said that an *indígena* woman would come from *el norte* ... Tonight, be ready at midnight. My brother, Teodoro, will come for you. He will lead you into the ancient city. There, if you are the woman sent by the gods, you will see the ancients.[112]

Teodoro arrived at midnight, carrying a flashlight, a lantern, and a machete, and led Clarke on a narrow path. They saw two red eyes glowing in the lantern light. A jaguar turned and leaped away. Teodoro said that "visual contact of a jaguar was rare," and seeing it was "a good sign." They saw a "glowing purplish light" ahead, which divided into several smaller lights. Teodoro whispered to Clarke that they are "lights of the ancestors." He led Clarke up temple steps, and told her they would wait at the top. After some three hours, Teodoro whispered that "they are here." Clarke saw "small balls of light" that "flickered around the ancient plaza and playfully danced back and forth ... one light broke off from its gliding antics and moved in front of me. The other lights floated into formation behind him. They hovered there, and then disappeared." Teodoro told Clarke, "You are one of us." Dawn soon arrived, and then "a large, circular, rotating wheel-like craft appeared overhead ... the revolving wheel disappeared toward the east" and was lost in the glare of the rising sun. Clarke asked Teodoro if he saw the UFO. He replied that "the old ones, the ancestors, came from the sky. It has been a long time since we saw them." Later in the day, her new guide, Mateo, arrived for Clarke. He asked her if she had seen the UFO that appeared over the city, then flew toward Copán.[113]

In part III, chapter 14, "The Sky Men of Quiriguá," Mateo, Clarke's guide through Guatemala, relates to her stories of his people (the Maya) about the Sky Men's origins. On their way to Quiriguá, as they pass through a banana plantation, they stop and chat with the foreman, Hugo. He tells them that the Sky People moved Quiriguá's enormous carved stelae from the quarry to the city. The largest stela, weighing sixty tons, is thirty-five feet tall, five feet wide, and four feet thick. He states that the Maya could not have moved them there millennia ago, nor could any current technology carry out that task. As they drive on, Mateo says to Clarke:

> I believe the ancients were more than Sky Gods with extraordinary powers. I believe they were star travelers from another planet. Just think about their names. Cauac Sky was also known as *K'ak' Tiliw Chan Yoat* or Fire Burning Sky Lightning God. After Cauac, there was Sky Xul, next came Sky Imx Dog, Scroll

---

112. Clarke, *Sky People*, 83–84.
113. Clarke, *Sky People*, 86–90.

Sky, and Jade Sky... Sky was an important name to the Maya. A child named "Sky" was destined to be a messenger between the Universe and Earth... Many elders told that in the beginning, the Maya came from the stars... I believe the elders spoke the truth... We are from the stars. No one knows how the ancient Maya achieved such astronomical precision or insights; they didn't have any astronomical observatories. They didn't have any Hubble telescopes, orbiting in space, and as of today no one has found any remnants of sextants or quadrants... I believe that the Sky People came to this planet and brought their knowledge with them and the Maya of today are the descendants of those space travelers.[114]

Clarke asked Mateo what he thought about the claim by Erich von Däniken that aliens came to Earth and constructed the Maya cities. Mateo said that von Däniken never asked the Maya people:

> His work is the best example of ethnocentrism practiced today. He believes some highly intellectual race came to Earth and forced the ignorant, savage Maya to build the cities. He does not recognize that the highly intellectual race is our ancestors. We are the same. In his arrogance he decided that Space Gods built the cities and then left. The Maya were no more than slaves. Of course, if he did admit that the Maya were the same as the Space Gods, and we are their descendants, then he might have to admit that the white man was not superior. But the Maya know the truth... the DNA of the Sky Gods [is] the blood of the Maya. Our language is the language of the Sky People.[115]

Clarke travels through Mexico in the final part of *Sky People*.

Part IV, chapter 42, "The Healers" presents another aspect of encounters with Sky People. It is told by Carla, the wife of Salvador. Their village is located near Uxmal. She relates that she and other villagers saw "a V-shaped craft with red lights... that hovered over her village, shining lights on the village below." The people were fearful, but the craft turned around and disappeared. She continues:

> Later that night, four lights appeared in our home. My husband was ill. The doctors said he had lung cancer from years of smoking and they sent him home to die. He had trouble breathing. He

---

114. Clarke, *Sky People*, 119–20.
115. Clarke, *Sky People*, 121.

> could no longer walk or feed himself. It took all of his energy to breathe. My sisters and I cared for him.[116]

Clarke asks Carla if Salvador is still alive. Her response is that he is very healthy. "How did that happen?" Arthur translates: "She says that the UFOS carried angels who healed him." Clarke is told that Salvador will be home soon; she would be able to talk with him directly. When Salvador arrives, he agrees to tell her what happened:

> I was close to death ... The priest had been called to my bedside twice, but I kept holding on, waiting for a miracle from Jesus. The doctors had given up on me ... The night the UFOS came, I could see the lights from my hammock. The whole outside was red ... It was later that night. I fell asleep. A bright light woke me. The room was like a full sun had come up, but that was not true. Five balls of light circled my hammock. They slowly went up and down my body. One centered over my head and stayed there ... It was warm and felt good. The others centered on my chest, which became very warm. Suddenly I could breathe. I sat up and the balls of light went out the door. I followed them and just as they reached the backyard, I saw them. Five men came out of the balls of light. They stopped and looked at me. I saw a beam of light come from the trees above, and they disappeared upward into the light. I watched as the V-shaped machine moved upward. Red lights outlined it. It climbed into the sky and then it was gone ... Carla slept. I woke her up. I knew I was healed. She was shocked and worried. She wanted me to sit down, but I was too excited. For the first time in years, I could breathe easily.[117]

Salvador told Clarke that this had happened four years previously. "The doctors said there was no sign of cancer. They did not understand."[118]

Star People and the New Others

Several Maya noted, in their particular stories (as the elder, Jimmy, had stated in *More Encounters*), that there was a difference between the Star People described by their elders—Visitors who were friendly and caring—and the new Others in recent decades—who were cruel and malevolent, who kidnapped young women to impregnate them, and came back in a few months to take the fetus and raise the baby; they kidnapped young men, too, to harvest their

---

116. Clarke, *Sky People*, 277.
117. Clarke, *Sky People*, 279–80.
118. Clarke, *Sky People*, 280. The chapter runs from 276–80.

sperm; and they subjected all manner of people to torturous examinations—much as described by several of John Mack's experiencers. It is evident that there are different species visiting Earth now, some benevolent and some malevolent. Many spoke, too, about Earth's impending destruction, which would result from wars, overpopulation, food shortages, and storms. The Maya who remained loyal to their traditions would be rescued, or sheltered underground or in the jungle until the devastation ceased. The fifth age of Earth would begin then.

A fundamental question remains for reflective people to consider, after reading the stories about Contact related by Mack and Clarke: Are all of the people who relate their experiences on the condition of anonymity either delusional or liars? If not, even people who have never seen an intelligently controlled UAP might think, "We are *not* alone," in the cosmos . . . or even on Earth.

The story of the Healers provides a good segue to the life and power, including healing power, of Wanapum elder David Sohappy from the Columbia River.

David Sohappy

The life and spiritual insights of David Sohappy Sr. (1925–91) presented here are based on my interactions with him over five years (1986–91). I met him while working for justice with the International Indian Treaty Council (founded in 1974), the first native peoples' Non-Governmental Organization (NGO) accredited to the United Nations (1977), in Category II Consultative Status with the UN Economic and Social Council (UNESCO). Although Allen Hynek did not have extensive contact with traditional Indian[119] elders and spiritual leaders, his mystical leanings, developed at the Yerkes Observatory, and his interest in spiritual consciousness and other aspects of spirituality (to which he returned, to some extent, in the last months of his life), would have helped him to appreciate and relate to the spiritual traditions and healing rituals of Sohappy.

David[120] was recognized as a spiritual leader, traditional healer, fisher on the Columbia River between Washington and Oregon, and social activist.

---

119. Traditional native peoples in the United States prefer "Indian" over "Native American," which many regard as a form of cultural genocide: it makes the centuries-old struggles of native people for justice, and for requiring governments to honor treaties made with them, disappear from history. So, there are the American *Indian* Movement (AIM), an activist organization, and the International *Indian* Treaty Council, a UN-accredited NGO that works for human rights for native peoples. David and Myra Sohappy were members of the board of directors of the IITC, as was Phillip Deere.

120. As noted earlier, ordinarily Indian elders are addressed as respected family

His native community was the Wanapum (River People), residents on the Columbia for thousands of years. His family had lived there for generations. Then, despite the 1855 Fort Yakama Treaty, which guaranteed them fishing rights on the Columbia in perpetuity, the Wanapum were forced from their traditional lands in the 1940s so that the Hanford Nuclear Reserve, to be placed on adjacent salmon spawning grounds, could be constructed. He successfully tried on several occasions to be arrested for civil disobedience as he sought to establish, via favorable court decisions, his people's claims to riverine land. He won several cases in the courts, including one in the US Supreme Court, *Sohappy v. Smith*. Even though a member of the pacifist *washat* religion, he was subsequently arrested in a nighttime US government military-style assault (heavily armed personnel in helicopters, motor boats, and police cars) on his and Myra's riverbank home, which he had built. He and David Jr., along with four other fishers, were sentenced to prison for "poaching." The law under which they were arrested did not yet exist: government officials said that they "anticipated" the law's passage. While in prison, he suffered a stroke; despite his paralysis in one arm, the prison officials denied him treatment, claiming that he had the "hysterical paralysis" that Indians sometimes experience when imprisoned. After the Sohappys had been in prison for twenty months of a five-year term, US Senator Daniel Inouye, on hearing their story, successfully pressed for their release.[121]

The United States and state (Washington; Oregon) government representatives mentioned only in passing that David Sohappy was a highly respected spiritual leader and healer. He was known for this role not only by Indian peoples in the Columbia River region, but far beyond, north into Canada and south into South America. He was on the board of the

members: "grandfather" or "grandmother." David Sohappy, among friends, preferred simply "David." His biographical data here is derived principally from my conversations with him at the International Indian Treaty Council conference held at Big Mountain, Arizona, in 1986; my conversations and interviews with him while he was in prison, where I interviewed him twice, in 1987–88; and his interviews in the film *River People*; my conversations with Myra Sohappy when she spoke at a conference that I organized at Carroll College in Helena, Montana, and stayed with my family in our Helena home; by telephone after her presentation at the UN International Human Rights Commission in Geneva, 1990; when I drove her in my car from Portland, OR (where she and David Jr. had addressed the steering committee for the Columbia River Pastoral Letter Project of the Columbia Watershed Catholic bishops) to her home on Cook's Landing on the Columbia River, during which she guided me to the Wanapum cemetery where David was buried, to visit his grave; when I visited her at the retirement home in Washington State after her stroke, where I pushed her wheelchair around the grounds; and occasionally thereafter by telephone.

121. Complementary and more extensive accounts of David Sohappy's life, activism, and spirituality are provided in Hart, *Sacramental Commons*, 97–109; and the multiple award-winning documentary film by Michal Conford and Michele Zaccheo: *River People: Behind the Case of David Sohappy* (1990).

International Indian Treaty Council NGO, and an elder in the Washat tradition (as was Myra).

David was a Dreamer, a specific and special role in the river people's religion. In biblical times and terms, he would have been regarded as embodying an integration of prophet, seer, and healer (much as Jesus is described in the Christian Scriptures). The Dreamer would go by him- or herself to remote riverine sites to pray for the people—as individuals or as a community. Individuals would approach the Dreamer at their home, or near their retreat on the river, to ask for healing for themselves or a family member; for spiritual guidance; and for practical advice. Community delegations would seek David's advice when deer, an important food source, could not be found during a hunt, to ask him where to look; or, when concerned because the salmon were not swimming upriver to spawn during their customary time in the spring, community leaders would ask him when the fish would be coming. After presenting to David their concerns and questions, and requesting assistance, the people would leave. They would return a day or so later for his answer. During the time they were gone, the Dreamer would pray about the matter that concerned them, and in a dream or vision would discern the response to give them on their return. Healing for a physical or psychological affliction would be done at the time asked. On such occasions, David, sometimes with Myra, would pray facing the four directions. Then David would go to the petitioner, usually seated on site, cup his right hand and touch the person's body where the problem lay, draw out the illness, and cast it away from the patient. Then he placed one hand atop the other, and passed his hands down from head to toe, without touching the person, to heal them. As his hands descended about four inches away from the one who needed healing, a strong magnetic force emanated from his hands. When he finished, a sense of euphoria engulfed the healed individual.

When I met David at an IITC conference on Big Mountain, Arizona, I did not know he was a healer. I was interested in his fishing rights activities (he was out on appeal awaiting a court decision, after conviction for "poaching" salmon when he was exercising his fishing rights, as stipulated by the Fort Yakama Treaty). In his presentation about his case in the morning, David had mentioned that he belonged to the Washat religion, a tradition called the "feather cult religion" and "drummers and Dreamers."[122] Just over a year before the IITC conference, I had had a series of five dreams about

122. When we spoke, David suggested that I read a book by an anthropologist who had described the healing ritual. He had not experienced it himself, but interviewed several Wanapum at a meeting where they had participated in it. The book is *The Feather Cult Religion*, published decades earlier. Astonishingly, I found it in the library of Carroll College in Montana, where I was a professor at the time. The participants' accounts, elaborated for the anthropologist, described experiences very much like my own.

Phillip Deere. He had passed on about a year before I met David. I spoke briefly with David about my dreams. He invited me to their campsite, where we shared their lunch of salmon and crackers. I asked David and Myra about my dreams. He and Myra interpreted my dreams, and then Myra asked me if I would like them to do a healing ceremony for me. I had never been to, let alone experienced, a traditional Indian healing ceremony. I responded affirmatively. They followed the ritual as I described it above. At the end, David said to me words of power and commissioning. I felt euphoric when the ceremony ended. I was healed immediately of an intestinal problem that had been afflicting me for days, which I had not recalled and related to them earlier.

The following day, as I emerged from my car on a dirt parking area, I was bitten by red ants. I am very allergic to insect bites, as was evident in that the bites on my stomach and leg were red, swollen, and painful. I sought out David, who was on his way to a plenary session of the conference. He paused to draw out the poison from my leg and stomach. Immediately, the pain stopped. An hour later, during a break in the session, I looked where I had been bitten under my T-shirt. There was no sign of a bite: the redness, swelling, and pain were all gone; I assumed that my leg had been similarly healed. I understood immediately that David Sohappy was more than a fishing rights activist. I made discreet inquiries about him, and was told that he was a very powerful healer, and could control weather, too.[123]

In a subsequent conversation with me when he was in the Geiger Correctional Institution in Washington, where he was sent after his appeal was denied, David told me about experiences he had had in the past. He said that, on one occasion when he was a youth fishing on the river, he fell into the water. He was frightened, thinking he would drown, but then felt a hand

123. On May 6, 1991, I had the most extraordinary experience of my life when I was praying for the first time in an Indian way atop Mount Helena in Montana. Among other aspects of the vision that came to me as I felt energy surging upward from my feet through my hands was an image of an *axis mundi*, and David's voice saying to me the words he had said during my healing ceremony at Big Mountain. I called Myra early the next week after I heard that David had died, and she told me that I had had my mountain vision on the same day. She then said to me, "I guess David went to say 'goodbye' to you on the way out." I refer to Mount Helena as a "mysterious, mystical mountain" because of my experiences there. Several years before this vision, I was on a path on a lower level of Mount Helena during an extraordinary display of the northern lights on a clear, starry night. I saw a variety of types of the lights on the mountains to the north. When I turned around and looked at the top of Mount Helena, I saw an amazing light spiraling upward. Several years after my vision, as I walked our dog, Sacha, on the lowest street around the mountain on a clear night, I saw, circling the mountain from midway up to just above the top, a transparent orange-brown tipi, reaching skyward. Through its transparency, I could see the stars in the night sky through the near side and beyond the far side of the tipi. I watched for a while in amazement, but Sacha was not impressed, pulled on her leash, and we went home.

pulling him from the water, while a voice told him that he still had important work to do. (Note the similarity of David's experience to experiences that Sequoyah Trueblood had: while a marine in combat situations, he was told that he was protected, and should not worry.)

When he became a Dreamer, David had numerous spiritual experiences. He told me, the second time that I visited him in prison, that he was guided and strengthened by the Power of the Universe. (When I saw a similar phrase in a comment by an experiencer in John Mack's *Abduction*, I thought about David immediately.) This Power empowered him to do healings. In his words:

> When a person believes in the [Washat] religion he goes to Mother Earth so he can get the good teachings that the Creator gives to the believers ... If the Creator wants you to know something he'll tell you. We never see God, only hear him. I was asleep at one time and I heard this voice tell me, "Listen to this, here is a chant you have to repeat all the time." ... So I have been following my dream all these years.

As a Dreamer, David was given a responsibility to guide his people. As a healer, he could not ask for money when he cured someone: his ability as a healer was a gift for the community. As a fisher, he provided for himself and his family. However, any time someone asked him for help, he had to drop everything and respond to that request—even if it came from "your worst enemy." As a Dreamer, he said,

> We're told in a dream what's going to happen. You hold services and tell people, "Here's what I dreamt, here's what we have to do next ... When we go to our services to help people, we pull down the *power of the universe*. People that can see, can see it coming."

In 2016, when I was conversing with one of David's attorneys, as I recall, he told me that on one occasion, when David was out on appeal during his fishing trial, the attorney went at night to the Columbia River location on Cook's Landing where David and Myra lived. He was told that David was down the hill, on the riverside. As he approached the river, he saw a glow on the bank. When he was near, he saw that David was looking out over the river, bathed in a light emanating from his body. Three years later, the attorney sent to me a lengthier story, in which he described his visit to David in prison, during which David glowed during the visit.

David Sohappy's life and extraordinary power emerge from his historical and cultural context as a Wanapum. For the Wanapum generally, but for the Dreamer in particular, consciousness of the interrelatedness, not only of all living beings but of the holistic cosmos's integral being, is extant. I described this in *Sacramental Commons*:

> In the Wanapum view, not only is creation as a whole sacred, but salmon and other fish (and other species) are honored beings within creation and are sacred also. The Wanapum see themselves related spiritually and materially to a universe permeated with the presence of the holy. Because of that relationship, they have traditionally acted responsibly and even regretfully in their use of other creatures, particularly when they had to take the lives of those creatures [to meet their own needs, such as for food]. They view themselves as part of a web of all life, a sacred whole that is woven from spiritual, social, and physical dimensions of reality.

The traditional Wanapum people engage the essence of Earth and Earth's beings, biotic and abiotic, and come to have a sense of the sacredness of existence and existents. They engage the Spirit by acknowledging creation as a divine work; by actively seeking, or being open to, divine encounters; and by striving to walk in a spiritual way in balance with the other members of the Spirit's creation. They experience spiritual realities in a special way at particular sites, which are designated as sacred, and by recognizing the special contributions of animals and plants to the Earth; they discover the spiritual powers in the land and, by participating in them, live in the multiple dimensions of reality. The Wanapum have a relational consciousness that stimulates their sense of kinship with all life, that is embodied in their unwritten laws, and that is concretized in the ethical actions that demonstrate their attitudes of caring about and being responsible for the ecosystems in which they live.[124]

John Mack's Experiencers and David Sohappy's Experiences

In *Abduction*, John Mack comments numerous times about how experiencers' lives were transformed after their ETI/IDI encounters. Most became more engaged in efforts to promote planetary ecological wellbeing, and several studied seriously the contributions to this effort that traditional native peoples make, especially as taught by spiritual leaders and healers. Some came to see themselves as a "shaman."

---

124. Hart, *Sacramental Commons*, 106–7. This passage was written in 2005 before I had heard of, let alone read, Mack's *Abduction*. In it, remarkably, the experiencers, and Mack in his analysis of and reflections on them, at times express ideas and a consciousness that are identical with or complementary to those of David Sohappy.

The term "shaman" has become commonplace, used particularly by anthropologists and New Age adherents. However, traditional Indian elders reject this word because it referred originally (and still does) to elders from the Tungus people in Siberia. The Tungus elders were healers but, depending on what they were asked to do or sought to do, called on good spirits or evil spirits to accomplish their goal; some were magicians. Indian elders in the Americas and elsewhere focus on spiritual powers, not magical powers: the latter are regarded as inferior, and as a way to promote the status and even economic benefit of the individual practitioner.[125] The healing and vision powers of Indian elders foster, by contrast, the wellbeing of an individual, a community, or Mother Earth and her children, biotic and abiotic.[126]

Mack and Sohappy converge in their thinking on the permeating cosmos presence of a Spirit, however understood. In *Passport to the Cosmos*, Mack observes that "I cannot avoid the fact that not much sense can be made of any of this material without positing an ultimate or overarching creative principle or intelligence in the cosmos that is doing its work through this and related phenomena that break into our material reality from unseen realms."[127] He sees the tie between Indian traditions and experiencers' altered consciousness and perspectives in that the experiencers "are often drawn to Native American spiritual leaders."[128] Experiencers' narratives and Indian elders' teachings, then, complement each other well.

More than a century has passed since Christian churches remembered biblical traditions related to social justice, and began to articulate them again, describing their relevance for diverse and changing social contexts. In the past decade and continuing into the future, new insights and deeper exploration of the old, particularly in regard to ecological devastation and remediation, have inspired new statements and commitments. These include the concepts of socioecological ethics and integral ecology, and principles and policies expressed in the Hague Principles and by the Intergovernmental Panel on Climate Change. These are elaborated in the next chapter.

---

125. Montana Chippewa-Cree elder Pat Kennedy, with whom I was friends, told me that a person on a vision quest should endure the trials for five or more—preferably seven—days. During the first four days, they would be tempted to accept lesser powers, which they could use for personal benefit, However, after these were refused the higher powers would be given. These words reminded me of the story of Jesus being tempted in the wilderness: after he rejected Satan's offers of economic, spiritual, and political power and Satan left, then angels arrived to minister to him.

126. This discussion is based on my almost forty years' work with the International Indian Treaty Council, during which I interacted with and learned from traditional elders' teachings, and from the statements of Indian activists that flowed from elders' insights.

127. Mack, *Passport to the Cosmos*, 272.

128. Mack, *Passport to the Cosmos*, 280.

6

Socioecology, Integral Ecology, Hague Principles, Intergovernmental Panel on Climate Change (IPCC): On Earth and in the Heavens

Earth today is in grave danger. Human-caused and human-exacerbated ecological devastation threatens the planet's ability to provide for the needs of all Earth's biota, and imperils Earth's very existence. Simultaneously, humankind's community-destructive social conduct is destroying relationships between people—as members of discrete communities, as residents within national borders, and as citizens of the world—and thereby threatens to destroy hope for a diverse intraworld community permeated by peace and justice.

The previous books in the trilogy[1] stated that before humankind ventures into space, it would be beneficial—for humans and for ETL—if the people selected for that role—who will be both voyagers from Earth and Earth's representatives to other worlds—were to change beforehand their current individualistic and Earth-destructive consciousness and its consequent conduct. Otherwise, humans will replicate in the heavens the devastation that they have wrought on Earth. Rather than say without basis that "we'll do better in space than we've done on Earth," people must take responsibility for their home planet now. As seen earlier, Stephen Hawking first declared that humanity must send a select few representatives into space to colonize other worlds in order to save the human species from extinction, because it was

---

1. Hart, *Cosmic Commons* and *Encountering ETI*.

destroying its home—and, thereby, itself. His conversion from that assertion was expressed in his essay in *The Guardian*, in which he declared that Earth is the only planetary home that humans know, that they do not know when they will be able to colonize another world, and that they should focus now on care for their Earth home.

It would be beneficial, too, for ETL and Others whom humans Contact on other worlds, that humans would have had the transformation just described. The arriving extraterrestrials—that is, humans from Earth exploring the cosmos and anticipating colonizing otherworld places—would then not be imperial invaders destroying life, in particular intelligent life, as their ancestors had done on Earth in the fifteenth through seventeenth centuries. As Stephen Hawking observed on several occasions, European Conquest and colonization "didn't turn out very well for the Native Americans." The contact between cultures had become a clash of cultures.

Previous chapters described possible diverse occasions of Contact, and potential results thereof. The current chapter offers sources and guidelines for humanity to choose conversion, to undergo transformation from a community- and planet-destroying way of life to an Earth community-based, planet-enhancing, and community-promoting manner of relational living. This effort will begin by positing practices that will be actualized in context through projects that develop and pursue a planetary relational consciousness. That consciousness would include awareness of sustainable ecological practices, and proposals and plans to embody them: on Earth and then in the heavens. This is necessary to ensure that all people have, for the long term, the necessities of life for nourishment, shelter, and health. The result would be a relational biotic-abiotic Earth community that is characterized by planet-wide environment-restoring ecological relationships, and social justice within and among human cultures in all places of habitation. Human explorers, in dialogue with other intelligent beings on other worlds, should be open to share with them socioecological praxis ethics principles for consideration. Human beings should, too, be willing to adapt, from Others with whom they come in Contact, equivalent or complementary ideas and principles that are being developed or are already in place in other cosmos locales.

The conversations would be more fruitful if other intelligent species already have developed, from within their own culture(s) in their own world, recognition of their responsibilities as *trustees* or, better yet, as *coequal members of the biotic relational community*—each of whom has its respective responsibilities according to its abilities and the extent of its consciousness; intelligent beings are not *owners* or *managers* of the land(s) and the natural goods of the places in which they live, work, and recreate.

Historically, many of Earth's religion scholars have taught that land and its natural benefits were a *gift* from God to humankind, whose members were to be its *stewards*. However, there are two significant misunderstandings hidden in these terms regarding intraworld conduct on Earth and a potential problem for formulating an interworld consciousness that respects the responsible "ownership" traditions and practices that other intelligent beings have developed in and for their own world's contexts.

In the first place, regarding Earth thinking, the recipient of a gift can ordinarily dispose of it as they wish: they can re-gift it, exchange it for something else, or return it for money to help meet pressing needs. In contrast, a *trust* is something held on behalf of another: it is entrusted to the recipient to be its *trustee*, to use in ways that are or would be approved by the one who entrusts it. At the same time, trustees recognize that, ultimately, control over what is entrusted to them is retained by the one who has entrusted it. In regard to Earth's places and goods, the one who entrusts them to human use might be understood to be the divine Creator Spirit, the biotic community as a whole, or only its human members or individuals, or Earth herself.

In the second place, a *steward* is a manager of another's property, in this case God's Earth, and is placed over others by God. But humans are not managers who have a higher status than other creatures, who understand every species' biological, ecological, and social needs. Humans lack the knowledge to exercise responsible and respectful control over every Earth creature and over creation as a whole. Earth in all its complexity, and Earth's living creatures in all their diversity (ranging from eagles in the air, through grizzly bears on the ground, and on to salmon in the rivers, or the ocean through which they journey), cannot be controlled, managed, or stewarded by human beings. Rather, humans should live in a relational community with all living beings and with Earth. Each being has its own intrinsic worth and responsibilities, and contributes to the whole. So here, too, humans should be conscious that they are called to be *trustees* who are solicitous for the well-being of Earth and all living beings, with whom they are intimately related and among whom they interact.[2]

2. This understanding first came to me in 1981, when I was director of the Midwestern US Catholic bishops' Heartland Project, and editor and principal writer of their land statement, *Strangers and Guests: Toward Community in the Heartland* (1980), which advocated for humans' *stewardship* of God's land. I published my advocacy of humans-as-trustees in my first book, *The Spirit of the Earth: A Theology of the Land* (1984): "When the land is seen as a *trust*, the primary attitude toward it is that it is to be *cared* for ... the one who holds something in trust is aware that its well-being and the well-being of others depends on how he or she fulfills that trust ... the trustee is accountable for it ... The land is seen as being on loan from the earth itself, from God, and/or from the human family: it has a social mortgage ... the land exists primarily for the other, the others, or the Other ..." (152). The perspective of humans as trustees evolved over time to be that humans

Socioecology

Since the latter part of the nineteenth century, Christian traditions (with roots in the prophets of Israel and in Jesus) have considered the idea of social justice, and elaborated it in books and documents. The Protestant thinkers who originated the *Social Gospel*,[3] and the popes who wrote *social encyclicals*,[4] understood well the unjust conditions that oppressed the vast majority of people, especially in capitalist countries and, particularly, working people. It was well into the twentieth century, however, before Christian scholars, community activists, and Church leaders began to address the environmental crisis threatening the wellbeing of Earth and all living beings. I began to link the issues of social justice and ecological justice beginning in the late 1970s, in my books, courses, public lectures, articles, and "ghost writing" for various Catholic and ecumenical church documents. At the beginning of the twenty-first century, as I was thinking about a unified concept and term to describe my work, the word *socioecology* came to mind, followed immediately by *socioecological ethics* and, a few years later, *socioecological praxis ethics*.

It is tempting to consider "ethics" in the abstract, as some do. This enables the subject and field to be developed in intellectually secure ivory-tower academic settings as "knowledge for knowledge's sake." There, the subject and its attendant principles are formulated as if they are not—and should not be—directed toward engaging with and resolving, or at least mitigating, real-world issues and events. Its proponents proclaim and project an imagined intellectual "objectivity," unencumbered by down-to-Earth considerations, in what is, in reality, their abstract, sociocultural personal pondering. In such aerie settings, when they present abstract ideas, and principles that elaborate them, these are countered with wordsmithing that others perform on their work, or by proposals for an alternative philosophical narrative from a distinct ideological base. The cycle keeps repeating. Intellectually, it is fascinating and challenging as new concepts are formulated and expressed in the same or contradictory terms, or as neologisms are creatively crafted. This mobius loop-type cycle calls to mind Karl Marx's mid-nineteenth-century

---

are comembers of a relational community, each member of which is equal to the others but has its own responsibilities, flowing from its particular capabilities, to contribute to the integral wellbeing of the whole Earth community.

3. These included Walter Rauschenbusch, Washington Gladden, Lyman Abbott, Richard Ely, and Josiah Strong.

4. The first social encyclical was Leo XIII, *Rerum Novarum* (On the Condition of Workers). It was commemorated in 1931 on its fortieth anniversary by Pius XI, *Quadragessimo Anno* (On Reconstruction of the Social Order), and by successive popes (Pius XII, John XXIII, Paul VI, John Paul II, Benedict XVI, Francis I) on every tenth anniversary thereafter.

words. In the eleventh (and last of) his "theses on Feuerbach," written for *The German Ideology* (1845), Marx declared famously that "The philosophers have only interpreted the world in various ways; the point is to change it."[5] People who suffer under oppression are not concerned about the latest ethical *theory*: they hope that ethical *action* will alter their condition by stimulating development of down-to-earth social theories and practices that initiate establishment of a just society, and sustain it over time.

Socioecology and Socioecological Praxis Ethics

The perspective, process, and practices of socioecological praxis ethics promote reflective action, in context, to address and eliminate specific situations of social and ecological injustice.

A *socioecological* understanding provides the foundation for developing this type of consciousness and conduct. It includes developing efforts to effect beneficial social change within and among intelligent beings' communities, integrated with the wellbeing of their world in its entirety, including all biota.

Praxis is the locus of a dialogic or dialectical process in which theory dialogues with practice, and present dialogues with future. Where efforts are collaborative because of complementary interests, values, and objectives, the process is *dialogic*. Where there is conflict between or among the communities engaged with each other, the process is *dialectic*: a clash of ideologies catalyzes social struggle to move society forward such that conflicts are overcome and a better world comes into being. One side is victorious, or all sides become accommodating to each other without violating their core principles and public practices. The classic formulation of a dialectic struggle is thesis <-> antithesis => synthesis. This might be expressed as a conflict between a present place, a *topia*, and an envisioned new place, a *utopia*, a "no-place" in the sense that such a place is not yet present but might become the new topia.

Dialogic process:

$topia_1$ <-> $utopia_1$ --> $topia_2$ <-> $utopia_2$ --> $topia_3$ <-> $utopia_3$ --> $topia_4$ <-> $utopia_4$ --> $topia_n$ <-> $utopia_n$ ... Ω/∞

Dialectic process:

$topia_1$ <-> $utopia_1$ / $utopia_2$ --> $topia_2$ <-> $utopia_3$ / $utopia_4$ --> $topia_3$ <-> $utopia_5$ / $utopia_6$ --> $topia_4$ <-> $utopia_7$ / $utopia_8$ --> $topia_n$ <-> $utopias_n$ ... Ω/∞

---

5. Marx, "Theses on Feuerbach," Thesis XI.

The *dialogic* begins with a shared vision (utopia$_1$) that developed congenially from a shared place (topia$_1$); in the resulting place (topia$_2$), a new vision is developed (utopia$_2$), and so on. The subscript $_n$ represents any and all succeeding topias and utopias in dialogic interaction, leading to progressively succeeding topias and utopias.

In contrast, the *dialectic* begins in a topia in which there are contrasting/conflictive/competing visions from parties in conflict; the conflict of visions leads to a new topia; the struggle continues as long as conflicts persist. Thus, as just stated, the subscript $_n$ represents all the topias and utopias that follow, in which conflicting utopias struggle in context for dominance. Karl Marx (and others) assumed there would always be a "dialectical" engagement; I propose that, instead, there might be a "dialogic" engagement if the parties engaged are open to compromise, or are accepting of the perspectives of the other, in whole or in part.

Ethics provides the underlying foundation and guide to effect social change. It includes the complementary values, expressed in principles, which are held by those collaborating to effect change, integrated into a common movement toward the utopia envisioned.

Socioecological Praxis Ethics

When the method of socioecological praxis ethics is initiated, those engaged in it will decide whether the ongoing process will be dialogic or dialectic. Its ongoing momentum will be toward positive social change; the means by which to achieve a just society will be determined in social conflict or social coordination and cooperation. The guiding phrase of Spain's Mondragón Cooperative Movement[6] is pertinent here: "We build the road as we travel."

The four basic steps in *socioecological praxis ethics* process are: 1. *socioecological analysis*; 2. *socioecological insight*; 3. *socioecological vision*; and 4. *socioecological project*. The steps might be taken sequentially or simultaneously, depending on social and ecological conditions in a particular context, and the experience(s) of those sharing a utopian vision to alter their topia.

---

6. José María Arizmendiarrieta (1915–76), a priest who had advocated for an independent Basque nation (and had been imprisoned for a time because of this), was appointed to Mondragón as a pastor in 1941. He began the Mondragón Cooperative in 1956, after providing its foundation in the Professional School for Mondragón youth, established for the 1943–44 academic year. Five of its graduates joined with him to found the cooperative. An historical outline of key dates is available on the Mondragón website, at https://www.mondragon-corporation.com/en/timeline/1957/. See also Hart, *Ethics and Technology* (1997), "Case Studies," "Chapter 3: Mondragón," 151–54. The current Mondragón website has updated information: https://www.mondragon-corporation.com/en/about-us/.

Socioecological *analysis* is an assessment of the most pressing social and ecological practices, and the systems that embody them, that oppress the most vulnerable biotic populations and abiotic contexts on the planet or in one or more of its distinct regions, in a given place and time. It seeks to identify the social causes of a specific community's oppression—who is responsible—and the means by which it has been implemented and maintained; the analysis includes proposing possible counter efforts through which oppression might be overcome.

Socioecological *insight* is consideration of values and principles, derived from humanist and spiritual traditions, that are relevant for and important to efforts to eliminate or at least mitigate oppressive systems and practices; the latter types of oppression restrict access to needed natural goods and prevent equitably distributed ownership of lands because the lands have been consolidated into the private possession of a few, dominant citizens. These injustices against the vast majority of people and other biota are often imposed and exacerbated by laws and policies that have been implemented and sustained by private property owners, individual and corporate. All of the preceding is likely enforced by police or private security companies that support unjust laws, which usurp community rights to lands and goods. Such institutionalized private ownership leads to environmental and ecological devastation, and socioeconomic harm. Social insights provide just alternatives to oppressive behaviors, such that lands and goods will be redistributed, as needed, to be shared justly to stimulate and sustain the wellbeing of all peoples, all living beings, and their shared Earth world.

Socioecological *vision* is a collaborative, imaginative formulation of what could be the outcome in a future time if the planet- and biota-harming socioecological situation were altered. The steps of assessing and analyzing *what is*, at this time, and contrasting this existing socioecological context to inspiring principles and values presented in the *insights* of diverse spiritual and social traditions' teachings, stimulates formulation of *what might be*—if not at this or an approaching proximate moment in time, then by being gradually developed through intermediate on-the-ground efforts, for ultimate realization in a future time. In this step, people "dream dreams" and "have visions" of that toward which they aspire and of how they might bring it to realization.

Socioecological *project* embodies the coordination of consciousness of the results of prior socioecological analysis of what is, contrasted with insights about what ought to be, which had stimulated envisioning how a new reality in which they are integrated would be implemented by their conduct in context at this time. The result is a new consciousness of what might be, as envisioned, and consequent commitment, through conduct in context, to engage in ongoing on-the-ground action to stimulate realization of the social vision in achievable socioecological projects. People engaged in this process should formulate achievable goals for the short term—*relative utopias*—while bearing in mind and working toward their ultimate vision—an *absolute utopia*.

Earth Wellbeing to ExoEarth Wellbeing

Socioecological praxis ethics[7] on Earth will extend to cosmos contexts as *cosmosocioecological praxis ethics* upon discovery of ExoEarth microbial life, evolving life, or intelligent life. It was first discussed in *Cosmic Commons*,[8] and succinctly re-stated in *Encountering ETI*:

> *Cosmosocioecological [praxis] ethics* extends and enhances socioecological ethics to embrace the seen and unseen, known and unknown dynamic universe, [which is] a cosmic unfolding of creation (and/or autopoietic generation) that is continuously *in statu viae* (a state of being-becoming). Humankind and all intelligent life are responsible for the wellbeing of those parts of the cosmos with which they become particularly interrelated when they pass through as explorers, or when they become and remain present as communities of colonizers and conscientious developers of natural goods.[9]

Principles for Earth and ExoEarth Projects

As humanity journeys from planet Earth into near and distant places, their new relational Earth consciousness would be assisted, in context, by their tentative guidelines for interworld and interspecies conduct, as subject to interworld creative amendment, as needed. On hearing this proposal, some people in troubling, trying, and even traumatic economic or ethnic circumstances have asked, "How can you think about conduct in space when there are so many problems on Earth?" A response to the question is to be found in the integration of socioecological praxis ethics, integral ecology, the Hague

---

7. Hart, *Sacramental Commons*; Hart, *Cosmic Commons*; Hart, *Encountering ETI*.

8. Hart, *Cosmic Commons*, 199–227.

9. Hart, *Encountering ETI*, 283. The section heading is "Cosmosocioecological Praxis Ethics" (281–83), but "praxis" was omitted inadvertently in the definition in the last paragraph. The entire term is used several pages later, in the section "Cosmosocioecological Praxis Ethics Dialogically Engaged" (284–86). A four-step process is described: social analysis, social insight, social vision, and social project—all developed through TI-ETI(-IDI) dialogue.

Principles, and recommendations for action in the reports of the Intergovernmental Panel on Climate Change (IPCC). This integration would provide a process, a way forward toward realizing a new intraworld consciousness and conduct; the latter would promote justice, peace, and planetary wellbeing on Earth. Similarly, in interworlds engagements, these documents would provide food for thought as humankind dialogues with other-than-human intelligent species.

Cosmosocioecological Praxis Ethics-in-Process: ExoEarth Contexts

Intelligent living beings on ExoEarth worlds who experience some form of oppression by a dominant and dominating group of other or Other intelligent beings hope that at some point a relational consciousness and ethics (although likely not expressed in those terms) will alter their condition. Other inhabitants, and the world itself, would benefit from a socioecological consciousness and consequent conduct that gradually effect a just and sustainable planetary community.

When the socioecological praxis ethics process is initiated on other worlds, those engaged in it—including the exoplanet humans, when they arrive—will assess whether the ongoing process will be dialogic or dialectic. Its ongoing momentum will be implementing socioecological praxis ethics to effect positive social change and enduring ecological wellbeing.

Cosmosocioecological Praxis Ethics, suggested in the previous two volumes of this trilogy as a "thought experiment," now can be viewed as a helpful way for TI/ETI/IDI to consider it in context. It is known now to be a fact, not a hypothesis or a theory, that Others exist. In light of new advances in humans' scientific knowledge, particularly in astrophysics, in humanist studies, such as metaphysics, in humans' social-scientific knowledge understood through sociology and psychology, and in the experiences of members of the Earth community as a whole, the "thought experiment" should be considered in a different way: humans now *know* that "We are *not* alone." What should we do?

Cosmosocioecological praxis ethics might be extended now to cosmos contexts: at first as a working hypothesis, but then to be used in context upon discovery of ExoEarth microbial life, evolving life, or intelligent life.

Cosmosocioecological refers to efforts to offer or extend beneficial social change and ecological commitments that developed within and among human communities, to be considered and adapted, as appropriate and acceptable, by Contacted intelligent beings. Human-originated understandings would serve, in new worlds' contexts, as examples of consciousness and conduct that might be integrated with the perspectives and practices that other intelligent beings had developed on their own world. The latter beings might accept such an integration in order to foster the wellbeing of their world, its diverse living beings, and its abiotic setting; reject it as incompatible with what they have developed themselves and intend to retain; or amend it to incorporate on-world communities' thought and action, consciousness and conduct.

Cosmo indicates places in innumerably diverse cosmos contexts. In each and all of them, voyaging intelligent beings should strive to dialogue with the distinct types of resident intelligent biota that they encounter on worlds unfamiliar to the travelers. Most (if not all) resident living beings, in whatever evolutionary state they have reached by the time humans arrive, likely will have physical characteristics substantially different from those of humans. They, too, would have evolved and would be evolving because of the interaction of their DNA with the microbes within planetary biotic zones in their planetary environment; the relationships they have, and the niches they have developed as they interacted with other biota; and the adaptations they have made to live in any or all of the areas of their world: forest, field, mountain, meadow, alongside rivers, on the plains, in oceans, or in areas of volcanic eruptions or tectonic plate movements. The most evolutionarily developed living beings' intelligence might be more advanced than human intelligence, or process ideas in a different manner. Perhaps they would have, too, radically different cultural mores or spiritual understandings and beliefs (if the latter exist in their consciousness and cultures). In all of this, the extent of resident and arriving intelligent beings' communication skills, openness to an "other," patience, receptivity, and adaptivity to alternative understandings and ways of thinking and reasoning, will enhance or inhibit Contact experiences.

Socio describes the social wellbeing of humans within and among human communities, on Earth and in the heavens, and of Others, within and among their communities, on their world and in the heavens. On Earth, or upon arrival on other worlds, human voyagers' social wellbeing will be interrelated and integrated with the wellbeing of all intelligent life with whom humans come into Contact—especially (but not solely) in places where humanity hopes to establish a colony.

Ecology in cosmos contexts is about relationships in which the wellbeing of a world and all its living beings is considered, including intergenerationally (E. O. Wilson's *eusociality*) and transcontextually (in all places). On Earth presently, and possibly on other worlds, the relationships exist in an evolutionary context, in which predator-prey relationships are operative. Each species prioritizes its own existence vis-à-vis others' existence and, within a species, individuals usually prioritize their own existence (except, of course, where love for another or others, or altruism, takes precedence over individualism, speciesism, or nationalism). In relationships between biota, the *intrinsic value* (inherent value) of all species and their individual members should be prioritized, to the extent possible, over their *instrumental value* (their value to another to meet the other's *need* or to satisfy the other's *want*).[10]

Praxis in cosmos worlds describes the locus of interactions between resident intelligent beings and immigrant intelligent beings, both of whom relate text-to-context and theory-to-practice in dialogue, in a particular place. Resident inhabitants would bring to the conversation their native cultures and values, and their familiarity with *abiotic* aspects of their place, such as types of terrain in their territory, weather, climate variations, soil types, air quality, potable water availability and accessibility, and *biotic* aspects, including types and characteristics of fauna and flora needed for food, fiber, or medicinal herbs, and information about potentially dangerous-seeming food sources (animal or plant), and of microbes that are present (to the extent known) so that humans would not be harmed by pathogenic transfers. Newcomers (including potential residents from distant planets and galaxies) would describe their culture and values, home and habitat requirements, needed nutrients and medicines, requirements for breathable air, uncontaminated soil, and unpolluted water; and, measures they would take to prevent pathogenic transfers from themselves to the present inhabitants of a place, including all biota: intelligent, evolving, or microbial.

Ethics in cosmos contexts considers the values and principles of intelligent life communities, as developed in their particular places. *Praxis ethics* in cosmos contexts, as in Earth contexts, is ethics-in-contexts, and ethics-from-contexts. It flows from a dialogic (and sometimes dialectic) engagement of text and context, in the hope of promoting positive interspecies and interpersonal relationships between and among intelligent biota. Cosmosocioecological ethics is, ultimately, contextual: it is developed in diverse worlds' contexts by human beings and other intelligent beings who consciously consider and prioritize previously formulated principles as they adapt to and adapt from each context that is their then-present social and ecological milieu. Humans, all intelligent living beings, and all other biota have *natural rights*, rights from nature: these natural rights are universal, for all biota and abiotic being, not solely for human beings and other intelligent beings, or solely for human beings, whether on Earth or in the heavens.

Cosmosocioecological praxis ethics, then, describes principles and practices intended to effect or affirm social justice and ecological wellbeing, on Earth and in other cosmos places. It is a participatory endeavor, in which

10. This is discussed more fully in Hart, *Sacramental Commons*, 121–25.

human explorers and native inhabitants of a world are involved; it is not an imperial invasion in which humans (or other intelligent beings) decide, from prior experience in their culture(s) alone, what should be operative values and principles in all contexts, Earth (or others' home planet) and ExoEarth/ExoPlanet. The guiding principles and practices would stimulate collaborative work to proceed from a current *topia* to a jointly envisioned *utopia*. Humans should consider, too, a new *prime directive*: not of non-interference in a planet's current struggles, but of engagement to address obvious social oppression and ecological destruction, and to promote love, justice, and peace in the worlds with which they come into Contact. Dialogic love expressed in compassion should be prioritized over a hands-off "non-interference" policy that leaves in place harsh political and economic dictatorships, and ongoing ecological devastation. This discretionary use of a prime directive is especially important if arriving humans (or other intelligent beings) observe that the harsh rulers are intelligent non-native invaders trying to conquer, subjugate, and control less weaponized cultures, for the invaders' exclusive benefit.

Cosmosocioecological praxis ethics would be a relational integration of social justice within and among intelligent beings, including in terms of how they relate to microbial beings and aspire to conserve the wellbeing of worlds (planets, moons, comets, etc.), and abiotic location(s), and biota in each and every context. This ethical method would enhance cosmos connections and relationships since it is developed in "dialogue" with social and cultural contexts, as guided by both core and negotiable values and principles. Rather than imperiously export and impose an Earth-specific (or other world-specific) ethics it provides, in context, for relational consciousness, conduct, consideration, and community to guide the process of ethical decision-making. Core, seemingly nonnegotiable values and principles from different intelligent beings' worlds coexist with each other, related to amendable, negotiable values and principles; they influence each other in a mutually beneficial manner. In this process, sociocultural, socioeconomic, and ideological conflicts can be addressed or avoided, and pathogenic transfers (biological and intellectual) can be averted.

Cosmosocioecological Ethics in Process in Place

The four-step process of *cosmosocioecological praxis ethics* would be adapted to specific cosmos contexts, and embrace, enhance, and incorporate, in a dialogic process in a world's place(s), complementary steps that had been taken by human (and other intelligent) explorers, prior to Contact, to contextualize *socioecological praxis ethics* on Earth (or Others' home worlds).

Cosmosocioecological Praxis Ethics Process: Contextual Consciousness, Context-Adaptive Ethics

Cosmosocioecological analysis, in space or in another dimension, is an assessment, on diverse other worlds or on distinct locales on other worlds, of the unjust social and ecological systems and practices that oppress the most vulnerable biotic populations in their home and habitat in a given place and time. This assessment can be done, it would seem, only through Contact and fruitful communication with diverse actors in each setting. Once sufficient data is collected and verified, critical analysis would seek to identify the social cause of beings' oppression—who is responsible—and the means by which it has been implemented and maintained—unjust laws and other social coercion; and, to consider and propose possible countering efforts through which it might be overcome. This will take time and patience, in order to identify types of oppression and those who enforce them to control intelligent Others, or to dominate less intelligent beings, including biota of different species. Analysis, too, will enable intelligent beings to discern ideological bases used to justify intelligent beings' degradation of their home planet, should this harmful conduct exist; discuss and alter practices that promote this destructive ideology; evaluate reasons for space exploration and settlement; and project possible consequences of the current rapacious Earth ideology and similar thinking on other planets.

Cosmosocioecological insight, in space or in another dimension, is consideration of values and principles from spiritual and non-spiritual traditions on other worlds that are relevant for and important to practice in place. Insight derives from faith traditions' and philosophical schools' (where these are present) values and principles, available international, planet-focused, and interworld documents, including, on Earth, reports and statements from such organizations as the Nobel Peace Laureate Intergovernmental Panel on Climate Change, United Nations documents such as the Universal Declaration of Human Rights and other UN documents and covenants related to fostering human rights. If extended to worlds other than Earth and implemented, the values and principles that are advocated would help to eliminate, or at least to mitigate, oppressive systems and practices, and thereby promote cosmos integral relational community. This might be achieved by widespread cooperative or communal ownership of territory in land, of natural goods' sites, and in order to eliminate excluding the many to benefit the few (those who have directly, or through the politicians whose campaigns they have funded, imposed proprietary restrictions on land ownership and use). This process would likely include elimination of restrictions of and limitations on types of private property ownership that have been reserved for the wealthy few; elimination of unjust laws, and of restrictive, oppressive limits on the common people's ownership of or access to lands and natural goods. Cooperatives could be developed as this occurs. Ordinary citizens need the lands for their wellbeing—even their very survival. As the new owners, they could prevent, by taking these actions, further ecological devastation wrought by irresponsible abuse of the land caused by private owners' or Others' acquisitiveness.

Cosmosocioecological vision, in space or in another dimension, is a collaborative, imaginative formulation of what could be the outcome in a future time—a *utopia*—if the socioecological situation—the current *topia*—were to be altered by implementing, in context, the social and ecological insights relevant to this place at this time. Some of these might have been under development already (at least conceptually) by intelligent native inhabitants, and subsequently could be enhanced and enabled by respectful dialogue between intelligent beings—human and other-than-human—in this place at this time. In their envisioning, intelligent beings would consider how the consciousness and conduct of human, ETI, and IDI explorers, entrepreneurs, scientists and engineers, government officials, and intelligent species' citizens in space, would develop and implement a new intelligent beings' cosmos perspective, in which all are integrated in, interdependent among, and interrelated with other biota and abiotic worlds.

Cosmosocioecological project, in space or in another dimension, would be a coordination of human consciousness and conduct with other worlds' intelligent beings' consciousness and conduct, in order to take steps to promote the respective worlds' commons good and common good.[11] The project would develop a preliminary and dynamic *Cosmos Charter*, to be adjusted as needed in diverse celestial contexts, as an ongoing work-in-progress that includes core principles and secondary, potentially negotiable principles. This would stimulate ongoing on-the-ground action to assist the realization of the cosmosocioecological vision, as developed locally, in distinct places with diverse populations and perspectives. It will likely take time for a social project to achieve its envisioned goal. Intelligent beings from different species who are engaged in this process should formulate achievable short-term goals—relative utopias—for their specific *topia*, while bearing in mind their ultimate vision—an absolute utopia for both their world and the cosmos as a whole (to the extent that it is known, and among intelligent species who are interacting collaboratively).

Humankind voyaging in space or in another dimension as it seeks a new home would have to explore how, or even if, cosmosocioecological

11. Hart, *Sacramental Commons*, 139–58 (see especially chapter 8: "Commons Good, Common Good, and Common Goods").

praxis ethics might be used in distinct places, as adapted to otherworld contexts with which, and the Others' communities with whom, humans have come into Contact.

The Earth Charter

Work already under way to integrate social justice and ecological wellbeing[12] was complemented, reinforced by, and embodied in principles discussed in the 1992 Earth Charter. That document, too, integrated human rights with Earth rights. The Earth Charter is discussed more fully in previous books.[13] The vision of Maurice Strong, who was a major force in developing the 1992 Earth Summit in Rio, was that the Earth Charter, which originated with him, would complement the UN Universal Declaration on Human Rights.

"Jobs *and* Environment"

Often in past years environmental groups did not consider seriously the plight of working people—particularly in the mining, timber, and chemical industries—who were employed by, and dependent upon for meeting their basic needs, corporations that were wreaking havoc on Earth's environment and biota. Few members of environmental groups working to end corporate devastation by limiting or shutting down egregious corporate industrial plants and practices suggested alternative employment for these workers. Obviously, the workers and their unions, reinforced by industry propaganda and lies, were hostile toward those who were threatening their livelihood and thereby the wellbeing of their family. Conversely, workers did not consider adverse environmental and biotic impacts of their jobs. Industries developed the slogan "Jobs vs. Environment" to deceive working people by portraying a purported conflict between the two. However, in some areas the workers themselves saw through this deception. For example, forestry workers, many of whom were hunters and fishers, realized that timber companies' proposals to clear-cut wide swaths of forests would deprive deer of their habitat, causing their disappearance from local areas; clear-cutting would also clog lakes and streams, killing fish by destroying their habitat. The foresters recognized that responsible logging would enable them to retain their employment and

---

12. Elaborated by this author in books, church documents, and journal articles such as Hart, "Poor of the Planet," 144–82.

13. Hart, *Cosmic Commons*, especially 112–14, 348–50; Hart, *Sacramental Commons*, 153–56; Hart, *What Are They Saying?*, 126–28. I participated in the development and dissemination of the Earth Charter.

source of livelihood, while they could continue to enjoy outdoor activities that provided recreation, family members' bonding, and food for the table.

People who had been integrating social justice and ecological wellbeing were pleased to hear about, and then to celebrate, the proclamation and publication of Pope Francis I's encyclical *On Care for Our Common Home*. For my part, I noted a strong correspondence and complementarity between *socioecology* in my work, and Francis's ideas on *integral ecology* in his encyclical.

Pope Francis I: Integral Ecology

Pope Francis I issued *On Care for Our Common Home* (*Laudato Si'*),[14] his major encyclical on the relationship between social justice and ecology, on May 24, 2015. In it, he declared that neither the ecological wellbeing of Earth and all living beings, nor social justice in human society, should be considered in isolation from the other. Rather, he said, an *integral ecology* is needed to link them together to promote social and ecological justice. Integral ecology and socioecological praxis ethics present complementary ideas and proposals about how to renew planet Earth while promoting and protecting thereby the wellbeing of humankind and all biota.[15]

The first paragraph of *Laudato Si'* recalls that the phrase comes from Saint Francis of Assisi's "Canticle of All Creatures,"[16] and means "Praise be to you, my Lord"; these words are repeated at the beginning of all the song's verses. Pope Francis then quotes the verse that celebrates "our Sister, Mother Earth, who sustains and governs us." He begins the second paragraph noting a startling contrast, in today's world, with the poetry of the song: "This sister now cries out to us because of the harm we have inflicted on her by our irresponsible use and abuse of the goods with which God has endowed her." People have come to regard themselves as Mother Earth's "lords and masters,

---

14. Francis, "*Laudato Si'*." The numbers in parentheses below indicate paragraph numbers in the encyclical.

15. An in-depth elaboration of the relationship between socioecological praxis ethics and integral ecology is found in Hart, "*Laudato Si'*," 37–53.

16. As noted earlier, Francis's song is called, too, "The Canticle of Brother Sun," and other, equivalent titles; it is translated from early Italian, when the language was developing from an integration of French and Latin. It is recognized by Italian scholars as the oldest poem in Italian, and as one of the first, if not the first, works in Italian literature. Francis sang the song, whose opening words are "Praise be to you, my Lord," as he approached villages. The Canticle's words are his, but the melody came from a ballad of the time that celebrated life in nature. Thus, when Francis's words about abiotic nature are integrated with the melody of a song about biotic nature, all creation is included and interrelated. Francis's listeners would know the melody already, and learn and integrate his complementary words.

entitled to plunder her at will." Humankind is faced with "global environmental deterioration" (3). He goes on to highlight strong words spoken by "the beloved Ecumenical Patriarch Bartholomew," head of the Orthodox Church: "to commit a crime against the natural world is a sin against ourselves and a sin against God" (8); this idea of "ecological sin" is new in Catholic thought. He cites Francis of Assisi again, in words that hint at the coming linkage of social justice and ecological justice as expressed in the phrase *integral ecology*: "Francis is the example par excellence of care for the vulnerable and of an integral ecology . . . He was particularly concerned for God's creation and for the poor and outcast . . . He shows us just how inseparable the bond is between concern for nature, justice for the poor, commitment to society, and interior peace" (10). Francis I then notes words of wisdom from the book of Wisdom: "Through the greatness and the beauty of creatures one comes to know by analogy their maker" (Wis 13:5) (12). In chapter 1, "What Is Happening To Our Common Home," Francis provides examples of environmental and ecological degradation:

> *pollution and climate change*—Francis states in this section that "the climate is a common good, belonging to all and meant for all" (23);
>
> *the issue of water*—"access to safe drinkable water is a basic and universal human right, since it is essential to human survival" (30);
>
> *loss of biodiversity*—different species "have value in themselves," they are not solely "potential 'resources' to be exploited" (33);
>
> *decline in the quality of human life and the breakdown of society*—there are "hidden areas where the disposable of society live" (45);
>
> *global inequality*—few people are aware "of problems which especially affect the excluded. Yet they are the majority of the planet's population, billions of people . . . a true ecological approach *always* becomes a social approach; it must integrate questions of justice in debates on the environment, so as to hear both the cry of the earth and the cry of the poor." (49)

In chapter 2, "The Gospel of Creation," Francis states (complementing E. O. Wilson's similar statement in *The Creation*) that "science and religion, with their distinctive approaches to understanding reality, can enter into an intense dialogue fruitful for both" (62); restates the teaching that creatures have intrinsic value: "other living beings have a value of their own in God's eyes: 'the Lord rejoices in all his works'" (Ps 104:31) (69); emphasizes that

"Creation is of the order of love. God's love is the fundamental moving force in all created things: 'For you love all things that exist, and detest none of the things that you have made'" (*Wis* 11:24) (77); and declares that it would "be [a mistake] to view other living beings as mere objects subjected to arbitrary human domination" (82). In "The Common Destination of Goods," Francis states:

> [Earth] is essentially a shared inheritance, whose fruits are meant to benefit everyone ... every ecological approach needs to incorporate a social perspective which takes into account the fundamental rights of the poor and the underprivileged. The principle of the subordination of private property to the universal destination of goods, and thus the right of everyone to their use, is a golden rule of social conduct ... Christian tradition has never recognized the right to private property as absolute or inviolable, and has stressed the social purpose of all forms of private property ... [Francis then quotes John Paul II's words to the poor of Oaxaca, Mexico in 1979]: "there is always a social mortgage on all private property, in order that goods may serve the general purpose that God gave them." (93)

The preceding statements provide a foundation for Francis to develop his fundamental ecological-environmental teaching: *integral ecology*.

In chapter 4, "Integral Ecology," Francis distinguishes "ecology" from "environment"; observes that all biota are related genetically; affirms that people are a part of, not separate from nature; states that social justice and ecology are intimately intertwined; and declares that all creatures and ecosystems have intrinsic value:

> Since everything is closely interrelated, and today's problems call for a vision capable of taking into account every aspect of the global crisis, I suggest that we now consider some elements of an *integral ecology*, one which clearly respects its human and social dimensions. (137)
>
> Ecology studies the relationship between living organisms and the environment in which they develop ... Time and space are not independent of one another, and not even atoms or subatomic particles can be considered in isolation ... living species are part of a network ... A good part of our genetic code is shared by many living beings. (138)
>
> When we speak of the "environment," what we really mean is a relationship existing between nature and the society which lives in it. Nature cannot be regarded as something separate from ourselves or as a mere setting in which we live. We are

> part of nature, included in it and thus in constant interaction with it ... It is essential to seek comprehensive solutions which consider the interactions within natural systems themselves and with social systems. We are faced not with two separate crises, one environmental and the other social, but rather with one complex crisis which is both social and environmental. Strategies for a solution demand an integrated approach to combating poverty, restoring dignity to the excluded, and at the same time protecting nature (139) ... ["Ecosystems"] have an intrinsic value independent of their usefulness. Each organism, as a creature of God, is good and admirable in itself; the same is true of the harmonious ensemble of organisms existing in a defined space and functioning as a system. (140)

Francis teaches, too, that indigenous peoples should have special consideration in discussions about land ownership and use, because of their intergenerational relationship with particular Earth places and their traditional understanding that they—and others—live in "sacred space":

> it is essential to show special care for indigenous communities and their cultural traditions. They are not merely one minority among others, but should be the principal dialogue partners, especially when large projects affecting their land are proposed. For them, land is not a commodity but rather a gift from God and from their ancestors who rest there, a sacred space with which they need to interact if they are to maintain their identity and values. When they remain on their land, they themselves care for it best. (146)

Returning to the principle of the common good, Francis reiterates that "Human ecology is inseparable from the notion of the common good, a central and underlying principle of social ethics" (156), and adds that "the common good calls for social peace ... which cannot be achieved without particular concern for distributive justice ... Society as a whole, and the state in particular, are obliged to defend and promote the common good" (157). In global society today, injustices oppress people, and so "the principle of the common good [is] a summons to solidarity and a preferential option for the poorest of our brothers and sisters" (158).

Finally, in the section "Justice Between the Generations," Francis declares that "the notion of the common good also extends to future generations ... Intergenerational solidarity is not optional, but rather a basic question of justice, since the world we have received also belongs to those who will follow us" (159).

Later in the encyclical, Francis calls for an "ecological conversion." He states that "the ecological crisis is also a summons to a profound interior conversion" because many people are not taking it seriously, or not seeing it as a requirement of their faith. But, Francis says, "Living our vocation to be protectors of God's handiwork is essential to a life of virtue; it is not an optional or a secondary aspect of our Christian experience." Here, he reiterates a teaching given by John Paul II in 1990, in *The Ecological Crisis: A Common Responsibility* (also titled *Peace with God the Creator, Peace with All Creation*). John Paul declares: "Christians, in particular, realize that their responsibility within creation and their duty toward nature and the Creator are an essential part of their faith" (150). Ecological responsibility, then, is not an "add-on" or optional practice for Christians; rather, it helps to define the very nature of being a "Christian."[17]

"Gift" or "Trust" Redux

Throughout the encyclical, a phrase is used that seems inappropriate to this writer, as noted earlier in this chapter. When Francis describes humans' relationship to the Spirit and to every other person and living being, who are humans' neighbors in creation, he states periodically that Earth is a "gift." Rather, Earth is *entrusted* to humankind and all living beings. It is a "trust," provided to all biota to meet their needs in interdependent relationships. A "gift" is something that the recipient can dispose of as they wish; a "trust" is something cared for and sustained for the one who entrusts it, and used to meet the needs of all. All recipients of a *trust*, within the parameters of their biological limitations, their ecological niche, their species and individual characteristics and abilities, and their stage of evolutionary development vis-à-vis other species, are immersed in an interrelational and interdependent association—in a community of all life, and a network of being in the integral cosmos. Biota intelligently or instinctually engage in species-specific conduct in abiotic contexts. The biological balance that emerges provides a stable setting for life's survival and continuing evolution.

When a single species—on Earth, humankind, which alone has the ability to dominate and even extinct other species, and to destroy its own and others' planet habitat—arrogates to itself life-and-death power and primacy over all living beings and even Earth herself, it usurps the rights of all species, disrupts their place in the biotic community, and imperils the balance that should characterize the relational community on Earth and the integral cosmos community. Such conduct causes, at times, a strong pushback from Earth: mining and fracking, for example, impact the geology of places where

17. Hart, *What Are They*, 13–14.

they have been rampant; Earth responds with earthquakes that destroy or severely damage urban structures and, when earthquakes occur in oceans or seas, they engender tsunamis that cause even greater damage to coastal areas.

Human-generated and human-exacerbated global climate change caused by burning coal and by auto emissions, among other factors, has resulted—as predicted by the scientists on the Intergovernmental Panel on Climate Change (IPCC)—in larger, more frequent, and more powerful hurricanes, longer and fiercer droughts in agricultural areas and massive floods there and elsewhere, and periodic deep freezes and scorching heat. Politicians, many of whose campaigns are funded by energy corporations or super-wealthy individuals (some politicians, for example, appear to be Koch addicts) ignore or deny ever-worsening Earth conditions that imperil all life. They have abandoned or deny their responsibility to people and country, favoring instead private corporations' profits. They are not fulfilling, either, their intergenerational responsibility—they have an apparent disregard for the future wellbeing of their children and grandchildren alive today, other children, and their descendants, who will have to live in an ecologically devastated Earth home tomorrow.

In the penultimate paragraph of the encyclical, Francis uses an internally contradictory phrase that incorporates both understandings: "we come together to take charge of [a managerial role] this home which has been entrusted to us [a trustee role]." This wording prompts questions that include: Are we managers over or trustees of creation? Do we see ourselves as members of a relational community in which each and every species—and every individual therein—contributes their particular abilities to effect and sustain a holistic integration of all, such that all are coequal members of the Earth community in which the Creator Spirit is immanent? A simple change of wording in the quotation—from "charge of" to "care for"—would profoundly change humans' attitude toward, and actions on, Earth. It would nicely complement, too, "entrusted to us."

In related phrasing, Francis states that "The created things of this world . . . are linked by unseen bonds and together form a kind of universal family, a sublime communion which fills us with a sacred, affectionate and humble respect" (89). However, he says, "This is not to put all living beings on the same level nor to deprive human beings of their unique worth and the tremendous responsibility it entails . . . At times we see an obsession with denying any pre-eminence to the human person" (90). Unfortunately, this denial of our intimate relatedness to and equality of stature with other living beings effects a rupture in the web of all life, since it asserts a dominant role for humankind that diminishes the stature and inherent worth of other living creatures. This perspective is not an "obsession." Rather, it is an elaboration, for the present and future, of humanity's profound immersion and participation in the community of all living beings, integrated well with their abiotic setting. In contrast to the mindset Francis proposes, humans can both see their equality with other biota, and recognize that those who have greater natural abilities have greater responsibilities in the ways they influence nature and natural processes (from those who have been given much, much is expected). This does not denigrate humans, but rather affirms them and enables them to express their relationship with all creatures in the community of all living beings. "From each according to their abilities," when describing all biota, indicates a cohesive bond among all, and demonstrates that "very good" creatures are able to live together with mutual (intelligent or instinctual) interaction. It also can generate a cosmic expansiveness, in which humans experience their place in the vast universe. People grow spiritually when they break the constraints of trying to be managers, and embrace instead a profound intimacy with all that is, and a profound respect for other types and expressions of creativity, intelligence, and other natural gifts within the integral being of the cosmos. All are the Creator's children, provided with abilities for their survival, for their genetic and mental capabilities and creativity to adapt to changing contexts. If humans view all biota and Earth as relations, new bonds of a shared family and community will be formed, and the strands of the web of all life will be strengthened.

It should be noted, too, that how humans view themselves in relation to other living beings on Earth, as managers or trustees, or as relatives in the biotic community, will carry over to their engagement with intelligent and less-evolved biota on other worlds. If humans view all creatures on Earth and in the heavens as relations, as advocated by Francis of Assisi and in indigenous spiritual traditions from around the world, people will be relatives to them and they to humankind: humans will not see them as subject to a human managerial role, in which people are "stewards" throughout the cosmos.

Laudato Si', then, reiterates and carries forward themes and principles expressed in socioecological praxis ethics, but includes, too, an extended elaboration of Christian, and especially Catholic, biblical, moral, and systematic theology. It stimulates Christians of all traditions—and peoples of other religious or humanist traditions—to reflect on their spiritual and social heritage when seeking ways to renew Earth, relate to all living beings, and do all of this with a special concern for the "least of these" about whom Jesus spoke. He taught that these "least ones" should be treated with justice and compassion, and that their right to basic necessities should be respected (as described in the Last Judgment story in Matthew 25:31–46).

Considerations of socioecological praxis ethics and integral ecology are complemented, reinforced, and carried forward by the Hague Principles.

This international proclamation invites and urges people to recognize and take seriously, in their conduct, principles for social justice and ecological wellbeing.

The Hague Principles

The Hague Principles for a Universal Declaration on Responsibilities for Human Rights and Earth Trusteeship,[18] issued on December 10, 2018, was developed primarily by scholars in the Netherlands. Subsequently, it was endorsed by individuals and organizations from around the globe. Its opening section, "Background," presents the historical context and thinking behind the document. In the first paragraph, the statement commemorates and celebrates the seventieth anniversary of the United Nations' 1948 adoption of a Universal Declaration of Human Rights, and observes that "The recognition of equal and unalienable rights of all human beings is an indispensable prerequisite for achieving just and sustainable societies." In the now "globalized world" in which we live, new challenges confront us, and will confront us, too, in the future: "We all belong to the community of life, the Earth community, which determines what rights and responsibilities we must recognize and honour for each other, for future generations, for all living beings and the Earth, our home."

The following paragraph opens with the warning that "The Earth community is in grave danger." Threats to Earth's and all biota's wellbeing include the human population explosion, "disparities in economic wealth," and human overconsumption of Earth's natural goods. These threats imperil "the entire Earth system with its interconnected components" which provide the foundation for human social and political wellbeing. Therefore, while people celebrate human rights achievements, they must go beyond these alone and accept responsibility "for the Earth community and the entire Earth system." Human beings must "act as Earth trustees." While over the decades numerous declarations and statements have exhorted people to accept their responsibility, the old documents must be supplemented by new ones. These should "formally recognise the human responsibilities that exist towards the Earth community and the Earth system."

Humanity, as individuals and collectively, must be "Earth Trustees" who effect "new arrangements of Earth Trusteeship" as an "active and all-encompassing way forward." (The authors, as they advocate for "trusteeship,"

---

18. On December 9, I was invited to be a signee of the Declaration and, after reading it, I signed promptly. Individuals and organizations are invited to add their affirmation of the principles in the document by becoming signatories.

progress a step forward from the "steward" managerial role for humanity suggested by Francis I.)

The second part of the document elaborates "Principles for a Universal Declaration on Human Responsibilities and Earth Trusteeship." Its preamble is a social, political, economic, international, and ecological assessment of the state of the world and of human actions needed to address present and impending dangers to the survival of Earth, all biota, and human social institutions. While people realize that their survival depends on "the health and well-being of other beings and ecosystems," the rampant "consumerist society and competitive nationalism" have continued to injure Nature and lead to "catastrophic climate change, unprecedented biodiversity loss, and eventual disintegration of the Earth system." People must consider that "the totality of beings and ecosystems on Earth forms a community of life (the 'Earth community')." Humans "have rights that suit their needs," and so do other beings "have the right to exist and flourish according to their specific needs"; these rights "have their source in being part of the Earth community." Collaboration is needed between "political, economic and cultural transformation movements" to respond to twenty-first-century challenges.

The Declaration elaborates three fundamental principles: "Responsibilities for Earth"; "Responsibilities within the Community of Life"; and "Responsibilities for Human Rights":

Principle 1 Responsibilities for Earth

1.1. All human beings, individually and collectively, share responsibility to protect Nature, of which we are an integral part, the integrity of Earth's ecological systems and Earth as a whole, home of all living beings.

1.2. Each state individually, and the international community of states collectively, acknowledge that they have, and share, responsibilities for Nature, in cooperation and in alliance with their citizens as equal trustees of Earth and the integrity of Earth's ecological systems.

Principle 2 Responsibilities within the Community of Life

2.1. Human rights are grounded in our membership within the community of life, the Earth community, which qualifies what rights we are called on to honor and what responsibilities we have for each other and for Nature.

2.2. Responsibilities for Nature, the Earth community and rights of Nature are grounded in the intrinsic values of nature and of all living beings.

Principle 3 Responsibilities for Human Rights

3.1. All human beings are responsible for the protection of human rights and for affirming human rights in their ways of thinking and acting.

3.2. Each state has a prime responsibility for the protection of human rights as a trustee of its citizens and all human beings.

[The Declaration concludes with a call to the UN] to initiate a process of consultation, negotiation and eventual adoption of a Universal Declaration on Human Responsibilities and Earth Trusteeship based on these principles.[19]

The Hague Principles are an important contribution to the body of documents and statements that advocate for integrating social justice within and among human communities and individuals, with the wellbeing of Earth and of all biotic community members; that recognize that Nature has natural rights; and that acknowledge that all living beings have intrinsic value.

Intergovernmental Panel on Climate Change (IPCC)

As was the case with this chapter's previous authors, statements, and concepts, the IPCC links ecology (with a focus on global climate change) and social wellbeing. Its science-oriented members state, for example, that anthropogenic global warming is causing the sea level to rise, which results in flooding of coastal areas and submersion of islands. This afflicts impoverished populations most, and therefore contradicts a UN pledge to "eradicate poverty." (Ironically, a result of human-caused and human-exacerbated climate change is that because of violent storms and rising seas afflicting coastal areas and islands, poor people are being "eradicated," not poverty.)

The IPCC describes on its website its rationale and its work:

> The Intergovernmental Panel on Climate Change (IPCC) is the United Nations body for assessing the science related to climate change.
>
> The IPCC was created to provide policymakers with regular scientific assessments on climate change, its implications and potential future risks, as well as to put forward adaptation and mitigation options.
>
> Through its assessments, the IPCC determines the state of knowledge on climate change. It identifies where there is

---

19. An annex to the Hague Principles helpfully lists the foundational documents used for the Declaration (which date from 1948–2017), with their web addresses.

agreement in the scientific community on topics related to climate change, and where further research is needed. The reports are drafted and reviewed in several stages, thus guaranteeing objectivity and transparency. The IPCC does not conduct its own research.

IPCC reports are neutral, policy-relevant but not policy-prescriptive. The assessment reports are a key input into the international negotiations to tackle climate change. Created by the United Nations Environment Programme (UN Environment) and the World Meteorological Organization (WMO) in 1988, the IPCC has 195 members.

The IPCC issues Assessment Reports (AR) periodically, preceded by Working Group (WG) Reports. Five AR have been published to date: AR1: Synthesis Report 1990; AR2: Synthesis Report 1996; TAR Climate Change 2001: Synthesis Report; AR4 Climate Change 2007: Synthesis Report; AR5 Synthesis Report: Climate Change 2014. The next report, AR6, will be released in June 2022. It will be preceded in 2021 by preliminary reports from its Working Groups: April, WG I: AR6 Climate Change 2021: The Physical Science Basis; October, WG II: AR6 Climate Change 2021: Impacts, Adaptation and Vulnerability; July, WG III: AR6 Climate Change 2021: Mitigation of Climate Change. In addition, the IPCC has had numerous specific issue-focused special reports.

In October 2018, heightened scientific concern about rapid deterioration of Earth's climate, and about the consequent acceleration of Earth's ecological devastation, prompted a special report: "Climate Change of 1.5°." It is described as "An IPCC special report on the impacts of global warming of 1.5 °C[20] above pre-industrial levels and related global greenhouse gas emission pathways, in the context of strengthening the global response to the threat of climate change, sustainable development, and efforts to eradicate poverty." Its opening "Summary for Policymakers" includes an introduction; A. Understanding Global Warming of 1.5°C; B. Projected Climate Change, Potential Impacts, and Associated Risks; C. Emissions Pathways and Systems Transitions Consistent with 1.5°C Global Warming; D. Strengthening the Global Responses in the Context of Sustainable Development and Efforts to Eradicate Poverty. In each of its assessments, the IPCC notes whether a particular statement indicates an event that is "unlikely" or "likely" to occur, or that the IPCC has a "medium confidence" or "high confidence" that it will occur. The boldfaced warnings in section A state, for example (italics in original):

---

20. An increase of 1.5° Celsius = an increase of 2.7° Fahrenheit.

A.1. Human activities are estimated to have caused approximately 1.0°C of global warming above pre-industrial levels, with a *likely* range of 0.8°C to 1.2°C. Global warming is *likely* to reach 1.5°C between 2030 and 2052 if it continues to increase at the current rate. (*high confidence*).

A.2. Warming from anthropogenic emissions from the pre-industrial period to the present will persist for centuries to millennia and will continue to cause further long-term changes in the climate system, such as sea level rise, with associated impacts (*high confidence*), but these emissions alone are *unlikely* to cause global warming of 1.5°C (*medium confidence*).

A.3. Climate-related risks for natural and human systems are higher for global warming of 1.5°C than at present, but lower than at 2°C (*high confidence*). These risks depend on the magnitude and rate of warming, geographic location, levels of development and vulnerability, and on the choices and implementation of adaptation and mitigation options (*high confidence*).

The subsequent five chapters of the Special Report are summarized as follows:

Chapter 1: Understanding the impacts of 1.5°C global warming above pre-industrial levels and related global emission pathways in the context of strengthening the response to the threat of climate change, sustainable development and efforts to eradicate poverty.

Chapter 2: Showing how emissions can be brought to zero by mid-century and stay within the small remaining carbon budget for limiting global warming to 1.5°C.

Chapter 3: Why is it necessary and even vital to maintain the global temperature increase below 1.5°C versus higher levels? Adaptation will be less difficult. Earth will suffer fewer negative impacts from the projected intensity and frequency of extreme events on resources, ecosystems, biodiversity, food security, cities, tourism and carbon removal.

Chapter 4: The global response to warming of 1.5°C comprises transitions in land and ecosystem, energy, urban infrastructure, and industrial systems. The feasibility of mitigation and adaptation options, and the enabling conditions for strengthening and implementing the systemic changes, are assessed in this chapter.

Chapter 5: The interactions of climate change and climate responses with sustainable development including sustainable development impacts at 1.5°C and 2°C, the synergies and tradeoffs of mitigation and adaptation with the Sustainable Development Goals/SDGs, and the possibilities for sustainable and equitable low carbon, climate resilient development pathways.

The IPCC site provides extensive updated information, periodically, on scientists', social scientists', and humanist scholars' findings about how human-caused global climate change is altering Earth, extincting species, and threatening humanity and human cultures. It presents well-researched data, and international experts' dialogic considerations of what that data means today and for the future.

The findings and conduct recommended by the IPCC are directly related to and relevant for Earth and Earth's biota (and indirectly related to and relevant for other worlds and their biota when humankind colonizes and establishes permanent residency in diverse cosmos places). In terms of the present, IPCC reports should immediately guide peoples and governments toward a dramatic conversion to ecological responsibility, so that they could conduct themselves accordingly. In terms of the human future on, and the ecological wellbeing of other worlds, IPCC reports serve as a warning about what has transpired on Earth that should be avoided in space. The reports provide guidelines to ensure that, immediately upon their arrival on other worlds and continuing thereafter, humankind's behavior will be better, from the start, than what it was on Earth. If this happens, people will not do to their other world homes the harm that they did to their Earth home.

Voluntary Displacement

Prior to sustained Contact, some representatives of humankind might choose to depart from Earth to explore the solar system and eventually the Milky Way Galaxy, seeking a new cosmos home on another world, and searching for ExoEarth intelligent beings. In the latter regard, Stephen Hawking states that people should search for ETI/IDI because, he said, humans are intelligent beings: "We are alive. We are intelligent. We must know"[21]; it is in our nature to be inquisitive and to explore.

---

21. See chapter 3.

A new generation of humankind, spurred on by human inquisitiveness, a sense of adventure, and a pioneering spirit, will leave Earth to search for new places to see and explore and, possibly, to colonize and settle upon if they appear hospitable. Should the latter settlement happen, then their voluntary displacement will evolve into their voluntary placement. Alternatively, their voluntary displacement could become an ongoing journey, even intergenerationally, as they decide that their place will be the craft in which they travel, with occasional stops on other worlds to satisfy their curiosity about what life is like there, and to enjoy temporary sojourns on diverse unfamiliar worlds encountered in space or in another dimension of the cosmos. On occasion, some or all of the voyagers might settle on the new worlds they find. In following this pathway into space (or into another dimension), the voyagers might well be, without realizing it, replicating what ExoEarth intelligent beings are doing—including some who have come to Earth, or at least to Earth's solar system.

Terraforming: Pros and Cons

Constraints of space and limitations of time will not permit in-depth consideration of proposals for terraforming[22]—altering other worlds so they are identical to Earth, *terra*, to the extent possible—in order to provide a hospitable habitat for humankind. In sum: the *pros* include forming a world that allows, as expeditiously as possible, for human habitation; putting in place microbial life that complements human and other Earth species' DNA, thereby eliminating pathogenic native microbes; providing for terra-based agriculture and forestry techniques imported from Earth to produce food, fiber, medicinal herbs, and building construction materials for the colonizers and, possibly, to secure space for livestock. The *cons* include the likely possibility that the terraforming process will extinct all living organisms, both beneficial and harmful, on the world as humans find it. These organisms might include both potential sources of food and medicines, and illness-generating and life-threatening biota.

Terraforming is yet another example and embodiment of the Discovery Doctrine[23] by which European seafaring explorers justified, for themselves, genocide against native populations who had been resident in their territories for thousands of years, who had agriculture, hunting, and fishing through which they provided for their needs in an Earth- and biota-respectful manner; converting natives' communal lands and territories to

---

22. See Hart, *Cosmic Commons*, 247–51, for a more extensive elaboration of terraforming.

23. This is elaborated further in Hart, *Terraforming Mars*.

fenced-in private property; and viewing the natural goods such as forests and waters as unlimited, to be used at will without regard for the future.[24] (An internet search by the reader will uncover detailed scientific and ethical discussions and descriptions of terraforming and its impacts, and indicate considerable sources with information worth pondering.) In science fiction narratives, Ray Bradbury's *Martian Chronicles* series and novel, and other science fiction stories written in the mid-twentieth century, illustrate human attitudes of dominating and "subduing" that underlie terraforming advocacy, and potential dangerous or at least harmful outcomes that might result from terraforming other worlds.

Interrelationship: Socioecological Praxis Ethics, Integral Ecology, Hague Principles, IPCC

Integration of the concepts, documents, values, and principles that were elaborated in the preceding pages will provide groundwork, guidelines, and guideposts for a path toward the Earth community's wellbeing, in itself and in relation to other worlds' communities. The integration provides a foundation, too, for ways humanity should act not solely on planet Earth, but on other worlds where humankind establishes bases and colonies in years to come. In order to stimulate this consciousness and conduct, humanity must be more aware that human "natural rights" are part of a greater whole, nature's natural rights—"nature" throughout the cosmos, that is, not nature limited to Earth; that humankind and all other biota and abiotic contexts have intrinsic value and should not be viewed as having only instrumental value determined by humans; and that Earth and all Earth's life, and other worlds and their biota, are specific relational communities that are ultimately part of a holistic cosmos ecosystemic relational community in an integral cosmos.

These considerations are incomplete. Principles to guide humankind's conduct on inhabited other worlds, and humankind's dialogic development of those principles for ExoEarth places, await sustained Contact with other-than-human intelligent beings, on Earth and in the heavens. These considerations, complemented by principles elaborated in a *Cosmos Charter* (see Appendix 2), provide seeds for development of responsible human

---

24. See Hart, *Cosmic Commons*, for discussion of the Discovery Doctrine as it was used in the fifteenth century and as it continues to be cited in the twenty-first-century in court cases about land ownership, especially chapter 2, "Terrestrial Discovery," 59–88, and footnotes citing other sources, including works by Indian scholars. For a discussion of how this might play out on ExoEarth worlds that humans visit, see chapter 4, "Extraterrestrial Discovery," 117–42; for a fictional presentation of issues, see the movie *Avatar*.

consciousness and conduct prior to ExoEarth voyages and ventures, as suggested in *Cosmic Commons*.

The ideas and principles derived from integrating socioecological praxis ethics, integral ecology, the Hague Principles, IPCC reports, and a *Cosmos Charter* would provide a firm foundation for exploring, and possibly becoming responsible inhabitants of, distant worlds, whether or not they have ETL.

At a future time, after initial ventures into the cosmos and settlement on worlds other than Earth, humans in the heavens might well educate people "back home" on Earth about how they have lived in accordance with socioecological values and principles they had learned on Earth. They might describe, too, how they have guided their own evolution on other worlds because of Contact with intelligent life, encounters with evolving life, or adaptation in a lifeless world. Mother Earth would be the living hub, for her distant children, as humankind on their home planet continues conversations with all the pioneers, and they share with each other the insights which they have developed.

Where Is the Proof? Redux

People who still today raise the question "Where's the proof?" mean that there is an absence of "proof" acceptable to them. At the same time, they reject types of *proof* acceptable to others—because of impeding factors for the "unbelievers": their lack of sufficient knowledge about data found or its implications for humankind; their absence from direct participation in events described, and engagement with data provided as proof of an event; their reductionist ideology that limits "proof" to physical or material evidence; and their innate fear of a Visitor, an *other*. The absence of public, direct Contact with ETI/IDI Visitors might be explained in part, too, by how humankind is like today in the conjectured assessment of Earth and humankind in the perspective of the rarely visible Visitors.

A New "Thought Experiment"

Imagine yourself during a future time, after humans have achieved global peace and social justice and become one people, discovering thereby the cultural and intellectual richness of their humanist traditions that, when tapped, freed up the collaborative instincts and creativity of the human species' community. This political, social, and economic achievement had stimulated an explosion of new ideas and new inventions: peace among peoples had been richly rewarded by sociality, eusociality, and social progress. Now, benefitting from the fruits of the ideas and work of a unified humanity, you voyage in a

SOCIOECOLOGY, INTEGRAL ECOLOGY, HAGUE PRINCIPLES, IPCC   223

spacecraft capable of cruising the galaxy and crossing cosmos dimensions. Along the way, you observe from space a world humankind is seeing for the first time. Curious about their characteristics and values, you eavesdrop on communications media conversations among their population; you view the images and listen to the dialogue on their broadcast "television" shows, including news stories and political speeches, whose content spreads out into space. You see walls separating large areas, and military personnel on both sides of these not–natural barriers. You see strife among diverse members and groups of the planet's intelligent species; sometimes outbreaks of violence, or sustained violent practices, are disturbingly frequent: between residents of one artificially but officially separated barrier-enclosed region and another, and among the residents of a single region. Widespread sickness and poverty evidence social-class distinctions. The massive sizes of a few gate-enclosed homes within a walled region that contrast with neighboring makeshift cardboard and plywood shacks occupied by large segments of the population reveal vast disparities between the poor and those who make them poor and maintain their poverty by paying them inadequate wages, denying them healthcare, and undemocratically suppressing their vote by gerrymandering districts and limiting their access to polling stations, among other means.

Suddenly, you awaken from your disturbing dream. You realize that it was not entirely a dream: you are on Earth in the twenty-first century, in a comfortable home or university residence, a member of a family that is one of the fast-disappearing typical middle class. You turn on the TV, and the morning news is on. Amid the stories you see labor demonstrations for a living wage, working women in an office demanding "equal pay for equal work," an ongoing conflict in the Israel-Palestine region, Latina/os and African Americans protesting housing and employment discrimination, and a black dummy from a store window display now wearing a noose around its neck and hanging from a tree outside a rural home. An unusual topic for the morning news is a short segment that briefly mentions there was a sighting of an apparently intelligently controlled UAP, hovering above a military base located a hundred miles away from your home, that shut down the MinuteMan ICBM missile launch system located there. "Nonsense!" you say in reaction—but then your dream returns vividly, and you become uneasy, even anxious.

In this variation of the thought experiment that was suggested in the first two volumes of the Cosmos Contact trilogy, a new question arises: what do you think might be your assessment of the human prospect, as an intelligent occupant of the craft described in the news story that was accompanied by long-distance footage taken with a cellphone camera? Think about your dream in greater depth. If you were in the craft, would you want to make Contact with the types of people whom you imagine humans on Earth to be? If they treat others of their species harshly and oppressively, how would they engage Visitors from an entirely different intelligent species whose physical appearance is dissimilar? Might you, as a Visitor, judge humans to be inferior beings, at an early stage of intellectual, emotional, maturity, and technological development, who might destroy themselves before they reach their full potential? Might they act as a pathogen when interacting with Visitors to Earth and encountered on other worlds? Now, reverse roles again. If you as a human are conscious today of humans' need to avoid transfers of dangerous pathogenic microbes from distant worlds to Earth, do you think that, shifting back again to your place on the hovering craft, you would think of words such as "pathogen" when you evaluate this violent, acquisitive, bellicose species, which appears to be a potential danger to ExoEarth life, evolving or intelligent? Would you view them as a danger to, and eventually to be a pariah among, other intelligent species in the universe? Would you decide to Contact them at their present evolutionary stage, with their present state of mind?

"Where's the 'proof' of ETI/IDI existence? Where's the evidence?" The evidence for one likely reason why intelligent ExoEarth beings have not "landed on the White House lawn" is all around and within human places of habitation—including, in the United States, in the environs of the White House, the very place that some people think Visitors should land to show that they exist.

Consider now an addendum to your waking reflections on your dream. In what ways might the scenario be altered if shared themes and principles, proposed in the selected passages cited earlier in this chapter, were to become and remain stimuli for humankind to do better on Earth before they venture into the vast, complex spatial and dimensional realities of the cosmos? To what extent would humans have a change of consciousness and conduct, and of relationships among the diverse members of the human species, before the departure of human voyagers, whether for extraterrestrial or interdimensional exploration? If what is proposed in the writings is an urgent prophetic message for our *topia*, how might people embrace it—how might *we* embrace it—as an urgently needed *utopia* to alter Earth and the human community? How might each of us seek to make it the new reality, embodying the best of our ideals? The new consciousness and conduct that humans would develop to accept and to begin to practice the integrated principles would bode well for a new *topia*. They would be, too, a foundation for a new *utopia* that would draw humankind even further toward achieving a relational Earth community—so that they would thereby participate as integral members of a relational cosmos community.

At the dawn of humans' space-time-interdimensional voyages, humankind needs a change of consciousness and a change in conduct—as noted in the previous volumes of this series—in order to avoid replicating throughout the cosmos the destructive ways humans today think and act on Earth. The human species must strive for planetary unity, not gear up for a new "space race," now with Russia and China, and soon, perhaps, with India, Israel, and a European space coalition, added to United States efforts. Capitalist corporate entities and wealthy individuals are already building rockets: they intend to exploit other worlds, not to benefit humanity, but to add to the extreme wealth of the entrepreneurs who finance them, who seek to find and exploit new sources of wealth on other worlds. Their conduct is in contravention of UN documents such as the 1967 Outer Space Treaty and the 1996 Declaration on International Cooperation in the Exploration and Use of Outer Space.[25] Such entrepreneurs, and people in their employ (including some politicians), consider neither the needs of peoples on Earth, nor impacts on other worlds and their biota (if there are living beings present, whatever their place in biotic evolution on their home and in their habitat). Humans and other biota cannot long endure, without reaction, this irrational and irresponsible behavior.

In order to avoid self- and others-destruction, humanity at its current crossroads in human history should consider to what extent it should have a relational consciousness to guide relational conduct in a relational Earth community integrated within a relational cosmos community. Self-interest (not selfishness, whether individual or class-based) and concern for other beings should stimulate people to act responsibly in space voyages so that they are not the feared Others of their nightmares, but benevolent intelligent beings who are intent on achieving a beneficial outcome of Contact—for the human species as a whole and for the worlds and beings they encounter. This would be facilitated by reflection on the wisdom of people who have been working to bring about a renewed Earth and restored respect for all living beings—and then incorporation of their principles in humans' care for their home planet, and during their explorations of and colonization in the spacious and interdimensional heavens.

---

25. United Nations, *United Nations Treaties*.

7

Conclusion: Community in the Cosmos Commons

Humans who discover and dwell in diverse cosmos places will adapt to a wide range of newly found other-world milieus. Through the ages, humankind's distinct ethnic communities have migrated throughout the world. They have found viable niches in diverse Earth contexts over the course of human biological and sociocultural evolution (sometimes, by unjustly displacing existing inhabitants). In the current era of space exploration, human social and ecological wellbeing on Earth and in the heavens would be enhanced through awareness of cosmos integral being, generated by a new cosmosocioecological consciousness. New milieus for humankind would be constructed and conserved through the practice of cosmosocioecological praxis ethics.

In the twenty-first-century process of transition from the old and transformation into the new, anxiety from an anticipated Third Displacement upon encounters with Otherkind could evolve into an adaptive openness to unanticipated experiences and events. The evolution will include embracing immersion in newly discovered spiritual, social, and spatial places, complemented by a perhaps shaky or nervous confidence in humans' ability to assess and adapt to them. The sense of Earth *displacement* might itself, in this process, be displaced—by the awareness and experience of a new material and metamaterial cosmos *placement* in a cosmos relational community.

A New World

E. O. Wilson, as elaborated earlier, discussed the possibility of the existence of extraterrestrial intelligent life in two of his recent books: *The Social*

Conquest of Earth and *The Meaning of Human Existence*. In *Social Conquest of Earth*, Wilson seemed to dismiss or even disparage the idea of spacecraft having visited Earth or passed near enough to be observed by the naked eye or at least through a telescope. However, in *Meaning of Human Existence* he is open to and affirming of the possibility of life elsewhere in the universe, as described in the chapter "A Portrait of E.T."[1] This new thinking is augmented by his Big Think interview on YouTube, mentioned previously. He speculates in it about ETI's possible characteristics in its existence on its home planet. He observes that "E.T. is out there. There just has to be in the hundred million-star system, [in the] galaxy [to which] we belong . . . other cases of life originating."[2]

Important evidence of ETI/IDI, even if not quantifiable, is found in oral statements of credible witnesses to ETI/IDI events, as described earlier. Previously, too, scientific investigations were undertaken, and scientists' affirmations of diverse Others of Otherkind were made by Allen Hynek, Jacques Vallée, Stephen Hawking, Wilson, John Mack's clients, and Ardy Sixkiller Clarke's interviewees. They indicated that ETI/IDI beings exist. Visitors' vehicles for space or interdimensional travel have been seen by individuals or groups of people as these craft flew by or hovered overhead; some seemed to be directed remotely and, on some occasions, made Contact by abducting people or by landing and communicating with them on Earth.

SETI and University of St. Andrews Scientists: UFO Sighting Scale

As sightings increased of reportedly intelligently controlled craft, scientists from the SETI Institute and the University of St. Andrews, Scotland revised, in 2018, the Rio guidelines that were developed in 2001 to rate and categorize the importance of reported UFO sightings. Rio 2.0 rates events' importance from 0–10 ("None" to "Extraordinary"). The scale offers shorthand science- and other academic field-based suggestions about how seriously a particular reported event should be taken.

Allen Hynek, in his capacity as scientific consultant on UFOs for the US Government via the US Air Force, developed the Close Encounters categories decades ago. CE-I, CE-II, and CE-III were to facilitate understanding how far from an observer an unidentified flying object appeared to be. The CE categories continue to be used today; the Rio 2.0 Scale complements them. According to SETI,

---

1. Wilson, *Meaning of Human Existence*, 110–22.
2. Big Think, "E.O. Wilson: ET Is Out There."

> [T]he Rio Scale is a tool used by astronomers searching for extraterrestrial intelligence (ETI) to help communicate to the public "how excited" they should be about what has been observed. The Scale measures the consequences for humans if the signal is from aliens, as well as the probability that the signal really is from aliens, and not a natural phenomenon or human-made. The scale gives a score between zero and ten, so that the public can quickly see how important a signal really is . . . The team has published an online Rio Scale Calculator, an interactive tool for scientists and science communicators to evaluate signals and give advice on how to use it for better reporting of ETI in the media.[3]

SETI Expands Its Space Exploration

Space telescopes have discovered millions of planets in the Milky Way Galaxy alone. Scientific estimates have suggested that the Galaxy has at least one hundred billion stars, forty percent of which, forty billion stars, have planets in the Goldilocks Zone. Given these projections, it is likely that many of these, being millions or even billions of years older than Earth, had and have intelligent species that are far older and more intelligent than humankind. That would likely mean that Otherkind—ETI and IDI—are more technologically capable than are humans at this point in human history, at humans' current stage of technological development. The famous Drake Equation, often quoted by some scientists prior to all the recent telescope discoveries, indicated that it was unlikely that intelligent life exists in space. In contrast, geologist and paleontologist Pierre Teilhard de Chardin, in his research almost a century ago (described earlier), stated, decades before Drake's equation became popular, that intelligent life likely does exist elsewhere than on Earth. He theorized that millions of intelligent species may be encountered in the universe. It seems likely now that Teilhard's projection was the more accurate one. It will be fascinating to see how close his projected number of intelligent species is to the number discovered by space telescopes and through direct Contact.

With theories, projections, and telescope data increasing almost daily, SETI has expanded the scope of its operations. Under the leadership of Andrew Siemion, director of the Berkeley SETI Research Center and incoming director of SETI Investigations at the SETI Institute, SETI is going in new directions while maintaining the old.[4] According to *National Geographic*

---

3. "How Can You," paras. 3, 9.

4. Shreeve, "Who's Out There?," 42–51, 61–75. The *National Geographic* issue is an extraordinary, data-filled, in-depth, and multi-topic publication that is focused on

Magazine writer Jamie Shreeve, "SETI 2.0 is trying to determine whether technological civilization is part of the cosmic landscape, like black holes, gravitational waves, or any other astronomical phenomenon." Siemion told Shreeve, "we're not looking for a signal. We're looking for a property of the universe."[5] Siemion was an early recipient of a major grant from Yuri Milner's Breakthrough Listen project. The grant provided SETI with funds to embark in new areas of research, while also effecting a major expansion of SETI telescope endeavors. The new areas of active research will include seeking signs of ETI existence such as technosignatures, not solely listening for ETI radio transmissions on massive arrays of coordinated radio telescopes.

ETI and IDI: Benevolent Species, Malevolent Species, or Both Types of Species?

An important question arises when extraterrestrial or interdimensional spacecraft are sighted: are their occupants or controllers malevolent or benevolent potential new "neighbors" for humankind?

Current scientific, social scientific, and psychological research and witness reports, and the extensive compilation of historical documents that describe Others' visits to Earth over millennia, seem to indicate that both malevolent and benevolent species and individuals are present in the cosmos. John Mack and Ardy Sixkiller Clarke relate witnesses' experiences with either or both types. Jacques Vallée conveys the accounts of Brazilian fishers who were shot with lasers, causing skin burns (Vallée provides photos of a victim[6]) when they went out to sea; they stopped fishing.

Vallée's Investigation of Hostile Alien Activity in Brazil

Astrophysicist Jacques Vallée visited a hilltop in Brazil where the bodies of two men had been found in 1996. They had been awaiting a visit from ETI. Locals said the men had been expecting some sort of communication from an alien craft, and had been found dead. They were wearing suits, lying atop a bed of leaves; their handmade lead masks were nearby. There were no signs of violence. Witnesses had seen a large oval object descend to the hilltop,

---

exploration for ExtraTerrestrial Intelligence; it is supplemented with photos, graphics, and artists' drawings (including a two-page spread, 42–43, that is an imaginative rendering of Breakthrough Starship mini-explorers in the area of Proxima Centauri b, four light years from Earth).

5. Shreeve, "Who's Out There?," 75.
6. Vallée, *Confrontations*, photos on page facing 147.

then rise and leave. In the years after the bodies were found, no vegetation has grown on the site.

After viewing the physical evidence at the scene of the incident, and hearing what local residents had seen at the time the men died, Vallée comments that circumstances surrounding the event might provide proof of UFO existence, but also prompt a drastic revision of hitherto held beliefs that alien beings were "gentle visitors," "scientific explorers," "mischievous aliens," or "shining presences." The alien hypothesis might have to include, Vallée observes, "a more complex and dangerous picture."[7] He observes further that "whatever else they may be, UFOs represent a technology capable of harmful actions."[8]

Aliens' Sixteenth-Century Battle above Nuremberg

Evidence that there are distinct and competing species is graphically—literally—presented in a woodcut engraving by noted artist Hans Glaser for the Nuremberg Gazette, published on April 14, 1561. It depicts a battle in the skies over the city, as described to Glaser by witnesses, in which sophisticated craft are engaged in combat.[9] The largest craft, apparently a mothership, was shot down. Observers at the time, being unfamiliar in the sixteenth century with propelled vehicles on the ground or in the sky, thought it was a battle between "angels" and "demons."

Hawking Reconsidered

Stephen Hawking was initially fearful about ETI, once he had acknowledged that his "mathematical mind" had reasoned to a "rational" position that intelligent beings exist in space. Then he became sufficiently concerned about possible negative Contact events to advocate that humans avoid Contact with ExoEarth intelligent beings. In the end, he was ambiguous about the aftermath of Contact with Otherkind, to the extent that he joined Yuri Milner in the "Breakthrough" ventures to make Contact.

When Hawking first expressed concern, as noted earlier, Robert Wright, in an op-ed response to Hawking in *The New York Times*, stated that biological or social evolution, which led to intelligent beings' capability to develop the technology and craft needed to explore the universe, required that they

---

7. Vallée, *Confrontations*, 3.
8. Vallée, *Confrontations*, 23.
9. Numerous websites describe this event, including the "Ancient Aliens" website; it has a brief account, "Ancient Aliens: The Battle of Nuremberg," which includes a photo of the woodcut.

CONCLUSION: COMMUNITY IN THE COSMOS COMMONS

had overcome violent conflict on their home planet. Then, living together in peace, they had the social ambience needed to evolve toward and work on a cooperative effort to invent the technology and have the social capacity to explore the universe together. Given abductees' experiences, it appears that Hawking and Wright were all accurate: there are both malevolent and benevolent ETI/IDI species cruising the cosmos.

In light of the preceding narratives, at or even before Contact, humankind must try to assess, to the extent possible, the intentions of Visitors, the Others nearing Earth. Some likely would be malevolent, perhaps shielding their intentions beneath a veneer of concern about Earth's and humans' survival (as told to Clarke by Indian elders). Others likely would be benevolent, genuinely interested in guiding humanity away from its self- and planet-destructive conduct (as Mack's interviewees stated). Both types of aliens have recognized the inevitable destructive consequences of current human conduct. One type wants to exploit that conduct and the consciousness behind it; the other type wants to eliminate it. The Others, in both cases, say that humankind needs a change of consciousness: for malevolent beings, so that people will be, ultimately, subservient to these Others and their projects; for benevolent beings, so that people will turn away from inevitable and impending death and destruction, and turn toward a peaceful, productive, and planet-restoring mode of existence.

All types of possible Visitors likely have the superior weaponry and vehicle maneuverability to prevail over less technologically capable humankind, to humans' detriment or for humans' benefit. An optimistic outcome of human speculation would be that the malevolent species, analyzing humans' positive attributes, such as love and altruism—which they themselves had lost when they evolved away from them, and now hope to regain—might determine that they should not eradicate humankind. Rather than eliminate the human species, in that case, the Others would strive to emulate humans' positive characteristics and, if the "hybrid project" is not succeeding, or as a complement to it, to cultivate congenial relationships with humankind rather than depopulate Earth. Yet another possibility is that, as portrayed in the "Star Trek" sci-fi series, there is a confederation of planets whose intelligent beings work together to promote peaceful coexistence among diverse species. Such a confederation would be in conflict with incorrigible bellicose representatives of some species; humans can only hope that the "good aliens" overcome the "bad aliens" on Earth and in the heavens.

Humankind in Space as "Bad Aliens": A Pathogenic Threat to "Good Aliens"?

The preceding analysis has an optimistic assumption, since it presents a highly subjective human perspective that humankind itself will not be among the "bad aliens"—effectively, a pathogenic interloper in the cosmos community. In order to be welcome in the cosmos relational community, humans need to eliminate the dominating Earth paradigm. It is inherent in economic systems that prioritize profits over people, and promote poverty for majority populations (the poor, and peoples of color) on Earth as a whole and within nations, individually and collectively. News reports describe current private corporation efforts that are being planned to mine other worlds to benefit a few people of one or several nations, despite provisions of international documents cited earlier that were passed by overwhelming majorities in the United Nations General Assembly.[10] The latter include the 1967 Outer Space Treaty, and the 1996 Declaration on International Cooperation in the Exploration and Use of Outer Space. These and other UN documents declare that "celestial bodies" encountered in outer space, and their natural goods, are the "common province of [hu]mankind"; outer space "shall be free for exploration and use by all States without discrimination of any kind, on a basis of equality and in accordance with international law, and there shall be free access to all areas of celestial bodies" (Art. I).[11] Celestial bodies' fruits should first benefit the poorest nations and the poorest people in all nations. UN documents are insightful and important because they were passed by the collective body of nations, representing the vast majority of peoples of the world:

> United Nations documents . . . represent the considered agreement of States around the world on principles, policies, and proposals that should be operative in present and future space exploration, and on possible settlements in space. They might be extrapolated to be applicable also in the event of Contact.[12]

In contrast to the ideals cited in the above and other UN documents, the corporate proposals now on (or under) the table aim to require private (corporate and individual) property ownership of land and its goods, to benefit primarily the wealthiest segments of countries.[13]

---

10. Hart, *Cosmic Commons*, 229–47.
11. Hart, *Cosmic Commons*, 233.
12. Hart, *Cosmic Commons*, 229–30.
13. In a meeting of the NASA Astrobiology Institute (NAI) Astrobiology and Society Focus Group of which I was a member, a professional who participated in the group stated that a member of his constituency wanted the group to ensure that "private ownership" would be operative and respected in space.

On Earth currently, the vision inspired by hope in the human future is that humanity will become more unified; this will require, beforehand, dramatic economic changes (including wealth redistribution). Humans' spacecraft, in that case, would not roam space to gain goods for the already wealthy, but to assist economically poorer nations and poor people in all nations. Should this perspective not inform humans' motives in space, humankind would be a "bad alien," a threat to be a social pathogen among worlds oriented toward equality of person and equitable wealth distribution.

A utopian vision of what Earth communities might become inspires some people to engage in efforts and projects to promote peace and justice when humanity is plagued by ethnic, economic, gender, and political oppression caused and maintained by political tyranny, overt or covert. The "haves" must become more respectful and justice-conscious vis-à-vis the "have nots," and conduct themselves accordingly. Otherwise, they risk endangering not only their own cosmos missions and future prospects for other human voyages, but also the possibility for peace and prosperity in space and interdimensionally.

Humankind and Human Place

Humans are children of the cosmos. Currently, in one region of the cosmos, humans seem to be children only of Earth, intelligent biological beings who evolved over millennia through continuing dialogic interaction between their DNA and their specific Earth terrestrial and microbial environments. On a cosmos scale, humans become part of a greater process at work, in which people can experience an interrelated community—whether they live on Earth, or on another world in the solar system, or in a more distant region of the cosmos. Humankind is stardust become thought. People have evolved and continue to evolve from the changing "stuff" of the "primeval atom," from whose primordial explosion emerged an inflationary expanding and unfolding of the universe. In that reality, humans eventually were born, evolved, and developed a capacity for self-reflection and cosmos reflection; they developed, too, the capacity to consider their own origins and the origins of other worlds with increasing clarity. Human beings, and other intelligent beings interspersed throughout the cosmos, are the universe thinking about itself in diverse locales, each acquiring new but still incomplete data about the complex cosmos.

Wherever humans and other intelligent beings come to be at home in the cosmos, they continue to retain essential elements of who they have understood themselves to be previously—wherever they have dwelled, or as they voyaged through the cosmos—spatially or interdimensionally.

As intellectually reflective stardust, humans realize now how insightful Charles Darwin was in his theory of evolution by natural selection, and how inspired he was when he penned the closing paragraph of *On the Origin of Species* (1859). Humankind has substantially accumulated more and more enhanced data than that which Darwin had or could imagine in the nineteenth century. However, the truth of his final, poetic statement in *On the Origin of Species* remains as current now as it was then. It will remain so, through centuries to come, as the magnificence of the cosmos, with its myriad of beings, continues to be emergent, not known in its totality:

> There is grandeur in this view of life, with its several powers, having been originally breathed into a few forms or into one; and that, whilst this planet has gone cycling on according to the fixed law of gravity, from so simple a beginning, endless forms most beautiful and most wonderful have been, and are being, evolved."[14]

Darwin did not speculate publicly about evolution on other worlds in the cosmos. However, other scientists, beginning in the nineteenth century, suggested that once life began on other worlds, it would evolve there, too. In light of the acknowledged presence of ETI and IDI, it is apparent that life did emerge on other places in the cosmos, and evolved to intelligent life.[15] One of Darwin's admirers, Pierre Teilhard de Chardin, SJ, not only affirmed Darwin's understanding of evolution, but extended it into space—just sixty years after the publication of *Origin*. Teilhard theorized that evolutionary development, including up to the origin of intelligent life, had occurred on other worlds throughout the cosmos. In the spirit of Darwin and Teilhard, humans continue to learn, and to marvel anew about life, as their ongoing cosmos journey progresses through space-time to new places.

The ideas, hypotheses, theories, and speculations presented here are intended to stimulate human interest in, and a growing awareness of, ever-increasing possibilities for diverse cosmos placements. Humankind no longer is Earth-bound, especially in terms of imagination but also because of exploratory Voyagers sent far into space, and rovers navigating the terrain of Mars. People are confined neither to material contexts nor mental constraints because of their limited knowledge of a single cosmos place. Humankind is at home on Earth and, in the future, will be concurrently at home throughout the cosmos as children of every place in which people settle and relate responsibly to the beings, biotic and abiotic, among whom they come to live.

---

14. Charles Darwin, *On the Origin of Species*, 490.
15. Levin et al., "Darwin's Aliens."

In integral cosmos being, the belief of the theist—that there is a Being from and in whom the cosmos was born, who continues to immanent all being—and the belief of the atheist—that all that is began through an unknown cosmos process, and then unfolded and evolved autopoietically, with no transcendent Being present in or related to it—ultimately are absorbed and integrated in a shared sense of common belonging, wherever human journeys carry the human species.

TESS and ETI; IDI?

NASA launched the Transiting Exoplanet Survey Satellite in 2018. It became a valuable complement to space- and Earth-based optical and radio telescopes, since it could detect the presence of planets as they transited—crossed between their star and the viewing telescope, as they orbited their sun—and became visible despite the intense solar light that, visually, ordinarily hid the planet and its journey. TESS has already helped to locate exoplanets. It is a significant addition to space telescope efforts to find planets. Planets it discovers will provide more possibilities, as they are analyzed, for the presence of ETI in the Milky Way Galaxy and beyond. No similar technological assist is possible (yet?) for detecting worlds in other dimensions.

The Kepler Planet Hunter Telescope, which retired last year after a productive sojourn in space, will soon be replaced by the James Webb Space Telescope. Kepler contributed significantly to the expansion of human knowledge of the number of planets in the visible universe, and the Goldilocks Zone orbits of some planets that were observed.

Astrophysicist Andrew Siemion declared that "Kepler was the greatest step forward in the Copernican Revolution since Copernicus."[16] In this insight, Siemion unknowingly links the First and Third Displacements: in astronomy; in history through an intellectual and scientific connection that has been developed over almost five centuries; and in actual and potential similar human displacement impacts. James Shreeve stated that Kepler's achievements in exoplanet discovery "changed the way we approach one of the great mysteries of existence. The question is no longer, is there life beyond Earth? It's a pretty sure bet there is. The question now is, how do we find it?"[17]

TESS and the forthcoming James Webb Space Telescope, and a variety of other space telescopes and planet-hunting technologies that are being used now, or are in the planning and development stage, focus on encountering

16. Shreeve, "Who's Out There?," 49.

17. Shreeve, "Who's Out There?," 49. To which question should be added another: How will humanity relate to intelligent life, at Contact and thereafter?

ETI or discovering Goldilocks Zone exoplanets. No similar effort seems to be underway to seek the dimensions of existence and places of origin for InterDimensional Intelligence. In fact, scientists have not reached a consensus even about whether cosmos dimensions, other than the one in which Earth exists, actually exist at all.

Religions' Rethinking

A fundamental question that has been posed to or about peoples of religious faith traditions (e.g., in the Peters Survey and elsewhere) is "How will religious believers react and respond to Contact with ETI–IDI?" The new reality today is that CE-I and CE-II Contact is known to have occurred between TI and ETI/IDI, and that CE-III Contact has occurred, but less frequently than CE-I and CE-II. Other questions being addressed to members of religious traditions include "How might religious believers respond to the reality of Contact with ETI and IDI?" and "How is a particular faith tradition to incorporate this reality into its belief system?" Doctrines might have to be amended to some extent, or solely reinterpreted to encompass the cosmos presence of Otherkind, other intelligent beings. Their civilization(s) and spiritual development are older than humans' by as much as millions (or even billions) of years. A corollary question is "Since humanity has been unable or unwilling to engender and foster a relational consciousness and relational community on Earth that integrates people of all ethnic groups and regards each and all as related, and thereby naturally worthy of respect and love, how would people be able to interact with intelligent beings of entirely different species?" To develop a response to this question, humankind should develop a cosmosocioecological consciousness as a guide, or at least as a major aspiration, for people who seek to live in harmony and community with each other and with intelligent Others.

Cosmos Community Consciousness and Conduct

As described in the introduction to this volume, *biology* (life on Earth) is now complemented by *astrobiology* (life in space among stars, in Earth's dimension). The study of life is gradually becoming *cosmobiology* (life on Earth, in space, and in all dimensions of existence), as awareness of life's cosmos possibilities stimulates a progression of terminology developed to attempt to include all known and proposed biota variations. Humans have acknowledged that life among the stars and life in other dimensions differ considerably from life on Earth. A similar progression of terminology is that *socioecological praxis ethics*[18] on Earth will become, in cosmos contexts, *cosmosocioecological praxis ethics* upon acknowledgment of the discovery of ExoEarth microbial life, evolving life, or intelligent life. *Ethics* is about the values and principles of communities, developed as ethics-in-context, and ethics-from-context, through a dialogic or dialectic engagement of text and context. How might terrestrial intelligent beings, encountering and engaged with extraterrestrial and interdimensional intelligent beings, arrive at an intellectual place where collaborative ethics might emerge and evolve? Might *cosmosocioecological praxis ethics* become operative as TI/ETI/IDI creatively and collaboratively initiate principles and practices that would bring about social justice and ecological wellbeing on Earth and other intelligent beings' worlds, and in the heavens beyond?

ETI or IDI... or Both?

During more than a decade I have explored the possibilities of intelligently controlled Unidentified Aerial Phenomena (UAP), journeying through different dimensions under the control of InterDimensional Intelligent beings (IDI), and of intelligently controlled Unidentified Flying Objects (UFOs) traveling through space. I have come to understand and accept their existence with more certainty in 2019 than in 2014 as I wrote *Encountering ETI*, in which I proposed that there are likely numerous species of other-than-human intelligent beings. These Others live throughout space in Earth's universe context, or in another (or other) dimension(s) of the vast cosmos. The beings with whom humans have had Contact, and others with whom humanity will have Contact, apparently originate from underground places on Earth, from space, or from another dimension and, in all cases might, as needed, pass from one to the other as they travel. There are then, from the evidence, both extraterrestrial intelligent beings and interdimensional intelligent beings who voyage through space or in another dimension, and ease from one mode into another to reach their destination or to continue their exploration. In sum: *both* ETI and IDI exist, as do ETI and IDI who voyage through space *and* among cosmos dimensions.

In the twenty-first century, distinguished scientists are stating openly and publicly that there is a strong possibility that there is extraterrestrial and interdimensional intelligent life; others openly state that ETI and IDI exist, and have made Contact. The argument that it would take generations for people to travel to the nearest planets, and because of that distance ETI has not arrived on Earth, and therefore ETI does not exist, is no longer valid (if

---

18. Hart, *Sacramental Commons*; Hart, *Cosmic Commons*; Hart, *Encountering ETI*.

ever it was valid: it assumes that spacecraft developed by Others are only as advanced as current human technology allows).[19] In the meantime, Earth "rocket scientists" and multiple scientists in other fields strive to design new forms of travel and new propulsion systems that would substantially diminish travel time for craft voyaging across vast distances in one dimension.

Scientists around the world have been developing innovative ways of increasing the velocity of spacecraft to enable them to travel rapidly from Earth's galactic neighborhood to distant destinations in space. Avi Loeb, whose work is described in chapter 4 and in the *National Geographic* article cited earlier, focuses on light sail travel. This is being developed through the Breakthrough Project. Another potential means of travel or, more accurately, an assist to or boost for travel, is described in the website Live Science. Columbia University astronomer David Kipping speculates that alien spacecraft might journey across the universe by shooting a laser at the "halo" atop a black hole, a location that would absorb the photons, enhance their energy, and propel them with the added energy halfway around the black hole in time to reenter and reenergize the spacecraft so that it might traverse vast distances more rapidly.[20]

A different mode of voyaging the cosmos, interdimensional travel, likely would enable much faster travel than space travel. Little is known, currently, about how human travelers might journey in this manner. Eventually, the theory of and technology for interdimensional journeys might be developed by human scientists and engineers on Earth, or be shared with humankind by IDI voyagers utilizing it.

Homelessness or Hopefulness: Humankind Displaced or Re-Placed?

Humankind stands on the threshold of a new awareness of its possible places in the universe, suggested and informed by new explorations of the vast cosmos—initially via optical and radio telescopes, planetary robotic rovers, and unoccupied spacecraft journeying through this solar system toward distant space. Subsequently, human astronauts will travel on space vehicles to worlds near and far; this will lead, eventually, to settlement on other worlds. Later still, humankind might travel interdimensionally, through portals or

---

19. This was scientists' and the general public's thinking (and mine) when I observed an intelligently controlled UAP above the Hudson River in 1963. Since then I have remembered my previous 'thinking' whenever I hear scientists or others declare with certainty that "this cannot be done" when what should be stated is, "This cannot be done with humankind's present science and technology."

20. Letzter, "Aliens Might Zap Black Holes."

CONCLUSION: COMMUNITY IN THE COSMOS COMMONS   239

wormholes or other, as yet unknown ways of going into and returning from other cosmos dimensions.

Prior to exploring and colonizing nearby planets and moons, however, humankind must end local and global conflicts on its own world. Wars are even now being fought over natural goods, water sites, and territory; they are promoted by self-centered politicians and greedy, acquisitive entrepreneurs and corporate executives, who often use as pawns unreflective members of diverse religious faiths. Such conflicts stimulate development and use of ever-more destructive weapons that, accompanied by accelerated human-caused and human-exacerbated global climate change, threaten human survival and the survival of all life on Earth. Even now, humans are accelerating the rate of extinction of all biota, as described in a 1,500-page report released on May 7, 2019, by the United Nations' Intergovernmental Science-Policy Platform on Biodiversity and Ecosystem Services.[21] In contrast to destructive conduct and thinking, the International Space Station provides a dramatic example of human possibilities for international, interethnic, and interracial collaboration to benefit all people.

If humanity survives and thrives, its future cosmos place will no longer be a single planet, Earth, in one solar system, in one galaxy, in the known visible universe. Humankind will come to dwell in numerous distinct cosmos places, on worlds now beyond human imagination. The Third Displacement, if all goes well, will stimulate a new consciousness of the immensity and complexity of the known universe, through humans' experiences, extrapolation of data, and hypotheses, and generate new visions and plans for humanity to transcend its current locale.

The shock of learning more about cosmos complexity and Otherkind inhabitants could be overcome and displaced by humans' excitement on arrival at new, fascinating places. However, the human species needs to achieve beforehand a new political maturity and an equitable sharing of Earth's goods, and advance scientifically and technologically. Should this happen, people will be enriched by an augmented sense that "we are all in this together" as a human species. Humans' sense of adventure, their curiosity, their creativity, and their unified community will enable them to face new challenges, and collaboratively develop creative responses to them.

Responses to Fundamental Questions

In the introduction, two fundamental questions were posed: "Is there intelligent other-than-human life in the universe?" (essentially, "Are we alone?") and "How could other-than-human intelligent beings traverse vast universe

21. United Nations, "Intergovernmental Science-Policy."

distances to arrive on Earth?" and its corollary, "How would humankind traverse vast universe distances to reach Others on other worlds?" The research and narratives presented in these pages provide at least tentative, if not definitive, responses to these questions. We are *not* alone as intelligent beings in the universe; and the sightings of and Contact with ETI and IDI confirm that it is possible for Visitors to come here from there, and innovative technologies now in process through the work of Earth's scientists and engineers have the potential to provide means for humans to go there from here. Humanity should reflect seriously on these realities. People need to consider thoughtfully what ethical, ecological, economic, and ecclesial (religious; spiritual) impacts might result from Contact, and how they might be addressed.

Realistic Idealism

It might seem to some people, as this book concludes presentation of possibilities for humankind after Contact, that the conclusions drawn from data presented on the preceding pages are too idealistic. Could a transformation of human consciousness and conduct, renewal of Earth, reconstruction of human communities, and peaceful and mutually beneficial engagement with intelligent beings from other places in the cosmos, actually occur? The answer is . . . perhaps. Humanity must replace an ideology of destruction with a perspective of construction, neighbor rejection with neighbor acceptance and love, and a sense of hope, rather than of despair, about the future—all the while recognizing the difficulties and obstacles to such a conversion. *Third Displacement* is permeated by ideals and idealism but, I think and hope, realistically so. Contrary ideologies are not omitted, but included and assessed.

Ideals must not be too idealistic but, on the other hand, people as individuals and as communities need dreams and visions—utopias—to help them avoid or endure a dystopian present and see the possibilities for a now seemingly deceptive dream that a utopia unseen could become a dream come true. In the words of the sages, "without a vision, the people will perish" (Prov 29:18). As described earlier, "utopia" might mean a fantasy, something not achievable; or, "utopia" is an envisioned and possible new reality toward which people and peoples should strive. Some people might despairingly fear that utopia is only a fantasy; others might embrace it as a projection and promise that what is not, could be, and work to make it a reality: a topia in which their descendants will live. The possible futures envisioned with a spirit of hopefulness will then be *realized*, and eliminate fear of an impending reality of displacement and homelessness. This is a time of dreams and visions, for all people, intergenerationally: "Your elders shall dream dreams, and your youth will see visions" (cf. Joel 2:28).

Cosmos Community of Communities

While Earth and Earth's communities are being transformed, humankind is venturing into space to explore planets, lunar bodies, and other celestial entities. Earth is in peril. If attitudes are not changed on Earth, space explorers will export economic, ecological, and other problems to distant places—unless deterred by other intelligent beings who view themselves as guardians of cosmos wellbeing. The quest for natural goods to support the human adventure and to enhance life on the home planet requires a new consciousness and new ethical commitments. These would guide humanity to respect and relate well not only to existing natural ecologies in new contexts, but also to the evolving life—intelligent to microbial—that they encounter. Such a transformation should stimulate Otherkind to view humankind as a welcome member of an existing relational community, rather than as a pathogen that would imperil cosmos community. The four-step process of cosmosocioecological praxis ethics, described in the previous chapter, would promote care for creation in terrestrial, extraterrestrial, and interdimensional settings.

In the near and distant future, then, there might well be, ultimately, no third displacement, no homelessness—physical or psychological. Cosmographically, humanity will come to be at home not only on Earth but on diverse worlds among the stars and in different dimensions. In all places, people would come to share with other intelligent beings, congenially and collaboratively, common places in cosmos communities in the integral cosmos commons.

Afterword

I have spent my academic career studying the question of the relationship of science to religion. Although the topic has many facets, the main issue is whether anything of lasting significance is going on in the universe (or in a multiverse if it exists). Does the universe have an overall aim, or is it instead a pointless movement of atoms hurling toward an ultimately lifeless and mindless abyss?

After reading this final volume in John Hart's adventurous trilogy, I find myself wondering how I might answer this question now.

Suppose I have acquired certain knowledge of the existence of intelligent others, as the book you have just read understands them? What difference would such a discovery make in how I address the momentous question of cosmic purpose?

Among other outcomes, over the course of billions of years, the universe has already given birth, at least on Earth, to living beings endowed with an interior life—that is, the capacity to experience. All sentient beings have at least some degree of "subjectivity."

Suppose, then, that in traversing the almost numberless planets, galaxies, and even other universes, I have encountered many other instances and degrees of "subjectivity." This would tell me more about the universe than I could have gathered from my terrestrial perch alone. A universe that gives rise in many spatial and temporal situations to experiencing subjects is an *awakening* universe. This is not a trivial quality.

But what if some of the "others" I encounter on my journey are *intelligent* subjects? What if they share my capacity not only to experience but also to understand, reflect, judge, know, deliberate, and decide?

Surely in reflecting on such encounters I would be justified in concluding that the universe at bottom is more than mindless meandering. It would strike me all the more as a *dramatic* awakening.

Awakening to what?

Ultimately, of course, to what *is*. To what is *intelligible*. To what is *true*. To what is *good*. To what is *beautiful*. That is, to what is *indestructible*.

The prospect of sharing the wonder of a dramatically awakening universe with such "others" is sufficient reason, I believe, for all of us to give our full attention to the reports that John Hart has put before us in his rich trilogy. For me, at least, the lavish volumes he has written are expressions not of idle curiosity but of ultimate concern.

John F. Haught, PhD
Distinguished Research Professor Emeritus
Georgetown University

APPENDIX 1

Analysis of Alleged ETI/IDI UAP Events in the US and UK

Incidents or events involving TI-ETI/IDI encounters, usually described from a distance (Allen Hynek's CE-I: Close Encounters of the First Kind), are increasingly reported in newspapers and on network television news programs. This is a marked departure from past journalistic practices in which such narratives were not reported at all, or were limited to front-page photo-accompanied stories in sensationalist tabloids on racks located next to grocery store checkouts. The principal reasons for the change are that a majority of people today accept that humankind has been and is being engaged by Visitors from other worlds, and that media corporations want to profit from this public awareness and interest. The headlines on television and in print usually use the generic "UFO" in its limited popular sense, that is, to mean always an *intelligently controlled* unidentified flying object, not a meteor or artificial satellite incorrectly identified as such. In light of the critical assessment of such narratives by astrophysicist Jacques Vallee and others, it would be helpful for the reader of these news reports to be an open-minded skeptic: to neither wholeheartedly accept nor wholeheartedly reject a story because of the reader's preexisting attitude of unquestioning UFO acceptance (Wow! More proof!), or unreflective UFO rejection (It can't be; therefore, it isn't), coupled with a realization, in either case, that US government black ops might have had a hidden hand in devising or manipulating a UAP event or events.

US: Nineteenth-Century Incidents

While I worked on *Third Displacement*, I learned about two purported UFO events that particularly intrigued me because they both were said to have occurred in the nineteenth century: in Montana in 1870, seventy-seven years before the Roswell crash, and in New Hampshire in 1871. I received first the 1870 Montana story, via the mail; it attracted me because it described a supposed event in my home state. My friend Jacques Vallee sent it to me in Montana, correctly assuming that I would be interested. When I researched the incident on Google using "Montana 1870 UFO sighting," I found the New Hampshire story, too. I was intrigued that both events were described as occurring within a year of each other, in the 1870–71 period.

Montana 1870 UFO

In 2013, UFO researchers from MUFON in Montana investigated a case dating to 1870 in which, it was alleged, an extraterrestrial craft was observed by Tom Melton, manager of the Knotts Stage Station south of Dillon. The UFO hurtled low and erratically through the sky and crashed into a mountainside near Bannock. More than a century after the purported event, local "treasure hunter" Warren Huxtable claimed that he had acquired the stagecoach employee's supposed diary, written in pencil. Huxtable said that he had read the August 14, 1870 entry which described the mountainside crash. He wrote to a friend at NASA, seeking advice. Subsequently, he was called by an unidentified person claiming to be from NASA, who asked Huxtable to give directions to reach the site; Huxtable declined. When he traced back and called the telephone number, which had a Virginia area code, a recording stated that the number was not in service. He was then visited by a team of aggressive men in a black SUV with Virginia license plates and a NASA logo on its sides; they forced him to take them to the site. They did field work for hours, including with lasers, which he was not permitted to watch. They returned back to where they had met Huxtable and, as they departed, they told him and the people who had been waiting for his return not to investigate further because a meteor and nothing else had landed there, and it was "dangerous" for investigators to go there. However, Huxtable continued his investigation. He invited UFO researchers (including two scientists, Joan Bird, PhD, zoologist, and William Puckett, MS, meteorologist) and local residents to accompany him to the site. He told them that he thought that he had found the crash site with some debris nearby. They went with him there, and found some metal objects, surmised to be artifacts from mining, which lab analysis subsequently verified. The UFO investigators concluded that the data was "inconclusive": they could neither confirm nor deny that the incident had really occurred. Later, Huxtable stated, he returned with Ground Penetrating Radar (GPR) which detected metal objects in the soil. A student at nearby University of Montana Western became interested in the story, contacted Huxtable, and received instructions from him about how to find the site. He went there, took photos of the area, and retrieved additional debris. In the debris he and the other investigators brought back from the site there was some which, although containing familiar metals, integrated them in unfamiliar alloys.

Over the past six years, other people have made site visits to Bannock. As I reflected on the original site visit report and on later data derived from online sources and received via email exchanges with Bird and Puckett, I found the information to be incomplete. I had several questions regarding Huxtable's claims and other aspects of the events described:

- Did a diary really exist? If so, for how long pre-Huxtable, or even recently, prior to the time of the site visit with experienced UFO investigators? (Huxtable said that he no longer had the diary, because his divorced wife had discarded it.)
- If it had existed, did a reputable historian or dealer in antiques or historic documents examine the diary to verify its date and author? (Huxtable said that the man from whom he had purchased the diary had died; no "experts" were consulted.)
- Did an independent source verify that Huxtable used a Ground Penetrating Radar instrument to go over the site at a later date, as he stated subsequently?
- Might Huxtable be a US government agent, perhaps related to the US military, similar to the backgrounds that Vallee had discovered about people involved in or related to events he investigated, directed to divert researchers from other investigations that had a greater likelihood of verifying the validity of UAP claims?

Since I had noted in the report narrative some similarities to Jacques Vallee's experiences with military-related/employed deceivers in the past, several other questions came to mind:

- Since there is a long history, over millennia, of ExoEarth intelligent beings' visits to Earth/Earth's atmosphere/humankind, might government agents who, in the Bannock case as in other cases, were part of the US military, a US spy agency, or a black ops group, have developed and used this story to divert people from their then-current research that would have had more likelihood of verifying the validity of UAP claims? As they had done with other supposed incidents in the past, could they have tried to entice UFO researchers into involvement with an event described as having occurred in 1870, witnessed by a stage company employee, and thus divert them from finding narratives of actual UFO encounters which government personnel are investigating?

- If the latter is the case, had the UFO investigators been viewed by government agents as uncomfortably close to finding and disclosing information that the government did not want people to know?

Further,

- Why did the UFO research team trust Huxtable—were his credentials impeccable? (In Jacques Vallee's *Revelations*, some people were not the person they presented themselves to be. The UFO team regarded Huxtable as an honest, congenial, credible—if somewhat eccentric—person, and a "storyteller.")

- To what extent have researchers investigated and verified his statement that, after they had departed, he had done a subsurface test and found something made of an unidentified metal? What kind of equipment did he use, and where did he obtain it and at whose expense? Huxtable mentions a "jumpy needle" on the GPR equipment he used. What caused that? (Researchers, lacking financial resources to do so, did not return to the site with their own GPR equipment to verify Huxtable's assertions and do their own onsite research. They, too, were curious about the "jumpy needle" he mentioned.)

- Since the imposing "NASA" visitors made laser forays across the gully, might there be an associated crash site there, if a spacecraft indeed had landed, but perhaps where most of the purported spacecraft hit the mountainside? Did Huxtable investigate there? If not, why not? On whose (public or private) property did the team do their investigation, and who is the landowner across the gulch? Are there any restrictions against digging on either site?

In my attempt to verify Huxtable's stories, I contacted my friend Joan Bird, PhD, who was part of the Bannock-area UFO research team. She is a scientist (zoology) and a long-time, experienced, and well-qualified researcher of UFO narratives, especially of events in Montana. She is the author of *Montana UFOs and Extraterrestrials* (2013).[1] Dr. Bird provided some

---

1. See Bird, *Montana UFOs and Extraterrestrials*.

ANALYSIS OF ALLEGED ETI/IDI UAP EVENTS IN THE US AND UK   249

of the information described above that came from the MUFON team. So, too, did another member of the team to whom she referred me, William Puckett, MS. He is a scientist (degrees in biology and meteorology),[2] a long-time UFO investigator, and the director of the Montana branch of MUFON.

The UFO research team members said that Huxtable seemed to be an honest person, and did not seem to be government-related. Joan Bird stated, about Warren Huxtable and the team's site visit:

> I sincerely doubt Warren is an agent. He's a character, a treasure hunter, and an intuitive, but I don't think he purposely misleads people. I think he's sincere, but he does have a reputation as a story teller, which is of course one way that people who report UFOs are dismissed.
>
> From what others said later, and thinking back on the surrounding terrain, I had a sense that we may not have been looking in quite the right place. To truly determine whether anything is there, I have thought we would need state-of-the-art ground penetrating radar, and that is not easy to come by. If anyone has used GPR and found anything, I am not aware of it.
>
> I suppose we could even consider that [the "NASA" group] was the Pentagon and their classified Advance Aerial Threat Identification Program that was investigating it, through their contractor Robert Bigelow.
>
> I think I can speak for both Bill Puckett, who was the Montana MUFON Director at the time, and myself, that we didn't have enough evidence to prove or disprove Warren's claim of a UFO crash.

Puckett's assessment of the visit and Huxtable was that

> Joan and I did take several measurements of the "alleged" UFO crash site near Bannock. According to Warren the crash occurred in 1870. I didn't find anything unusual other than some magnetic anomalies which could be possibly explained by natural fluctuations. I was most intrigued by the fact that the area appeared to be "artificially" carved out and looked "out of place" in the natural terrain. This was revealed by photos taken around a mile from the site.
>
> Perhaps NASA (or maybe they were CIA) didn't want civilians potentially to find UFO artifacts. They told Warren after a day of investigating that a meteor crash occurred there. This

---

2. William Puckett was a meteorologist, in turn, for the National Weather Service and for the Environmental Protection Agency (EPA). He is also a consultant for UFO documentaries on TV.

was "bunk" as there were no meteor rocks in the area . . . Yes, he is a story teller, but yet seems to have had some interesting experiences . . . Warren tends to spin tales, but yet does seem to have had some real UFO experiences.

Although I received these responses from members of the MUFON research team who made a MUFON field visit, I decided to leave all of the questions here. This enables the reader to see how I evaluated the Bannock narrative events, and to reflect themselves on how they might react and respond to the story. Through this process, they might formulate their own questions about this and other—alleged or actual—UFO events.

All this having been said, I do not mean to impugn Huxtable's character or truthfulness. He might well be a sincere person who is honestly conveying to the UFO investigative team what he had been told about the story, his reading of a stage station manager's diary, his understanding of historic Bannock-area UFO events, and his involvement with them more than a century after they are said to have occurred. However, his stories do not contain sufficient verifiable information to justify confirmation of the event by independent investigators.

The Bannock events, those that are claimed for 1870, and those that occurred around the time of the site visit in 2013, illustrate well the difficulty—including for scientists—of determining the veracity of reports about UAP/UFO/IDI/ETI events; additional difficulties are encountered in efforts to analyze them and assess the credibility of those who describe them, and then to accept or reject them wholly or partially.

New Hampshire 1871 UFO

As I searched the web for Bannock corroboration and additional site details, I discovered that a fascinating complementary UAP event apparently occurred in the winter of 1870–71 on Mount Washington, New Hampshire. One of the two photographers who were members of a scientific expedition observed and photographed a massive frost formation capping the mountain, against whose backdrop a dark, cigar-shaped object with seemingly rough edges on all sides is seen clearly. The object in the photo could be a gap in the frost caused by a ravine or other natural geological depression; a tall object visible because it protrudes above the frost; or an airborne object between Mount Washington and the photographer.

The expedition was undertaken by members of the 201 Mount Washington Scientific Corps, which was doing a geological and meteorological study of the mountain under the direction of State Geologist Dr. Charles Henry Hitchcock. More than a century later, the photo was described as the oldest picture of a UAP; it had been taken to be seen through a (now-antique) stereoscope viewer.[3] Notations around the border of the stereoscope photo displayed on the internet state the names of the photographers, "Clogh and Kimball," the name of the scientific expedition, the time period during which it was exploring, and the fact that the stereoscope was "Entered according to Act of Congress in the year 1871, by Clogh [sic] & Kimball, in the Office of the Librarian of Congress, at Washington." The font used seemed an older type; the surname of the first photographer is misspelled, which seems unlikely for a submission to the Library of Congress (LOC): an incorrect "Clogh" is written, rather than "Clough."

I decided to research the LOC, using the photo and its border inscription. Unable to find anything after exploring several research links, I sent an email to the library via the "Ask A Librarian" link, describing the photo and the margin notes. About a week later I received a detailed reply from the Reference Librarian of the Prints and Photographs Division. She thought that she had found the stereoscope photos matching my description. To verify that she found the same photo, I sent to her a copy of the version I had; there was a match. Subsequently, she sent me a digital photocopy of several of the stereoscope pictures. These include both the entire stereoscope card with two photos side by side, and half of the stereoscope card with one photo, but enlarged. Another full card has two other photos, in which several dark openings or mountainside protrusions of various shapes are visible. The pictures are very clear. In the margins of the original, "Clough" is spelled correctly, and the inscriptions are written in a beautiful elegant style seen on nineteenth-century picture captions and personal letters. In addition to the

---

3. The developed product was for a stereoview dual photo. See http://www.theblackvault.com/casefiles/ufo-over-mt-washington-new-hampshire-1870/. The photographers' names on the stereoscope are "Clogh [sic] & Kimball." A Google search of "Clough & Kimball" resulted in more information about this company, additional photos from the expedition, a clear photograph of the "UFO," and details about and photos from other work by Clough & Kimball over the decades since the Mount Washington photos were taken. In December 2018 I contacted the Library of Congress through their "Ask A Librarian" link to see if they had a record of the submission of the photo to the library. I received a response from the reference librarian of the LOC Prints and Photographs Division on December 27, 2018, which included pictures of the original stereoscope photos in the LOC. In another search, I found this article: Larsen, "Oldest Known UFO Photo Refuted." Larsen, after several years' research, had found in the New York Public Library a photo of the original stereoscope picture. He also found reference to a book written by a scientist on the expedition, Dr. Charles Henry Hitchcock: *Mount Washington in Winter, or The Experiences Of A Scientific Expedition Upon The Highest Mountain in New England—1870-71*. I found and purchased the book, which provided more details about the mountain's frost formations, especially in chapter 16, "The Frost-work and Clouds," 285–92. Hitchcock's book is available from Amazon, as are several other reprints, because the copyright has run out; I ordered a reprint.

stereoscope photos, an accompanying separate sheet, stamped with "Library of Congress Division of Prints," lists twenty-five photos, at the end of which a sentence states that copies would be mailed to "any address upon receipt of price—$3.00 per dozen." The photo described on internet sites as possibly the "oldest UFO photo" is number seventeen, "FROST ARCHITECTURE"; number 18 is "FROST FEATHERS."

I examined the photographs carefully, including by using a large magnifying glass. I recalled that Samuel Sherman, the person who bought a supposed "original" at auction for $385 in 2002, had stated at the time that he would make it available for scientific examination. To my knowledge, this never happened. I wondered when I read that story if he had discovered, after seeking additional information about the photo (or paying for his own "scientific study"), that it was not what he had thought it to be when he bought it.

As I examined the photos, several ideas came to mind. First, that the cigar shape, an apparently rectangular shape of the dark object, *might* indicate it was in the air away from the mountainside, and was some sort of spacecraft; it's jagged sides, however, called that into question. Second, that if it had appeared to the photographer that the dark form was suspended above rather than laying on the mountainside or protruding from the frost, the amazed photographer would have taken additional pictures. Third, if it appeared to be moving rather than stationery, the greatly astonished photographer would have taken as many pictures as possible in either case—suspended or in motion—and would have put a different caption on photo 17. It might be possible to conjecture, looking closely at the object, that it is stationery, suspended off the mountain, but that a professional photographer did not notice such a separation between mountain and dark rectangle seems unlikely.

The next and final step in my research was to try to find and purchase a copy of Dr. Hitchcock's book. I searched the internet using his name, and found biographical information about him. I found, too, a link to Amazon, which sold the book. I purchased a reprint, and read about the Mount Washington scientific survey as described in *Mount Washington in Winter, or The Experiences Of A Scientific Expedition Upon The Highest Mountain in New England—1870-71*. It contains chapters written by members of the expedition who had climbed the mountain and wintered there. Hitchcock, the state geologist, communicated with them by telegraph from his office in Hanover, New Hampshire (the expedition had carted up the mountain the wires and other equipment needed to have a telegraph station). In chapter 16, "The Frost-work and Clouds," expedition member J. H. Huntington celebrates the natural grandeur of Mount Washington. In his descriptions of clouds, he observes that sometimes "innumerable mountain peaks protrude and seem like islands in an ocean bounded only by the sky. In winter these cloud effects continue often a whole day almost unchanged."[4] (In winter, likely fewer peaks, not "innumerable" in extent, protruded above the massive frost cap on the mountains.)

When my research was complete, I concluded that the hypothesis that a UFO is visible in the 1870–71 photograph can be conclusively dismissed. The overwhelming likelihood is that the photo's dark object, visible against a whitecapped Mount Washington, is exactly what the photographer called it: part of the mountain's "Frost Architecture."[5]

UK: Twentieth Century Incident

Rendlesham Forest

The events at Rendlesham Forest in England have been publicized as "The Other Roswell." Sometimes this is supplemented by a comment and claim that there is more information about the incidents there than is available about Roswell (where the US government has suppressed information about Roswell events since 1947).

The Rendlesham Forest events are particularly fascinating because there are credible people arguing pros and cons about how true is what was reported to have happened. Both groups include people who, under ordinary circumstances, would be considered "credible witnesses"—"ordinary circumstances" mean, in this instance, without hypnosis and sodium pentothal mind-altering psychological torture at the hands of government agents.

Initially, and for several years, I accepted the "evidence" that was offered by Rendlesham aficionados in the United States and United Kingdom. However, when I read the Rendlesham narrative, there were details—or the

---

4. Hitchcock, *Mount Washington in Winter*, 289. A reasonable extension of this imagery, it seems to this writer, would be to assume that the tallest peaks would rise, too, above the frost covering the mountain, and that the fierce winds on the mountain, measured with the expedition's anemometer to exceed at times one hundred miles per hour, could clear off the frost cap atop mountains' peaks.

5. A fascinating addendum to this research: I saw a photo posted online of one of the historical markers in the area of Mount Washington. Its inscription, in white letters on a green background (as were other signs commemorating historic events): "BETTY AND BARNEY HILL INCIDENT—On the night of September 19–20, 1961, Portsmouth, NH couple Betty and Barney Hill experienced a close encounter with an unidentified flying object and two hours of 'lost' time while driving south on Rte 3 near Lincoln. They filed an official Air Force Project Blue Book report of a brightly-lit cigar-shaped craft the next day ... This was the first widely-reported UFO abduction report in the United States." The sign was installed in 2011; see it and others here: http://www.images-of-new-hampshire-history.com/New-Hampshire-Historical-Markers.php.

lack thereof—that did not jibe with what should have been an accurate and realistic report of events that occurred. Several of these details seemed to coincide with what US government official statements said about Roswell, and government officials' denial that anything extraordinary had happened there—to the extent of threatening witnesses. I suppressed my doubts because the Rendlesham narrative seemed to be—and I hoped it would be—a true presentation about what happened there.

A part of the Rendlesham story that made me uneasy initially, even though I accepted the broader overall narrative as accurate, included the statement that Sergeant James Penniston's notebook, apparently, had not been taken from him before or during his debriefing by on-site military superiors or members of the Air Force Office of Special Investigations (AFOSI), an agency whose sometimes brutal methods of interrogation were undertaken with impunity. Why did they not (if indeed they did not) confiscate his notebook, or temporarily do so in order to alter it, especially since it included not only written notes, but his drawings of what he had seen? Why did Penniston not mention the binary code therein when he spoke with Georgina Bruni?[6] Why did he state only years later that he had copied a binary code that contained a message from the occupants of the landed craft?[7] Was the code added to his notebook at a later time? The OSI is regarded as thorough, and it is not conceivable that they would have let Penniston keep his notebook. Why, then, did he still have it in his possession? Or, had it been taken from him during his debriefing, and altered, perhaps even by him while under hypnosis and drugged? Were the binary codes added then, or later—along with an implanted memory that he had written them himself, and another memory that he had continually had the notebook in his possession?

In reflecting on his experience, Penniston states that the craft had technology far superior to humans'; "suddenly, there was no doubt. I realized that I was 100 percent certain that we are part of a larger community beyond the confines of our planet."[8] (His use of "community" is commendable, and opens to the possibility of a positive relationship with ETI/IDI.)

When Penniston and John Burroughs returned to the site after briefly reporting to the base and turning in their weapons, Penniston saw and photographed broken branches, scorch marks, and three indentations in the soil in a triangular arrangement, which he took to be evidence of the place where the triangular craft he had seen had landed: "I was relieved to find proof that this had really happened."[9] He took his film to the base lab; he was told when

6. Bruni, *You Can't Tell the People*, 172–86.
7. Pope et al., *Encounter in Rendlesham Forest*, 228–45, 265–70.
8. Kean, *UFOs*, 181.
9. Kean, *UFOs*, 183.

he returned later that the photos came out poorly. A major question here is, why was Penniston "relieved to find proof" about what he thought he had seen? Was the event not strongly etched in his mind, in which case additional physical evidence would not have seemed necessary? (Perhaps the incident had been so unusual that he needed physical proof it had occurred. However, is it possible that false memories about event details had been planted in his mind, and he was unsure of them because the sodium pentothal-hypnosis procedure had been done earlier, and he did not recall that physical-psychological intrusion?) Complementary to the lab's story that his photos were not good ones are other incidents, not related to Rendlesham, where a film or photos displaying UAP "disappeared" when in military hands.[10]

What struck me, too, was that military personnel who were present for the Rendlesham events sometimes provided contradictory accounts of details—even, at times, giving different dates for some incidents, information about the extent of ranking officers' involvement in them, or even the shape of the craft seen—or crafts seen: circular or triangular? Moreover, technical difficulties seemed to abound, such as malfunctioning radios and, strangely, that the light-alls, portable banks of floodlights, could not be taken to the forest area immediately as needed because either their generators needed to be charged, or they had insufficient gasoline . . . or both. Would a US air base in the United States or on foreign soil, supposedly ready to respond to aggression by hostile powers, be so poorly prepared? Or, was there a covert US agency ensuring that illumination and communication devices could not be used—in this case rendering them useless not only in this event but in a real emergency if there had been an act of aggression by a foreign power?

In contrast to Penniston's apparent retention of and control over his notebook describing and illustrating events in Rendlesham Forest, in the Roswell area US government representatives threatened ranchers and members of their families who had seen the crash sites not to say anything about the sites; some of these witnesses had taken "souvenirs" there, which were confiscated by investigators. Military personnel in the hundreds were dispatched to the site to comb it carefully and remove the smallest scraps of debris in order that there would not be evidence of a spacecraft crash.[11]

    10. See, for example, the experience of baseball minor league manager Nick Mariana in Great Falls, Montana. In August, 1950 (just three years after Roswell) he saw two circular objects flying past two tall smokestacks. Subsequently, he showed his UFO film to the local Rotary Club; then, Air Force personnel at Malmstrom Air Force Base near Great Falls asked if they could borrow it. He lent it to them, and had a difficult time in getting it back. When he did recover it and ran it, he discovered that the clearest footage of the two objects had been removed; the film had been spliced to cover that spot. See Bird, *Montana UFOs and Extraterrestrials*, 15–76.

    11. More details about Roswell, and also my interviews with Colonel Dr. Marcel, are

A major shadow that looms over the Rendlesham story is that witnesses to events were "debriefed" or aggressively interrogated by OSI members—including by use of hypnosis and drugs, the combination of which could alter or eliminate real memories, and implant false recall of what happened. As Colonel Halt would observe years later,

> [A]gents from the Office of Special Investigations (OSI), the Air Force's major investigative service, were on the base and secretly investigated the case in the days following . . . the OSI didn't want anyone involved whom they couldn't control. OSI operatives harshly interrogated the young airmen, some of them in shock at the time, who were key witnesses. These men reported later that the agents told them not to talk about the UFO events, or their careers would be in jeopardy.[12] Drugs such as sodium pentothal, often called a 'truth serum' when used with some form of brainwashing or hypnosis, were administered during these interrogations, and the whole thing has had damaging, and lasting, effects on the men involved . . . Repression by the OSI is not uncommon in the military, but nobody involved will even admit that.[13]

It is especially disturbing to hear a retired colonel describe OSI "interrogations" as "brainwashing," and state that such "repression" is "not uncommon" or, simply put, is common.

Georgina Bruni presents compelling data and insights about effects of the use of hypnosis combined with sodium pentothal. She writes:

> [Witnesses] might have been given screen memories [catalyzed by] the administration of drugs combined with hypnosis. [If the victim of this process started to recall actual events] the created

---

elaborated in *Encountering ETI*. He was an otolaryngologist (ENT specialist) who was a decorated combat helicopter pilot and a flight surgeon in the first Iraq War. (My sources here are numerous books about Roswell, and my email interviews with the late Colonel Dr. Jesse Marcel Jr.) As a child he had handled debris from the crash site that his father, Major Jesse Marcel Sr.—then head of security at the Roswell Army Air Force base (at the time, the only atomic bomb facility in the world)—had brought home to show his wife and son. When Dr. Marcel passed on, he was reading *Encountering ETI* to provide a cover blurb. He was one of the people to whom I dedicated the book. See Hart, *Encountering ETI*, 106-33. I last spoke with Jess Marcel the night before he passed on; we were due to have lunch the following week.

12. Adrian Bustinza adds that his life was threatened during his interrogation. He was instructed to say and do as he was told, or else there would be consequences: "Bullets are cheap, a dime a dozen." Bruni, *You Can't Tell the People*, 205-6.

13. Kean, *UFOs*, 188.

screen memory (false story) would be distorted [and] recalled incoherently.

[Another procedure] would be to induce hypnotic amnesia, which causes the subject to forget all he is programmed to . . . the subject may never know that he was meddled with. [The procedures were] designed to be used by the Central Intelligence Agency and the US military.

Bruni consulted with British hypnotist David Bonner. A member of the National Register of Hypnotherapists and Psychotherapists, he told Bruni that sodium pentothal was not just a "truth drug": it could be used, coupled with hypnosis, for "suppressing or implanting information, overriding the truth, blocking off certain memories and breaking down resistance." He added that "'trigger' words, sounds, and smells could be planted in the mind and be used at any time for whatever reason, even years later."[14] This information from Bruni and others was a red flag for me: how many Rendlesham Forest events' witnesses had been subjected to this type of drug-hypnosis treatment, and how many things did they "recall" that did not actually occur?

When I first read about Rendlesham events, I heard on an online BBC story the partial tape recording made by Colonel Halt. It seemed authentic—and also surprising: How did Halt retain some control over this tape? Why did the US military release it? (Responses to "Freedom of Information Act" requests are only as helpful as the extent of cooperation with them that a government or agency of government extends upon receipt of a request by an ordinary citizen, a politician, or an organization. A claim of "national security" regarding some details "covers a multitude of sins"—and violations of law, as well.). In light of Vallee's assessment (see chapter 4), that apparently the entire Rendlesham Forest event was orchestrated by US spy agencies (to which should be added "torture experts"), Colonel Halt might well have been part of this effort from the beginning. A clue here is the recollection of Sergeant Adrian Bustinza that when he went into the Forest, he saw Halt standing by the craft, apparently communicating with someone within it (or, from elsewhere via radio transmission). Bustinza said that "he thought he heard Halt say he would contact the electronics division and they would try to get a part from another world."[15] Later, Halt claimed that Bustinza had not been on site (because he was not ordered there, so he should not have been there), but reversed his assertion when other airmen stated firmly that Bustinza had,

---

14. Bruni, *You Can't Tell*, 317–18. Cf. with the film *Conspiracy Theory* (1997): actor Mel Gibson's character periodically feels compelled to buy copies of J. D. Salinger's novel *The Catcher in the Rye* (1951); government agents can then locate him by book sales.

15. Bruni, *You Can't Tell the People*, 202.

in fact, been there.[16] It appears that Halt became aware that his exchange with someone in the craft—or communicating via a radio transmitter or other device—was overheard by Bustinza, and Halt decided to deny that Bustinza was there in order to strengthen his claim that Bustinza would not have been able to overhear the exchange about a "part."

Another interesting bit of data is that Halt lent his tape to Colonel Gordon Williams, who played it for his staff and his superior, General Robert Bazley. They responded to it with "stunned silence."[17] Later, General Bazley, "unbeknownst to me, started playing it at cocktail parties."[18] In contrast to the "stunned silence" reception earlier, on some occasions people reportedly laughed when they heard the tape. Why was it so entertaining? Because it furthered the illusion that an intelligently controlled UFO was approaching the forest, while partygoers knew that the event was contrived? Perhaps they were laughing at Halt, too, because of his ignorance and naivete, or with Halt because he played his role well. The different responses seem odd: some people (the uninformed) were in shocked silence when they heard the tape, while others (those aware of its role in the engineered event) laughed about a colonel's recording of a supposed alien encounter.

A possible clue to Halt's actions and character is in Georgina Bruni's *You Can't Tell the People: The Cover-up of Britain's Roswell*. Bruni states that "according to Halt he interviewed the witnesses about a week later. However, Airman Edward N. Cabansag claims he was instructed to report to Lieutenant Colonel Halt on the morning of December 26th, a few hours after he had gone off duty. This being the case, it means that Halt was involved in the debriefings from day one."[19]

Another puzzle: the document that witnesses were compelled to sign, which had been prepared for them, supposedly describing Rendlesham events, was not accurate, according to witnesses' later statements. However, they feared personal and professional consequences if they did not sign it.

It appears that Colonel Halt was intimately involved in the preparation and field orchestration of Rendlesham Forest events.

Another twist in the story regarding the origins of the craft seen at Roswell—whether Earth-origin military machines, or space-origin UAP—was generated by *The Daily Express* when in 1983 it broke the first major story about Rendlesham Forest events. The headline was "UFOs? They're Our Boys Really!" The story went on to state, in Bruni's words, that "Lord Clancarty, who headed the House of Lords All-Party UFO Study Group, had said that

16. Bruni, *You Can't Tell the People*, 200.
17. Pope et al., *Encounter in Rendlesham Forest*, 73.
18. Kean, *UFOs*, 186–87.
19. Bruni, *You Can't Tell the People*, 195.

"the UFOs were British and American secret projects. 'I know for sure that such man–powered machines are being used by both the Americans and the British.'"[20]

Often overlooked in some analyses of Rendlesham Forest events is that the nearby town of Orfordshire in Suffolk, "was, and probably still is, home to some of Britain's most secret government research facilities," according to Bruni. She describes several such facilities, and reports she found about the types of research they were doing. She makes no explicit statement of links between the facilities and the Rendlesham events, but the suggestion that there is some connection is strongly implied.[21]

Finally, I am skeptical about the role of Nick Pope in books cited and other works. This skepticism is triggered, in part, by Jacques Vallée's description of his experiences over decades with people who initially attempted to hide their present or prior role with military intelligence or other government agencies. Pope's brief bio on the cover of *Encounter in Rendlesham Forest* states that he "used to run the British government's UFO project at the Ministry of Defense." Several times in his books he has stated that he remains bound to secrecy about details related to his former employment and employers, and must not disclose information that is not declassified.

The book jacket's front cover declares and boasts: "This controversial new book is largely based on recently declassified government files and is the only UFO book ever to have needed security clearance from both the American and British governments." Two questions immediately came to mind: "What was censored by those governments and deleted from the manuscript?" and "Why did the US government clear this book (other than because the events were orchestrated and spy agencies are pleased with the results of their work, especially in its dissemination) and want it to be published, when for decades it has denied Roswell narratives, and officially continues to state that UFOs do not exist?" The US government, too, tries to prevent independent scientific inquiry into and analysis of UFO events, uses ridicule to discredit witnesses, prohibits US government funding agencies from providing financial support for independent scientific research on the topic, and promotes reluctance among scientists who have witnessed UAP events or are curious about them to express any of this, for fear that they might lose their job, a promotion, research support, or even being hired at all if they have no current position or if they seek a different position.

I acknowledge that there might have been published accurate details with which I am not familiar, or that there are military policies unknown to civilians. I state for the record that I do not impugn the motives or narratives

20. Cited in Bruni, *You Can't Tell the People*, 61.
21. Bruni, *You Can't Tell the People*, 17–23.

of Sergeant Penniston: in fact, ordinarily I would regard him as a very credible witness. However, he was drugged and hypnotized for his interrogations, which both affected his memory of what he had experienced, and added new "memories." Therefore, he is very likely presenting, in what he recalls as being "true," data that he does not realize has been implanted in his memory without his knowledge or consent. I think it is possible, too, that Nick Pope is honestly describing events but does so with restrictions imposed on him by his previous government positions.

Discernment and Disappointment

I was disappointed to conclude in my assessment of both of the 1870s events that neither one was historically accurate. However, since it was slightly possible, though not likely, that the Bannock event had actually occurred, I place it in a category of "inconclusive evidence for case resolution." As with others who have observed ETI/IDI craft, I hope to find conclusive evidence of complementary events that withstands scientific scrutiny and critical assessment by outside analysts. Then an incident's occurrence can be accepted "beyond a reasonable doubt" ("doubt" because I have not witnessed personally events that are described) as a real ETI/IDI event.

In the Rendlesham Forest story, initially I doubted several details, but brushed aside my uneasiness about this because I thought that there seemed to be so much "evidence" presented about the events, and so many ordinarily credible witnesses, that more than balanced my concerns. I was not sufficiently knowledgeable about military procedures, spy agency intrusions, and secret ops personnel's psychological, intellectual, and chemical manipulation of participants in, and witnesses to apparent ETI/IDI arrivals on particular Earth sites. The (unknown to me as spurious) "evidence" seemed to overcome apparent contradictions in information provided by participants (including in both the information they gave about what they heard or did personally, and in how their information was not in accord with others' information about what had occurred at the same site and in the same time period), gaps in information about some incidents, and other flaws in the narratives.

A nagging question about the entirety of this story is this: Why did the US government (or a secret agency of the government) develop and orchestrate Rendlesham events? If it was an exercise to distract the UFO/IDI community away from other incidents, which might have been more arduously pursued if focus had remained on them, it has been highly successful. If it was to test types of psychological warfare on unwitting subjects in order to determine how others might react or respond, that has not yet been unearthed. (Involuntary testing and endangerment of unaware subjects—which violates research protocols—has had several precedents. Decades ago, for example, the US military sent soldiers onto lands where atomic bombs had just been detonated to determine what might be the impacts of radiation on civilians or soldiers in the immediate aftermath of an attack. The soldiers entering the highly contaminated irradiated sites were subjected to massive doses of radiation, with now-predictable results.[22]) There might be yet another reason: that there was some UAP activity at the time, and the agencies hoped to distract people from inquiring about incidents or reporting them; or, to discredit reports about the activity, and about past and future UAP, by casting doubt on what witnesses to these events had described or might describe. Should this be the case, pro and con groups' members would both be correct in what they argue for: that UAP were active, and that government agents tried to control the narrative. At the time of this writing, there is insufficient data to determine conclusively the extent to which there was—or was not— UAP activity that was controlled in the Rendlesham area by Visitors to Earth.

I am not, of course, a complete skeptic regarding the reality of encounters between human beings and, indirectly, the occupants or controllers of intelligently controlled craft. To be a skeptic entirely, I would have to deny or self-censure my own observations of incidents in which I saw an intelligently controlled UAP, as described in the introduction. As stated earlier, too, I do not "believe" in such incidents: belief is a metaphysical category related to transcendent realities. I do *think* that narratives by credible witnesses are true accounts of what they have experienced during encounters—of any or all of Hynek's three kinds—with UAP. I *know* that I have observed, on two occasions, the flight of intelligently controlled UAP. And, I will continue to be an "open-minded skeptic" when I hear reports, see them on television, or read about them in newspaper stories or online. If I have questions or doubts, I will try to resolve them, rather than set them aside or dismiss them.

22. See, for example, Haberman, "Veterans of Atomic Bomb Blasts." This site has a link to a documentary, "Atomic Vets," that provides details about numerous occasions when soldiers—and, secretly, civilians—were unaware victims of atomic bomb and then nuclear bomb tests, depleted uranium in tank and artillery shells, and other secret exposure. The US government and Veterans Affairs denied that dangerous exposure had occurred, and when they did admit this, limited the types of illness that would receive compensation. Angry "Atomic Vets" declared that they had been "guinea pigs," and said that the government was waiting until most had died before granting full compensation; some vets had discovered, too, that their children had birth defects as a consequence of their father's exposure. (During the Vietnam War, soldiers were subjected to Agent Orange and, in the United States, microbes were released in the New York subway system to see how quickly they would be spread by commuters.) In the aftermath of Rendlesham Forest, veterans such as Jim Penniston have been denied access to their medical records and unable to have a record of the types of drugs that were administered to them that have had ongoing, adverse impacts on their health. See Pope et al., *Encounter in Rendlesham Forest*, 247–48, 253–54.

I will continue to research ETI/IDI narratives, and to accept as true those related by credible witnesses.

I wonder if at some point I will have another "close encounter."

APPENDIX 2

Cosmos Charter[1]

Planetary and interplanetary well-being are currently on some people's minds. They are concerned and even anxious about the possibility of an impending Earth—and cosmos—displacement. Many have observed intelligently controlled UAP—or think that credible witnesses' reports about such events are true. They are considering what might be—or become—their cosmos place(s). Some seek a commonality of elements and interests in diverse religions and spirituality. On a social level, people have begun and continue to develop and implement policies and practices—embodied in local, national, and international law—that require governments, socioecological organizations and movements, and individuals to bring about an equitable (re)distribution of property in land, in goods, and in monetary wealth, while caring for their Earth home and all her living beings.

The Cosmos Charter elaborates requirements for peace with justice in the near and distant future, on Earth and on other worlds that humankind will see, and perhaps will survey and settle. People hope to be responsible residents, in terms of who they are today and will be tomorrow, and where they are today and might be tomorrow. The Charter provides a vision, an ideal, a *utopia* toward which people should strive: first, as Earth's most evolved intelligent species, and second, in collaborative consideration with other-than-human species, as coinhabitants of the broader cosmos relational community in the integral cosmos. The Charter is foundational, not fixed,

---

1. Published originally, in its first draft, in Hart, *Cosmic Commons*, 358–67. Foundations of the *Charter* in UN and other documents, including the *Earth Charter*, are elaborated in chapter 3, "Terrestrial Transformation," 89–114; and in chapter 11, "Cosmic Charter," 331–58.

and will adapt to or adopt from complementary considerations proposed by ETI and IDI.

Cosmos Charter

Preamble

The cosmos is a vast and complex expanse with multiple dimensions in time and space. All comprise a single reality, and are related to each other in the integral being of all that exists. The existents, energies, elements, entities, and entropy of the universe are intertwined, integrated, interrelated, and interdependent. In incompletely known and complex ways, they influence and impact each other in time and through distinct dimensions of reality.

Intelligent beings are conscious, reflective, creative, curious, and contextually adaptable inhabitants of the cosmos, in whole or in part. They have developed modes of cosmos travel that enable them to voyage expeditiously and safely through what would be, in observable space-time, immense spatial distances and distinct zones of time: past, present, and future. In their voyages, they come into Contact with other intelligent beings who comprise diverse species with distinct technological capabilities and possibilities; disparate environmental contexts on sometimes distant planets or celestial bodies; and new (to them) and innovative native cultures and the institutional—political and economic—and transcending—philosophical and spiritual—social structures that comprise and organize their relationships to each other as social beings in social contexts. Intelligent beings consciously integrate with each other for mutual benefit, and to envision, develop, and realize common wellbeing. In newly discovered environmental and cultural contexts, too, they become aware of diverse types of ecological integration: among members of intelligent species, between communities of intelligent species, between intelligent species and less complex species, and between all species and their planetary setting.

In their initial encounters and engagement, intelligent beings will seek to develop such relationships and structures as will enhance their consequent interaction. In order to proceed pacifically and to provide mutual benefits, intelligent species strive to effect equitable allocation of mutually sought territory and natural goods, as provided in various contexts by the dynamic cosmos, each or all of which might be necessary or useful for particular beings' organized community entities during some or many of their stages of social development: to meet the shared needs of their own societies or of other societies with which they come into Contact.

Signatories pledge to develop, establish, and support a Cosmos Charter Confederation, with associated governance, for mutual wellbeing and interactive support as an interrelated cosmic community. A Cosmos Charter Council will provide such governance, and oversee and facilitate implementation of Cosmos Charter provisions, such as would benefit each and every Signatory to the greatest extent possible in an interdependent and interrelated association. The membership of the Cosmos Charter Council shall include a representative selected by each Signatory or groupings thereof that might be developed.

Signatories of the Cosmos Charter agree that all planets, celestial bodies, and other habitable or natural goods-rich places that are discovered by any of them independently or collaboratively shall, if not inhabited at the time discovered, become the common territory of all signatories, and its natural goods, if not currently under the authority otherwise of a governing entity, shall be the common goods of all signatories. The common territories shall be administered by the Cosmos Charter Council.

Signatories agree that cosmic space, planets (including origin planets and discovered planets) and celestial bodies (including origin celestial bodies and planets' satellites) shall be used only for peaceful purposes.

The Cosmos Charter is a work in progress, subject to internal evolution—as approved by its signatories after the Cosmos Charter Council has reviewed and considered them and presented them to signatories—stimulated by ideas and insights suggested by diverse intelligent beings in distinct social settings and disparate cosmic contexts.

The Cosmos Charter is presented for consideration by all intelligent beings in diverse planetary and other cosmos settings as a foundation for ongoing congenial and collaborative efforts to provide for the needs of all intelligent life; to safeguard the wellbeing of simple and complex biota evolving in distinct places; and to ensure the wellbeing of the commons ground and commons goods on which all life depends for its survival and communal wellbeing. To these ends, the principles that follow are proposed as a dynamic foundation for intraspecies, interspecies, interplanetary, interstellar, and interdimensional collaboration and community.

Part 1: Common Ground: Origin Planets

Each signatory is responsible for securing the social, cultural, and ecological wellbeing of planets and other places on which they evolved or on which they resided when they signed the Cosmos Charter and became members of the Cosmos Charter Council, and which they inhabit or will inhabit.

Article 1. Respect and conserve planetary common ground: Planets and other inhabited places shall be carefully conserved, to maintain their abiotic contexts and biotic habitats.

Article 2. Provide territorial space and natural goods access needed to ensure species diversity, wellbeing, and survival in natural evolutionary processes, and to provide security against being extincted by intelligent beings.

Article 3. Conserve the integrity of cosmos communities' ecological systems, with special concern for biological diversity and the natural processes that sustain life.

Article 4. Conserve contiguous ecosystems necessary for species to survive and to thrive.

Article 5. Intelligent beings from more technologically advanced and economically stable societies should assist intelligent beings who lack the capability for space exploration but otherwise are sufficiently mature to do so responsibly and well without violating their culture or place, to develop this capability through enhanced scientific education and technological assistance.

Article 6. Transparency should characterize specific space missions' purposes and activities, and the dissemination of the results of exploration and research on celestial bodies.

Article 7. Intelligent beings' politically organized bodies should exercise control over private enterprises under contract to them or under their sponsorship; and, intelligent beings' politically organized bodies should provide universal access for all intelligent beings' mutual education and potential collaboration, including in areas developed by private enterprises within signatories' jurisdiction, to their space-related sites on origin planets or other places where they have been constructed.

Part 2: Commons Good and Commons Goods: Origin Planets

Ensure equitable access to, and, distribution and use of, biotic and abiotic planetary natural goods.

Article 8. Respect the biotic diversity and evolutionary integrity of all biota present as native inhabitants of planets and celestial bodies, whether found on first exploration, during colonization or natural goods acquisition, or at any other time during the course of development and use of the land, water, minerals, and other natural goods of planets or celestial bodies.

Article 9. Ensure that mining processes and mineral production and refinement are not destructive to natural environments and ecologies, and that mining sites, after responsible use, are restored to a viable state suitable for biotic introduction and reintroduction.

Article 10. Develop social consensus societies that respect the insights and practices of all intelligent beings, and are permeated by justice, governed in a participatory manner, dynamically sustainable over time, and embody and promote peace among all intelligent beings.

Article 11. Acknowledge and ensure the intrinsic value of all biota and all abiotic places, and only alter that status to instrumental value for limited members of a species and limited ecosystem areas during periods when, and in places where, they are needed to provide necessary sustenance or goods for intelligent life.

Article 12. Maintain sufficient habitat for the wellbeing of biota to be safeguarded when biota are removed or abiotic places are impacted by intelligent beings' acts.

Article 13. Strive to ensure that all intelligent beings' communities have access to and the ability to acquire such land and natural goods as are needed for their sustenance.

Article 14. Ensure that the least benefited intelligent beings' communities have priority rights to share common ground and common goods in order to improve their economic base, promote social wellbeing, and enable their cultures to be sustained.

Part 3: Common Ground: Discovered Planets and Celestial Bodies

Respect natural processes in place: geological and meteorological integrity, and biotic evolution.

Article 15. Respect all intelligent species' integrity, and all species' evolutionary development, in native niches.

Article 16. Equitably allocate celestial bodies' territory. Provide territorial space and natural goods access needed to ensure species' survival and well-being within natural evolutionary processes, to provide security against being extincted by intelligent life.

Article 17. Ensure that intelligent species have equitable access to, allocation of, and distributions from territory and natural goods on newly discovered planets and celestial bodies, or parts thereof when they are sufficiently extensive to allow for non-competing claims to and development on an entire planetary or celestial body surface.

Article 18. Promote collaborative development and exchange of natural goods for mutual benefit and well-being, with particular regard for the least economically benefited intelligent beings' communities.

Article 19. Provide equitable opportunities for diverse species' exploration, colonization, and natural goods development on newly discovered planets and celestial bodies, or allocated parts thereof.

Article 20. Formulate and promulgate inter-intelligent beings laws, policies, guidelines, and other agreements that will provide for the Cosmos Charter Council, as a mediating third party, to resolve competing claims on territory or natural goods; and, agree to accept the Cosmos Charter Council's mediation as an arbiter, and its subsequent impartial decisions and determinations.

Article 21. Natural goods, when needed in places other than the setting in which they were found, should be removed carefully and conscientiously; areas from which they have been removed should be restored to their original state, to the greatest extent possible, with provision for native biota reintroduction or introduction into restored places or regions.

*Part 4: Commons Good and Commons Goods:
Discovered Planets and Celestial Bodies*

Conservation of natural characteristics and natural goods of worlds discovered by signatories, and equitable distribution or allocation of all newly discovered territories and their natural goods.

Article 22. All places discovered by one or several signatories immediately become common Cosmos Charter territory *unless they are occupied and used by indigenous intelligent beings*, in which case the original occupants shall remain the owners and users of the territory. Unoccupied newly discovered places enter under the jurisdiction of the Cosmos Charter Council, which will allocate or distribute them to benefit signatories according to their need, prioritizing the survival or wellbeing of signatories to favor those most in need of territory or particular natural goods.

Article 23. No intelligent beings' political entities shall have a claim of sovereignty over or ownership of discovered planets or celestial bodies, whether by first detection, first robotic research vehicle, first arrival, first placement of a particular cultural artifact, first scientific expedition, or first preliminary settlement with a base for research, mapping, or other initial assessment and demarcation of site geophysical characteristics, biotic habitation, or geographic boundaries.

Article 24. No private organization, corporation, association, agency, or individual shall have ownership of discovered places, but may have the use thereof as stipulated by statutes in or governing parties under the Cosmos Charter.

Article 25. Exploration of space generally, and of proximate celestial bodies particularly, is to be done collaboratively, carefully, and conscientiously.

Article 26. Where the survival or wellbeing of intelligent beings is threatened by bellicose invaders, the interstellar defense body of the signatories, whose members shall be representatives of diverse intelligent beings and chosen by the Cosmos Charter Council, should intervene with such force as is necessary to maintain signatories' security and integrity, whether or not the team's members are of the same intelligent species.

Article 27. Origin planets and their satellites, other planets and their satellites, and other celestial bodies should not be endangered or harmed as a consequence of intelligent beings' exploration or use.

Article 28. Special, protected science preserves should be established on pristine places at the earliest opportunity; and, data derived from scientific research and experiments by any intelligent life community entity should be shared among all, disseminated either directly or under the auspices of the Cosmos Charter Council.

Part 5: Common Good on Common Ground

Equitable provision for the habitable space and natural goods needs of Cosmos Charter signatories in all Cosmos Charter Confederation territories.

Article 29. The occupation and use of Confederation territories shall be available for all interested intelligent beings' entities to promote collaboratively the mutual common good, for themselves and other intelligent beings.

Article 30. Material goods and other material benefits derived from exploration and use are to provide particularly to meet intelligent beings' needs, including especially those in the least developed regions of the cosmos and the least prosperous intelligent beings on all planets and celestial bodies; and, priority shall be given to intelligent beings most in need of a particular territory or of natural cosmos common goods found there; where there is equal need for places or goods, signatories shall develop conjointly their equivalent and equitable distribution.

Article 31. Species-open sites should be designated to provide areas in which intelligent species might collaboratively or independently explore for natural goods to be responsibly extracted or altered on site, or territory that would be habitable for intelligent species to be integrated with the setting and rhythms of their new context.

Article 32. Intelligent beings' politically organized bodies have ultimate ownership of and responsibility for objects they or those under their auspices have launched into space.

Article 33. Intelligent beings' politically organized bodies should avoid contamination and other adverse environmental impacts on others' inhabited or occupied places, and the biota and abiotic goods present on them.

Article 34. Access should be provided to all collaboratively developed areas of planets of origin and celestial bodies, and to intelligent beings' distinct places, following advance notice and without disturbing local ecologies, cultures, and inhabitants.

Article 35. Intergenerational present and future needs should be projected for intelligent beings, and responsible practices utilized to meet them, especially through the equitable conservation and distribution of material goods and beneficial places found in space.

Part 6: Interdependence, Integration, and Interrelationship

Governance and guidance of Cosmos Charter signatories and control of common places.

Article 36. Cosmos Charter signatories shall promote dialogic engagement in cosmic contexts as constitutive of cosmic community, and a way to promote a peaceful and mutually beneficial relationship among all signatories.

Article 37. Interstellar law developed by the Cosmos Charter Council should be operative in all space explorations and all interactions among representatives of distinct intelligent beings.

Article 38. Cultural artifacts should be respected and left *in situ*, because they pertain to and contain the cultural memories of previously existing intelligent inhabitants of and civilizations in a place, and are part of the common heritage of all intelligent life in diverse stages of material and sociocultural evolution; and to respect and honor cultures of intelligent species that evolved in diverse places through eons of integral being.

Article 39. Collaborative space projects, and development plans that would foster collaboration on a mutually acceptable basis, should be undertaken by beings with diverse financial resources or technological abilities.

Article 40. Sites proximate to places inhabited or used by diverse particular intelligent beings should be available for shared use as a launch site for ongoing and outgoing space exploration for other intelligent beings, and a place to which they or others might return, and with mutually agreed-upon arrangements for responsible use.

Article 41. Dangers discovered in space or on a space body that pose a threat to any intelligent beings on site or in their places of origin, or in colonies or bases elsewhere, should be immediately disclosed to all astronauts and their respective governing authorities.

Article 42. Astronauts, as interstellar representatives of all intelligent beings and not solely of their origin planet or other place, should be given hospitality by any and all intelligent beings' stations in times of need.

Part 7: Cosmos Community in Cosmos Commons

A Cosmos Charter Council shall be established, comprised of a representative from each Cosmos Charter signatory. The Council shall promote cosmos community in places where its signatories reside in the present and future in the cosmos commons. Cosmos community wellbeing will be enhanced through establishment of a Cosmos Charter Confederation.

Article 43. The Cosmos Charter Council shall be established as an intergalactic and interstellar body charged with promoting peace and just allocations of territories and goods for which there are seemingly equal claims of discovery of planets and celestial bodies, or of goods on species-open sites. A Cosmos Charter Confederation shall be developed as the interstellar organization that includes all origin planets and subsequent worlds discovered and developed by signatories. Its individual signatories govern territories under their specific jurisdiction, while the Cosmos Charter Confederation integrates all signatories into a cohesive, interrelated, mutually supportive entity.

Article 44. The Cosmos Charter Council shall make all decisions regarding allocations to enable signatories' occupation and use of newly discovered places.

Article 45. The Cosmos Charter Council shall make all decisions regarding the distribution of natural goods on Charter territories. Natural goods are to be used in context or removed from context without disrupting planetary abiotic dynamics or biotic evolution.

Article 46. The Cosmos Charter Council shall ensure that if any intelligent indigenous beings exist on newly discovered territory, the areas in which they live and the natural goods in those or contiguous territories shall remain under their control and for their use. They shall be invited to participate as incorporated signatories in the Cosmos Charter, the Cosmos Charter Council, and the Cosmos Charter Confederation.

Article 47. The Cosmos Charter Council shall ensure that planets that are intelligent beings' places of origin, or other celestial bodies and their abiotic context and biotic inhabitants, would not be endangered or harmed as a consequence of intelligent beings' exploration or use.

Article 48. The Cosmos Charter Council shall ensure that material goods acquired during space exploration and use are to be equitably distributed so as to benefit all intelligent beings according to their needs, without consideration of their economic system or financial wellbeing, or the stage of their scientific development.

Article 49. The Cosmos Charter Council shall ensure that material benefits derived from exploration and use are to provide particularly for intelligent beings' needs, including especially the needs of those in the least developed regions of the cosmos, and to benefit first the least prosperous intelligent beings on all planets and celestial bodies, to be ensured by concerted collaborative efforts to utilize space-generated benefits and goods to meet intelligent beings' responsible development goals for themselves (when they are in need) and for others (when politically and economically stable species seek to provide for the needs of less-developed species).

Conclusion

The Cosmos Charter offers a vision and a hope that the space and places of the cosmos shall be regarded as a common, shared, intergenerational benefit for the wellbeing of all intelligent beings. The Cosmos Charter signatories pledge that when newly discovered worlds are not already the habitation of intelligent species, at whatever their evolutionary stage, they shall be available to and for all intelligent beings, allocated equitably to each as a whole, or to discrete members of their communities, according to their needs. Intelligent beings not already signatories will be invited, upon or subsequent to Contact, to become signatories of the Cosmos Charter in order to promote the Cosmos Commons Good, characterized by peace, justice, and ecological wellbeing, for mutual benefit, throughout the cosmos.

Signatories will be especially concerned to do no harm to members of their own or another species, and to do no harm to the communities and metropolises into which intelligent beings have been organized or within which they have coalesced as social beings seeking and stimulating the social, biotic, and planetary commonweal.

The Cosmos Charter is a dynamic document that will evolve over time and in space as events—including encounters with newly evolved intelligent beings in diverse cultures—and continuing consideration of socially and ecologically progressive ideas, proposals, and projects, based on experience in context, are evaluated and then incorporated when determined to be beneficial to present, future, and potential signatories.

A shared vision and hope prompt the signatories to interrelate peacefully and to integrate diverse ways of thinking and acting into a coherent whole that acknowledges interdependence. Signatories pledge to strive collaboratively to realize cosmos unity and mutuality in pursuit of the cosmos commons good, the common good of the biotic community of which all are members, and the common good of signatories' communities, for present and future generations.

APPENDIX 3

Continuing Considerations and Conversations

Reflection on interspecies cosmos Contact, humans' Third Displacement, and possibilities for a cosmos relational community would be helpful to understand human place in the present, and possible place(s) in the future. Exploration and exposition of data and events that might catalyze a third displacement fall into categories that are distinct, but at times overlapping.

The following questions should help to focus discussion. They are not intended to be used in any particular order. Individuals and discussion circles should select and deliberate them in a way that will stimulate or assist collaborative work.

Comparative terrestrial-extraterrestrial research perceptions, priorities, and practices would address such questions as: What assumptions are associated with the Outer Space Treaty and other relevant documents and policies that are related to microbial life and environments, on Earth and other celestial bodies? What additional considerations for current SETI Principles and Outer Space Treaty implementation might be suggested in the light of social and ethical understandings of integral being and transcosmos (in the universe and in interdimensional realities) natural rights, such that these rights are integrated with research goals and scientific and technological accomplishments? How does the now-indisputable presence of ETL in the solar system catalyze revision of existing treaties and policies relevant to ongoing exploration, and protection of ExoEarth life and environments? What comparative cultural, religious, and ethical concerns are relevant to discussions about and considerations of ETL and its environments, during the post-discovery phase of research and exploration? How would these perspectives contribute to discussions and considerations upon discovery of ETL?

The potential for terrestrial-extraterrestrial biological impacts and exchanges would raise such questions as: How might the search for and verifiable discovery of ETL, ETI, and/or IDI aid in understanding the significance of evolving life in the dynamic universe? How might the desire to discover beneficial organisms or ExoEarth[1] planetary goods ("resources") influence research, field work, and exploration with the concomitant danger that commercial profit could be prioritized over the wellbeing of people and other living beings? How might humans avoid altering life and life's possibilities on other worlds (through impacts on its actual or potentially actual existence and evolutionary trajectory), and thereby potentially adversely impacting the ultimate reality or potential ultimate reality not only of biota, but of life's abiotic contexts, and of integral being? Needless to say, not all of these questions—perhaps few of them—can be answered prior to human space journeys, but they might be at least guiding concerns during cosmos voyages.

Comparative analysis of TI-ETI and TI-IDI social thought should prompt consideration of the following questions: How might reflection on the significance of evolving lives in the dynamic cosmos stimulate consciousness of integral being and ultimate reality, and influence an ethical interaction between Earth- and ExoEarth-based entities? How might an "ethics of encounter" be developed, which would consider issues of encounters with life that appears to have greater or lesser intelligence; encounters with intelligent life that is morally benevolent, or malevolent, or neutral; or encounters with new, complex, and diverse components of a dynamic cosmos and abiotically dynamic planets, and evolving life on the latter? How might an ethical cosmos consciousness flow into cosmos commitments? How might ecological considerations (including ecosystem relationships, and considerations about interference in present stages of a planet's biotic evolution), in movements to and from ExoEarth contexts, influence humans' sense of responsibility toward and, consequently, human conduct in, distinct contexts?

Speculation about ultimate realities might prompt further questions: What kind of psychic, spiritual, and material sense of dis-placement (or even of non-placement: no sense of particular attachment to, or meaning in, a place) might humans have if living beings elsewhere are more, equally, or less intelligent? How would the discovery of other forms of life (intelligent or otherwise) impact human understandings of divine being and integral being? How might it impact the human psyche in terms of humans' place in the cosmos and in the evolution of life in habitable places? How might responses

---

1. "ExoEarth" is a more accurate designation than "extraterrestrial": life or intelligent life Contacted might be extra-terrestrial or extra-terra-dimensional (interdimensional).

to questions of place diverge if integral being includes divine being, or if integral being does not include divine being? (E.g., do human norms originate in human culture per se, in an ultimate reality that coincides with and is immanent in nature, or in an ultimate reality that transcends—while including—nature and culture, whether or not that reality, as integral being, includes divine being?) To what extent might the discovery of ExoEarth intelligent life positively or negatively impact humans' religions and spirituality? Would humans expand their understandings by incorporating complementary transcending understandings from other intelligent beings; seek to impose human understandings on other beings for their incorporation; or accept that in the material universe, and in its metamaterial or metaphysical aspect, there might be diverse manners of understanding, relation to, expression by, or engagement with transcendent being, or with other aspects of integral being and ultimate reality?

Bibliography

Ancient Aliens. "Aliens in Art: Battle of Nuremberg." https://www.theancientaliens.com/alien-art-battle-of-nuremberg.

Archbishop Demetrios. "Love and Care for Strangers: *Philoxenia* in Christian Tradition." *BTI Magazine* 12.1 (2012) 4–7.

Armstrong, Neil, et al. *First on the Moon—A Voyage with Neil Armstrong, Michael Collins, and Edwin Aldrin*. New York: Barnes & Noble, 2002.

Ayala, Francisco J. *Darwin's Gift to Science and Religion*. Washington, DC: Henry, 2007.

Basalla, George. *Civilized Life in the Universe: Scientists on Intelligent Extraterrestrials*. Oxford: Oxford University Press, 2006.

Batchelder, Lasandra. "Legendary Interview: Jacques Vallee on the Extraterrestrial Evidence Top Ufology." *YouTube*, January 24, 2018. https://www.youtube.com/watch?v=pqsaWloOA2o.

Berliner, Don, and Stanton T. Friedman. *Crash at Corona: The U.S. Military Retrieval and Cover-Up of a UFO: The Definitive Study of the Roswell Incident*. New York: Paraview, 2004.

Berry, Thomas. *The Christian Future and the Fate of the Earth*. Edited by Mary Evelyn Tucker and John Grim. Ecology and Justice Series. Maryknoll: Orbis, 2009.

———. *The Dream of the Earth*. San Francisco: Sierra Club, 1998.

———. *The Great Work: Our Way Into the Future*. New York: Bell Tower, 1999.

———. *The Sacred Universe: Earth, Spirituality and Religion in the Twenty-First Century*. Edited and with a foreword by Mary Evelyn Tucker. New York: Columbia University Press, 2009.

Berry, Thomas, and Brian Swimme. *The Universe Story: From the Primordial Flaring Forth to the Ecozoic Era: A Celebration of the Unfolding of the Cosmos*. San Francisco: HarperSanFrancisco, 1992.

Big Think. "E.O. Wilson: ET Is Out There and He/She Probably Looks Like This." https://bigthink.com/think-tank/eo-wilson-et.

Bird, Joan. *Montana UFOs and Extraterrestrials: Extraordinary Stories of Documented Sightings and Encounters*. Helena, MT: Riverbend, 2012.

Boyle, Alan. "Hawking Goes Zero-G: 'Space, Here I Come.'" *MSNBC*, April 26, 2007. http://www.nbcnews.com/id/18334489/ns/technology_and_science-space/t/hawking-goes-zero-g-space-here-i-come/.

"Brazil Air Force to Record UFO Sightings." *BBC News*, August 11, 2010, https://www.bbc.com/news/world-latin-america-10947856.

Bruni, Georgina. *You Can't Tell the People: The Cover-up of Britain's Roswell*. Foreword by Nick Pope. London: Sidgwick & Jackson, 2000.

Birchall, Guy. "Out of This World: Why Stephen Hawking and the World's Top Scientists Say This Massive Object Hurtling through Space Could Be an Alien Spaceship." *The Sun*, December 13, 2017. https://www.thesun.co.uk/news/5130300/why-stephen-hawking-and-the-worlds-top-scientists-say-this-massive-object-hurtling-through-space-could-be-an-alien-spaceship/.

Carey, Thomas J., and Donald R. Schmitt. *Witness to Roswell: Unmasking the Government's Biggest Cover-up*. Foreword by Edgar Mitchell. Afterword by George Noory. Pompton Plains, NJ: New Page, 2009.

Chang, Kenneth. "A Journey Into the Solar System's Outer Reaches, Seeking New Worlds to Explore." *The New York Times*, December 30, 2018. https://www.nytimes.com/2018/12/30/science/nasa-new-horizons-kuiper-belt.html?emc=edit_th_181231&nl=todaysheadlines&nlid=607146151231.

"Churchill Ordered UFO Cover-up, National Archives Show." *BBC News*, August 5, 2010. http://www.bbc.co.uk/news/uk-10853905.

Clarke, Ardy Sixkiller. *Encounters with Star People: Untold Stories of American Indians*. San Antonio: Anomalist, 2012.

———. *More Encounters with Star People: Urban American Indians Tell Their Stories*. San Antonio: Anomalist, 2016.

———. *Sky People: Untold Stories of Alien Encounters in Mesoamerica*. Pompton Plains, NJ: New Page, 2015.

Climate Communication. "Heat Waves." https://www.climatecommunication.org/new/features/extreme-weather/heat-waves/.

Collins, Sarah. "Gaia Spots a 'Ghost' Galaxy Next Door." https://phys.org/news/2018-11-gaia-ghost-galaxy-door.html#jCp.

Cooper, Keith. "Astrobio Top 10: Liquid Water Discovered on Mars." *Astrobiology Magazine*, January 1, 2019. https://www.astrobio.net/news-exclusive/astrobio-top-10-liquid-water-discovered-on-mars.

Corso, Philip J., and William J. Birnes. *The Day After Roswell*. New York: Pocket, 2008.

Costa, Cheryl, and Linda Miller Costa. *UFO Sightings Desk Reference, United States of America 2001–2015: Unidentified Flying Objects: Frequency—Distribution—Shapes*. Syracuse: UFO Scholar, 2017.

Crowe, Michael J. *The Extraterrestrial Life Debate, Antiquity to 1915: A Source Book*. Edited with commentary by Michael J. Crowe. Notre Dame: University of Notre Dame Press, 2008.

Cuénot, Claude. *Teilhard de Chardin: A Biographical Study*. Translated by Vincent Colimore. Edited by René Hague. Baltimore: Helicon, 1965.

Darwin, Charles. *On the Origin of Species: A Facsimile of the First Edition*. Introduction by Ernst Mayr. Cambridge: Harvard University Press, 2003.

Dick, Steven J., ed. *Many Worlds: The New Universe, Extraterrestrial Life and the Theological Implications*. Philadelphia: Templeton Foundation, 2000.

Duffy, Kathleen. *Teilhard's Mysticism: Seeing the Inner Face of Evolution*. Maryknoll: Orbis, 2014.

"DNA." https://www.britannica.com/science/DNA.

ExoNews TV. "Pope Endorses Evolution of Alien Life and UFO Activity as Part of God's Plan." *YouTube*, October 29, 2014. https://www.youtube.com/watch?v=9KGwx0SXNlQ.

Farrell, John. *The Day Without Yesterday: Lemaître, Einstein, and the Birth of Modern Cosmology*. New York: Thunder's Mouth, 2005.

Fingas, Jon. "Queen Guitarist Brian May Wrote a Song for NASA's Historic Flyby." *Engadget*, January 1, 2019. https://www.engadget.com/2019/01/01/queen-brian-may-song-for-ultima-thule-flyby/.

Fizbit, Fatima. "What Is the Theory of Panspermia?" *Astronomy*, April 1, 2008. http://www.astronomy.com/news-observing/ask%20astro/2008/04/what%20is%20the%20theory%20of%20panspermia.

Fortini, Arnaldo. *Francis of Assisi*. Translated by Helen Moak. New York: Crossroad, 1985.

Francis, Pope. "*Laudato Si'*." http://w2.vatican.va/content/francesco/en/encyclicals/documents/papa-francesco_20150524_enciclica-laudato-si.html.

Friedman, Stanton T. *Top Secret/MAJIC—Operation Majestic-12 and the United States Government's UFO Cover-up*. Foreword by Whitley Strieber. Philadelphia: Da Capo, 2008.

Funes, José Gabriel. "L'extraterrestre è mio fratello" ["The Extraterrestrial is My Brother"]. http://www.vatican.va/news_services/or/or_quo/interviste/2008/112q08a1.html.

Ghosh, Pallab. "Hawking says Trump's Climate Stance Could Damage Earth." *BBC News*, July 2, 2017. https://www.bbc.com/news/science-environment-40461726?fbclid=IwAR1mCvJFhoiMoF7yMgSmFOWyWhoqeTqGH6ti6h1fzr7VldGoBSl2VLh-cCU.

Ginsburg, Idan, et al. "Galactic Panspermia." *The Astrophysical Journal Letters* 868.12 (Nov 19, 2018) 1–9. https://arxiv.org/pdf/1810.04307.pdf.

Greenberg, Alissa. "Stephen Hawking Endorses New Hunt for Alien Life, Despite Fear of Being 'Conquered and Colonized.'" *Time*, July 22, 2015. http://time.com/3967126/stephen-hawking-seti-extraterrestrial-life-breakthrough.

Haberman, Clyde. "Veterans of Atomic Bomb Blasts: No Warning, and Late Amends." *The New York Times*, May 29, 2016. https://www.nytimes.com/2016/05/30/us/veterans-of-atomic-test-blasts-no-warning-and-late-amends.html.

Hart, John. "Cosmic Commons: Contact and Community." *Theology and Science* 8.4 (2010) 371–92.

———. *Cosmic Commons: Spirit, Science, and Space*. Vol. 1 of *Cosmos Contact: Close Encounters of the Otherkind* Eugene, OR: Cascade, 2013.

———. *Ethics and Technology: Innovation and Transformation in Community Contexts*. Cleveland: Pilgrim, 1997.

———. *Encountering ETI: Aliens in* Avatar *and the Americas*. Vol. 2 of *Cosmos Contact: Close Encounters of the Otherkind*. Eugene, OR: Cascade, 2014.

———. "*Laudato Si'* in the Earth Commons—Integral Ecology and Socioecological Ethics." In *The Wiley Blackwell Companion to Religion and Ecology*, edited by Josh Hart, 37–53. Foreword by Ecumenical Patriarch Bartholomew I, Orthodox Church. Oxford: Wiley Blackwell, 2017.

———. "The Poor of the Planet and the Planet of the Poor: Ecological Ethics and Economic Liberation." *University of St. Thomas Law Journal* 5.1 (Winter 2008) 144–82.

———. *Sacramental Commons: Christian Ecological Ethics*. Foreword by Leonardo Boff. Afterword by Thomas Berry. Lanham: Rowman & Littlefield, 2006.

———. "Salmon and Social Ethics: Relational Consciousness in the Web of Life." *Journal of the Society of Christian Ethics* 22 (Fall 2002) 67–93.

———. *The Spirit of the Earth: A Theology of the Land*. Ramsey: Paulist, 1984.

———. "Terraforming Mars and Marsforming Terra: Discovery Doctrine in Space." *Theology and Science*, 17:3, 355-365, DOI: 10.1080/14746700.2019.1632531, 2019.

———. *What Are They Saying About Environmental Theology?* What Are They Saying About Series. New York: Paulist, 2004.

Hart, John, ed. *The Wiley Blackwell Companion to Religion and Ecology*. Foreword by Ecumenical Patriarch Bartholomew I, Orthodox Church. Oxford: Wiley Blackwell, 2017.

Harvard University. "A Profile of Astrophysicist Avi Loeb." *YouTube*, June 9, 2016. https://www.youtube.com/watch?v=BKm26WtYXgI.

Haught, John F. "What If Extraterrestrials Exist?" In *Science and Faith: A New Introduction*, 163–76. New York: Paulist, 2012.

Hawking, Stephen. *A Brief History of Time: From the Big Bang to Black Holes*. Updated and Expanded Tenth Anniversary Edition. New York: Bantam, 1998.

———. *The Illustrated A Brief History of Time*. Updated and expanded edition. New York: Bantam, 1996.

———. *My Brief History*. New York: Bantam, 2013.

———. "Questioning the Universe." https://www.ted.com/talks/stephen_hawking_asks_big_questions_about_the_universe/transcript?language.

———. "This Is the Most Dangerous Time for Our Planet." *The Guardian*, December 1, 2016. https://www.theguardian.com/commentisfree/2016/dec/01/stephen-hawking-dangerous-time-planet-inequality.

Henderson, Neil. "Files Reveal 'Rendlesham Incident' Papers Missing." *BBC News*, March 3, 2011, http://www.bbc.co.uk/news/uk-12613690.

Herd, George. "UFO Wales: New X-Files Shine Light on Alien Sightings." *BBC News*, July 12, 2012. https://www.bbc.com/news/uk-wales-18798862.

Hitchcock, Charles Henry. *Mount Washington in Winter, Or the Experiences of a Scientific Expedition Upon the Highest Mountain in New England—1870-71*. Reprint, Boston: Chick & Andrews, 1871.

Holder, Rodney D., and Simon Mitton. *Georges LeMaître: Life, Science, and Legacy*. Astrophysics and Space Science Library 395. New York: Springer, 2013.

Holman, Bill. *Smokey Stover, the Foo Fighter*. Racine, WI: Whitman, 1938.

"How Can You Tell if that ET Story Is Real? St Andrews Scientists Revise the Rio Scale for Alien Encounters." *SETI Institute*, July 24, 2018. https://www.seti.org/press-release/how-can-you-tell-if-et-story-real-st-andrews-scientists-revise-rio-scale-alien-encounters.

Howell, Elizabeth. "Drake Equation: Estimating the Odds of Finding E.T." https://www.space.com/25219-drake-equation.html.

Hrala, Josh. "Stephen Hawking Warns Us to Stop Reaching Out to Aliens before It's Too Late." *ScienceAlert*, November 4, 2016. https://www.sciencealert.com/stephen-hawking-warns-that-we-might-not-want-to-reach-out-to-aliens.

Hui, Sylvia. "Physicist Hawking Says Human Race Must Look to Outer Space for Survival." *Helena Independent Record*, June 14, 2006.

Hynek, J. Allen. "Address to the UN General Assembly." https://magonia.com/wp-content/uploads/j-allen-hynek-onu.pdf.

———. *The UFO Experience: A Scientific Inquiry*. Chicago: Regnery, 1972.

———. *The Hynek UFO Report*. New foreword by Jacques Vallée. New York: Barnes & Noble, 1997.

Hynek, J. Allen, and Jacques Vallée. *The Edge of Reality: A Progress Report on Unidentified Flying Objects*. Chicago: Regnery, 1975.
Hynek, J. Allen, et al. *Night Siege: The Hudson Valley UFO Sightings*. 2nd ed. St. Paul: Llewellyn, 1998.
"In Pictures: The UFO files." *BBC News*, May 14, 2008. http://news.bbc.co.uk/2/hi/in_pictures/7398491.stm.
Intergovernmental Panel on Climate Change. http://www.ipcc.ch/publications_and_data_reports.shtml.
———. "Findings of the IPCC Fourth Assessment Report: Climate Change Mitigation." www.ipcc.ch/publications_and_data/ar4/wg3/en/contents.html.
———. IPCC Special Report on Climate Change. https://www.ipcc.ch/sr15/.
"Jacques Fabrice Vallée." https://rro.org/people/v/ValleeJacques/.
Jessup, Philip C., and Howard J. Taubenfeld. *Controls for Outer Space—and the Antarctic Analogy*. New York: Columbia University Press, 1959.
John Paul II, Pope. *The Ecological Crisis: A Common Responsibility: Message of His Holiness Pope John Paul II for the Celebration of the World Day of Peace, 1 January 1990*. Washington, DC: United States Catholic Conference, 1990.
Kwon, Jung Yul, et al. "How Will We React to the Discovery of Extraterrestrial Life?" *Frontiers in Psychology* (Jan 10, 2008). https://www.frontiersin.org/articles/10.3389/fpsyg.2017.02308/full.
Kaminski, Bob. *Lying Wonders: Evil Encounters of a Close Kind*. Mukilteo, WA: Wine, 2006.
Kaplan, Sarah, et al. "China Lands Spacecraft on the Far Side of the Moon, a Historic First." *Washington Post*, January 3, 2019. https://www.washingtonpost.com/science/2019/01/03/china-lands-spacecraft-far-side-moon-historic-first/?utm_term=.751744357abd.
Kean, Leslie. *UFOs: Generals, Pilots, and Government Officials Go on the Record*. Foreword by John Podesta. New York: Three Rivers, 2010.
Kim, Heup Young. *Christ and the Tao*. Eugene, OR: Wipf & Stock, 2010.
———. "*Theodao*: Integrating Ecological Consciousness in Daoism, Confucianism, and Christian Theology." In *The Wiley Blackwell Companion to Religion and Ecology*, edited by John Hart, 104–14. Foreword by Ecumenical Patriarch Bartholomew I, Orthodox Church. Oxford: Wiley Blackwell, 2017.
King, Ursula. *Spirit of Fire: The Life and Vision of Teilhard de Chardin*. Maryknoll: Orbis, 1996.
Koerner, David, and Simon LeVay. *Here Be Dragons: The Scientific Quest for Extraterrestrial Life*. New York: Oxford University Press, 2000.
Krasney, Zoe. "What Were the Mysterious 'Foo Fighters' Sighted by WWII Night Flyers?" *Air & Space Magazine*, August 2016. https://www.airspacemag.com/history-of-flight/what-were-mysterious-foo-fighters-sighted-ww2-night-flyers-180959847/.
Larsen, Ragnar. "The Oldest Known UFO Photo Refuted." *LockLip*, December 29, 2015. https://www.locklip.com/5889-2/.
Leake, Jonathan. "Don't Talk to Aliens, Warns Stephen Hawking." *The Sunday Times*, April 25, 2010. https://www.thetimes.co.uk/article/dont-talk-to-aliens-warns-stephen-hawking-rftn7kpjgbx.

Lemaître, Georges. "A Homogeneous Universe with Constant Mass and Increasing Radius Explaining the Radial Velocity of Extragalactic Nebulae." *Monthly Notices of the Royal Astronomical Society* 91 (1927) 483–90.

Letzter, Rafi. "Aliens Might Zap Black Holes with Lasers to Travel the Galaxy." *Live Science*, March 15, 2019. https://www.livescience.com/65005-black-hole-halo-drive-laser.html.

Levin, Samuel, et al. "Darwin's Aliens." *The International Journal of Astrobiology* 18.1 (2017) 1–9. https://doi.org/10.1017/S1473550417000362.

Loeb, Abraham. "Are We Really the Smartest Kid on the Block?" https://www.cfa.harvard.edu/~loeb/Kid.pdf.

Loeb, Avi, and Manasvi Lingam. "Implications of Captured Interstellar Objects for Panspermia and Extraterrestrial Life." *The Astrophysical Journal Letters* 156.5 (October 16, 2018) 1–10. https://arxiv.org/pdf/1801.10254.pdf.

Louth, Andrew. *Maximus the Confessor*. Early Church Fathers 1. London: Routledge, 1996.

Lukas, Mary, and Ellen Lukas. *Teilhard: The Man, the Priest, the Scientist*. Garden City: Doubleday, 1977.

Mack, John E. *Passport to the Cosmos: Human Transformation and Alien Encounters*. New York: Crown, 1999.

———. *Abduction: Human Encounters with Aliens*. New York: Scribners, 2007.

Marcel, Jesse, Jr., and Linda Marcel. *The Roswell Legacy: The Untold Story of the First Military Officer at the 1947 Crash Site*. Foreword by Stanton T. Friedman. Franklin Lakes: New Page, 2009.

March, James, dir. *The Theory of Everything*. Cambridge, UK: Working Title Films, 2014.

Marx, Karl. "Theses on Feuerbach." Translated by W. Lough. https://www.marxists.org/archive/marx/works/1845/theses/theses.htm.

Maximus Confessor. *Maximus Confessor: Selected Writings*. Translated with notes by George C. Berthold. Introduction by Jaroslav Pelikan. Preface by Irénée-Henri Dalmais. The Classics of Western Spirituality. Mahwah: Paulist, 1985.

McGrath, Alister. *The Reenchantment of Nature: The Denial of Religion and the Ecological Crisis*. New York: Doubleday, 2002.

Meyers, Steven Lee, and Zoe Mou. "'New Chapter' in Space Exploration as China Reaches Far Side of the Moon." *The New York Times*, Jan 2, 2019. https://www.nytimes.com/2019/01/02/world/asia/china-change-4-moon.html?emc=edit_th_190103&nl=todaysheadlines&nlid=607146150103.

Michaud, Michael A. G. *Contact with Alien Civilizations: Our Hopes and Fears about Encountering Extraterrestrials*. New York: Copernicus, 2007.

"Ministry of Defence Files on UFO Sightings Released." *BBC News*, August 11, 2011. https://www.bbc.com/news/uk-14486678.

More, Thomas. *Utopia*. Edited with revised translation by George M. Logan. Norton Critical Edition. 3rd ed. New York: Norton, 2011.

NASA. "Old Data Reveal New Evidence of Europa Plumes." www.nasa.gov/press-release/old-data-reveal-new-evidence-of-europa-plumes/.

———. "NASA Retires Kepler Space Telescope, Passes Planet-hunting Torch." https://www.nasa.gov/press-release/nasa-retires-kepler-space-telescope-passes-planet-hunting-torch.

———. "Astronomy Picture of the Day: Ultima Thule from New Horizons." htpps://apod.nasa.gov/apod/ap190129.html.
New World Encyclopedia. "Axis Mundi." https://www.newworldencyclopedia.org/entry/Axis_Mundi.
O'Connell, Mark. *The Close Encounters Man: How One Man Made the World Believe in UFOs*. New York: Dey Street, 2017.
———. "J. Allen Hynek." http://www.cufos.org/Hynekbio.html.
Peacocke, Arthur. *All That Is: A Naturalistic Faith for the Twenty-First Century*. Edited by Philip Clayton. Minneapolis: Fortress, 2007.
———. *Creation and the World of Science: The Re-shaping of Belief*. Oxford: Clarendon, 1979.
———. *Evolution: The Disguised Friend of Faith?* London: Templeton Foundation, 2004.
———. *Paths from Science towards God: The End of All Our Exploring*. Oxford: Oneworld, 2001.
Peters, Ted, ed. *Astrotheology: Science and Theology Meet Extraterrestrial Life*. With Martinez Hewlett, Joshua M. Moritz, and Robert John Russell. Foreword by Paul Davies. Eugene, OR: Cascade, 2018.
Peters, Ted, and Julie Froehlig. "The Peters ETI Religious Crisis Survey." http://www.counterbalance.org/etsurv/PetersETISurveyRep.pdf.
Peters, Ted, and Martinez Hewlett. *Evolution from Creation to New Creation: Conflict, Conversation, and Convergence*. Nashville: Abingdon, 2003.
Pope, Nick, et al. *Encounter in Rendlesham Forest: The Inside Story of the World's Best-Documented UFO Incident*. New York: Dunne, 2014.
"The Probability of Panspermia." *Astrobiology Magazine*, September 28, 2012. https://www.astrobio.net/also-in-news/the-probability-of-panspermia/.
Randolph, Richard, et al. "Reconsidering the Theological and Ethical Implications of Extraterrestrial Life." *CTNS Bulletin* 17.3 (1997) 1–8.
Rosenberg, Eli. "Former Navy Pilot Describes UFO Encounter Studied by Secret Pentagon Program." *Washington Post*, December 18, 2017. https://www.washingtonpost.com/news/checkpoint/wp/2017/12/18/former-navy-pilot-describes-encounter-with-ufo-studied-by-secret-pentagon-program/?utm_term=.de1052f9ea81.
Salas, Robert L. *Unidentified: The UFO Phenomenon: How World Governments Have Conspired to Conceal Humanity's Biggest Secret*. Foreword by Stanton T. Friedman. Pompton Plains, NJ: New Page, 2015.
Salas, Robert L., and James Klotz. *Faded Giant*.Charleston, South Carolina, BookSurge, 2005.
Saplakoglu, Yasemin. "Is Humanity Ready for the Discovery of Alien Life?" *Scientific American*, February 16, 2018. https://www.scientificamerican.com/article/is-humanity-ready-for-the-discovery-of-alien-life/.
Selk, Avi. "Harvard's Top Astronomer Says an Alien Ship May Be Among Us—and He Doesn't Care What His Colleagues Think." *Washington Post*, February 5, 2019. https://www.washingtonpost.com/lifestyle/style/harvards-top-astronomer-says-an-alien-ship-may-be-among-us--and-he-doesnt-care-what-his-colleagues-think/2019/02/04/a5d70bb0-24d5-11e9-90cd-dedb0c92dc17_story.html?utm_term=.b100146b8227.
Shreeve, Jamie. "Who's Out There?" *National Geographic*, March 2019.

"Stay Home ET. Hawking: Aliens May Pose Risks." *Phys.org*, April 25, 2010. https://phys.org/news/2010-04-home-stephen-hawking-aliens-pose.html.

"Stephen Hawking Warns over Making Contact with Aliens." *BBC News*, April 25, 2010. http://news.bbc.co.uk/2/hi/8642558.stm.

Swartz, Josh. "Harvard Astronomer on Why Aliens Aren't Science Fiction." *Endless Thread*, January 30, 2019. https://www.wbur.org/endlessthread/2019/01/30/oumuamua-alien-probe-avi-loeb.

Swords, Michael and Robert Powell, eds. *UFOs and Government: A Historical Inquiry*. San Antonio: Anomalist, 2012.

Teilhard de Chardin, Pierre. *Christianity and Evolution: Reflections on Science and Religion*. Translated by René Hague. New York: Harcourt, 1974.

———. *The Divine Milieu*. Rev. ed. New York: Harper & Row, 1968.

———. "Fall, Redemption, and Geocentrism." In *Christianity and Evolution: Reflections on Science and Religion*, translated by René Hague, 36–44. New York: Harcourt, 1974.

———. *The Heart of Matter*. Translated by René Hague. New York: Harcourt, 1978.

———. *Human Energy*. Translated by J. M. Cohen. New York: Harcourt, 1969.

———. *The Human Phenomenon: A New Edition and Translation of* Le Phénomène Humain. Translated by Sarah Appleton-Weber. Brighton: Sussex Academic, 2003.

———. *Hymn of the Universe*. Translated by Simon Bartholomew. New York: Harper & Row, 1961.

———. *Letters to Two Friends, 1926–1952*. Translated by Helen Weaver and edited by Ruth Nanda Anshen. New York: New American Library, 1967.

———. "Note on the Modes of Divine Action in the Universe." In *Christianity and Evolution: Reflections on Science and Religion*, translated by René Hague, 25–35. New York: Harcourt, 1974.

———. *The Phenomenon of Man*. 2nd ed. New York: Harper & Row, 1965.

———. "A Sequel to the Problem of Human Origins: The Plurality of Inhabited Worlds." In *Christianity and Evolution: Reflections on Science and Religion*, translated by René Hague, 229–36. New York: Harcourt, 1974.

———. *Science and Christ*. Translated by René Hague. New York: Harper & Row, 1968.

———. *Writings in Time of War*. Translated by René Hague. New York: Harper & Row, 1968.

Theokritoff, Elizabeth. "The Vision of St. Maximus the Confessor: That Creation May All Be One." In *The Wiley Blackwell Companion to Religion and Ecology*, edited by Josh Hart, 220–36. Foreword by Ecumenical Patriarch Bartholomew I, Orthodox Church. Oxford: Wiley Blackwell, 2017.

Thunberg, Lars. *Man and the Cosmos: The Vision of St Maximus The Confessor*. Foreword by A. M. Allchin. Crestwood, NY: St Vladimir's Seminary Press, 1985.

Toolan, David. *At Home in the Cosmos*. Maryknoll: Orbis, 2001.

United Nations. *Antarctic Treaty*. https://www.ats.aq/documents/ats/treaty_original.pdf.

———. *The Declaration on the Rights of Indigenous Peoples: With an Introduction for Indigenous Leaders in the United States*. Tucson: University of Arizona Indigenous Peoples Law and Policy Program, 2012.

———. "Intergovernmental Science-Policy Platform on Biodiversity and Ecosystem Services Report." https://www.ipbes.net/news/ipbes-global-assessment-summary-policymakers-pdf.

———. "Millennium Development Goals (MDGs)." https://www.who.int/topics/millennium_development_goals/about/en/.
———. *United Nations Treaties and Principles on Outer Space*. New York: United Nations, 2008. http://www.unoosa.org/pdf/publications/st_space_11rev2E.pdf.
———. *Universal Declaration of Human Rights*. https://www.un.org/en/universal-declaration-human-rights/.
———. *World Charter for Nature*. https://www.un.org/documents/ga/res/37/a37r007.htm.
Vallée, Jacques. *Confrontations: A Scientist's Search for Alien Contact*. Vol. 2 of the *Alien Contact Trilogy*. San Antonio: Anomalist, 2008.
———. *Dimensions: A Casebook of Alien Contact*. Vol. 1 of the *Alien Contact Trilogy*. San Antonio: Anomalist, 2008.
———. "Five Arguments Against the Extraterrestrial Origin of Unidentified Flying Objects." *Journal of Scientific Exploration* 4.1 (1990) 105–17.
———. *The Invisible College: What a Group of Scientists Has Discovered about UFO Influence on the Human Race*. Rev. ed. San Antonio: Anomalist, 2014.
———. *Messengers of Deception: UFO Contacts and Cults*. Brisbane: Daily Grail, 2014.
———. *Passport to Magonia: From Folklore to Flying Saucers*. Brisbane: Daily Grail, 2014.
———. *Revelations: Alien Contact and Human Deception*. Vol. 3 of the *Alien Contact Trilogy*. San Antonio: Anomalist, 2008.
Vallée, Jacques, and Chris Aubeck. *Wonders in the Sky: Unexplained Aerial Objects from Antiquity to 1879 and Their Impact on Human Culture, History, and Beliefs*. New York: Penguin, 2009.
Villaluz, Kathleen. "Stephen Hawking Warns the World Against Contacting Aliens." *Interesting Engineering*, July 28, 2017. https://interestingengineering.com/stephen-hawking-warns-against-contacting-aliens.
Wilkinson, David. *Science, Religion, and the Search for Extraterrestrial Intelligence*. Oxford: Oxford University Press, 2013.
Williams, Martin, dir. *The Brady Bunch*. Season 1, episode 2, "Aliens." Aired April 25, 2010, on Discovery Channel. https://www.discovery.com/tv-shows/into-the-universe-with-stephen-hawking/full-episodes/aliens.
Wilson, Edward O. *The Creation: An Appeal to Save Life on Earth*. New York: Norton, 2006.
———. *The Meaning of Human Existence*. New York: Liveright, 2014.
———. *The Social Conquest of Earth*. New York: Liveright, 2013.
Wright, Robert. "Ethics for Extraterrestrials." *The Opinionator* (blog), May 4, 2010. http://opinionator.blogs.nytimes.com/2010/05/04/the-moral-alien/.

Index

axis mundi, 26, 59–61, 188

Breakthrough Initiatives, 111–14, 123, 133–35, 229–30, 238
Center for UFO Studies (CUFOS), 65, 67, 74, 135–36
"Center of the Universe" elders' experience, 26, 46, 60, 61
Chang'e 4 lunar rover, 3
Clarke, Ardy Sixkiller, 18, 138, 152n40, 167, 168–85, 229, 231
    Encounters with Stat People, 170–76
    More Encounters with Star People, 176–80
    Sky People, 180–85
Close Encounters, 4n9, 10, 14, 15, 17, 23, 34, 65, 70n12, 137, 227, 245
    categories, 67–70
    Rendlesham Forest, 91
    scientists' reactions to, 71–74
    Vallee's critique of, 76–77
CNES-GEIPAN (France National Space Agency/Centre for UAP Phenomena), 2, 8, 75
CNSA (China National Space Agency), 2, 3, 4
cosmolocality, 7, 11, 13, 16, 55, 61–62
cosmosocioecological praxis ethics, 8, 11, 15, 16, 21, 27, 199–206, 226, 237, 241

Darwin, Charles, 32, 54, 56, 61, 80, 234
Deere, Phillip, 138, 149–50n30, 167–68, 185n19, 188
displacement, human, 6, 7, 11, 12, 13, 14, 17, 22, 23, 29–33, 35, 38, 46, 54–57, 61, 62, 76, 116, 145–46n12, 159, 162, 165, 226, 235, 239, 240, 241, 263, 273
    voluntary, 219–20
Earth Charter, 206
ESA (European Space Agency), 2, 8, 15, 67, 87, 95

Francis of Assisi, 11, 52–54, 208, 213
Francis I, Pope, 195n4,
    ETI and, 132
    Hague Principles and, 215
    integral ecology exposition, 207–11
Goldilocks Zone, 12, 14, 67, 87, 111, 121, 124, 126, 228, 235–36

Hague Principles, 13, 191, 213, 214–16, 221–22
Handsome Lake, Seneca prophet, 144n9
Hawking, Stephen, 25–26, 98, 106–16, 117, 118, 119, 120, 129, 133, 177, 192, 193, 219, 227, 230–31
    Deus ex Machina in his thought, 25–26, 106–7

ETI: changing position on,
  108–13
  'Oumuamua and, 113–14
  Socioecological concern,
  evolving, 114–16
Hudson River, 23–24, 64n1, 238n19
hybrid project, 18, 28, 146, 163–67,
  179, 170, 231
Hynek, Allen, 4n9, 5n11, 13, 15, 62,
  64–74, 93–94, 124, 125, 135,
  140, 185, 227

idealism, realistic, 240
Indian, 9, 22, 185n119
integral being, 7n13, 21, 22–23, 27,
  35, 38, 46, 51–52, 163, 190,
  213, 226, 264–70, 273–75
Intergovernmental Panel on Climate
  Change (IPCC), 191, 200,
  204, 212, 216–19
ISS (International Space Station), 1,
  28, 96, 135, 239

Kennedy, Pat, 191n125
Kim, Heup Young, 57–59
  Theodao of, 57–58
  Theanthropocosmic vision of,
  58–59

land as *gift* or *trust*, 194, 211–14
LeMaître, Georges, 22–23, 44, 130
Loeb, Abraham (Avi), 98, 123–29,
  177, 238
  ETI: assertion of their reality
  and presence, 123–28
  Panspermia speculation, 126–28
  Breakthrough Initiatives, and,
  133
Logos and *logoi*, 32, 41–44, 46–51,
  57–59, 162–63

Mack, John, 17–18, 38, 79n42, 117,
  138, 139, 140–62, 166nn79–
  82, 167, 168, 169, 173, 185,
  190, 191
  Abduction, 141–48
  psychiatric insights, 146–48
  representative cases, 142–46

Passport to the Cosmos, 148–49
  impacts on Mack's thinking,
  149
  Indian elders' experiences,
  149–58
  Mack's reflections on elders'
  narratives, 158–59
  Mack's reflections on
  impacts of abductees,
  160–61
  spiritual awareness of
  abductees, enhanced,
  159–61
  Mack and Saint Francis, 163
  Mack and Vallee, 163–65
Maximus Confessor, 47–48, 50–51,
  57, 59, 162, 163
May, Brian, 3n6
Mutual UFO Network (MUFON),
  67n8, 135–36, 246
Mutwa, Credo Vusumazulu, 150,
  156–58, 167

NASA Astrobiology Institute, 4, 6,
  10, 232
natural rights, 7–8, 202, 216, 221,
  273
natural good, 8n16
natural goods, 8, 15, 21, 26, 31, 107,
  109, 120, 151, 193, 198, 199,
  204–5, 214, 221, 232, 239,
  241, 264–71
New Horizons voyager, 3, 6
Nicholaus of Cusa, 51–52, 151
Nuremberg, 1561 aliens' aerial
  battle, 230

'Oumuamua, 36
  Avi Loeb and, 123–25, 127–28
  Stephen Hawking and, 113–14

Panspermia, 126–28, 129–30, 177
  Anaxagoras speculates about,
  109n49
  Avi Loeb and, 126–28
  Stephen Hawking and, 109

INDEX   289

pathogenic threat in space, humans as, 230
Peacocke, Arthur, 46
Peixoto, Bernardo, 150–52
Peters ETI Religious Crisis Survey, 36, 236
philosophy and science, 128–29

relational community, 13, 17, 21, 23, 33, 55, 105, 163, 193, 194, 194–95n2, 204, 211, 212, 221, 226, 232, 236, 241, 263, 273
  members distinguished from gift recipient, steward, trustee, 194
Rendlesham Forest, England, 21n29, 87, 253–61
  Jacques Vallee and, 88, 89–91
Roswell, New Mexico, 91, 103, 108, 139, 170, 171, 246, 253–59

science and religion complementarity, 14–15, 100, 122, 131, 208
SETI Institute, 6, 23, 25, 107, 108, 117, 228–29, 273
  University of St. Andrews and, 227–28
SoCIA, 136–37
socioecological praxis ethics, 8, 12, 16, 22, 193, 195, 196–200, 207, 213, 221–22
  process steps, 198–99
Sohappy, David, 185–91
  John Mack and, 190–91
Sohappy, Myra, 186, 188

terraforming, 220–21
Teilhard de Chardin, SJ, Pierre, 36, 37, 96, 98–104, 130, 131, 228, 234
  ETI and, 103–4
  Maximus and, 50
  science and spirituality, 99–102
  sounds of created being, fused, 101

universe vibration, 101–2
  Vallee and, 82
  Wilson and, 122
Theokritoff, Elizabeth, 48–49
topia and *utopia* dialogic and dialectic processes, 196–97
Trueblood, Sequoyah, 152–56
Thunberg, Lars, 49–50

UAP (Unidentified Aerial Phenomena/on), 13, 14, 16, 20, 21, 24, 70, 88, 91–95, 124, 131, 177, 185, 223, 237, 238n19
Ultima Thule, 3

Vallee, Jacques, 74–94, 229–39
  abduction reports analysis, 78
  Brazil investigations, 229–39
  Confrontations content, 81–86
  critique of ETI assertions, 76–79
  Dimensions content, 79–81
  Hynek and, 93–94
  hypnotist ineptitude, 83–84
  Interdimensional Intelligence, and, 75–77
  "missing time" critique, 85–86
  Rendlesham Forest events contrived by US government, 88–92
  Revelations content, 86–92
  Governments' manipulation and construction of "UFO events", 86–87
  UMMO critique, 87–88
Vatican Observatory and ETI, 131–32
visitors, 13, 33–37

Wilson, Edward O. (E.O.), 78, 116–23
  ETI and, evolving position on, 117–22, 226–27
  science and religion complementarity, 122–23
world, plurality of, 39–44

www.ingramcontent.com/pod-product-compliance
Lightning Source LLC
Chambersburg PA
CBHW032052220426
43664CB00008B/968